Scottish Society in the Fifteenth Century

Scottish Society in the Fifteenth Century

edited by
Jennifer M. Brown

Edward Arnold

© Edward Arnold 1977

First published 1977
by Edward Arnold (Publishers) Ltd
25 Hill Street, London W1X 8LL

ISBN 0 7131 5944 8

Phototypeset in VIP Bembo
by Western Printing Services Ltd, Bristol

Printed by photolithography and bound
in Great Britain by The Pitman Press, Bath

Contents

Illustrations

Plates

Note: Plates 1 to 12 appear between pages 152 and 153, plates 13 and 14 between pages 194 and 195.

Figures

Contributors

John W. M. Bannerman is lecturer in Scottish History, University of Edinburgh.

Jennifer M. Brown is lecturer in Scottish History, University of Glasgow.

Ian B. Cowan is reader in Scottish History, University of Glasgow.

Barbara E. Crawford is lecturer in Medieval History, University of St Andrews.

S. G. E. Lythe is emeritus professor of Economic History, University of Strathclyde.

Norman A. T. Macdougall is lecturer in History, Langside College of Further Education, Glasgow.

John MacQueen is director of the School of Scottish Studies, University of Edinburgh.

James J. Robertson is senior lecturer in Law, University of Dundee.

Geoffrey Stell is investigator, the Royal Commission on the Ancient and Historical Monuments of Scotland.

Acknowledgements

A book of essays, being a cooperative venture, has its own particular pleasures. One is the privilege which the editor has of being able to record appreciation: first, and obviously, I wish to thank the contributors, for agreeing to write, and for doing so with an enthusiasm and thoughtfulness which has made the hectic periods, inevitable in the compiling of the book, more than bearable, and the more peaceful ones greatly rewarding; and secondly, the publishers, for their helpfulness over all matters, whether trivial or important, and for the patience and tolerance they have unfailingly shown to that nervous breed, the academic author. Thirdly, I want to express my gratitude to all those who have in so many ways encouraged and aided the production of this book, from the time when the warm reaction to what was then only an idea made it seem worth pursuing the project. I would like especially to mention Professor A. L. Brown, to whom I owe a particular debt, which it is a pleasure to record here, for all that I have gained from being able to draw on his extensive knowledge of fifteenth-century English society, my colleague Dr I. B. Cowan, whose generous assistance extended far beyond the contribution of his article (chapter 6), Professor Gordon Donaldson, Professor A. A. M. Duncan, Dr G. G. Simpson, Professor T. C. Smout, Dr D. E. R. Watt and Mr C. P. Wormald. In particular, I would like to thank Dr N. A. T. Macdougall, who has been a close friend since the days when we both embarked on the stormy and then largely uncharted seas of research into fifteenth-century Scotland; it was as a result of discussion with him that the idea of the book came into being; and both in the planning and in the time when it was being written, his help, support and always constructive advice have added substantially to the pleasure, and eased considerably any problems, of editing this book. Finally, I thank my son Andrew, for remaining sane and cheerful, and keeping me so, in the last distracted days before the manuscript was sent to the publishers, and for seeing it safely into the post.

JENNIFER M. BROWN

Abbreviations

ADA	*The Acts of the Lords Auditors of Causes and Complaints,* edited by T. Thomson (Edinburgh, 1839)
ADC	*The Acts of the Lords of Council in Civil Causes,* edited by T. Thomson (Edinburgh, 1839)
Acts of Council (Public Affairs)	*Acts of the Lords of Council in Public Affairs: Selections from Acta Dominorum Concilii,* edited by R. K. Hannay (Edinburgh, 1932)
APS	*The Acts of the Parliaments of Scotland,* edited by T. Thomson and C. Innes (Edinburgh, 1814–75)
ALI	*Ancient Laws of Ireland* (Dublin, 1865–1901)
Asloan Manuscript	*The Asloan Manuscript,* edited by W. A. Craigie (STS, 1923)
AU	*Annals of Ulster,* edited by W. M. Hennessy and B. MacCarthy (Dublin, 1887–1901)
BM	British Museum
BN	Bibliothèque Nationale, Paris
Cal. Docs Scot.	*Calendar of Documents relating to Scotland,* edited by J. Bain (Edinburgh, 1881–8)
Cal. State Papers (Milan)	*Calendar of State Papers and Manuscripts existing in the Archives and Collections of Milan,* edited by A. B. Hinds (London, 1912)
Cast. and Dom. Arch.	D. Macgibbon and T. Ross, *The Castellated and Domestic Architecture of Scotland* (Edinburgh, 1887–92)
CG	*Críth Gablach,* edited by D. A. Binchy (Dublin, 1941)
Chron. Bower	*Joannis de Fordun Scotichronicon cum supplementis et continuatione Walteri Boweri,* edited by W. Goodall (Edinburgh, 1759)

Chron. Fordun	*Johannis de Fordun Chronica Gentis Scotorum*, edited by W. F. Skene (Edinburgh, 1871–2)
Chron. Wyntoun	*The Original Chronicle of Andrew of Wyntoun*, edited by F. J. Amours (STS, 1903–14)
Coupar Angus Rental	*Rental Book of the Cistercian Abbey of Coupar Angus*, edited by C. Rodgers (Grampian Club, 1879–80)
CUL	Cambridge University Library
CPL	*Calendar of Entries in the Papal Registers relating to Great Britain and Ireland: Papal Letters*, edited by W. H. Bliss and others (London, 1893–)
DN	*Diplomatarium Norvegicum*, edited by C. A. Lange and C. R. Unger (Kristiana, 1849–)
Dunfermline Registrum	*Registrum de Dunfermelyn* (Bannatyne Club, 1842)
Dunkeld Rentale	*Rentale Dunkeldense* (SHS, 1915)
St Andrews Acta	*Acta Facultatis Artium Universitatis S. Andree*, edited by Annie I. Dunlop (SHS, 1964)
Eccles. Arch.	D. Macgibbon and T. Ross, *The Ecclesiastical Architecture of Scotland* (Edinburgh, 1896–7)
Edinburgh St Giles Registrum	*Registrum Cartarum Ecclesie Sancti Egidii de Edinburgh* (Bannatyne Club, 1859)
EHR	*English Historical Review*
ER	*The Exchequer Rolls of Scotland*, edited by J. Stuart and others (Edinburgh, 1878–1908)
FMLS	*Forum of Modern Language Studies*
HMC	*Reports of the Royal Commission on Historical Manuscripts* (London, 1870–)
JEGP	*Journal of English and Germanic Philology*
Moray Registrum	*Registrum Episcopatus Moraviensis* (Bannatyne Club, 1837)
NLS	National Library of Scotland
PSAS	*Proceedings of the Society of Antiquaries of Scotland*
RCAHMS	Royal Commision on the Ancient and Historical Monuments of Scotland
Recs. Scot. Church Hist. Soc.	*Records of the Scottish Church History Society*
Reg. Supp.	Vatican Archives, Registra Supplicationum

RES	*Review of English Studies*
RMS	*Registrum Magni Sigilli Regum Scotorum*, edited by J. M. Thomson and others (Edinburgh, 1882–1914)
Rot. Scot.	*Rotuli Scotiae in Turri Londinensi et in Domo Capitulari Westmonasteriensi Asservati*, edited by D. Macpherson and others (Record Commission, 1814–19)
RSS	*Registrum Secreti Sigilli Regum Scotorum*, edited by M. Livingstone and others (Edinburgh, 1908–)
SBRS	Scottish Burgh Records Society
Scots Peerage	*The Scots Peerage*, edited by J. Balfour Paul (Edinburgh, 1904–14)
SGTS	Scottish Gaelic Texts Society
SHR	*Scottish Historical Review*
SHS	Scottish History Society
SRO	Scottish Record Office
SRS	Scottish Record Society
STS	Scottish Text Society
TA	*Accounts of the Lord High Treasurer of Scotland*, edited by T. Dickson and J. Balfour Paul (Edinburgh, 1877–1916)
TGSI	*Transactions of the Gaelic Society of Inverness*

1

Introduction
Jennifer M. Brown

'The first half of the fifteenth century saw the struggle between crown and nobility rife throughout western Europe. . . . The domestic history of Scotland was . . . to be full of the abortive efforts of successive kings to bring the powerful nobility under control of the central government.' This quotation comes from the opening and closing sentences of the first paragraph of E. W. M. Balfour-Melville's biography of James I, written in 1936.[1] It is a succinct statement of a view of fifteenth-century Europe current at the time when Balfour-Melville wrote. Historians emphasized the aggressive nature of the society of northwestern Europe, and painted a picture of that society as decadent, in the grip of the final decline of 'medieval' ideas in both church and state, apparently obsessed with the idea of death in the aftermath of the psychological and physical devastation of the Black Death, and certainly lawless, restless, turbulent. Not many years before *James I* was published, the Dutch historian, Huizinga, had brought out his famous book *The Waning of the Middle Ages*, in which he looked at the art of northern Europe and saw there macabre morbidity.[2] Late-medieval governments were allegedly dominated by the largely insoluble problem of overmighty magnates. Charles Plummer quoted with approval the statement that 'the two cankers of the time were the total corruption of the church and the utter lawlessness of the aristocracy'; he coined the phrase 'bastard feudalism' to describe a relationship which had changed from the 'primitive relation of a lord to his tenants' to one in which the lord shielded from the consequences of their crimes his 'horde of retainers', who provided a private army to be used in furthering his own ambition.[3] Plummer himself did not argue that the 'older feudalism' was without evils and it was left to others to develop the idea of contrast between an earlier age of loyalty and faith

1 E. W. M. Balfour-Melville, *James I, King of Scots, 1406–1437* (London, 1936), p. 1.
2 J. Huizinga, *The Waning of the Middle Ages* (London, 1924).
3 Sir John Fortescue, *The Governance of England*, edited by C. Plummer (Oxford, 1885), pp. 14 and 15.

and the decadent disorder and self-interest of late-medieval society.[4] Wherever one looked, the picture was indeed bleak.

This view was first effectively challenged by the great English historian, K. B. McFarlane. The revisionist approach which he initiated began with his attack on the interpretation of 'bastard feudalism' as a fundamental evil in society. His study of the late fifteenth-century Flemish artist, Hans Memling, suggested that the popularity of Memling's 'harmonious, candid and serene' art strongly counteracted the idea of morbid preoccupation with death and hell. Similarly, his Ford lectures and other studies of the English nobility attacked the 'bogy of the textbooks – the overmighty subject'.[5] Since McFarlane questioned and overturned the older shibboleths in England, they have never been reinstated in their stark and uncompromising form. Yet so firmly did they take root that, some forty years after the questioning began, two recent books on fifteenth-century society still showed a conscious need to combat them, and show their defects.[6] The idea of a society in decline and disorder dies very hard.

In Scotland, it has scarcely begun to die at all. Perhaps because the fifteenth century has been to a large extent neglected, there has been no Scottish Huizinga to draw oppressive conclusions about the *danse macabre* carved in Sir William Sinclair's wonderfully elaborate fifteenth-century collegiate church at Roslin. The problems of Scottish society have been discussed almost exclusively in terms of conflict between crown and nobility. There seemed good reason to take this view. In this little-known century of Scottish history, a few grim events stand out and are regarded as characterizing the age: James I was murdered by a magnate faction in 1437; James II's reign was dominated by conflict between the king and the supreme overmighty subjects of fifteenth-century Scotland, the earls of Douglas; and James III provided the final and most dismal spectacle in a dismal century, when he was killed in battle against his nobles in 1488. These dramatic

4 For example, Helen Cam, 'The Decline and Fall of English Feudalism', *History* xxv (1940), pp. 210–33; this article is interesting because it contains a very explicit statement of this idea, which was still acceptable in 1940 but was on the point of being not only questioned but rejected as an adequate comment on late-medieval society.

5 K. B. McFarlane, 'England: the Lancastrian Kings' in *Cambridge Mediaeval History* viii, edited by C. W. Previte-Orton and Z. N. Brooke (Cambridge, 1936), pp. 363–417; two articles of major significance, 'Bastard Feudalism', *Bulletin of the Institute of Historical Research* xx (1943–5), pp. 161–80, and 'Parliament and Bastard Feudalism', *Transactions of the Royal Historical Society* 4th series xxvi (1944), pp. 53–79; *Hans Memling* (Oxford, 1972); and *The Nobility of Later Medieval England* (Oxford, 1973) – the quotation is taken from p. 282.

6 J. R. Lander, *Conflict and Stability in Fifteenth-century England* (London, 1969), pp. 11–18, opens with a chapter entitled 'The Dark Glass of the Fifteenth Century'; and the first chapter of F. R. H. Du Boulay, *An Age of Ambition: English Society in the Late Middle Ages* (London, 1970), pp. 11–16, is called 'The Myth of Decline'.

flashpoints are thought to have punctuated a long, dreary, slogging power-struggle between king and magnates, in which neither side actually won, although both gained temporary victories and suffered temporary setbacks. The Stewart kings apparently had some success in bringing 'the powerful nobility under control', but in each case they died young, leaving a child to succeed them, and the initiative passed back to the magnates. In Scotland, as in the rest of Europe, the crown was dependent on the magnates, at both a formal and an informal level, for successful control of the country. The degree of dependence was heightened, however, by the appalling bad luck of the Scottish monarchy; three minorities in three reigns is unique. And if, as the traditional view suggests, the crown had to depend on a nobility which was lawless, self-seeking and lacking in political responsibilty, then the fifteenth century can indeed be written about in terms of conflict and, for that matter, written off as one of the least rewarding periods of Scottish history.

One difficulty in understanding this century is that there has been comparatively little written about it at all, and certainly very little which offers any dimension other than that of political conflict. Until very recently there were only two major works, Balfour-Melville's biography of James I, and Annie I. Dunlop's biography of James Kennedy, bishop of St Andrews, who died in 1465.[7] Both books suffered to an extent from the fact that they were biographies, with something of a tendency to become hagiographies, though Dr Dunlop did provide justification of her title, *Life and Times*, in an interesting and wide-ranging chapter on 'Kennedy's Scotland'. Both were certainly written in the context of the attempts by the crown to establish strong central government and the frustration of these attempts by the nobility. Balfour-Melville, having set the scene in these terms, ended on the remarkably strong note that 'the tragedy of James I lies in the wreck of his high purpose upon the stubborn individualism of the Scottish nobles in an age which saw throughout Europe the last recrudescence of feudalism before it withered in the dawn of modern times.'[8] Almost by definition, kings had high purposes, nobles base and selfish ones. The idea of conflict and failure was carried over into more specialized works: Robert Rait in his work on the Scottish parliament, and I. F. Grant, writing on the economy, both discussed their themes against the background of magnate dominance, while for the law, it was the 'Dark Age', and for the church, 'a period of decline'.[9] John MacQueen's study of Robert Henryson, one of the

7 Annie I. Dunlop, *The Life and Times of James Kennedy, Bishop of St Andrews* (Edinburgh, 1950).

8 Balfour-Melville, *James I*, p. 280.

9 R. S. Rait, *The Parliaments of Scotland* (Glasgow, 1924); I. F. Grant, *Social and*

major Scottish poets of the age, did open up a new and fascinating dimension.[10] But although Henryson was writing in the reign of James III, there is a tendency to link him with the interest in learning and the arts associated with the traditionally more attractive reign of James IV, the reign to which historians and students alike turn with relief, because it seems to have so much more to offer than the squalid quarrelling of two-dimensional kings and magnates.

Recently, the fifteenth century has been given comprehensive treatment in Ranald Nicholson's volume in the *Edinburgh History of Scotland*. This immensely detailed work provides a wealth and range of information not hitherto easily available. In no sense is it restricted to the older narrow view. But even here the idea of conflict has left its mark, in the more sophisticated theory that the monarchy in the fifteenth century was engaged in a long attempt to transform into courtiers a feudal baronage with great power in the localities, and that James IV ultimately succeeded to a considerable extent in doing so.[11]

The neglect of fifteenth-century Scotland until recent years is not, however, the only problem. There is also the difficulty of understanding the values and *mores* of Scottish society. Scotland was a small country, remote on the periphery of Europe. In 1474, the duke of Milan caustically refused Louis XI's suggestion that one of his daughters might marry James III's son and heir on the grounds that he would not want to send any of his daughters 'so far off as Scotland would be'.[12] Scotland was impoverished, certainly by comparison with her powerful southern neighbour. Her government institutions had recognizable similarities with those of England, but were relatively underdeveloped. She had nothing approaching the highly trained secular legal profession which existed in England nor any central courts of justice. Both secular and ecclesiastical architecture were on an altogether smaller scale than in England; the cathedral of Lismore, for example, was smaller than many English parish churches. Her church was, in one sense, wholly prosaic and the great mystics of late-medieval England had no counterparts in Scotland. She had contacts with Europe, but inevitably her influence was small, her main role being, apparently, to draw English fire when necessary in the interests of France. Her volume of trade was considerably less than that of England.

Much more is known about England and, to an extent, comparison

Economic Developments of Scotland before 1603 (Edinburgh, 1930); G. C. H. Paton, 'The Dark Age, 1329–1532' in *An Introduction to Scottish Legal History* (Stair Society, 20, Edinburgh, 1958), pp. 18–24. See also below, chapter 6, p. 115 and n. 10.

10 J. MacQueen, *Robert Henryson: a Study of the Major Narrative Poems* (Oxford, 1967).

11 R. G. Nicholson, *Scotland: The Later Middle Ages* (Edinburgh, 1974).

12 See below, chapter 5, p. 109.

with Scotland's nearest neighbour is not only tempting but also valid in that it puts Scottish society into some kind of perspective. When, much later, James VI argued the case for union of the nations as well as the crowns, in his speech to the English Commons in 1607, he did so on the grounds of common language and customs as well as of a single monarchy and geographic unity.[13] Two late-medieval Scottish kings, David II and James I, spent years in captivity in England and returned to Scotland apparently impressed by what they had experienced. Whether explicitly or not, it was easy for historians to measure Scottish government and society against that of England. But the comparison may well be pressed too far. For example, the dominant concept of conflict between crown and magnates rested on the assumption that the crown wanted a strong centralized administration and therefore needed to reduce the local power of the magnates. It was not actually asked whether Scottish kings wanted any such thing, merely assumed that they did. The contemporary kings of England, arguably the most governed country in Europe, were managing distinctly better; and in so far as the Stewart kings' control of their country fell short of that of the English monarchy, so they failed.

Historians writing about Scotland in the nineteenth and early twentieth centuries were largely inspired by their own contemporary values. Government from the centre relying on a professional bureaucracy, impartial justice in the central courts, at least official resistance to the idea that ties of kinship should influence appointments in church or state – these were all more acceptable than the notion of decentralized power vested in local lords, to which they were strongly antipathetic. It was a matter for criticism that the men who seized control during the minorities, the Livingstones in the minority of James II, the Boyds in that of James III, not only did well themselves but substantially benefited their families.[14] Yet today there is possibly less certainty in the view that a strong central authority seeking to exercise tight control over the localities necessarily provides the best answer to the problem of how to govern effectively. As a result, it may be easier to consider less critically the kin-based society of fifteenth-century Scotland where, for all except the few politically powerful magnates, local and personal ties were far stronger than national ones,

13 *The Political Works of James I*, edited by C. H. McIlwain (New York, 1965), pp. 290–305.

14 Lucy Mair, *Primitive Government* (London, 1970), p. 237, sums this up very well when she writes: 'The modern theory is that ties of kinship have no rational basis; they provide means of advancement to persons who would not get far on their merits; it may not be wrong that people should want to help their kinsmen, but it is wrong that they should be able to.' In fifteenth-century Scotland, it was not thought wrong.

an attitude which comes through with great clarity in Dr Bannerman's discussion of the Lordship of the Isles.[15]

There is another and more precise reason for questioning the traditional view of the fifteenth century. Some fifty years ago, C. L. Kingsford, in his brilliant lecture on 'Fifteenth-century History in Shakespeare's Plays', established the existence of the Tudor myth about fifteenth-century England, that myth which ultimately reached its greatest heights in the portrayal of the monster that was Shakespeare's Richard III.[16] Scotland had no Shakespeare. What she did have was a sixteenth-century myth about the fifteenth century, as Dr Macdougall shows.[17] In particular there was a legend which developed in the course of the sixteenth century about James III, the man said to have surrounded himself with lowborn favourites – an architect, a musician, a tailor and a fencing-master, the king who had no inclination for war, and who antagonized his nobility, his natural counsellors, because he ignored them, and thereby came to grief, dying an ignominious death in flight from battle against his magnates. This has come down to us, in its most entertaining form, in the racy and lively chronicle written in the 1570s by Robert Lindsay of Pitscottie, although even after Pitscottie wrote, further details were added;[18] and it shows remarkable tenacity in its survival. Thus the architect Cochrane is still to be found building the magnificent great hall in Stirling castle, although there is no evidence that James III had a favourite who was an architect, and the building accounts leave no shadow of doubt that the hall was erected in the reign of James IV. The fact is that much of the long-accepted story of the reign of James III can no longer be believed, and sixteenth-century accounts of events in the fifteenth century cannot be regarded as trustworthy.

This in turn raises a new problem, for the quantity of contemporary evidence about fifteenth-century Scotland is not large. There are, as with any medieval society, questions to which no satisfactory answer can ever be given, and the patchiness of contemporary record leads to danger of distortion. It is inevitable that there is much less information about the lower ranks of society than about kings and nobles, traders and the higher clergy. But by contrast with England, the amount of evidence even for what should have been the most fully recorded aspect of Scottish society, royal government, is pitifully small, and before the reign of James III, not wholly reliable. So much evidence

15 See below, chapter 10, pp. 209–40.
16 C. L. Kingsford, *Prejudice and Promise in Fifteenth Century England* (Oxford, 1925), pp. 1–21.
17 See below, chapter 2, pp. 10–32.
18 Robert Lindsay of Pitscottie, *The Historie and Cronicles of Scotland* (STS, 1898–1911).

about the government institutions of fifteenth-century England survives that there may be a danger of overestimating the extent of control from the centre, and the smoothness with which government worked. In Scotland, by contrast, there is so little evidence that it is too easy to assume that it was relatively primitive.

Dr Macdougall is right, however, to stress that pessimism about the amount of available contemporary evidence is only 'to some extent' justified. As more aspects of the period begin to be opened up and analysed, the limitations become obvious, but what also becomes obvious is that there is plenty of scope for enquiry. There is enough material to make possible a greater understanding of Scottish society than we have at present. There are, for example, indications of a social shift, with the greater landowners coming to be less distinct, socially and economically, from those of lesser rank. Not enough is known about the relative wealth of aristocracy and gentry to apply with certainty to Scotland Du Boulay's comment on fifteenth-century England that 'the redistribution of wealth called for modes of behaviour to justify the "noveau riche" on the one hand, and to assert on the other the immemorial predominance of the lord.'[19] But the sumptuary legislation of Scotland in this period, attempting to define dress, the arms a man could bear and the size of his retinue, and the emergence of a parliamentary peerage, suggest that there were social pressures on the magnates of fifteenth-century Scotland as elsewhere in Europe, and indicate that far from enjoying too much power, they were having rather more of a struggle than their predecessors to assert their 'immemorial predominance'.[20]

The theme of conflict which has dominated historical writing on fifteenth-century Scotland has spilled over into discussion of other aspects of society. The purpose of this book is to make possible a more balanced analysis of the period by bringing together surveys of a wide range of topics by specialized scholars. Each subject is considered in its own right, without preconceptions about the political, social and economic weakness of Scottish society, in contrast with contemporary England and the more powerful nations of northern Europe. This has produced a reassessment of the various aspects of Scottish life in

19 Du Boulay, *Age of Ambition*, p. 61.

20 For example, *APS* II, pp. 18, 49 and 100, on dress and weapons. The first of these acts is dated 1430. Legislation about size of retinue began earlier, in 1366; *ibid.* I, p. 499. It had a different dimension from the other legislation; but it had in common the idea that size of retinue (about which it was always imprecise) was again determined by rank. It was never an attempt to prevent lords riding out with retinues. Lawrence Stone, *The Crisis of the Aristocracy, 1558–1641* (Oxford, 1965), p. 27, describes sumptuary legislation in England as 'attempts . . . to put authority of the state behind the enforcement of the ideals of hierarchy and social stability', a judgement which would equally apply to Scotland.

the fifteenth century which suggests that in each there was much that was positive and vital. In secular architecture, for instance, the idea that magnates and lairds shut themselves up in stone buildings, in the safety of which they could remain secure against their aggressive neighbours and challenge the authority of the crown, while in the more civilized south men were turning away from medieval stone to modern brick, is modified; and Mr Stell points out that the ability of the lairds as well as the magnates to build in stone argues both sufficient wealth to do so and a self-consciousness about social status, the desire to cut a dash. In Scotland, a stone building was desirable not just for defence, but because it was a status symbol. Moreover, what emerges from Professor MacQueen's consideration of the literature of the period is the degree of sophistication of Scottish writers, their understanding and use of literary genres, the amazingly complex and elaborate structure of James I's *Kingis Quair*, and the extent, never before brought out with such emphasis, of royal and aristocratic interest in and patronage of the arts. These articles demonstrate that there is a different side to the magnates and gentry, who thus begin to lose their two-dimensional quality.

Again, the theory that, with the Wars of Independence and the severing of friendly relations with England, Scots law began to show signs of decay after its period of healthy development under English influence in the twelfth and thirteenth centuries, cannot be sustained. The direction of development may have changed somewhat, but Mr Robertson shows that exciting and important development there was. And while, in European terms, trade and industry were not significant, in Scottish terms they were. This was the age of successful self-assertiveness by the merchants at the expense of the craftsmen; and while the economy was 'abnormally focused on rural activity and on the products of nature', it was 'without doubt . . . far from static', as Professor Lythe convincingly argues.[21] This is, perhaps, a particularly pioneering article, because the absence of statistics for trade, population and produce has tended to create a special degree of pessimism in the economic historian; Professor Lythe's analysis shows that, once again, the pessimism is exaggerated. And in political and social contact, as in trade, it appears that there is good reason to turn one's eyes from the south towards the Baltic, where Dr Crawford puts Scotland in a rather different light, not as a poor and overshadowed country, but as one with much to offer and with the power, on occasion, to dictate terms. Even in contact with England and France it becomes clear from Dr Macdougall's analysis that the weaker nation was not always at the beck and call of the stronger; the Stewart kings, if

21 See below, chapter 4, p. 67.

anything, showed a remarkable lack of appreciation of how poor and weak they were.

The church in fifteenth-century Scotland has suffered from rather different preconceptions, to an extent the effect of the Great Schism, and more obviously the imminence of the Reformation. Only at the end of the century, however, as Dr Cowan shows, were there any signs of a weakening of the effect of the church on men's lives, whether spiritually or in the field of law and education or as the source of much of the art, music and culture of the age. There is little room here for assumptions of the inevitability of the Reformation, and none at all for the idea which crept into older works on the Scottish church that Scotland was by nature Calvinist rather than Catholic.

Finally, there is the discussion of the social structure, the state of the local church, and the artistic and literary culture of the Lordship of the Isles, a province of Scotland which did in many ways differ from other parts of the country, but which also showed similarities and certainly points of contact. Here Dr Bannerman provides the opportunity to look at a local society in detail and in depth. It is a fascinating study; and it demonstrates in extreme form the limitations and weaknesses of trying to measure Scottish society against that of England. It is not that it is found wanting; it is profoundly different.

In the last resort, what makes a society successful, vital and rewarding, depends not on the judgements of other contemporary societies or of later ages, but on whether its own conventions give it cohesion and purpose, some measure of law and order, a degree of development and a range of interests. These articles show that if historians begin with the values of fifteenth-century Scottish society, rather than being influenced by inevitably unfavourable comparisons with more powerful and more centrally governed states, a much more positive picture begins to emerge.

2

The sources: a reappraisal of the legend
Norman A. T. Macdougall

It has become customary for Scottish historians to preface any discussion of the fifteenth century by bemoaning the lack of available source material. Their pessimism is to some extent justified, and it must be admitted that we shall never obtain a sharply defined picture of fifteenth-century government and society from surviving records and chronicles. There does however exist a body of official material, especially from the 1460s onwards, although it is still often fragmentary and inconclusive. The register of the great seal contains some 1,730 entries for the period 1424–1488; there exists a reasonably full register of parliamentary acts, statutory and judicial; the records of the lords of council sitting as the supreme civil court survive from 1478; and there is even a tantalizing glimpse, a mere sixteen months in 1473–4, of court receipts and expenditure preserved in the treasurer's accounts. Above all, the exchequer rolls, though far from complete, provide us with evidence about the administrators of crown lands – stewards, chamberlains, bailies and receivers of rents – and of custumars and bailies of royal burghs, and give information about the extent of crown lands, the names of individuals entrusted with the keeperships of royal castles, or granted annual pensions by the king, the itinerary of the royal household, and the growing wealth of the Edinburgh merchant classes.

It is therefore unfortunate that the traditional picture of fifteenth-century Scotland, still broadly accepted today and paraded in textbooks with misguided tenacity, should be founded much less on information obtainable from the public records than on the stories purveyed by sixteenth-century chroniclers, whose motives in writing varied from a desire to glorify a particular political power group or family to blatant post-Reformation bias. True historical scholarship in Scotland, as Trevor Roper has pointed out,[1] did not really begin until the publication in 1729 of Thomas Innes's *Critical Essay on the Ancient Inhabitants of Scotland*; and a spirit of critical enquiry into sources to

1 H. R. Trevor-Roper, 'George Buchanan and the Ancient Scottish Constitution', *EHR* Supplement 3 (1966).

separate truth from myth is not to be looked for in sixteenth-century Scotland. Indeed, the five principal writers of that period who concerned themselves with the fifteenth century, Adam Abell, Bishop John Lesley, Giovanni Ferreri, George Buchanan, and Robert Lindsay of Pitscottie, all saw their function as continuing the work of Boece in setting forth a series of moral tales on the virtues and vices of kingship; and in the process they contributed to the growth of a legend regarding the second half of the fifteenth century, especially concerning the character and policies of James III, which may with some justification be regarded as the Scottish equivalent of the Tudor myth of Richard III.

Such distortions, it is true, are not so much in evidence before 1437, when we can consult contemporary chroniclers for a fairly detailed account of the reign of James I. This is provided by Walter Bower's continuation of Fordun's *Scotichronicon*, which ends with the king's assassination and the execution of his murderers in 1437.[2] Furthermore, the anonymous author of the *Liber Pluscardensis*, although deriving much of his information from Bower, gives his own account of Scottish military assistance to the French between 1420 and 1431, and follows the career of James I's daughter Margaret from her marriage to the dauphin Louis to her death in 1445.[3] His chapters on Scottish assistance to France in the 1420s are particularly well informed, suggesting a first-hand account, possibly the work of Maurice Buchanan, one of the ambassadors who accompanied Princess Margaret to France in 1436, and subsequently acted as her treasurer there. At any rate, for the period before 1437 we possess two complementary contemporary or near-contemporary chronicle narratives. A study of these together with the official records gives us a clear impression of the events and policies of James I's reign, and allows us to form some estimate of the king's character.

From 1437 to 1482, however, confusion reigns. The entire period is covered by only two chronicle fragments, probably contemporary, both of which are extremely short and offer little or nothing by way of interpretation of the events which they describe. The first of these forms part of the Asloan Manuscript; headed 'ane schort memoriale of the scottis corniklis for addicoune', it occupies some fifteen folios of the manuscript and consists of two separate series of entries, the first running from 1428 to 1460, the second from 1420 to 1455. Both contain gaps and both are incomplete at the end.[4] The other source is even shorter; bearing the title 'Heir is assignt the cause quhy our

2 *Chron. Bower*, book xvi.

3 *Liber Pluscardensis*, edited by F. J. H. Skene (Edinburgh, 1880), book x, chapters 25–32; book xi, chapter 4.

4 NLS, Acc. no. 4233, ff. 109–23; printed in *Asloan Manuscript* I, pp. 215–44.

natioun was callyt fyrst the Scottys', this chronicle – a mere ten folios – is appended to the earliest manuscripts of Andrew Wyntoun's *Orygynale Cronykil of Scotland*, and it covers the history of Scotland from its legendary beginnings down to 1482;[5] but only the last two folios deal with the fifteenth century at all. In short, contemporary narratives of the whole of James II's reign and twenty-two years of the reign of James III consist of a mere seventeen folios in all; and the vital last six years of the reign, 1482–88, are not described by any contemporary. This paucity of evidence, together with the comparative lack of official records, especially before 1466, makes the growth of later legends about the period more readily understandable.

The danger of sixteenth-century misconceptions or embroidered fantasies distorting our view of the fifteenth century is considerable in the period before 1460, when we do not even possess an official register of parliament's acts, and a chronological framework of events is difficult to establish. The tendency therefore has been for writers to rely heavily on the five narrative sources available for James II's reign – the contemporary 'schort memoriale' in the Asloan Manuscript; John Lesley's vernacular history, written between 1568 and 1570;[6] George Buchanan's *Rerum Scoticarum Historia*, probably largely complete by the early 1570s but not published until 1582;[7] and Robert Lindsay of Pitscottie's *Historie and Cronicles of Scotland*, completed between 1576 and 1579. This last, the most colourful of all sixteenth-century narratives, is for James II's reign merely a translation, with some additions by Pitscottie himself, of the eighteenth book of the *Scotorum Historiae* of Hector Boece, first published in 1526.[8] A comparison of these five sources reveals the growth of sixteenth-century distortions of the major events of James II's reign, above all by Pitscottie.

The 'schort memoriale', which is contemporary or near-contemporary, is by far the most accurate of the four. Precise dates, often to the day and month, are given of events which the writer describes, and where it is possible to check these with official records, they are usually correct. Nevertheless, this is a frustrating source, for it is not a straightforward narrative of the political events of James II's reign. The major crises, such as the fall of the Livingstons, the murder of the earl of Douglas by the king, and James's own death at Roxburgh in 1460, are indeed described; but they occupy considerably less space

5 BM, Royal MS. 17 d xx, ff. 299r–308r.

6 John Lesley, *The History of Scotland from the Death of King James I in the Year 1436 to the Year 1561* (Bannatyne Club, 1830), pp. 11–32.

7 George Buchanan, *Rerum Scoticarum Historia*, translated by J. Aikman (Glasgow and Edinburgh, 1827–9) II, book xi.

8 Robert Lindsay of Pitscottie, *The Historie and Cronicles of Scotland (STS, 1899–1911)* I, pp. 12–147; Hectore Boece, *Scotorum Historiae* (Paris, 1526).

than the writer's accounts of local feuds and border warfare, natural disasters such as the flooding of Govan in November 1454, calamities like the outbreak of the plague at Dumfries in 1439, and the problem of dearth and rising prices in the same year. This recurrent interest in local events in the west suggests that the writer lived in that area of Scotland, possibly in or around Glasgow, for he cites the dates of the deaths of the provost and the bishop, and even the exact day of the first mass said by the new bishop, William Turnbull.

Where events of political importance are concerned, the chronicler is often extremely brief. Thus the notorious 'Black Dinner' of 1440 is dismissed in a single sentence: 'Item, Im iiij^c xl Erll willame of douglass archebaldis sone beand than xviij yeris of age and his brother dauid douglass was put to deid at Edinburgh.' No motive is suggested for this summary execution, nor is there any account of its consequences.[9] Fortunately subsequent events receive rather fuller treatment, and it is possible to form some estimate of royal policies during the 1450s. Although the writer displays no obvious bias in favour of the king (he describes the murder of the eighth earl of Douglas as 'foule slauchter' and criticizes the ensuing royal raid on his brother's lands[10]), he portrays James II as a powerful monarch enjoying the support of the great majority of his nobility even during times of crisis. Thus in 1452, after James's murder of Douglas, there is no suggestion that the king was in any real danger as a result. On the contrary, when the writer goes on to relate the reaction of the murdered earl's kinsmen, who arrived in Stirling a month after the murder dragging James II's safe-conduct to Douglas at a horse's tail through the town, he remarks that 'thai [the Douglas faction] excedit nocht of gud men vj^c.' This statement should be compared with a later comment; under the date June 1452, that is three months later, the writer credits the king with assembling an army of 30,000 men for an attack on the Douglas lands in the south.[11] Even if we allow for huge exaggeration in the numbers involved on both sides, the chronicler's implication is still clear. At a time when they might have expected considerable popular sympathy, the Douglases were unable to muster an army remotely comparable in size to that of the crown. Their principal ally, Alexander, earl of Crawford, had already been defeated at Brechin, significantly not by James in person, but by the earl of Huntly: 'and thair was with the erll of huntlie fer ma than was with the erll of craufurd becauss he displayit the Kingis banere and said It was the Kingis actionune and he was his luftennend.'[12]

Thus the contemporary view of James II was of a powerful, aggres-

---

9 *Asloan Manuscript* I, pp. 233–4. 10 *ibid.* I, pp. 241–2.
11 *ibid.* I, pp. 241 and 242. 12 *ibid.* I, p. 238.

sive and yet popular monarch enjoying wide support throughout his eleven years of active rule, and the chronicler records 'gret dolour throu all Scotland' at the news of his accidental death at Roxburgh.[13] This view was echoed in the first half of the sixteenth century by the monastic chronicler Adam Abell of Jedburgh, writing about 1533.[14] But the post-Reformation writers, Lesley, Buchanan and Pitscottie, while admitting James's ability, suggest that the royal position in relation to the Douglases was much weaker than contemporary evidence would lead us to believe. Furthermore, in the century separating the reign of James II from the appearance of the principal sixteenth-century histories, there had clearly emerged colourful tales about the more dramatic events of the reign which fitted well into the demands of Renaissance historiography for descriptions of clashes of personalities. Largely as a result of the lack of reliable contemporary written accounts of the reign, therefore, sixteenth-century writers turned to oral evidence, ballads or prose tales, to fill out their narratives, and their picture of James II, if not wholly false, is undoubtedly distorted.

The first of these works to appear, Bishop John Lesley's vernacular history, covers the reign fairly sparsely,[15] using parliamentary acts as a framework. He comments on social and economic problems, and this suggests a familiarity with the 'schort memoriale' or some similar contemporary source. For example, he refers to the dearth and plague of 1438–9, regarding both as 'just and dew punishment for the offencis baithe of the reularis and people' during the feuds and slaughter which he has just described as features of the previous two years.[16] But his main interest is political history, and the struggle between the king and the Douglases forms a large part of his narrative. Lesley sees the Douglas family as powerful but, at least until 1450, cooperating with rather than menacing the crown, and he follows the author of the 'schort memoriale' in suggesting that the aggression which culminated in the eighth earl's murder by the king in 1452 was initiated by James II. This view of the struggle is to some extent borne out by official records, which indicate that the animosity between king and earl was caused by James's determination to grant the earldom of Wigtown, claimed by Douglas in right of his wife, to the queen, Mary of Gueldres.[17] Douglas, on his return from a pilgrimage to Rome, was summoned to an interview with the king at Stirling but, according to

13 *ibid.* I, p. 230.
14 Adam Abell, *The Roit or Quheill of Tyme*, NLS, MS. 1746, ff. 109v–10r.
15 Lesley, *History*, pp. 11–32.
16 *ibid.*, p. 14.
17 *RMS* II, nos. 447, 503 and 544.

Lesley, refused to attend until he received an assurance under the great seal that no harm would come to him, 'as wes commonlie reportit'. James accused him of making bonds with the earl of Crawford and the Lord of the Isles, as well as with his brothers the earls of Moray and Ormond; 'and becaus the Erle ansuerit to the King owre frilie and bauldlie, he wes presentlye in the castell of Striveling slane at fas-transevin 1451' (recte 1452).[18] Lesley's account undoubtedly tele-scopes events to provide a suitably dramatic narrative, but his princi-pal point, that Douglas was to a great extent the victim of royal aggression, seems not unconvincing.

The remainder of Lesley's chapter on James II, however, is rather less credible. The murder, according to Lesley, led to such serious retaliation by the Douglases that the king considered fleeing to France. Advised against this course by the loyal James Kennedy, bishop of St Andrews, James was also heartened by the defeat of Douglas's ally, Crawford, at Brechin in May 1452. Lesley, however, still credits the new earl of Douglas with an army of 30,000 men, much larger than the king's, and apparently only the wise advice of Bishop Kennedy led to James's survival and the gradual elimination of his enemies.[19] Lesley has now clearly entered the realm of legend. Possibly he confused the original statement by the writer of the 'schort memoriale' that the king had quickly raised an army of 30,000 men. Certainly James had no reason to flee to France at this time. Nor can the major advisory role attributed by Lesley to Bishop Kennedy be substantiated. In the whole of the 'schort memoriale', Kennedy is mentioned only once, and this is a reference not to 1452, but to 1445.[20] The silence of official records about Kennedy's movements between 3 May 1451, when he was in Bruges, and 18 April 1452, when he reappears in Edinburgh as a charter witness,[21] suggests that he played little part in the crisis.

If Lesley falls into the error of relying too heavily on oral tradition when recorded facts are lacking, George Buchanan and Robert Lind-say of Pitscottie carry the same process much further. Both writers stress the threat to the crown posed by the Douglases, and Buchanan goes so far as to suggest that the eighth earl was aiming at the throne in 1451.[22] The most significant departure from Lesley's account, how-ever, lies in Buchanan's and Pitscottie's efforts to provide a motive for James II's murder of Douglas at Stirling in 1452. According to Bucha-nan, Douglas seized and put to death Maclellan, tutor of Bombie, who

18 Lesley, *History*, p. 22.   19 *ibid.*, pp. 23–5.

20 *Asloan Manuscript* I, p. 220.

21 Annie I. Dunlop, *The Life and Times of James Kennedy, Bishop of St Andrews* (Edinburgh, 1950), p. 135; *RMS* II, no. 544.

22 Buchanan, *History* II, p. 90.

had killed one of his adherents, despite James II's pleas on his behalf made directly to Douglas through Maclellan's uncle, Sir Patrick Gray. This arbitrary act, together with the Douglas-Crawford-Ross bond which James wished to break, led directly to Douglas's murder by the king at Stirling. Significantly, Buchanan suggests that the murder may have been premeditated, and names Sir Patrick Gray as one of the assassins.[23] In one of the few additions which he makes to Boece's *Scotorum Historiae*, Pitscottie gives an even more lurid version of the same tale. Sir Patrick Gray, described as 'the Kingis principall captaine and secreit serwant and familiar to his graice', was given dinner by the earl of Douglas while Maclellan was beheaded outside. Subsequently Douglas took Gray to view the body and made a grim joke of the execution. Maclellan's offence seems to have been that he would not 'ryd with the Erle of Douglas contraire the King and his authoritie nor zit to oppres the common weil of the cuntrie bot keipit him quyetlie within his boundis doand na man na wrang.' The murder of Douglas by the king was, according to Pitscottie, the immediate outcome of Maclellan's execution.[24]

This strange tale of the tutor of Bombie is not to be found in any earlier source; and indeed there is no evidence in contemporary official or private records that such a person ever existed. The conclusion must be that Buchanan and Pitscottie, seeking a motive for the king's murder of Douglas, were provided with tales of the earl's arbitrary acts which undoubtedly became garbled as they were passed on. Thus in Buchanan's account, Maclellan is executed for killing one of Douglas's supporters, while Pitscottie claims that his crime was to refuse to assist the earl against the king.

The century between the events of James II's reign, as described in the 'schort memoriale', and the completion of the histories of Lesley, Buchanan and Pitscottie, saw a remarkable shift of emphasis in written treatment of political events. All three sixteenth-century chroniclers made a considerable contribution to legend by exaggerating greatly the strength of the Douglases, and relative weakness of the king, contrary to the available contemporary evidence. Buchanan and Pitscottie sought to underline this strength by describing the aggression of the Douglases in the south and southwest, culminating in open defiance of the crown in the slaughter of Maclellan of Bombie. Only Lesley, who does not have this story, appreciated that the aggressor was the king, and his references to James's invasion of the eighth earl's lands reflect the crown's determination to recover the earldom of Wigtown in 1451. On the whole, however, the general disparity between contemporary and sixteenth-century accounts of the reign

23 *ibid*. II, pp. 90–93.   24 Pitscottie, *Historie* I, pp. 90–94.

cannot satisfactorily be explained because, apart from Lesley who claimed to have consulted public archives and some private monastic records, the chroniclers give no indication of their written sources for the pre-1460 period; and without such information, it is difficult to understand their attitudes to political events at that time.

No comparable obscurity surrounds the chroniclers' treatment of the reign of James III. Indeed, the gradual flowering of the legend regarding the king's character and policies may be clearly traced from the late fifteenth century until the early 1580s. By the latter date James III was portrayed as a recluse, alienated from his nobility and dominated by young or baseborn counsellors, in particular Cochrane the stonemason, who had turned him against his brothers and caused the murder of the younger of the two, John, earl of Mar. In addition the king, according to the legend, was no leader in war, was guilty of amassing great wealth for himself at the expense of his subjects, and was negligent in carrying out his duties, particularly in the field of criminal justice. With only minor modifications, this sixteenth-century legend has been accepted by modern writers. Thus the late Professor Dickinson, while mentioning the favourites, attributed the failures of government to the king himself, suggesting that 'in his love of the arts, James was surrounding himself with men who, to the nobles, were simply "fiddlers and masons"; and in his failure to govern, and his contempt of warlike exercises and manly sports, he was contrasted, to his disadvantage, with his brothers, the duke of Albany and the earl of Mar.'[25]

The sequel to all this, of course, was the king's downfall – an unpopular monarch, unfit to rule, deposed by his indignant nobility and finally killed after a battle in which he acted conspicuously throughout as a coward. This makes a marvellous moral tale, a warning to kings to govern well; treachery is requited, the nobility of Scotland upheld, and the story is set forth of an individual who was a failure both as a man and as a king. Yet even more strikingly than in the case of the previous reign, this traditional viewpoint is based on highly suspect chronicle narratives rather than on official records. As we have already seen, contemporary accounts of this period are limited to two folios appended to Andrew Wyntoun's *Orygynale Cronykil*, terminating abruptly in 1482. The problem is therefore to identify the sources of the dramatic tableaux which form so much of the sixteenth century accounts of the reign – the death of the earl of Mar, the power of Cochrane and the other favourites, the hangings at Lauder Bridge, and James's cowardice and murder by a priest after Sauchieburn.

25 W. C. Dickinson, *Scotland from the Earliest Times to 1603* (Edinburgh, 1961), p. 227.

The starting point for such an investigation must be contemporary views of the king himself, and two vernacular poems are of assistance in this field. The first of these, Hary's epic poem *The Wallace*, which Dr McDiarmid has convincingly argued was written about 1476–8,[26] is largely composed of bitter invective against the English, and may be taken to be a violent condemnation of James III's pro-English attitude after the alliance of 1474. Significantly, one of Hary's sources was Sir James Liddale, the duke of Albany's steward.[27] Since Albany had been prepared to resist a projected English invasion as recently as April 1474,[28] and had almost certainly been opposed to alliance, it seems likely that Hary was one of his supporters, and that *The Wallace* provided Albany with useful propaganda to justify and magnify the importance of his opposition to James III a few years later. This view of Albany as a popular national hero rather than a squalid conspirator was the beginning of the James III legend.

The second poem is a satire, probably written between 1482 and 1488,[29] and including direct rather than implied criticism of the monarch. Entitled *The Thre Prestis of Peblis*, the poem consists of three tales told by three Peebles priests to entertain each other, similar to Chaucer's *Canterbury Tales* on a much smaller scale. The first two tales are satires of the Scottish king. The writer complains that he consorted with young counsellors rather than his nobility; that the administration of justice became corrupt through the king's ready acceptance of bribes and granting of remissions for serious crimes; and that he was unfaithful to his queen. This last charge is most clearly set out in the second tale, the story of the burgess's daughter and the king. Attracted by the beauty of the daughter of a burgess named Innes, the king informed the royal fool Fictus that 'this nicht I wald have hir to my bed.' The fool, however, approached the queen and advised her to slip into the king's bed instead of the burgess's daughter, and for three nights she shared her husband's bed. When the king expressed his satisfaction with the new arrangement, Fictus revealed to him that he had in fact been sleeping with his wife. The astounded king asked the queen to forgive him, which she immediately did.

This tale is not of course to be taken literally as representing an event which actually occurred in James III's household. It is in fact an old tale, which later supplied the plot of Shakespeare's *All's Well that ends*

26 *Vita Nobilissimi Defensoris Scotie Wilelmi Wallace Militis*, edited by M. P. McDiarmid (STS, 1968) I, p. xxiv.

27 SRO, Yester Writs, GD28/170.

28 *TA* I, p. 44.

29 *The Thre Prestis of Peblis* (STS, 1920), pp. ix–xi, identifying the king in the poem; and lines 811–1004, suggesting an estrangement between the king and queen, can only refer to the crisis of 1482.

Well, and in the context of James III probably drew its relevance from a brief period during the king's captivity after the Lauder Bridge crisis when the queen was negotiating with her husband's captors, and husband and wife seem to have become estranged. That this estrangement did not last, however, is amply proved by James III's efforts, after his wife's death in 1486, to have her canonized by Pope Innocent VIII.[30]

The other complaints made against the king by the author of the *Thre Prestis*, that he shunned his nobility and turned to young counsellors, as well as accepting bribes to grant remissions for serious crimes, are fairly conventional ones. They appear, for example, in Lindsay's *Satire of the Three Estates*, in which the royal target, James V, is nevertheless treated quite sympathetically. The same is true of James III: at no point does the author of the *Thre Prestis* accuse him of being personally covetous; there is no suggestion that 'young counsel' led the king fatally astray, indeed the counsellors are only mentioned in the second of the three tales; and above all, there is no sign at all in this contemporary satire of the named favourites, the strange conglomeration of stonemasons, tailors, shoemakers, musicians, and fencing masters who figure so largely in the sixteenth century and later accounts and who would surely have been worth satirizing if they had been known to the author of the *Thre Prestis*. In the following reign, William Dunbar was quite specific in his condemnation of James IV's protégé, Damian, abbot of Tongland.

In James III's case, therefore, the complaint about 'young counsel' was probably greatly exaggerated by reference to the Scottish king's contemporaries in England and France, Edward IV and Louis XI. In England, the elevation of the relatives of Edward IV's queen, Elizabeth Woodville, widow of a former Lancastrian, was much resented by the loyal Yorkist nobility, in particular the king's younger brothers, the dukes of Clarence and Gloucester. In France, Louis XI's reliance on loyal nonentities is even more striking, illustrated most clearly by his reliance on his barber, Oliver le Dain, who was used as a royal envoy and justiciar and created count of Meulan. Significantly, the irate nobility hanged Le Dain for treason within a few months of Lousi XI's death. Thus the criticism in the *Thre Prestis* that the king was taking advice from people of no experience who were not his 'natural' counsellors, has its parallels, much more striking ones, in other countries; and the author's sympathetic treatment of the Scottish monarch extends to a tribute to his fine horsemanship, a statement which on its own casts doubt on the later tales of the fleeing coward of Sauchieburn.

30 Reg. Supp. 870, f. 121r; *CPL* xiv, p. 4.

Apart from official or private record evidence, the only other contemporary references to the reign which we possess are limited to two folios at the end of the brief chronicle appended to Wyntoun.[31] The anonymous author of this fragment may well have been a supporter of James III's rebellious brother, Alexander, duke of Albany, whose career is described even after his banishment in 1479, and whose treasons are conveniently omitted. The chronicler deals at some length with the years 1479, 1480 and 1482, and where his account may be checked against official records, his accuracy regarding dating is impressive.

Under the heading 1479, the writer describes the death of James III's younger brother, the earl of Mar: 'that zere was mony weches and warlois brint on crag gayt; and Jhone the erle of mar the Kingis brothir was slayne becaus thai said he faworyt the weches and warlois.' This curious macabre story has a striking parallel in an English event of the previous year. In February 1478, Edward IV's younger brother, George, duke of Clarence, was executed on charges which included conspiring with sorcerers to destroy the king, an elaborate indictment which was probably a device to conceal the much more worldly charge of treason. It seems highly probable that the story of Clarence's conspiracy with necromancers spread rapidly to Scotland, and that it influenced the chronicler in providing an explanation of Mar's death in the following year. Continuing the Clarence analogy, it is possible that Mar was convicted not of sorcery but of treason, and it is significant that the writer does not blame James III openly for Mar's death.

The chronicle continues with a brief account of the outbreak of war between England and Scotland in 1480. But it is in his description of the events of the crisis year 1482 that the writer is at his most interesting. He claims that there was 'gret hungyr and deid' in Scotland on account of 'the blak cunzhe in the realm strikkin and ordinyt be King James the thred, half pennys and three penny pennys innumerabill of coppir And they yeid twa zere and mair' – the first reference to the notorious black money. The other source of hardship, according to the writer, was the Anglo-Scottish war, which resulted in 'gret distructioun . . . of corne and cattell'. He goes on to relate that in July 1482, James III intended to invade England. When he had reached Lauder, 'the lordis of scotland held thair consaill in the kirk of lauder and cryit downe the blak silver and thai slew ane part of the kingis housald and other part thai banysyt.' Thereafter they took the king and put him in Edinburgh castle 'in firm kepying', where he remained from the Magdalene day (22 July) until Michaelmas (29 September). Apart from his introduction of the black money, the king is criticized in that 'he wrocht mair the consaell of his housald at war bot sympill na he did of thame that war lorddis.' Economic recovery seems to have followed the lords' 'crying down' of the black money, 'for the bol [of meal] that was for four punds [as a result of the crisis] was than for xxii shillings of quhyt silver'.[32]

Unfortunately, the chronicler breaks off at this point, having provided only a very brief narrative of the 1482 crisis with which to supplement the official records. It may however be doubted whether he either knew, or was prepared to relate, much of what was happening in Scotland in the summer of 1482. For example, he credits James III with preparing to invade England when in fact, this is the reverse of the truth. A very large English army under Richard, duke of Gloucester, assisted by James's exiled brother Albany, had invaded southern Scotland,[33] and James's muster at Lauder was purely for defence. Again, no mention is made of Albany's treasonable association with the English and his fantastic claim to be king of Scotland, a remarkable omission which is consistent with the writer's pro-Albany attitude throughout. Furthermore, he appears to have no clear idea of what 'black money' was. He calls it 'copper' first, suggesting a drastic debasement, but later describes it as 'black silver', which might well be a reference to billon placks, a mixture of silver and copper which had been authorized by parliament in 1466 and 1473, and which remained in circulation for more than ten years. He may therefore be confusing the war crisis of 1480–82, when the king may have conducted a drastic debasement, with stories of earlier parliamentary debasements and re-enhancements of the coinage which inevitably upset basic prices. It is perhaps significant that the chronicler does not in any way associate the king's 'sympill' or low-born counsellors with the introduction of the debased coinage; this was part of the later legend.

This contemporary fragment, therefore, established the existence of the legend of the earl of Mar's slaying because of his association with witches and warlocks, and also the notion that the king was heavily dependent on 'simple' counsellors. But none of these are named, nor are the stories of James as a recluse and coward who could not cooperate with his nobility to be found anywhere in contemporary literature.

The unexpected death of James III in 1488, fighting against rebels whose nominal leader was his son, altered the picture completely. In order to justify itself, the new government had to suppress any virtues which the dead king might have had, and to illustrate that, far from being rebels, they had acted for the good of the realm. Their late

32 *ibid.*, f. 308r.
33 Cora L. Scofield, *Edward IV* (London, 1923) II, p. 344.

sovereign had been misled by mean and lowly counsellors, and the magnates had taken up arms to remove these men and replace them with the monarch's 'natural' counsellors, the rejected nobility. In the ensuing struggle, the king, as they gave out in the parliament of October 1488, 'happinit to be slane'. This apology for the rebellion, expressing regret at the late king's death but suggesting that he brought it upon himself, was the official story, sent round the courts of Europe in 1489.[34] A rebellion led by disappointed office-seekers and former supporters of James III frightened the new regime into offering a reward of a hundred marks to anyone who would come forward with information leading to the arrest of the murderers of the late king.[35] It was never claimed, and by 1492, James III's name had totally disappeared from official records. However, his failure and death in the rebellion of 1488, followed by the long reign of his son James IV, a man obviously popular with his nobility, made possible an immediate extension of the James III legend. Tales of the late king's tyranny and incapacity were bound to grow in his son's reign and, as the events themselves receded in people's memories, the atmosphere was gradually created which permitted the spreading of the Scottish equivalent of the Tudor myth of Richard III.

A further stimulus was however necessary to foster the legend of James III, and it was provided by the choice of John, duke of Albany, as governor of the realm during the minority of James V. Albany, the son of James III's treacherous brother Alexander, duke of Albany, forfeited in 1483, occupied the office of governor for nine years, from May 1515 until May 1524. During this period he spent only about three and a half years in Scotland itself, the remainder in his native France; then from 1524 until his death in 1536 he was permanently in France. However, he not only left behind him a large following of pro-French Scotsmen, but also played an active part in Scottish foreign affairs until his death, being closely concerned with the abortive negotiations for a marriage between James V and Marie de Bourbon as late as 1535. The importance of Albany, both at home and abroad, throughout this period must have revived interest in the career of his father, Duke Alexander, whose reputation would now require to be rescued. Over a generation had passed since Alexander's forfeiture in 1483, and his English treason could now conveniently be forgotten and his career be made to appear that of a nobleman who consistently adhered to the Franco-Scottish alliance. This, in its turn, would involve a condemnation of his royal brother James III for his pro-English policies and tyrannical mistreatment of his younger

34 *APS* ii, p. 211.
35 *ibid.* ii, p. 230.

brothers, both themes which would probably be popular with the supporters of John, duke of Albany. In this way the legend was given a new lease of life to serve the needs of a sixteenth-century political power group.

However, not all sixteenth-century writers were aggressively pro-Albany and anti-James III. Indeed, John Major, whose *History of Greater Britain*, published in 1521, makes clear his disapproval of John, duke of Albany, remarks at one point that 'you shall find many a King, both at home and abroad, who was worse than James III.'[36] More significantly, in his *Lives of the Bishops of Mortlach and Aberdeen*, published a year later, Hector Boece describes James III as the king who had subdued the Highlanders and brought to the whole of Scotland a well-established peace, and later in the same work he praises the king as a devout and merciful man.[37] Furthermore, Boece, who made a theme of tyrants deposed by their indignant subjects in his *Scotorum Historiae* published in Paris in 1526, did not number James III among them; in fact, his short note on the king is sympathetic and anti-baronial in character.[38]

However, the passing comments of these writers were hardly enough to salvage the dead king's reputation. In 1533, Adam Abell, who describes himself as an Observantine friar of Jedburgh, completed a chronicle entitled *The Roit or Quheill of tyme*. This is a short work, owing much to Boece, briefly recording Scottish history from its fabulous beginnings down to the writer's own time, and it includes a short section on James III which adds substantially to the legend.[39] Much of Abell's account of the reign is a eulogy of Alexander, duke of Albany, who is even praised for bringing an English army to Edinburgh in July-August 1482 and freeing James III from the conspiratorial lords who had seized him at Lauder – an ingenious departure from the truth, since official records make it clear that Albany intended to depose the king. Throughout, Abell is vague about dates and inconsistent in his attitudes. For example, he contrives to be sympathetic towards James III, 'ane dewot man', and pro-Albany at the same time, and he blames unspecified conspirators for the king's death. In his thumbnail sketch of James, his reliance on earlier writers is considerable. The King is portrayed as devout, an echo of Boece, as unfaithful to his queen, a criticism levelled at him by the author of the *Thre Prestis*, and as addicted to 'privat consall of sympill men', the complaint of the

36 John Major, *A History of Greater Britain* (SHS, 1892), p. 368.

37 *Hectoris Boetii Murthlacensium et Aberdonensium Episcoporum Vitae* (New Spalding Club, 1894), pp. 73 and 76–7.

38 Boece, *Scotorum Historiae*, Regum Scotorum catalogue (Paris edition, 1526).

39 NLS, MS. 1746, ff. 110v–12r.

writer of the short comtemporary chronicle. Thus there is nothing really new in Abell's description of James's character.

In his account of the earl of Mar's death, however, Abell adds to the legend in a single sentence: 'The herll of Mar', he says, 'wes slane be consall of ane trucur callit cochrene.' This is the first reference in any chronicle to the notorious favourite, forty-five years after his supposed execution at Lauder Bridge. Cochrane is associated directly with the death of the earl of Mar, a claim made by no contemporary, and with the coining of the 'blak copir' in 1482; and Abell is the first chronicler to describe the executions at Lauder as hangings. The victims were Cochrane 'and the laif of his priwat consall' and no other favourites are mentioned by name.

Abell makes two further significant contributions to the legend. First, under the year 1486, he describes Albany's escape from Edinburgh Castle, where he had been imprisoned as a result of evil counsel given to his brother, the king. He escaped by slaying his keeper 'and syne be lynnyng clathis he passit awa downe at ane windo and salit to france.' The date is impossible, since Albany had already been dead for a year in 1486. The story could relate to either 1479 or 1483, occasions on which Albany had fallen out with James III and fled abroad from his castle of Dunbar, but there is no record evidence whatever to suggest that he was imprisoned in, or escaped from, Edinburgh castle. It would appear, therefore, that the tale of Albany's escape came to Abell or his source in the form of an undated 'prison-and-escape' story without any real motivation.

Secondly, Abell gives a brief account of James III's last campaign in 1488. With Albany's supposedly benign influence removed, he disposes of the king in two sentences: 'Than the forsaid coniuratouris the Kingis bredir slane thai conspirit aganis the King and gaif him batell beside striwiling and thare wes he slane. He wes confessit before with maistir Johne Yrland proffesor of theologie.' The implication is clear; with Albany dead, the main source of James's power was gone, and there was no further check on rebels.

The importance of Abell is not that he has these tales, for they turn up in the accounts of later writers. However, most later writers rationalized and dated them by collation with the parliamentary records, first published in 1566, and so gave them a specious air of authentic history. In Abell's chronicle, they appear without any chronological framework worth the name, and the chain of cause and effect which he suggests is slender, if not wholly absent. In fact, his account of the reign consists of little more than three stories – the death of the earl of Mar on the advice of low-born royal favourites, especially Cochrane, the career of Alexander, duke of Albany, and what might be called the story of Stirling, that is, the battle of Sauchieburn and the death of the king. Significantly, in the sentence after he states that James was slain, Abell remarks that the king was shriven by a priest, John Ireland, who was in fact the royal confessor, before the battle. Already we see the source of the later confused and distorted stories that the king was murdered by a supposed priest after the battle.

In the mid-1530s, about the same time as Abell completed his chronicle, John Bellenden produced a translation and amplification of Hector Boece's *Scotorum Historiae* of 1526 which made a curious contribution to the James III legend. Although the reign is not covered at all, Bellenden adds a genealogy of the Stewarts at the end of the volume, and remarks that the earl of Mar 'was slane in the Cannongait, in ane baith fatt'.[40] A 'baith fatt' is a bathing vat, and is presumably similar to, if not identical with, a brewer's or dyer's vat. The statement by Bellenden that Mar was killed in one of these receptacles indicates a further borrowing from the story of the death of the English duke of Clarence, who was currently said to have been executed by being drowned in a butt of Malmsey wine in 1478.[41] The tale of Mar's death in a similarly bizarre fashion, probably drawn directly from the Clarence story, must already have been incorporated into the legend.

Thus stories about James III continued to grow, and the principal sources for chroniclers of the period were probably tale-bearers, whose existence and potential danger was the theme of a number of acts of parliament from the time of Robert I until the end of the seventeenth century. These individuals, known as lesing-makars, were by definition those who uttered 'false and slanderous accusations calculated to prejudice the relations between the sovereign and the lieges',[42] in fact professional slanderers of the crown. Acts of parliament condemning lesing-makars were framed in 1318 and again in 1424, apparently with little effect.[43] In 1540 there appeared a further statute, ordering 'gif ony maner of persoun makis ony ewill information of his hienes to his baronis and liegis, that thai sal be punist in sic maner . . . as thai that makis lesingis to his grace of his lordis, baronis and liegis'; that is, that anyone trying to make a profession of stirring up trouble between crown, nobility and people by tale-bearing should

---

40 Hector Boece's *Chronicles of Scotland*, translated into Scots by John Bellenden (edition of Thomas Davidson, Edinburgh, *c*.1536). book xii, ff. lxxvr–v.

41 Dominic Mancini, *The Usurpation of Richard III*, edited by C. A. J. Armstrong (Oxford, 1936), pp. 76–7.

42 *A Dictionary of the Older Scottish Tongue from the Twelfth Century to the end of the Seventeenth*, edited by Sir W. A. Craigie and A. J. Aitken (Chicago and London, n.d.) III, p. 694. 'Lesing' is defined as 'the action of telling lies, lying, falsehood'.

43 *APS* I, p. 112; II, p. 8.

suffer the statutory penalty laid down in the previous century – forfeiture of life, lands and goods.[44]

This statute of 1540, framed in more emphatic terms than the earlier ones, suggests that tale-bearing had continued unchecked during the reign of James III and throughout the two generations which had passed since his death, the period when much of the legend grew up. Unfortunately, the statute does not state whether these stories were ballads or prose tales. However, certain themes recur like *leitmotifs*, and these rarely correspond with contemporary criticisms to be found in *The Thre Prestis of Peblis* or the acts of James III's parliaments. Instead, they are dramatic events – the death of Mar, the escape of Albany from Edinburgh Castle, the hanging of the royal favourites – and as time passes, they become more and more dramatic. Thus the fragmentary contemporary chronicle had made much of the economic crisis of 1482, down to quoting the exact rise in the price of grain as a result of the debased coinage; but half a century later, these problems are only mentioned at all by the chroniclers in order to introduce the story of Lauder Bridge and the hanging of Cochrane and the other favourites.

Thus it seems unlikely that post-Reformation writers, Lesley, Ferreri, Buchanan and Pitscottie, would have been able to present an accurate picture of the reign even if this had been their principal aim. Faced with two separate types of source – the legend, already enshrined in existing chronicles or passed on by word of mouth for two generations, and the parliamentary acts, first published in 1566 – their dilemma lay in trying to reconcile the two. This would prove difficult if not impossible in every case without rejecting the legend out of hand, for parliamentary records contain no complaints about low-born favourites, no reference to hangings at Lauder Bridge, to Mar's bizarre execution or to James's cowardice and murder by a priest. Nevertheless, the records make it abundantly clear that Albany was guilty of treason on at least two occasions, and was justifiably forfeited for these offences. The legend of Albany's heroism and political sagacity was however already established, so that the chroniclers, using parliamentary records in order to provide a framework for their narratives and yet at the same time retaining Albany's unsullied reputation, were attempting to reconcile the irreconcilable; and in the process, they added considerably to the legend.

This dilemma is apparent in John Lesley's vernacular history, completed between 1568 and 1570, the first full narrative of the reign of James III to be written.[45] Lesley's sources, by his own account, were the English histories of Polydore Vergil, Robert Fabyan and Edward

---

44 *ibid.* II, p. 360.   45 Lesley, *History*, pp. 7–9.

Hall, the Scottish public archives, and private records preserved in monasteries, of which he specifically names Paisley and Scone.[46] The English chroniclers are used only to provide some account of Scotland's foreign relations and the monastic records describe isolated events of local importance such as the promotion of Henry Crichton, abbot of Paisley, to Dunfermline as the result of royal supplications. Thus Lesley's principal sources would appear to be two in number – the public archives, which are unspecified but probably included the printed parliamentary statutes of 1566 and a diplomatic collection of documents, transcripts of royal letters, truces, alliances and treaties; and the legend, which provided him with a eulogy of Albany, an embroidered story of Mar's death and the royal favourites, the hangings at Lauder, and the king's murder in 1488.

Much of Lesley's potential value as a source for James III's reign is therefore vitiated by his combination of these two very different types of evidence, and we may note a number of contributions to the legend as a result. Thus he relies on the 1482 chronicle, Abell and Bellenden in describing the fate of Mar, convicted of witchcraft and murdered in the Canongate; and he adds his own information, the date 1480, Craigmillar as the place of Mar's imprisonment, and the story that he bled to death rather than drowned.[47] The inclusion of the date 1480, a year later than that suggested by the contemporary chronicler, gives an air of authenticity to Lesley's tale which it does not deserve; his parliamentary sources would give him the date of Mar's forfeiture, and he has merely used a more than ordinary historical intelligence to link this with tales of Mar's fate which had long been circulating. And so it goes on. The 1482 crisis is explained in terms of the king's lowly familiars, above all Cochrane, who is now given the Christian name of Thomas, is associated with the coining of the 'black money', and is described as a mason whom the king had made earl of Mar. This was simply an elaboration of the well-established theme that Cochrane had been responsible for Mar's death. Lesley adds the information that the favourite received the earldom as a reward for poisoning James III's mind against his brother, thereby creating an explanation for the crisis of 1482, and ensuring that Cochrane's inevitable fall would be from a great height. Lesley adds one further complaint which indicates the extent of his confusion: the king, he suggests, had fallen into disrepute by his estrangement from the queen, living voluptuously with a

46 J. Lesley, *De Origine, Moribus et Rebus Gestis Scotorum Libri Decem* (STS, 1888) I, pp. xx–xxi. This was Lesley's second history of Scotland, written in Latin and published in Paris in 1578. However, since he can only have consulted Scottish records before going into exile in 1568 (that is, before he wrote the vernacular history), we must infer that the same sources were used for both works.
47 Lesley, *History*, pp. 43–4.

whore called Daisy. As 'Daisy' is merely a contraction of 'Margaret', the queen's name, it becomes apparent that this is a garbled version of the theme of the second tale in the *Thre Prestis*, which turns up again in Abell's account and which had its origin in the king's physical separation from the queen.

The favourites named by Lesley as having been hanged at Lauder 'with certane uthers' are three in number, 'Thomas Cochran Erle of Mar, Williame Roger, and James Hommyll tailyeour'. There was a Thomas Cochrane in the royal service at this time, a minor household official, possibly usher of the king's bedchamber, who was presented by the king to the lands of Cousland near Edinburgh, died and was forfeited some time before May 1483.[48] The name only appears twice in contemporary official records, and there is no evidence whatever to support the story that the king made Cochrane earl of Mar. Even less is known about the English musician William Roger; possibly he is to be identified with the king's 'familiar squire' who received the lands of Traquair in Peeblesshire after the fall of the Boyds, resigning them about the time of the general revocation of 1476.[49] However Giovanni Ferreri, who otherwise follows Lesley's narrative very closely, was later to describe Roger as the founder of a school of musicians who remembered him as late as 1529,[50] and as Ferreri was in Scotland between 1528 and 1537, his information for this statement may well have been at first hand. Absence of the other record evidence regarding Roger's career suggests that his position at court was not an important one, and he may have played no more part in political life than the lute players to whom the king made small payments in 1473 and 1474.[51] Finally, James Hommyll presents no problem. As Lesley states, he was the king's tailor, frequently mentioned in the treasurer's accounts, and he survived into the following reign.

Thus Lesley, though building on well-established tales, added considerably to the Lauder legend by giving the incident a false motivation. What probably happened was that the king was seized by a group of conspirators, and a few household servants who happened to be present were killed. But later accounts, in order to justify the actions of those involved, shifted the emphasis from the principal event, the seizure of James III, to the killing of the servants, who to merit their deaths required to have created for them careers as evil counsellors. It is true that Lesley, in completing his account of the Lauder affair, mentions as the sole survivor among the favourites a youth of eigh-

48 *ADC*, pp. 49 and 82.

49 *RMS* ii, no. 1418.

50 *Appendix to Hector Boece, Scotorum Historiae*, second edition, by Giovanni Ferreri (Paris, 1574), ff. 391 r–v.

51 *TA* i, p. 59.

teen, John Ramsay, whom the records show to have risen high in the royal service during the 1480s.[52] But nothing whatever is known of his career before 1482, and it is likely that, like the others, he was a minor servant in the royal household who had the misfortune to be in attendance on the king at Lauder.

The great weakness of Lesley's account of the reign, however, lies in his consistent praise of the duke of Albany, even in 1482–3, when his English treason was clearly set forth in the parliamentary records and diplomatic documents of the period. In this attitude Lesley was treading an already well-worn path; and like Abell, he followed Albany's career through to its conclusion, describing his death at a tournament in Paris in 1484, and mourning him as 'ane fadir in chevalry'.[53] Once deprived of his pro-Albany source, however, Lesley shows little or no understanding of the events of the 1480s. Thus the motives of the 1488 rebels are of the highest, and they were determined 'to restore the libertie of the cuntrey, and to purge the same of all wicked counsall and abuses' – the traditional complaint about evil advisers surrounding the king. Lesley's description of 1487–8 is hopelessly at odds with the facts. For example, he states that 'the King passit to Striveling to remane, leaving the prince his sone in Edinburgh castell with the Quene his modir';[54] in fact, the king was to be found almost constantly at Edinburgh,[55] the prince was brought up in Stirling, and the queen was dead. To revert to Lesley: giving battle to the rebels, who demanded that he abdicate in favour of his son, James was slain by anonymous wicked men at Bannockburn mill. Thus Lesley ends his description of the king on a sympathetic note; evidently the 'wicked men' who murdered the king are not to be identified with the well-meaning nobility who were fighting to remove his supposed evil counsellors. Perhaps to draw the distinction more clearly, Lesley suggests that, before the battle, the rebel prince gave orders that no one was to lay violent hands on his father.

Little need be said about Giovanni Ferreri's continuation of Hector Boece's *Scotorum Historiae*, published in Paris in 1574. The author covers the reign of James III and, as he had had two spells as a teacher at Kinloss Abbey in the 1530s and 1540s, some originality might have been expected in his narrative. Clearly, however, he did little more than copy Lesley, to whose account of the reign Ferreri's work bears a striking similarity. Probably he copied much of Lesley's narrative when the latter was in exile in Paris; and so he added little to the

52 The first known royal grant to Ramsay was made on 6 September 1483, when the king described him as his 'familiar squire of his chamber'; *RMS* ii, no. 1565.

53 Lesley, *History*, p. 51.

54 *ibid.*, p. 55.

55 *RMS* ii, nos. 1691–1730 (October 1487–May 1488).

legend, except to change Cochrane's Christian name to Robert and to add three more favourites, Preston, Torphichen and Leonard. Leonard is described as a shoemaker, Torphichen as a man-at-arms who is possibly to be identified with Sir William Knolles, preceptor of Torphichen; and Thomas Preston, according to Ferreri an innocent nobleman hanged at Lauder, may have been the individual who brought in an English ship, loaded with wine, and was paid £90 out of the Edinburgh customs for his trouble. This slender evidence would suggest that Preston's status was that of a well-to-do Edinburgh merchant burgess; and it is possibly the same man who is described as forfeited and dead before Christmas 1482.[56]

The remaining chroniclers of the period, Buchanan and Pitscottie, are hardly worth discussing as serious history. George Buchanan, who underwent a remarkable change from Catholic humanist in the 1550s to Protestant revolutionary by the end of the 1560s, was primarily concerned in his *Historia* to justify the political theory that a tyrant might be deposed by his people; and his target was Mary, queen of Scots. In order to convince his readers of the justice of Mary's deposition, Buchanan quoted precedents from Boece's legendary kings in the *Scotorum Historia*, and he quoted 1488, which was not a deposition at all, but after the passage of a century and the growth of the legend could be made to look like one. Thus book XII of the *Historia*, which relates to James, is a contribution to legend, but not to history.[57] As an example both of Buchanan's moralizing and his extension of the legend, his conclusions on James III are worth quoting. The king, he claimed, was 'a prince not naturally of a bad disposition, but corrupted by evil communication; for when in childhood he had given some indication of an excellent genius, and a mind truly royal . . . he was hurried headlong into every species of vice by men of the very lowest description.'[58] Lesley and Ferreri had at least treated the king sympathetically at the end, but Buchanan, in order to support his own theory of popular sovereignty, introduced a determined bias against James III which extended the myth.

Robert Lindsay of Pitscottie, a Fife laird, was like Buchanan a Protestant apologist and propagandist. However, in describing the latter half of the fifteenth century, he has no consistent attitude, except perhaps the glorification of his Lindsay ancestors, and his information is all hearsay, a collection of strange, unlikely, and sometimes absurd tales strung together, often without any apparent function or relevance. Pitscottie's *Historie* is unredeemed by any use on his part of the

56 *ER* IX, p. 218; *RMS* II, no. 1533.

57 An excellent analysis of Buchanan's motives is to be found in Trevor-Roper, 'George Buchanan and the Ancient Scottish Constitution'.

58 Buchanan, *History* II, p. 159.

public archives, and the prominent men whom he quotes as his sources, Sir Andrew Wood of Largo, Sir David Lindsay of the Mount, John Major, Patrick, fourth Lord Lindsay of Byres, and Sir William Bruce of Earlshall, all Fife men, were not Pitscottie's contemporaries, since he was not born until about 1532. It is unlikely that Pitscottie ever had the opportunity to read the histories of Lesley and Ferreri, and so his account of the reign of James III lacks even the chronological framework which these writers imposed on their narratives by constant reference to acts of parliament.

All the well established tales, often considerably expanded, are to be found in Pitscottie – the killing of the earl of Mar because a witch had prophesied to the king that he would be slain by the nearest of his kin (a distortion of the story in the 1482 chronicle); the glorification of Albany and consequent deprecation of James as 'ane man who desirit nevir to hear of weiris nor the fame thereof'; the seizure and hanging of Cochrane and the other favourites (who are however not named) at Lauder; and the rebellion of 1488, ending with the tale of James's flight from the field of Sauchieburn on a great grey horse given to him by Pitscottie's ancestor, Lord Lindsay of Byres, and his fall and subsequent murder in Bannockburn mill by an individual who claimed to be a priest and offered to shrive the king.[59] This last tale is merely a distortion of that part of the tradition which appears with Abell's statement that James III was shriven by John Ireland before the battle and there is nothing really new here. Apart from the addition of highly coloured details, therefore, Pitscottie extends the legend in only one respect: he suggests that Stirling was James III's favourite town, and attributes to the king the founding of the chapel royal and the building of the great hall at Stirling (both James IV's creations). This error probably arises out of the fact that Margaret of Denmark and her sons lived at Stirling Castle, and that James III was eventually killed near Stirling; but his favourite town, as official records clearly show, was Edinburgh.

Space precludes further discussion of the progress of the legend in later centuries, when it assumed fantastic proportions, including efforts in the seventeenth century to upgrade the favourite Cochrane from the lowly status of stonemason into the architect who designed the great hall at Stirling Castle, a claim eagerly seized upon by twentieth-century writers, but not made even by Pitscottie; an eighteenth-century pamphlet war on the merits or demerits of Cochrane as prime minister of Scotland; and a nineteenth-century play which attributed James III's death at Sauchieburn to the failure of the Bathgate miners to rally to him at a critical point in the battle. It is to be

59 Pitscottie, *Historie* I, pp. 152–210.

hoped, however, that enough has been said about the sixteenth-century myths of the fifteenth century to make clear the steady growth of the legend. The fact that the details of this legend do not appear in writing until the late sixteenth century suggest that those who wrote them down were drawing heavily on unwritten stories which had been circulating earlier, stories which were probably encouraged by the fact that James IV had nominally overthrown his father, and regent Albany was the son of James III's treasonable brother. Oral tradition is not a good source for the accurate transmission of information, particularly when there are probable grounds for its distortion.[60] The result in this case is clearly seen in Pitscottie's *Historie*, a confused collection of picturesque stories which are either pure legend, or distort the truth to such an extent as to make the entire work worthless as a source for the fifteenth century. Pitscottie is an extreme case; but there is no doubt that a sufficiently accurate, if incomplete, picture of the fifteenth century can be drawn from contemporary records, and this makes it possible to consign many of the stories of the sixteenth-century chroniclers to the realm of legend where they belong.

60 One of the themes in Jan Vansina, *Oral Tradition: a Study in Historical Methodology* (London, 1973), is the development of myths designed 'to justify the existing political structure' (p. 51). The reasons for distortion in the transmission of oral testimonies are discussed on pp. 76–7.

3

The exercise of power
Jennifer M. Brown

1 The king

Government in fifteenth-century Scotland was monarchical government, the most familiar form of medieval government and having much in common with other western European monarchies. Scottish kings, like their contemporaries, worked through formal institutions, their chancery and exchequer, council and parliament. These institutions were less sophisticated and complex than their English or French counterparts. At the most formal and technical level, Scottish royal clerks were perfectly competent in producing official documents, as comparison between English and Scottish privy-seal and signet letters illustrates.[1] But there was no equivalent in Scotland of, for example, the vigorous English house of commons, highly self-conscious about its rights and privileges. Nor did there exist established central courts of justice or a secular legal profession; it was only in this century that there came into existence a central court at all – the session, brought into being by James I to relieve the council of some of the burden of judicial cases. Moreover the Scottish crown was not wealthy by any standards and certainly not in comparison with the English; the incomplete financial records make it impossible to be certain about the king's revenue, but it would appear that it was at best one tenth of that of the English monarch, and very probably less.[2]

The Scottish crown was, therefore, comparatively impoverished, both in real terms and in the sense that its central institutions were relatively undeveloped. In addition there was the appalling problem of successive royal minorities, amounting overall between 1406 and 1488 to thirty-eight years, compared to the forty-four when an adult king was on the throne. Yet from another point of view, the Scottish

---

1 I am indebted for this point to Professor A. L. Brown of the University of Glasgow.

2 A. L. Murray, 'The Comptroller, 1425–1488', *SHR* LII (1973), p. 13; Ranald Nicholson, *Scotland: the Later Middle Ages* (Edinburgh, 1974), pp. 453–4. It is suggested that the estimate for *c.* 1486, £16,380 Scots, is too high. This indicates that James III was doing well if he got an income of about £5,000 sterling. An English king would have at least £50,000 and often considerably more.

monarchy of the fifteenth century enjoyed a position of greater strength than that of England. It was unchallenged. Only once was there anything which can be accurately described as a usurpation attempt, and that was the unsupported claim to the throne by James III's brother in 1482. Nor was it endangered from without, for the last serious threat of English overlordship came from Edward III. Indeed, far from being defensive, the Stewart kings showed a new, outward-looking self-confidence. For the first time since 1286, they looked further afield than their own country or England for brides; a daughter of James I was married to the dauphin, and James II regarded himself as of sufficient European importance to offer to arbitrate in a dispute between the French king and his heir. If there were weaknesses, there was also certainly strength. The problem is the source of that strength.

The question of what monarchy meant in Scotland would be difficult to answer even with a great deal more information than exists. Commentary on an accepted form of government was rare in the middle ages, and virtually non-existent in Scotland, while what there was tended to be very general, going no further than the dictum of the English lawyer, Sir John Fortescue: 'Regis namque officium pugnare est bella populi sui, et eos rectissime iudicare.'[3] General as they were, however, these two principles were fundamental, and they provide some kind of yardstick in assessing what was expected of a Scottish king, as is indicated by the known reactions to the actions of the kings themselves.

The first principle was taken literally. The idea of the king taking the field in battle died out in Britain in the mid-eighteenth century, earlier than in Europe. But until then, in spite of occasional disasters, such as Neville's Cross in 1346, when David II was captured by the English, saddling his country with the problems of an absentee king and a large ransom, and Roxburgh and Flodden, when James II and James IV were killed, both leaving a child to succeed them, it was never seriously questioned that kings should lead their armies in person. Thus in March 1482, faced with the threat of an English invasion, it was resolved in parliament that if the English wardens led the invading force it should be met by the Scottish wardens and lieutenants given sufficient power for the time; but if the 'saide Revare Edward [Edward IV] happinis to cum in propir persoun, to be resistit be oure soverane lord in propir persoun'.[4] A century later, while there was no occasion for the principle to be called into operation, its continued acceptability is attested by the growing legend of James III, which depicted him as a man who had no ability in warlike pursuits and failed as a military

3 Sir John Fortescue, *De Laudibus Legum Anglie*, edited by S. B. Chrimes (Cambridge, 1949), p. 2.
4 *APS* ii, p. 139.

leader, ultimately dying a coward's death in flight from battle.[5] Even shortly after Flodden, a disaster on an unparalleled scale in a country where battle with the English normally meant defeat, John Major could write an account of that earlier disaster, the death of James II at Roxburgh in 1460, which showed no sign of any feeling that the price might be too high: 'for vigorous kingship, most writers give the first place to this monarch, seeing that he gave himself with all zeal to things of war and naught else; and in time of war he was fellow to every private soldier. I, however, prefer before him his father, the first James, alike for his natural endowment and his fortitude in the field.'[6]

The first of Fortescue's principles is straightforward enough. The second is more complicated, for it meant far more than is immediately implied by the word 'iudicare', and indeed, it is curious that it is expressed in terms of justice rather than of good government. Two long-accepted and standard comments on medieval kingship are that government was the king's government, personally controlled and inspired by him, and that the king was the fountain of justice; but in the fifteenth century, reference was normally made only to the second of these.[7] In fact the idea that a king should provide justice for his subjects was very comprehensive. It did not simply mean that he had a duty to make available justice in his courts, although that was part of it, and in the fifteenth century there was increased demand for royal justice. It included also the obligation to deal justly with his subjects, to cope adequately with rebellion and disorder, to create conditions in which people could obtain justice, with all the benefits of peace and security for person and possessions which would follow from that; in other words, to provide strong government as well as effective courts.

But to defend one's country and to govern it, kings required money, or, at any rate, so the kings of England and France thought. So also, to an extent, did the kings of Scotland, the problem being that they had much less of it. Their lack of money had a profound effect on how they exercised royal power. They could not, even if they wanted, aim at anything like the degree of centralization of the governments of England and France, nor begin to build up power at the centre at the expense of power in the localities; for they could not pay officials in the way that the English crown could pay, for example, its wardens of the marches, nor could they pay the judges and lawyers. And at no time did they have the money to raise a contract army.[8]

5 See above, chapter 2, p. 17.

6 John Major, *A History of Greater Britain* (SHS, 1892), p. 386.

7 S. B. Chrimes, *English Constitutional Ideas in the Fifteenth Century* (Cambridge, 1936), p. 15, cites Fortescue on one occasion writing about the king's duty as administrator as well as judge; this is an unusually wide view, even for Fortescue himself.

8 They did, of course, give wages and pensions to their household servants and other

Yet the problem is not simply that the Scottish crown was too impoverished to emulate its European contemporaries. Poverty can be a relative thing. By comparison with the revenues of the kings of England and France, that of the kings of Scotland was so small as to appear derisory. But their expenditure as rulers of a smaller country with a much smaller population was also very much less. Moreover, it is difficult to say with certainty that the Scottish monarchy was particularly poor, in the sense that it did not have money for the things that it wanted. The evidence is so far from complete that only once is it possible to estimate the king's revenue – £16,380 Scots for the year 1486 – and even that is probably too generous. The evidence is also conflicting, for it suggests grave financial problems, sometimes crises.[9] But it also shows, for at least parts of the period, a surprising degree of spending power, and on one occasion the possession by the crown of a very considerable amount of money. All the Stewart kings were conspicuous spenders, interested in building, in presiding over a court which, though smaller than those of fellow monarchs, was by no means one of which they need feel ashamed, in being patrons of the arts, if again on a comparatively limited scale, in spending great sums on artillery, on the navy, on dress, on making a show which befitted a king. James I was apparently in debt at his death in 1437, though that was a situation far from unique to Scottish kings. James III was in financial straits in 1482 yet, after his death at Sauchieburn in 1488, boxes were found, including one picked up on the battlefield, containing sums of money amounting to £24,517 10s, an amount perhaps equal to two years' revenue. It has been rightly pointed out that this 'serves as a warning to those who try to write the financial history of his reign from the exchequer rolls alone'; but it is simply not known how he managed to acquire this money.[10]

What this seems to suggest is a curious hand-to-mouth quality about the attitude of the fifteenth-century kings to their cash revenue, a desire to have money for specific purposes, but a lack of long-term economic thought and an indifference to capitalizing on such opportunities as they had. A striking feature of this century is the great

servants outside the household, but these were not large; A. L. Murray, *Exchequer and Crown Revenue, 1437–1542* (unpublished PhD thesis, Edinburgh, 1961), pp. 222–5.

9 The introduction, for example, of a drastically debased coinage by James III, the 'black money' was one of the causes of resentment in the period immediately preceding the Lauder crisis of 1482. Nicholson, *The Later Middle Ages*, pp. 499–500.

10 Murray, 'The Comptroller', p. 29. In an interesting article on the use of feudal practices of little social relevance, R. G. Nicholson points to the success of James IV in making money by adapting these practices to a money economy, in the development of feuing, sales of land and apprisings, but, as he says, although this did not begin only in James IV's reign, it was of far less financial significance before then; 'Feudal Developments in Late Medieval Scotland', *Juridical Review* 18 (1973), pp. 1–21.

increase in the amount of land possessed by the crown. Both James I and James II were in marked degree acquisitive, indeed avaricious. Both added considerably to the royal demesne, principally through the forfeiture of a few great families; the extensive lands of the Douglases, which came to the crown after their forfeiture in 1455 as a single windfall, were a dramatic addition. Yet these lands were not used, to anything like the extent they could have been, to build up cash revenue. This was not simply because of lack of currency; it has been argued, in a discussion of crown lands in the late fifteenth and early sixteenth centuries, that 'the continued appearance of rents [of crown lands] in kind in the rentals and exchequer rolls should be ascribed to the conservatism of the financial system, not to the poverty of the country or the shortage of coin.'[11] In 1455 and again in 1458, suggestions for change actually came not from the crown but from parliament.

The first move was the act of annexation of 1455, the attempt to make the crown husband its resources. This began with the statement that 'the poverte of the crowne is oftymis the caus of the poverte of the Realme' – admittedly hardly profound economic comment – and went on to insist that certain lands, lordships and castles, which were listed, should be annexed to the crown and inalienable by it without consent of parliament. The act went on to make the amazing provision that if the king did grant any of these lands without consent, they were recoverable by the crown, and the recipient would be obliged to pay back any profits he had made. It stated that James was sworn to observe this, and that his successors would be likewise bound in their coronation oaths. This was followed up in 1458 by a suggestion which, if adopted, would have increased the crown's money revenue: parliament thought it 'speidfull that the king begyne and gif exempill to the laif' by feuing his lands.[12] But the crown did not adopt the idea, to any significant extent, until the reign of James IV, when its cash income was indeed increased by this method.

What parliament wanted was, presumably, a situation similar to that demanded much more frequently in England, that the king should live of his own.[13] There is no evidence in Scotland of a tradition of conflict between king and parliament about this principle. But if it was not a matter for regular discussion, the point made in 1455 was the same, that the king had sufficient lands to do two things, both admirable – one, to give grants to those who served him well and merited

---

11 Murray, *Exchequer and Crown Revenue*, p. 187.   12 *APS* II, pp. 42, 49.

13 B. P. Wolffe, *The Crown Lands, 1461–1535* (London, 1970), pp. 1–28. No Scottish king used as propaganda, as Edward IV did, the promise that he would relieve his subjects of financial burden by living of his own, although no Scottish king had quite the need to advertise the advantages of his kingship that Edward IV had.

them; the other, to support his household and government without recourse to other means, provided that he acted on the first point with moderation. But there was one element lacking on the Scottish side, taxation; only in a negative sense can it be regarded as an issue, to the extent that, if the act was observed, regular taxation would not be necessary. This, even more than the failure to take up the idea of feuing, is the remarkable and crucial difference between the kings of Scotland and their northern European contemporaries. They did not tax regularly. David II had done so, in the last decade of his reign, but that was exceptional, and can be explained largely in terms of the ransom he was obliged to pay.[14] Yet James I was also saddled with a ransom, and he did not manage to impose regular taxation. It is not enough to explain this on the grounds that there was resentment against taxation itself, and against James's use of his ransom as an excuse while pocketing the money for other purposes. Probably there was resentment, but the question is the wider one of why the Scottish kings did not make use of a practice which was long established in England and becoming so in France.

No doubt part of the explanation of the contrast between Scotland and France in this period lies in the fact that the French kings could do what the Scottish kings could not, namely use war as a legitimate reason for taxing regularly, and having begun, simply continue.[15] Lack of taxation in itself helps to explain why Scottish government was much less complex than that of England or France; without it, there was less money to pay royal officials, but also less need for them, for the administrative sophistication of these other countries. It helps, moreover, to explain the failure of James I's attempt to involve the lairds, the equivalent of the English knights of the shire, in parliament; there was less incentive for them to turn up, to assert their rights, when their pockets were touched very much less. The argument at this stage becomes circular. But there is a central point at the heart of it. It is not just that Scottish subjects consistently managed to put up successful resistance to attempts by the crown to levy taxation regularly. The kings themselves did not think as their contemporaries thought in England and France. They did not try to tax regularly. Even when

14 Nicholson, *The Later Middle Ages*, p. 454, points out that James III's revenue cannot have been greater than David II's, in the last year of his reign, a century earlier. Most of James's income came from crown lands, most of David's from taxation and the great customs.

15 P. S. Lewis, *Later Medieval France: the Polity* (London, 1968), pp. 104–7. G. L. Harriss, *King, Parliament and Public Finance in Medieval England to 1369* (Oxford, 1975), pp. 509–17, shows the effect of war on English public finance and on the role of Lords and Commons in parliament in financial matters. These developments in England and France are not paralleled in Scotland, although Scotland had had its time of war also, from the late thirteenth to the mid-fourteenth century.

they did require to raise an army, or needed money for embassies or a royal marriage, they did not necessarily demand taxation and, on the occasions when they did, their demands were limited. This suggests a different approach to the business of governing their country on the part of the kings of Scotland, and makes the yardstick which could be used in England and France – the degree of success which kings had in building up government at the centre – much less applicable.

There were positive reasons why Scottish kings should not have tried to tax. Given the much smaller population, they would, for example, have had to tax infinitely more heavily than the kings of England or France to pay for an army of comparable size. It is not surprising that they did not try to do so; it was a matter of common sense. But there is a danger here of imposing too great a degree of rationalization. There remains the question of whether they began with the assumption that it was unrealistic to try to impose regular taxation and that therefore they had to accept a different style of government, even if it was second best, or whether they simply assumed that their style of government was suited to the country they ruled and that as a result they did not consider substantially different possibilities.

In fact, they relied heavily on the personal cooperation of their most powerful subjects, more heavily than other fifteenth-century monarchs, although this was a matter of degree not of kind. Thus when they were involved in war, they depended on the landowners using their personal power to turn out their men. This did mean that they had problems not faced by kings who could pay their troops. There is a certain irony, for example, in the later legend of James III, in that on four occasions James proposed military campaigns which foundered on the refusal of the magnates to fight. Any war must have a measure of popular support. But James III's experience demonstrates the peculiar relevance of this in Scotland, to an extent not found, for example, in England, where kings could pay for their armies. In 1400, Henry IV, the usurper, attempting to increase his prestige, sought to do so by mounting an expensive and, as it proved, humiliating campaign against Scotland. It was made clear in parliament that it was the king's decision, but the fact that the enthusiasm of both Lords and Commons was less than the king's did not prevent the campaign from taking place. Henry raised an army, not by indenture, but by summons to those who had personal bonds with him. It cost over £10,000; the money came mainly from loans, which the king repaid by the third year of his reign.[16] This is something which could not have been undertaken by the Scottish crown.

16 A. L. Brown, 'The English Campaign in Scotland, 1400' in *British Government and Administration: Studies presented to S. B. Chrimes*, edited by H. Hearder and H. R. Loyn

Even when the Scottish kings did raise money, the contrast with England was dramatic. In 1482, £13,000 was allocated from the English exchequer to finance an army of 20,000 men under Richard duke of Gloucester, to take Berwick and return home in twenty-eight days; a further £595 was paid out for a force of 1,700 men to remain in the north with Gloucester for fourteen days thereafter.[17] In Scotland, in April 1481, under threat of an English invasion, parliament agreed to raise a 'contribucioun' of 7,000 merks Scots each from the clergy and barons, and 1,400 from the burghs, with exemption for those landed men who went in person to Berwick. In March 1482, with invasion certain, the estates agreed that, as the king had already financed the strengthening of the fortifications of Berwick and would pay for a garrison of 500 men for three months, they would provide and pay for 600 soldiers, to be stationed along the borders. The detailed attention given to this makes curiously pathetic reading when set against the machine-like efficiency of the English plan of campaign. All that was done to ensure that, when these small garrisons of sixty or more frequently twenty men were mown down by the English, there would be a Scottish army to meet them, was to direct the sheriffs to hold weapon-showings every fifteen days, and to be ready to call out the lieges, well armed and with provisions, and turn up as quickly as possible when summoned.[18] The obligation of able-bodied men to fight for their country was a common one; in Scotland it did not necessarily involve payment from the crown.

The king was therefore particularly dependent on the cooperation of men of influence in the localities, and this gave heightened importance to the popularity of the campaign. Neither James I nor James II had any difficulty in raising armies to besiege Roxburgh, the English-held town which was a thorn in the side of the Scots because it was an English enclave within Scotland. James I's campaign in 1436 failed. But this did not lessen the enthusiasm to try again, as is reflected in the contemporary chronicler's account of the great host which accompanied James II in 1460. No estimate can be made of what was meant by 'ane gret ost', but the army's own enthusiasm is indicated by the fact that even when the king had been killed when watching a gun which exploded, it remained to capture Roxburgh.[19] These cam-

(Cardiff, 1974). pp. 40–54. Another example is the Agincourt campaign where the enthusiasm felt for Henry V should not obscure the earlier doubts about the proposal to fight; E. F. Jacob, *The Fifteenth Century* (Oxford, 1961), pp. 138 and 141. While not so heavily dependent as a Scottish king on the reaction to his proposed campaigns, an English king could not, of course, be indifferent to it, as is shown by J. R. Lander, *Crown and Nobility, 1450–1509* (London, 1976), pp. 220–41.

17 N. A. T. Macdougall, *James III: a Political Study, 1466–1488* (unpublished PhD thesis, Glasgow, 1968), pp. 138–9.

18 *APS* ii, pp. 134 and 139–40.   19 *Asloan Manuscript* i, pp. 229–30.

paigns, and occasional forays into northern England, popular with the border lords, attracted support; they had the double advantage of offering the chance of fighting the traditional enemy, England, while not involving the Scots in a pitched battle where the odds were weighted against them. Indeed, the desire to avoid engaging the English in battle was a marked feature of military policy since the reign of Robert II, arousing the contempt of the French troops who came to Scotland in 1385, but remarkably successful in its effect of leaving invading English armies with no one to fight and nothing to do but create a certain amount of havoc in the lowlands, and retreat.[20]

The other important element which had a bearing on men's willingness to fight was the personal prestige of the king. Both James I and James II commanded respect, and proposed popular campaigns. The other military enterprise which roused tremendous and remarkable enthusiasm was the Flodden campaign in 1513. This was a distinct break in the pattern of not fighting the English, and it was a battle fought as a result of James IV's ambitious foreign policy, in French interests. What the overwhelming support for it reflects is the extent of the popularity which the king enjoyed. In sharp contrast are the reactions to the military proposals of James III.

Early in his reign, James sought to raise armies for campaigns which were both over-ambitious and frivolous. In 1471 he proposed to take over part of the duchy of Brittany, and in 1473 to acquire Saintonge and annex the duchy of Gueldres. In no way could this be regarded as defence of the kingdom and indeed, one of the main points of the clergy's opposition in 1471 was the danger of leaving Scotland vulnerable to English attack.[21] In 1473, parliament again objected strongly to James's plans, this time telling him bluntly 'to tak part of labour apon his persone & travel throw his Realme & put sic Justice & polycy in his awne realme that the brute & the fame of him mycht pas in utheris contreis'.[22] This stricture gives one contemporary evaluation of what was wanted of the king – to get on with the business of governing his country, and not to seek renown in risky and grandiose schemes for foreign adventuring.

A decade later, lack of enthusiasm for a particular campaign and hostility to the king came together to create a situation which ended with the brutal humiliation of James III. A number of the magnates, summoned to the muster of the army at Lauder in July 1482, chose to ignore the threat from the invading English army, which included Alexander, duke of Albany, making a bid to seize his brother's throne; instead, they forced a showdown with James, who was brought back

20 Nicholson, *The Later Middle Ages*, pp. 196–8; Brown, 'The English Campaign in Scotland, 1400', pp. 43–4.

21 *APS* II, p. 102.   22 *ibid.* II, p. 104.

to Edinburgh and temporarily incarcerated in the castle by his half-uncles, the earls of Buchan and Atholl, and the bishop-elect of Moray. Defence of Berwick, the main target of the English attack, was much more justifiable than James's earlier schemes. But there is room for doubt about the extent of Scottish commitment to retaining Berwick. For the English, in spite of the criticisms of one contemporary, on the grounds of the expense and difficulty of holding the town, it was a matter of prestige; they had held it from 1356 until 1461, when it was handed over to the Scots by Henry VI and Margaret of Anjou, desperate for support after the Lancastrian defeat at Towton.[23] To James III also, Berwick was important; after its loss, he made it an issue in negotiations with England during the last six years of his reign. But his concern does not seem to have been shared by others. An offer to consider handing over Berwick and Roxburgh made in 1433 by the English, anxious to weaken the Franco-Scottish alliance, was rejected, and the Scots concentrated their military efforts only on Roxburgh, lying within Scotland. Nor was there any military attempt to retrieve the loss of 1482. The refusal to defend Berwick suggests that they did not regard it as a matter of top priority at a time of internal crisis, when grievances against the king's government had come to a head.

What this episode demonstrates is that this king did not command the respect and support of his greatest subjects. Thus his chances of persuading them to support him were reduced and, lacking the resources to pay for an army, James's intention to fight could be checkmated. But the refusal to support the king was a symptom and not the cause of trouble. In 1473, James was told by parliament what was the business of a king; indeed, successive parliaments, in the 1470s and 1480s, criticized him for his laziness, his interest only in the profits of justice. That he failed to raise an army in 1482, and was faced instead with an opposition which this time resorted to violent means, is a measure of the extent to which his authority had broken down.[24] The feature common to both parliamentary criticism and violent opposition was that the way in which James had acted as king was regarded as unacceptable. Parliament in 1473 had indicated where he had gone wrong when it begged the king to 'put sic Justice & polycy in his awne

23 The Second Croyland Continuator, in *Rerum Anglicarum Scriptorum Veterum*, edited by W. Fulman (Oxford, 1684), p. 563. It was certainly Berwick that the English were after. The presence of Albany was no doubt useful as a threat – as Edward IV had used the earl of Douglas and the Lord of the Isles in 1462, when the Scottish government was still supporting the Lancastrians – but there was no intention of mounting an expensive campaign on Albany's behalf, and no attempt to force the Scots to accept him as king when there was obviously no support for him in Scotland.

24 Even if the ringleaders in the Lauder crisis were motivated by personal reasons, James had, apparently, remarkably little support, except temporarily from the arch-bishop of St Andrews, Scheves, and Andrew, Lord Avandale, chancellor until June 1482; Macdougall, *James III*, chapter 4, 'The Crisis of 1482–3 and its Aftermath'.

realme'. It was talking about the other great principle that the king should follow, the principle that he should do justice. In fifteenth-century Scotland, the general lack of enthusiasm for warfare and the particular reaction to James III suggest that here, as elsewhere, this was by far the more important principle.

Reliance on personal cooperation, not paid service, is as evident in the way in which the fifteenth-century kings governed their country as it is in the way they defended it. This is in no way lessened by the fact that there were, not surprisingly, developments and improvements in administration; the business of government tends at any time to produce increasing quantities of red tape. For example, greater attention was paid to the keeping of records, and to making them easier to use and refer to by having them in book form rather than rolls. There was an increasingly bureaucratized attitude to authentication, and the order of chancery – signature, signet, privy seal and great seal – was established certainly by the reign of James IV, and probably earlier. The number of royal officials in financial administration grew; in the reign of James I, the treasurer and comptroller replaced the chamberlain as the crown's chief financial official, and *ballivi ad extra* appeared on the royal demesne.[25]

But administrative developments do not necessarily mean increased centralization. How remote was the desire to increase central power at the expense of local power is nowhere more clearly seen than in the attitudes of both king and subjects to the way in which the king should fulfil his second obligation, to provide justice. Both law and the lawyers were becoming more professionalized, and there was set up, by James I, a royal court intended to remove pressure of business from council and parliament.[26] But the original idea of how this court should function was not that it should be a central court; rather, it was peripatetic, meeting three times a year in different parts of the country. There was no encouragement for people to come to the capital when they sought royal justice. Indeed, it is not altogether clear where the capital was in the early fifteenth century, for it was not until the reign of James III that Edinburgh shook off rivalry from Perth and Stirling as the place where the king's business was done, where council and parliament met.[27] James III, the one king who did try to bring people to the centre, rather than making royal justice available to them

25 J. Maitland Thomson, *The Public Records of Scotland* (Glasgow, 1922), pp. 29, 58 and 64–6. Murray, 'The Comptroller', pp. 1–29.

26 See below, chapter 7; A. A. M. Duncan, 'The Central Courts before 1532' in *An Introduction to Scottish Legal History* (Stair Society, 20, Edinburgh, 1958), pp. 330–39.

27 All but two of James I's parliaments and general councils were held in Perth; one was in Stirling, one in Edinburgh. In James II's reign, the figures are Edinburgh 13, Stirling 9, Perth 6. Every one of James III's parliaments and general councils were held in Edinburgh, except for one, held during his minority at Stirling. It is not impossible

in the localities, by letting the sessions fall into abeyance and replacing them by lords of council hearing cases almost exclusively in Edinburgh, and by refusing to go on justice ayres, thereby earned for himself the reputation of being lazy and indifferent. His successor found a much better balance. Criminal justice was pursued by the king in the localities and, while the lords of session now met in Edinburgh, they administered justice at fixed terms, and shires were grouped into areas for summons. This made it infinitely easier for those who wanted to bring their case before the king's court; it is an indication of how little men in the fifteenth century had equated royal justice with a central court that such apparently obvious provisions were not made until the end of the century.

Moreover, giving time to judicial business was something which was expected of men of political power, the men involved in the king's government. They were not paid to do so. Parliament in 1458 gave them short shrift for suggesting that their expenses might be met and, having considered 'the gret gude of the Realme', it decided that the lords of session 'of thir awne benevolence sulde beir thir awne costis'.[28] In the end, successful and permanent central courts for civil and criminal justice did need more than reliance on people to do the work 'of thir awne benevolence', but the payment of judges and the development of a lay legal profession centred in Edinburgh belonged to the sixteenth century. Professional knowledge of the law was still the preserve of churchmen, who might hope for advancement through royal service. With them sat lay lords, amateurs who dispensed justice in local courts, in private settlements (about which more will be said in the second part of this chapter) and as members of the king's council. Their right to do so was not challenged by the crown and their duty to do so was expected by it.

In practice, of course, only a small proportion of the landowners sat as judges in the king's court. It was certainly the intention to share out the work, and this may have happened before the court came to be held in Edinburgh. The sederunts, however, which survive from the reign of James III onwards, show the same people turning up again and again.[29] Most lords, apart from a few of the greatest magnates and some others, were reluctant to take the time and trouble to come to the king's council, court or parliament; the king's natural counsellors were by no means endlessly eager to give him their advice. The

that a reason for Perth's loss of popularity as the centre of government, and the move south, was the murder of James I at Perth in 1437.

28 *APS* ii, p. 48.

29 This was demonstrated by Professor A. L. Brown who has made a statistical analysis of the sederunts of James III's reign and the early part of James IV's. I am indebted to him for the information.

Scottish parliament, by comparison with that of England, was more restricted and less sophisticated in its view of its place in government and, as late as the end of the sixteenth century, it was still possible to debate the superiority of parliamentary statute over council ordinance, an issue settled in England in the mid-fourteenth century.[30] The problem was rather to persuade people to turn up than to persuade them to modify their demands. A crucial factor, again, is taxation. The fact that English kings regularly taxed their subjects has much to do with the development of the lower house in the English parliament. Although it is impossible to be certain, because the loss of the official record of proceedings before 1466 means that it is not known who came to parliament until after that date, it is probable that there was a connection between the lack of taxation and the comparative lack of interest of the lairds and burgesses; the only obvious explanation for an unusually large attendance of lairds and burgh commissioners at the parliament of March 1479 is that this was one of the rare occasions when taxation was levied.[31]

Yet limited though it was, the Scottish parliament should not be written off as weak and ineffective, the rubber stamp for the crown.[32] The introduction of the lords of the articles, the people who did the work of drafting and agreeing on legislation to be presented to the full parliament, may have something to do with the difficulty of securing attendance, although the practice of giving people leave to go home was stopped after 1425. It is more likely that it reflects the strength of parliament and the desire of the crown to control it, and certainly with the much fuller evidence available in the reign of James VI, it is clear

30 Councils could deal with matters of considerable importance. It is rather surprising to find, for example, that James I's 'parliamentary' act of 1428, attempting to introduce shire commissioners and a speaker, was passed not by a parliament, but by a general council; the act was to apply to both councils and parliaments. *APS* ii, p. 15.

31 *APS* ii, 120–21. One hundred and four people turned up, the largest number to attend any of James III's parliaments and they included forty-one lords of parliament and lairds, and commissioners from twenty-eight burghs. In March 1482, when the cost of the war was part of parliamentary business, there was again a large attendance, including thirty barons and lairds, and commissioners from twenty burghs; *ibid.* ii, pp. 136–7. There is not always a correlation; the last two parliaments held by James III, in October 1487 and January 1488, were also unusually well attended by barons and lairds, forty-three and forty, although less so by the burgh commissioners, eleven and fourteen. It would be stretching the argument beyond conviction to regard as the explanation for the numbers in 1488 the £250 to be raised for an embassy, £100 each from prelates and barons, and £50 from the burghs. A more possible explanation is that justice, both royal and local, was very much a matter of concern in both; *ibid.* ii, pp. 175 and 180–82. But the figures do suggest that money was one of the reasons, while not the only one, why more people than usual made the effort to come.

32 R. S. Rait, *The Parliaments of Scotland* (Glasgow, 1924) regarded parliament as the mouthpiece for the crown, or for the ruling clique in the minorities; in the section 'From James I to the Reformation', pp. 30–47, parliament is described as 'thoroughly obedient' and reference is made to its 'accustomed role of registration'.

that this was the case. The initiative taken by parliament over James II's finances, the repeated criticisms of James III, show that it did not regard itself as existing simply to represent the royal will. Indeed, it may have developed in the course of this century an increased degree of self-awareness, though lack of evidence makes it possible to trace this only in the most general terms. James I used parliaments extensively. His parliaments produced a flood of legislation on all manner of things, from the important to the trivial. To have a parliament regarded as a body of importance and authority was much more use to him than to have a rubber-stamp. By the reign of James III, there is some suggestion that there had been a change of emphasis; legislation tended to begin with a statement not of what the king, or king and parliament, thought, but what the lords of the three estates thought, and this may be more than a verbal detail. In any event, it is extremely unlikely that parliament was a subservient body. The degree of dependence on the cooperation of the landowners did not stop at the business of raising an army and, when the landowners were summoned, not to fight, but to attend parliament, they did not come simply to acquiesce.

Lack of money, comparatively undeveloped government institutions, royal justice still a matter for the council, with the new court set up in this period surviving sometimes with difficulty, sometimes, probably, not at all, the necessity of relying on personal cooperation and therefore ultimately on personalities – all these may seem to give grounds for the long-held concept that the Scottish monarchy of the fifteenth century was itself weak. But when fifteenth-century Scotsmen talked about the strength or weakness of the crown, its success or failure in governing, they did not think primarily about the efficiency or degree of sophistication of the king's formal administration. They thought in much more personal terms. There are two comments on the effectiveness, or lack of it, of the crown which are worth considering in this context; both are linked to particularly dramatic and ruthless actions, the first by a magnate, the second by a king. In 1398, the chronicle of Moray, written in an area of the country which had suffered, during the 1390s, from the rampant disorder created by Robert III's brother, Alexander, earl of Buchan, the 'Wolf of Badenoch', lamented that:

> in diebus illis non erat lex in Scocia sed quilibet potencior minorem oppressit et totum regnum fuit unum latrocinium. Homicidia depredaciones et incendia et cetera maleficia remanserunt inpunita et justicia utlegata extra regni terminos exulavit.

By contrast, parliament in 1458 took the almost unique step of praising a king, James II, acknowledging that

God of his grace has send our soverane lorde sik progress and prosperite that all his rebyllys and brekaris of his Justice ar removit out of his Realme and na maisterfull party remanande that may caus only breking in his Realme sa that his hienes be inclynit in himself and his ministeris to the quiet & commoune profett of the Realm and Justice to be kepit amangis his liegis

and expressed the hope that James would continue to deserve praise by putting into effect the acts of this parliament.[33]

Both these comments refer to justice and neither is concerned only with justice in the courts. The Moray chronicler can hardly have believed that to bring the king's brother before the courts was a practical solution. He painted his picture of unpunished crime and violence against the backcloth of the breakdown of political power; Robert II and Robert III, both well-intentioned but pathetically weak personalities, had lost political control, to the extent of failing to hold their family in check. The effect of this, as experienced in Moray, was not the only possible one. Although there was faction fighting, there were repeated attempts in this period to stop the rot, to give impetus to government and to provide effective justice by transferring authority to other members of the royal family. This suggests that not all who held political power thought only of the chance offered by the absence of a strong monarchy to further their own interests by means more violent than usual. The situation in Moray was particularly bad because the extension of royal power to the locality through the local magnate had become uncontrolled power exercised by an individual magnate, without fear of reprisal. The significance of the most dramatic of the many acts of violence committed by the Wolf of Badenoch, the burning of Elgin Cathedral in 1390, is that it demonstrates in extreme form what could happen when the monarchy was weak. It is a comment on the importance of individual ambition and personality in the case of the magnates. But it was not usual, even in a Scotland traditionally regarded as lawless, for a powerful lord to burn a cathedral because the bishop had stopped paying for his protection. This event, and the whole of Buchan's career, have been rightly linked with the weakness of the crown. What is not so readily explained is why this was so, why it mattered that the king should be personally effective, and what effect he was supposed to have. Whatever royal authority meant, it did not mean tight control from the centre. What then would make it possible for a stronger personality on the throne to do better for those of his subjects remote in Moray?

This is not a problem which can be discussed in absolute terms and

33 *Moray Registrum*, p. 382; *APS* ii, p. 52. It should be stressed that the Moray chronicler, though writing what purported to be a general comment on the state of the kingdom, was in fact describing the situation in the north.

at best it is a matter of relative success or failure. But the compliment paid to James II reveals something of what men at the time thought was the answer. The rebels and breakers of justice whom James had removed from the realm, the masterful party which no longer existed, almost certainly refer to the Black Douglases, finally defeated after several years of conflict with the king, and driven out of the kingdom in 1455. If so, parliament in 1458 was congratulating a king for actions which were as extreme as the actions of a magnate deplored in the 1390s. The Douglases cannot simply be explained away as rebels or overmighty subjects. Certainly by the mid-fifteenth century they had reached a position of exceptional power, based on their three earldoms, that of Douglas, with its extensive lands in the southwest, and Moray and Ormond, acquired in the minority of James II, and giving them influence in the north; and a fourth Douglas brother was lord of Balveny. Yet however potentially dangerous this was, one has to turn to writers of the following century, notably Lindsay of Pitscottie, to find detailed accounts of their misuse of power and open defiance of the king. These accounts may have been based on stories handed down. But they are still open to doubt, for they are hardly likely to have been inspired by the losing and exiled side, the Douglases, and much more likely to derive from the propaganda of the winning side; and it is hard to give any credence at all to one of the best of the stories of Douglas outrage, the account of their execution of the tutor of Bombie, who has left not a trace of his existence in any contemporary record. Nor does the idea that the king's onslaught on the Douglases can be explained on the grounds of their treasonable dealings with England carry weight until after James's murder of Earl William in February 1452.[34] The apparent reason for the murder, Douglas's refusal to break his bond with Alexander, earl of Crawford and John, Lord of the Isles, cannot be regarded as the valid reaction of a king who rightly wanted to stamp out the pernicious practice of the magnates of making bonds with one another, thus building up alliances which threatened the crown. No late medieval king thought in this way, and indeed James himself made bonds, being the only king who made use of this normally non-royal practice.[35] What is left is the scanty

34 For tutor of Bombie, see Robert Lindsay of Pitscottie, *The Historie and Cronicles of Scotland* (STS, 1899–1911) I, pp. 89–92; J. M. Brown, 'Taming the Magnates?' in *The Scottish Nation*, edited by G. Menzies (London, 1972), p. 47. *Asloan Manuscript* I, p. 237 describes Douglas fighting successfully in the north of England in 1449 in what seems to have been more than a border raid. In a tantalizing fragment of a story in the same chronicle, Sir James of Douglas is described as being 'with the king of yngland lang tyme and was mekle maid of', why, as the chronicler says, 'men wist nocht redelye'; but this was involved with an embassy negotiating for truce, and it is difficult to know what weight to give to the sinister element – or, indeed, whether that was simply hindsight; *ibid.* I, p. 239.

35 Two bonds exist, one certainly and the other probably connected with the

contemporary evidence which, small though it is, points to the fact that initially James was the aggressor, taking the provocative action of seizing the Douglas lands of the earldom of Wigtown in 1450–51, during the earl's absence abroad, not as a measure against an overmighty family, but because he wanted them for his wife.[36]

In any event, a king who murders is hardly showing concern for royal justice. The murder of an earl by a king was as unique as the burning of a cathedral by an earl. It happened not because James regarded it as justifiable treatment of an overmighty subject, but because he lost his temper, as indeed his lords had feared he would do.[37] Yet he was saved from the consequences of his own action because the magnates were prepared to support him. Not only was the new earl of Douglas, brother of the murdered earl, forced to come to terms with the king to whom, in the immediate aftermath of the killing, he had publicly renounced allegiance, but when the final crisis took place in 1455, the Douglases were left to fight alone, deserted by their former allies. The reference in 1458 to 'rebellys and brekaris of his Justice' was not as inaccurate a description of the Douglases after 1452 as before. Even so, the whole episode, the reaction of the magnates who backed the king, and the tribute paid to James, who had acted in this affair not only strongly but outrageously, suggest a new dimension in the problem of understanding what people meant when they

Douglas crisis. James, earl of Douglas, came to terms with the king in August 1452. In January 1453 there was a second agreement, more favourable to the earl and it included a bond by the earl to James II, promising manrent. It is known only from a copy, wrongly ascribed to the year 1402, which is impossible, there being no Earl James at that time, and the terms of the bond exactly fit the agreement of 1453. It is unfortunate that the original does not survive, for it refers to 'thir my lettres written with my hand' and to the king's 'lettres written with his hand', which would be interesting evidence of literacy. It is printed in *The Additional Case of Elisabeth, claiming the Title and Dignity of the Countess of Sutherland* (Sutherland Case, 1771), appendix X. The other bond is a bond of maintenance given to James Tweedie of Drumelzier on 8 March 1455, in return for Tweedie's manrent and service. This bond, made to a laird whose lands lay in southern Scotland, suggests a connection with the build-up to the final onslaught on the Douglases, ending with their defeat at Arkinholm on 1 May 1455, and although Tweedie was a reasonably important laird, it is unlikely that he was singled out as the only one to whom James made such a bond. *HMC, Various Collections* v, p. 11.

36 *Asloan Manuscript* I, p. 239 describes William, earl of Douglas, coming to the parliament of June 1451, and putting himself in the king's grace; and 'at the Request of the qwene and the thre estatis' James received him into his grace, and gave him back the lands he had taken, with the exception of Wigtown. 'And all gud scottismen war rycht blyth of that accordance.' This suggests that James's actions had caused unease and that there was sympathy with Douglas.

37 *ibid.* I, p. 240, refers to the agreement made by all the lords who were with the king in Stirling before the murder that 'suppose the king wald brek the band forsaid [his safeconduct to the earl] that they suld let it at thair powere'; this certainly suggests fear of what the king might do.

admired a Scottish king for providing 'quiet & commoune profett' and 'Justice' in his realm.

Why did James get away with murder? There is little doubt that those who feared what might happen felt misgivings, embarrassment, even perhaps horror when it did happen. The exoneration of the king produced by the parliament which met in June 1452 illustrates the dilemma. It is quite remarkably vague; it seems that those asked to inquire into the circumstances of Douglas's death took the easy way out, and gave the king an answer which was no answer, saying that he had acted defensibly in doing something for which there was no real defence.[38] How much easier it was in 1458, when the Douglases, now a real rather than a potential threat, had been crushed by the king, for then uncertainty and embarrassment could give way to admiration which was genuine enough.

Yet even in 1452 there was no alternative. James had not provided justice, had stepped outside the law, had acted with a violence and barbarity condemned in lesser mortals. But he had all the prestige and power of monarchy on his side. He was, admittedly, helped by being able to use patronage, though even this shows how confident he was. It was hardly lavish, there was no question of it being liberally distributed by a terrified king and, indeed, within a few years, some of it had been withdrawn.[39] Part of the explanation of why the king's position was so strong is to be found in the attitudes and position of the magnates, which form the theme of the second part of this chapter. But in terms of royal power, James was right to be confident. The Scottish monarchy was strong because of what it had to offer – political and social stability. It alone could keep a balance of power in the state, could bring to an end too great a concentration of power in the hands of one family, Stewarts or Douglases. Far from not being given support by their greatest subjects, the evidence suggests that kings received a considerable amount, even in outrageous circumstances. The emphasis on the risk to a king who was not backed up by a strong centralized administration, and therefore relied on personal co-operation, has been overstated. The greater risk was to the subjects, dependent not on state control, but on the personality of an individual monarch. There was no way of doing without the king; he was utterly necessary, the lynchpin of society. If he was weak, like Robert III, then

---

38 *APS* II, p. 73.

39 *Asloan Manuscript* I, pp. 242–3 gives a list of creations made in the parliament of June 1452; two Crichtons received the earldoms of Moray and Caithness, and Lord Hay the earldom of Erroll, and a number of people including former Douglas adherents like Fleming of Cumbernauld, were made lords of parliament. But neither Crichton had his earldom for long. Both were in the king's hands by 1454, and there is some doubt whether the Crichtons ever actually held them. A. I. Dunlop, *The Life and Times of James Kennedy, Bishop of St Andrews* (Edinburgh, 1950), pp. 148–50.

individuals, though not the nobility as a whole, might cause havoc, while others made an attempt to stagger on, keeping some measure of control, until death removed him. If he combined laziness and indifference with a high degree of whimsical arbitrariness, as James III did, then he might build up sufficient resentment to provoke the political solution of rebellion, although only a handful were prepared to take this course. But the idea that there was conflict between crown and nobility is two-dimensional. It does not allow for the interplay of individual personalities, nor does it give sufficient weight to the fact that, in a situation where personality was of supreme importance, the fifteenth-century kings, including James III, had the inestimable advantage of being exceedingly tough and powerful men. It made them extraordinarily difficult to deal with, and certainly to oppose, without recourse to extreme action. It gave them the ability to rule with considerable power.

2   The lords

When the first printing press was set up in Scotland in 1508, one of the earliest books produced was a translation of a French work into Scots entitled *The Porteous of Noblenes*. This described the twelve virtues of a nobleman. First on the list was faith, and second loyalty or truth. The two are closely related, the first making in more general terms the same point as the second; God has ordained everything in its proper place, to provide concord and unity, 'sum till haf lordschipe and otheris to lif in subiectioun . . . for treuth and lawte nobliss war first ordanit and stablit abone the commoun peple and thairfor to thaim was gevin hie honour manrent and service of thar subiectis. Thai ar nocht sa hie set nor ordanit for to reif or tak be force in ony way bot thai ar haldin in werray richt and resoun for to serf thair king and defend there subiectis.'[40]

A literary account of nobility is evidence of theory rather than practice. But that does not mean that the theory was only that of the author, writing about what he wanted to see, as opposed to what he did see. The demand for the book, which was, presumably, why it was one of the first to be printed locally, suggests an interest in a theoretical description which was reflected in social reality, not remote from it. The book is not at all profound in its thought, but it does state a norm, and has tough things to say about those who depart from the norm. Not surprisingly, it is not possible to give a single example of a magnate who matched the author's ideal. However, it can be shown that the ideal had much in common with the way in which fifteenth-century magnates used their social and political power.

40 *Asloan Manuscript* I, pp. 172–4.

There were very good practical reasons why the crown should be able to persuade the magnates that their personal ambitions, to increase their wealth, status and power, would be better realized through service than defiance, even passive defiance. It was not only in theory that the king could give and the king could take away. The point had been made very clearly by the reduction of the power of the Stewarts in the reign of James I, and the fate of the Douglases under James II, families whose crime was to have too great a concentration of power, even if, initially at any rate, they had not used it against the crown.[41] There was no doubt which was greater, royal or magnate power. But this did not produce merely an uneasy alliance between kings and magnates, with hostility never far below the surface and likely to erupt when opportunity offered. There was a more positive side. For both kings and nobles, self-interest and the concept of a balance of power in the state went together and were not mutually exclusive.

The crown was not alone in fearing or resenting one family or faction which was too powerful. The collapse of Stewart and Douglas domination was not watched by a surly and fearful nobility, afraid that what the king had done to these families he might do to them. It was made possible by the support of a nobility which welcomed the wider spread of lands and offices. The new earl of Huntly, beginning the build-up of Gordon power in the north, where first the Stewarts and then the Douglases and their ally Crawford had had control, the border families who replaced the Douglases as wardens of the marches, the five families raised to the rank of earl by James II to fill the vacuum created by the removal of the Stewarts, all these had every reason to do more than acquiesce when the king flexed his muscles. In a strongly hierarchical society, where political power lay first with the king, but secondly with the greatest landowners, there were strong advantages for both in the restoration of an equilibrium which the power of the Stewarts and Douglases had upset; and it is a drastic underestimate of the political responsibility which fifteenth-century magnates were quite capable of showing to think of this only in terms of material gain. There is much more than that behind the Auchinlek chronicle's description of how, at the battle of Brechin in 1452, 'thair was with the erll of Huntlie fer ma than was with the erll of Craufurd becaus he displayit the kingis banere and said it was the kingis actioun and he was his luftennend'; and it is not surprising that 'schortlie the erll of Huntlie wan the feld.'[42]

---

41 Brown, 'Taming the Magnates?', pp. 49–55. Fortescue described James II as having 'putt owt off the same lande the Erle Douglas whos livelod and myght was nere hand equivalent to his owne, moved therto be no other cause, save only drede off his rebyllion'; Sir John Fortescue, *The Governance of England*, edited by C. Plummer (Oxford, 1885), p. 130.   42 *Asloan Manuscript* i, pp. 237–8.

For the crown, this was the final stage in the resolution of a problem which every medieval king had to face, but which was particularly pressing in Scotland because of the unusually high degree of dependence on the magnates: how to find a balance between giving the great men of the kingdom too much power, so that they were at least potentially dangerous, and giving them too little, so that they were ineffective. Obviously it was a gamble. Rewarding a loyal supporter with lands and offices was natural and expected of a king, but it contained the inherent problem of whether the man and his descendants would remain loyal, and whether gratitude to the crown would form any part of their thinking about their possessions. James, last earl of Douglas, renouncing his allegiance to James II, presents a striking contrast with his ancestor, the good Sir James, to whose service as one of Robert Bruce's principal supporters the earl owed much of the foundation of the family's wealth and power. Yet the historian is probably more aware of this problem than the late medieval monarchy was. It would be absurd to suggest that Bruce should not have liberally rewarded Douglas because of a hypothetical fear about his descendants. It is wrong to regard the crown as impotent in the face of an overmighty subject because it did not have, for example, a standing army. The lesson of the Douglases is not that the crown should put heavy restraints on the power of its natural counsellors, its representatives in the localities, but that if any of these natural counsellors did become threateningly powerful, the king could always find greater support, could raise an army, and would win.

Discussion of magnate power in the first half of the century is set particularly in the context of conflict with the crown, because of two unacceptably powerful families. After 1455, this is a dead issue; it is a mistake to think that better relations between king and nobles become a feature of Scottish political life only after 1488, in the reign of the attractive and popular James IV. In the second half of James II's reign, exactly these better relations, overshadowed though not in fact non-existent before 1455, become very clear. James's early death, followed by another minority and the tense and difficult reign of James III in turn obscure this brief period, and make it temptingly easy to regard the particular nature of the conflict between crown and nobles in the first half of the century as the hallmark of the whole period. But James III was a very different man from his father and grandfather, and the problems of his reign were profoundly different from theirs. His high-handed and ill-considered actions in the end provoked some of the magnates into taking action against him. But the rebels of June 1488 lived on to become the major figures in the new government of James IV. They did not change their spots; they were not overmighty, lawless barons for the first half of the year, and new, cooperative nobles only in the second.

Again, these better relations after 1455 came about not because the nobility was now substantially weakened. Given the nature of royal government, a weak nobility was of little use to the king. The vacuum created by the removal of the Stewarts and Douglases was filled. There were now men who had the problem of converting their rise in status from the formal dignity of a new title to the position of pre-eminence in practice in the locality where formerly they had been one of a number of lesser men of local influence. The main issue in the second half of the century is how they established themselves.

The grant of a title, the grant of land, was the starting point. But what ultimately gave one man more power than another was the extent of his personal influence, the number of dependants on whose support he could count. In the late sixteenth century, this point was made in two accounts of the nobility, estimating their social and political importance. In one, the earl of Montrose is described as 'an Erle of small power, having but few gentlemen of his surname', while in the other, Lord Ogilvy is 'a man of no great lyving but of a good number of landed men of his surname which make his power in Angus the greter'; and in general, both accounts concentrate on the size of following rather than the extent of landholding.[43] That following is described time and again in late-medieval sources, both record and chronicle, in the phrase 'kin freindis allya parttakaris tennentis servandis and dependaris', the comprehensive list of supporters without whose backing no noble, lord nor laird acted, whether settling a local feud by arbitration or maintaining one by violence, or coming up to Stirling or Edinburgh to parliament, council or court. It is an accurate description, not a conventional jingle of the 'et aliis' type, and it reflects a shift in emphasis in the concept of lordship and service.

This shift was a move away from the feudalized form of the contract between lord and man, where service was linked to material reward, normally in land, sometimes in cash. This is not the place to attempt to enter the debate about 'feudalism', that word which 'prête à confusion'.[44] But unless it is used in its most general sense, as almost equivalent to 'medieval', so that it becomes 'in all essentials identical with landed lordship',[45] it is inappropriate to describe fifteenth-century Scotland as a feudal society. Legal terminology survived and Francis Bacon's tag 'vocabula manent, res fugiunt' is entirely applica-

43 *Estimate of the Scottish Nobility during the Minority of James VI* (Grampian Club, 1873), pp. 7–28; BM, Additional MS. 38,823, ff. 9r–12v.

44 F. L. Ganshof, *Qu'est-ce que la Féodalité?* (Brussels, 1947), p. 11.

45 Otto Brunner, 'Feudalism: the History of a Concept' in *Lordship and Community in Medieval Europe*, edited by F. L. Cheyette (New York, 1968), p. 48.

ble.[46] What did not survive was the direct connection between land and service. The unequal bargain by which one side gave something intangible in return for a tangible reward from the other gave way to a different contract. New priorities were established. The good lord of late medieval society was not primarily the lord who gave lavish grants of land; he was the lord who offered effective protection.[47]

It is possible that the change was, to an extent, more apparent than real. Knowledge of the feudal contract comes from the charter recording the tangible element in more detail than the intangible, and it may be that this gives undue importance to the economic part of the agreement.[48] Certainly it is given greater weight than the personal service of vassal to lord, while that service was increasingly restricted and limited. But it is wholly improbable that, in a society where one's locality and local affinities were what mattered to most people, the need for the personal protection of the local lord became submerged. Hence there was, in fourteenth-century Scotland, as in England and France, a move away from the restricted forms of feudal service, which ultimately reduced it to absurdity, and a greater emphasis on more general personal service. Thus *auxilium*, narrowed down until it referred to the limited number of occasions when the vassal was obliged to open his purse to his lord, became a comprehensive promise of service to the lord in all his actions. Service in war was no longer subject to limitations of time and place, but was to be given, along with service in time of peace, whenever the lord required. The tension between lord and man reflected in the promise by the vassal not to harm his lord, a promise regarded as sufficiently important to be included in the oath of fealty, and in Flanders made the subject of a separate oath, was no longer evident; in the fifteenth century, the man promised 'nowthir to her thar [his lord and his heirs] scath na se it bot warne thaime ther of and let it at my power'.[49] The fourth of the major obligations which constituted service to a lord, the giving of counsel, remained not surprisingly unchanged; this was the one obligation which it was in the vassal's interests not to restrict, for it gave him the

46 Bacon's tag is quoted by Alfred Cobban, *The Social Interpretation of the French Revolution* (Cambridge, 1968), p. 26.

47 Good lordship, the common phrase in England, was rare in Scotland and only in documents in the Maxwell and Oliphant collections is it used with any frequency. The common Scottish word was maintenance.

48 A. A. M. Duncan, *Scotland: the Making of the Kingdom* (Edinburgh, 1975), pp. 407–9.

49 Marc Bloch, *Feudal Society*, translated by L. A. Manyon (London, 1965) I, p. 220. The promise not to harm the lord survived in the fourteenth century, but with the positive promise to warn the lord of harm and prevent it, added to it, as given in the text of an oath of fealty in *Moray Registrum*, pp. 377–8. The fifteenth-century example comes from a bond of manrent made to William Cunningham of Snaid and his heirs; SRO, Yester Writs, GD 28/120.

right as well as the duty to offer advice to the lord on actions in which he might be involved. And in return for all this, the lord offered the equally general promise of maintenance and protection, assistance in the man's affairs, prevention of harm to him and counsel.

From the mid-fifteenth century, these obligations were crystallized in written vernacular bonds, of maintenance and manrent. A few were made before that time, but from then on they became commonplace documents, until the early seventeenth century, and it was in the 1440s that personal service was given the name 'manrent'.[50] This word had come into Scottish usage in the late fourteenth century, but was a rare and literary word meaning homage, in the sense of an act of homage. Now it came to describe lifelong or hereditary personal service as well as the oath which initiated that service, given verbally by the man placing his hands on the gospels but not kneeling before his lord, in a ceremony which included or was followed up by the exchange of contracts.[51]

The question of why men saw a value in writing down their personal obligations can be answered partly in terms of a desire to ensure loyalty, but not in terms of an increased need to do so. The idea that men were less naturally imbued with loyalty in the later middle ages than earlier is not convincing.[52] There is neither more nor less sinister significance in the desire to record a personal obligation than in the desire to record a grant of land with the services owed for it. In general terms, what lay behind the practice of giving written bonds was not a decline in the concept of loyalty, but a greater interest in committing an agreement to writing. The amount of documentation from the fifteenth century cannot be explained simply in terms of

50   There are some 700 bonds of manrent surviving from this period. 'Manrent' is the middle-Scots form of the late Anglo-Saxon word 'mannraedan', meaning allegiance, dependence; etymologically it is the same as 'homagium'. It was, in Anglo-Saxon, English and Scots, always a rare word until it became associated with personal service as described in the bond to which it gave a name, the first surviving example being dated 1442.

51   Many of the bonds include the statement that an oath was sworn on the gospels. There is only one detailed account of the ceremony, a notarial record of the making of a bond in 1524; Argyll MSS, Inveraray Castle I, nos. 19 and 20; Transcripts of Argyll Muniments in Inveraray Castle III, p. 179.

52   An extreme statement of this was made by Helen M. Cam, who wrote of late medieval English indentures of retinue as 'a parasitic institution . . . far removed indeed from the atmosphere of responsibility, loyalty and faith which had characterised the relationship of lord and vassal in the earlier middle ages'; 'The Decline and Fall of English Feudalism', *History* xxv (1940), pp. 216–33. This was devastatingly answered by K. B. McFarlane, the great late medieval historian whose work opened up a new and positive approach to fifteenth-century England which has held good ever since. McFarlane suggested that those who believed in a 'golden age when men's appetites were subdued by simple faith' should seek it before 1066 when 'there are practically no records'; *The Nobility of Later Mediaeval England* (Oxford, 1973), p. 114. The traditional view of late medieval Scotland inclined towards that of Helen Cam.

greater chance of survival; it was no longer only one's title to land which was likely to be recorded, but more ephemeral matters as well. Increase in literacy and increase in the number of notaries public in this century both indicate the milieu in which the writing of personal bonds can be set.[53]

Their attraction is obvious enough. Written bonds were not made with the men who formed the lord's ordinary retinue, his household men and servants, the 'servandis and dependaris' of the descriptive list.[54] They were sought from men who were themselves powerful in the localities, who had, by virtue of their social position, followings similar to, if smaller than, those of their lords – kin, friends and so on. For the lord, the bond of manrent meant the assertion of superiority over such men, and the extension of his influence by bringing into his following not merely individuals but groups of people. This was the more effective because the problem of divided loyalties, which arose from the vassal seeking fiefs from as many lords as he could, was eradicated. It was very rare indeed in late medieval Scotland for men to give bonds to more than one lord. Loyalty was of course not absolute. The bond might be used to force a local family to accept a lord's superiority, so that rather than enjoying his protection, they had it inflicted on them; the tense and sometimes openly hostile relations between the Gordon earls of Huntly and the powerful Aberdeenshire family of Forbes were punctuated by the making of bonds of this kind. Nevertheless, it was generally the case that most bonds did produce for the lord the assurance of support, with the proviso that, as the men who gave them were men of standing, they had the right to be consulted and could refuse to act. No laird ever became the slavish adherent of his lord.

The practice of making bonds has another crucial aspect. Those who made bonds of manrent were the 'allya and parttakaris' of the lord – allies, those bound, and those who would take his part – while his 'freindis' were men of equal rank with whom he exchanged bonds of friendship. But first in the list came the kin. There is no need to stress here the importance of the Scottish kingroup in this period for it has always been recognized as a fundamental force, in social and

---

53 G. G. Simpson, *Scottish Handwriting, 1150–1650* (Edinburgh, 1973), pp. 8–12; Maitland Thomson, *Public Records of Scotland*, pp. 86–96.

54 'Retainer' in Scotland is different from 'retainer' in England. English indentures of retinue were made with men of the same social standing as those who in Scotland made bonds of manrent. But Scottish usage was the original one of someone who was kept, not in the sense of being paid a fee, but by being given his keep, that is, a member of the lord's household. Thus household and retinue service were interrelated, the second being part of the first. Those who made bonds were, on particular occasions, added to the ordinary retinue. J. M. Brown, *Bonds of Manrent in Scotland before 1603* (unpublished PhD thesis, Glasgow, 1974), pp. 178–9.

political life. What the bond did was to create a relationship with those who were not of the lord's kin which imposed on them the obligations which bound those who were. This was explicitly stated. The word 'kindnes' – kinship – was repeatedly used to describe the relationship. In 1491, George, earl of Huntly and Patrick, earl of Bothwell promised, in their indenture of friendship, to be 'tendir kynde and lele as the fadre sonnys and brethir aucht to be'; and Huchon Rose of Kilravock and Alexander Fraser of Philorth, making bonds to William, thane of Cawdor, both promised to act as if they were carnal sons of their lord, who in turn obliged himself to act as their carnal father.[55] The bonds provide a wealth of evidence that lords and their men were expected to act as kinsmen, evidence which exists precisely because they were not kinsmen, and therefore made written bonds setting out the obligations which were implicit and unwritten for the kin. What these bonds make clear is that in the late middle ages, kinship and lordship were what one suspects they had always been, complementary.

The importance of kinship is reflected in the matter-of-fact, even casual way in which it was used. How astonished Henry IV must have been, when in 1400 he received a letter from the earl of March, who sought his help, not as king of England, but because he was March's kinsman in the fourth degree.[56] In the early 1450s, when James II was attempting to counteract Douglas power by strengthening another family of influence in the southwest, the Kennedys of Dunure, he did so by giving them a string of royal charters affirming their position as head of their kin with all rights pertaining to 'kenkynnoll'. This was the family whose presumed ancestor, Roland of Carrick, had received a charter from his uncle, Neil, earl of Carrick, designating him head of his kin, presumably on the grounds that Neil's heir of line, being a woman, could not hold this position.[57] There was no such reason for the reiteration of Kennedy's position in the 1450s. What may lie behind it is a breakdown of unity in the Kennedy kingroup, an idea supported by the fact that at this time Kennedy was making written agreements with some of his kinsmen. To find the crown backing Kennedy's position in this way underlines the importance of kinship.

But this does not mean that the obligations of kinship were always obvious, however remote the degree. A major problem in any kin-based society is that each kingroup merges with others, and therefore some sort of principle by which a man's loyalty can be determined has

55 *Miscellany of the Spalding Club* (1841–52) iv, pp. 187–8; *The Book of the Thanes of Cawdor* (Spalding Club, 1859), pp. 60–62 and 69–71.

56 *Royal and Historical Letters during the reign of Henry IV*, edited by F. C. Hingeston (Rolls Series, 1860) i, p. 24.

57 *RMS* i, nos. 508 and 509; SRO, Ailsa Muniments, GD 25/1/ 29, 45, 52, 60, 63, 66 and 70.

to be established; the need for definition was an intensely practical one. It was not simply a matter of blood-tie. What blood-tie? Did one owe loyalty equally to the kin of the father and the kin of the mother? Was a fourth cousin in a kingroup whose normal limit was third cousinage, but who lived on the spot, rejected by the kin, whereas a second cousin who lived a hundred miles away was an accepted part of it? These are questions which it is easier to answer in the sixteenth century, because of the greater quantity of evidence. By that time, the word 'surname' had clearly become synonymous with 'kindred'. This became the simple acid test. If one's surname was Gordon, then one was part of the Gordon kingroup, even if the relationship was remote.[58]

What this means is that the Scottish kingroup was agnatic; the males of the family were the constant factor, the females being added to or removed from the kindred by marriage. When a woman was married in late medieval Scotland, she was regarded rather as providing a link with another kingroup than as becoming completely assimilated into her husband's kin. She did not take his name. She was considered, for example, as a Gordon who had married a Hamilton, not as someone whose marriage had made her a Hamilton.[59] It is probable that the kingroup survived in Scotland as a powerful force, at a time when in England interest in the family had become 'a fad, a craze, a quasi-intellectual hobby of the idle rich',[60] precisely because it was agnatic, and was therefore not vitiated by the great weakness of cognatic kinship. The assumption of agnatic kinship was that a man's brothers and sons were more likely to support him than his brothers-in-law and sons-in-law, who had a prior claim on their loyalty. If, on the other hand, one regarded one's obligations towards the kin of one's father and mother as equally binding, one's position in a quarrel became intolerable.

There is less evidence about fifteenth-century kinship but no reason to doubt that it was agnatic. The surname was not yet widely used to denote the kingroup, but it was coming to be so used. In 1430 it was used as an administrative convenience by the government, to identify people in the courts. Entails were beginning to specify heirs male who

---

58 So remote, indeed, as to defy knowledge. Thus in 1590, John Grant of Freuchy was justly incensed by the murder of one Alan Grant and another Grant whose Christian name is not recorded, on the grounds that they were of his kin, or 'at leist being ane of his surename'; W. Fraser, *The Chiefs of Grant* (Edinburgh, 1883) III, pp. 177–8.

59 This is illustrated in a letter written in 1568 by Adam Bothwell, bishop of Orkney, to his brother-in-law Archibald Napier of Merchiston, in which there occurs the phrase: 'Alwayis [I] besekis you as ye luif your awin wele, the wele of your houss, and us your freindis that wald your wele', thus drawing a distinction between 'your houss' or kindred, and 'freindis', who included the writer, related by marriage; Mark Napier, *Memoirs of John Napier of Merchiston* (Edinburgh, 1834), p. 111.

60 Lawrence Stone, *The Crisis of the Aristocracy, 1558–1641* (Oxford, 1965), p. 23.

bore the family name.[61] It is extremely unlikely that its advantages were not equally appreciated in the localities, where there was as much need of definition of the kingroup as in the sixteenth century. Why else should Alexander Seton of Gordon, who succeeded to the Gordon inheritance through his mother, change his name to Gordon after being created earl of Huntly if there was not good reason to emphasize his position as head of the Gordon kindred by taking the name? And there is an isolated example of the word surname being used exactly as it was in the sixteenth century, to describe a kingroup: 'the surnam and nerrest of blude' of William of Preston of Gorton were given the right, by the burgh of Edinburgh in 1455, to carry the armbone of St Giles when it was borne through the church of St Giles, because Preston had acquired the relic in France, and given it to the church.[62] This suggests that the commonplace practice of the sixteenth century, while not entirely established in the fifteenth, was coming into existence. There may well be a link between the obvious advantages of that practice, and the fact that 'in the lowlands surnames had become all but universal before the end of the fifteenth century.'[63]

In any case, it was geographic unity that gave the kingroup its final form and cohesion. The Gordons, for example, were originally small-scale landowners in Berwickshire. By the end of the fifteenth century, when they had become the dominant family of the north-east, the few Gordons left in Berwickshire, although they shared the family name, were in no real sense part of the Gordon kin. The same is true of the Hays who became earls of Erroll; as a kingroup they existed in Aberdeenshire and not in their original lands in Perthshire. The one exception is the remarkable family of Campbell. The earls of Argyll did retain their connection with cadet branches of the family in Perthshire and Moray, although the strain put on the relationship by geographic remoteness is reflected in the fact that, in the second case, written bonds were given. The earl's position is shown by the regular acknowledgement of the higher allegiance owed to him by those who gave bonds to the Campbells of Glenorchy and Cawdor; and it may be that the steady increase in power of the earls of Argyll, which reached staggering proportions in the seventeenth and eighteenth centuries, owed much to their success in retaining control of a kingroup which extended far beyond their own area of direct control in Argyll.

The loosening-up of restrictions on the service of a man to his lord, their association with the obligations of kinship, and the lessening of

61 *APS* II, pp. 17–18; for example, *RMS* II, nos. 792, 884, 989, 1045, 1064.

62 *Charters and other Documents relating to the City of Edinburgh, 1143–1540* (SBRS, 1871), p. 79.

63 G. Donaldson, *Scotland: James V–James VII* (Edinburgh, 1965), p. 12.

the problem of conflicting loyalties, worked very much to the advantage of the superior, whether earl, lord or laird, whose kin, friends and allies, the most important members of his following, were bound to him by a common ideology. One effect of this is all too well known, that local power was an important factor in causing disorder, lawlessness and violence. There is no need to labour this point; it has been given considerable and sometimes exclusive attention. There was indeed violence and disorder, although the assumption that it was particularly bad in Scotland is a very different and less certain matter. It depends on the idea that the less strong central government was, the more lawless would be the localities. But at the end of the sixteenth century, in his manual of kingship, *Basilikon Doron*, James VI reminded his son that 'the most part of your people will ever naturally favour justice.'[64] This is not something which alters according to the degree of strength of the government; it is a natural human instinct in any circumstances to want to preserve life, lands and goods. If a society lacks the benefits of the modern police force and insurance company, it will find other ways to meet the need to preserve order. This is precisely what the local lord, the man of influence, could and did do.

In 1409, an indenture of friendship was made between Robert, duke of Albany, governor during the captivity of James I, and Archibald, earl of Douglas. This promise of mutual support has been interpreted in a distinctly sinister light, as providing evidence both of Albany's ambition to become king and of the weakness of the government. In fact, it is almost wholly devoted to a description of the way in which these magnates would deal with dispute among, and crime committed by, their followers, or disagreement between themselves; it was proposed that they and members of their councils would arbitrate, and that they would withdraw their protection from any of their dependants who refused to accept their arbitration.[65] This indenture is the first surviving example of its kind, the earliest of a great number of such contracts. It is no more sinister than a similar agreement made by William, Lord Graham and John, Lord Oliphant a century later, in 1500, that 'gyff ony of thar frendis men and servandis and allya has actionis agane utheris thai sall cum to thar lordis and schaw thar action and caus befor tham that it may be considerit and sene and therefter the lordis to decreit and deliver. And gyff it can nocht be decidit be thar lordis it salbe leful to the parti plenzeand on otheris to pass to the law' – that is, the courts. This does not involve an attempt to bypass justice by keeping criminals out of the court. A slightly later agreement

64 *Basilikon Doron of King James VI*, edited by J. Craigie (STS, 1944) I, p. 63.
65 W. Fraser, *The Douglas Book* (Edinburgh, 1885) III, pp. 369–71.

suggested that dispute might be settled 'by siche of frendis or lawe as thay think expedient';[66] in other words, it was a matter of convenience. But it does suggest how people thought about justice; reasonably enough, they considered what was most convenient, what would give them a quick answer and, in view of the delays to which cases before the session could be subject, this is not surprising.

It also shows the survival of a kind of justice which had nothing to do with the courts. Here the lord was acting as head of kin, taking responsibility for the disputes and crimes of his kinsmen and his men. It is, in fact, a survival of the system of justice associated with the bloodfeud. It may seem unlikely that the bloodfeud should exist in late medieval Scotland; and it was modified, in that there was no longer a fixed tariff of compensation payments according to status, as there had been in prefeudal Scotland. But the principle that the head of the kin or the lord of the victim of crime had not only the right but also the responsibility of forcing the man who committed the crime to compensate the injured man, or in the case of murder, his closest relatives and dependants, was still an entirely acceptable and regular method of dealing with crime. Bloodfeud is a misleading word. The point of course was, not that the feud was bloody, but that the escalation of bloodshed was halted by settlement and compensation. Thus in 1486, John, Lord Maxwell and Cuthbert Murray of Cockpule made an agreement to end their feud, which included Cuthbert and his kin and friends enduring the humiliating penance of having to appear publicly in their 'lynyng claithis in the maist lawly wis thai can' to seek forgiveness; in addition Maxwell and Murray bound themselves in maintenance and manrent, and promised to pay for masses to be said for the souls of their dead kinsmen. Finally, both sides agreed to give letters of slains, that is, letters saying that rancour for the crimes was now remitted, the feud was at an end, and the parties would remain in amity one with the other.[67]

In 1443 was made a settlement remarkable to modern eyes. This is known from a supplication for a dispensation for Reginald Johnson of the Isles and Catherine Patrick, wishing to marry in order to preserve

---

66 J. Anderson *The Oliphants in Scotland* (Edinburgh, 1879), pp. 47–8; SRO, Abercromby of Forglen Muniments, GD 185 box 2 bundle 6.

67 W. Fraser, *The Book of Carlaverock* (Edinburgh 1873) II, pp. 446–7. The public ceremony which Cuthbert had to endure was common in these agreements, frequently including the offering of naked sword by the point to the man from whom forgiveness was sought. There is an interesting article on this by George Neilson, 'The Submission of the Lord of the Isles to James I: its Feudal Symbolism', *Northern Notes and Queries* (1901), pp. 113–22. This shows that the ceremony was known in Europe, and its form depended on rank; knights used the sword, their weapon and the symbol of beheading, the manner of execution befitting their status, while lesser men, like the burgesses of Calais submitting to Edward III in 1347, had ropes around their necks – the symbol of hanging, the baser form of death.

peace and amity among their kinsmen, who had been at feud because Reginald's father had slain Catherine's father.[68] The idea that a murdered man's daughter should marry the son of the murderer may seem bizarre in the extreme. Yet it is a very good example of the principle involved in these settlements. The murderer had deprived Catherine of her natural protector, her father and, in order to redress that loss, he was providing her, as her father would have done, with a husband. The intention was to restore as far as possible the status quo which the crime had destroyed, an idea which is stated very clearly in a letter of slains given at the end of the fifteenth century by the kin of the late John of Caldwell, forgiving the Cunninghams for his murder, and agreeing to 'stand in hartlie freindschip and kyndnes . . . lyk as the slachtyr of the saide Johne of Caldwel had nevir bein committit'.[69]

The bloodfeud exists in a society where central government is not strong. But that is not equivalent to saying that there is no order in society. Recent writing on the dark-age bloodfeud, or on modern kin-based societies where it still survives, show a refreshing tendency to regard it as a positive and effective method of preventing feud rather than a lamentable reflection of violence and lawlessness. One of the best analyses of the bloodfeud makes the point that 'to the legal historian feud dies a slow inevitable death, yielding to the superior equity of royal justice; chaos and bloodshed give place to good order because they must. But it is possible to see the matter otherwise.'[70] Indeed it is, and not only for the historian or social anthropologist. The fifteenth-century Scottish monarchy also saw the matter otherwise. In 1425, an act of parliament gave expression to James I's much-quoted principle of justice 'als wele to pur as to rych but fraude or favour.' What tends not to be quoted is the following act, which insisted on assythment in cases which had happened before the king's return to Scotland; assythment is the normal Scots word for compensation.[71]

Moreover, James's principle meant that rich and poor should get justice, but not that there should be a uniform system of justice for all men. At the lowest level, there was the distinction that the rich could buy their pardons while the poor could not; every Scottish king sold remissions for crime, and this was acceptable enough except in the case of James III, who was criticized because this was the only part of justice to which he paid much attention. But cynicism is quite out of place. Crime was not something for which the state took responsibility.

---

68 Reg. Supp. 391, f. 223v; I am indebted to Dr I. B. Cowan for drawing my attention to this case.

69 SRO, Register House Charters no. 596.

70 J. M. Wallace-Hadrill, 'The Bloodfeud of the Franks' in *The Long-haired Kings and other Studies in Frankish History* (London, 1962), p. 146.

71 *APS* II, p. 8.

Responsibility for pursuing a criminal, whether it resulted in a case before the courts or a private settlement, was still put on the kingroup. It was then expected not that the criminal should be punished by the state, but that he should make reparation to those he had wronged, and this is both an acceptable and a valid social principle, one which, it has been suggested, is too much lacking in modern criminal law. It was not only in private settlements that compensation payments were made. The late-sixteenth century lawyer, James Balfour of Pittendreich, in his *Practicks*, cited case law to give examples of this, and described the attempt to assess realistically who lost most because of crime and therefore deserved most compensation; thus unmarried daughters should have twice as much compensation as sons, and the heir should have less than the younger sons.[72] The monarchy approved and encouraged the use of the bond to bring men at feud into amity; and, at the end of the sixteenth century, James VI was still ratifying this practice.[73]

For the crown, there was the additional consideration that a murder in the locality did not justify the execution of a man of influence who was useful. Time and again the crown used the power of such men in the localities to its advantage, relying on the principle of personal influence. In 1501, James IV directed Alexander, earl of Huntly, 'to ressave in our soverane lordis name bandis and oblissingis of erlis lordis baronis and hed kynnismen within his realme in the north partyis of the Month, efter the tenour and effect of the writingis gevin to him thairuppoun; and gif neid be in our soverane lordis name and auctorite to compell thaim thairto'.[74] Presumably these were bonds promising service to Huntly as the king's representative in the north. The significant point is that James seems to have been far more aware of the advantages of encouraging men of local influence and position to bind themselves to Huntly than he was of the potential disadvantage, that Huntly might use his following only in his own interests in the north or in defiance of the crown. In the difficult areas of the Borders and the Highlands, the government introduced in the fifteenth century and used frequently in the sixteenth the general band, making lords and chiefs responsible for bringing to justice their men and tenants. Inevitably this was by no means always effective, but again it shows the value that the government placed on the use of the

---

72 *The Practicks of Sir James Balfour of Pittendreich* (Stair Society, 21 and 22, 1962–3), II, pp. 516–18.

73 Twice James directed that a bond of manrent be made, or ratified, to end dispute, in the second case the reason stated being that it was 'gevin for ane necessar and guid caus viz for keping . . . the parties thairin . . . in perpetuall quietnes in all tyme cuming'; *The Lag Charters*, edited by A. L. Murray (SRS, 1958), pp. 55–6; *APS* III, pp. 624–5.

74 *RSS* I, no. 722.

principle which was the basis of the individual agreement, the personal responsibilities of lord and man.[75]

At the end of the sixteenth century, when there had been considerable developments in central government, administration was more sophisticated, there were central law courts for civil and criminal justice, and taxation was becoming frequent, James VI wrote a book to instruct his son not how to theorize about monarchy by divine right, but how to be in practice an effective king. This contains his famous condemnation of the nobility, of their 'natural sickness . . . a fectlesse arrogant conceit of their greatnes and power', of their 'barbarous feides', of the way in which 'without respect to God, King or common-weale [they] bang it out bravely, hee and all his kinne against him and all his.' It is a marvellous passage, written in James's most pithy and memorable prose. But when Prince Henry read on, he was given the other side of the picture. The magnates were still the king's greatest servants and natural counsellors, for 'vertue followeth oftest noble blood.' If the king was father of his subjects, he should honour his nobles who kept his laws as 'Peeres and Fathers' of the land. The best service they could give 'is in their persons to practise, and by their power to procure due obedience to the lawe'; for 'they must be your armes and executers of your lawes.'[76] A century after *The Porteous of Noblenes* was written, James VI was still saying the same thing, and expressing an attitude to magnate power which was moderate and realistic. It was one with which his fifteenth-century predecessors would have wholly agreed.

75 T. I. Rae, *The Administration of the Scottish Frontier, 1513–1603* (Edinburgh, 1966), pp. 116–19.
76 Craigie, *Basilikon Doron* I, pp. 83–4, 87–8.

4

Economic life
S. G. E. Lythe

Because the economic life of fifteenth-century Scotland can be studied only on the basis of fragmentary evidence, conclusions about its general state are likely to vary enormously in character and emphasis. Thus the biographer of James IV, while believing that because of freedom from English invasion the century had 'been a period of comparative prosperity', concluded that 'at the end of the third quarter . . . Scotland was, even by medieval standards, an uncomfortable and uninviting country.'[1] By contrast Hume Brown believed that 'the Scottish peasantry enjoyed life on easier terms than those of the same class in any other country in Europe' and that 'the middle classes in the country had a very tolerable share of the good things of life.'[2] In a measure modern historians have reflected the conflicting views of contemporary commentators; but these must be treated with due caution for the contrast between the rosy picture drawn by Pedro de Ayala at the end of the century and the embittered comments of Aeneas Sylvius and Froissart at its beginning may reflect no more than the public relations nature of their activities, based, at best, on fairly restricted personal experience.[3]

The impossibility of sophisticated examination is immediately illustrated by the absence of data on such basic elements as the size and distribution of the population. Ingenious calculations, based on highly tenuous premises, have suggested that late fourteenth-century Scotland (that is, after the Great Pestilence) had somewhere between 250,000 and 350,000 people, and Hume Brown believed that the fifteenth-century population was 'not probably more than a quarter of a million'.[4] There is some consolation for the historian in Professor

1 R. L Mackie, *King James IV of Scotland* (Edinburgh, 1958), p. 3.

2 P. Hume Brown, *Scotland before 1700 from Contemporary Documents* (Edinburgh, 1893), pp. xi and xiii.

3 The relevant sections of these contemporary accounts are reprinted in *A Source Book of Scottish History*, edited by W. C. Dickinson, G. Donaldson and I. A. Milne (London, 1958) II, pp. 2–6; and P. Hume Brown, *Early Travellers in Scotland* (Edinburgh, 1891), pp. 8–15, 25–9 and 39–49.

4 T. Cooper, 'The Numbers and Distribution of the Population of Medieval Scot-

Postan's dictum that for his purposes, the dynamics of population are more significant than its absolute numbers, and it would certainly seem an arguable proposition that, despite the continuance of feuding, the incidence of Malthusian checks decreased by comparison with the fourteenth century. It is true that there were periodic outbreaks of variously named epidemics in the 1430s and again in the later part of the century, but by contrast with 1350 or 1530 they seem to have been relatively limited both in extent and intensity.[5] Whether the reduction in mortality by plague and war was reflected in any sustained rise in total population is pure speculation; all one dare say is that the evidences of vigour in Scottish society in the later part of the fifteenth century may suggest that, in common with much of western Europe, there was by then a greater buoyancy in the active adult sector of the nation.

For without doubt, whatever the catalysts may have been, the Scottish economy of the fifteenth century was far from static. The popular concept of a 'medieval' society, extending from some vague date in the twelfth century on to the Reformation or beyond, has no validity even in the rural sector where, almost inevitably, custom and convention counted most heavily. It scarcely needs saying that the Scottish economy was, by the the standards of western Europe, abnormally focused on rural activity and on the products of nature. That this rural society had suffered more than most from insecurity of tenure at all levels was commonly asserted by contemporary observers and their generalizations have coloured modern popular accounts. In fact the pattern was neither simple nor unchanging. Dr Grant quoted, with approbation, the view of R. L. Jones that 'the variety and confusion of tenure before the feu–ferme act of 1457 has never been fully appreciated. Every possible combination of lease and ward and blench–farm seems to have been adopted.'[6] A crude summary would be that while in 1400 there were still vestigial remains of thanages and of serfdom, and ancient land units such as the 'davoch' still persisted, by 1500 the Lowlands at least were beginning to move towards systems of tenure with terminology which would have been familiar to an eighteenth–century family lawyer. The principle of the perpetual feu was already recognized, and it is justifiable to regard its extension to land tenure as one of the clear symptoms of change in the fifteenth century. Resting on the basis of an initial downpayment, the

land', *SHR* xxvi (1947), p. 3; J. C. Russell, *British Medieval Population* (Albuquerque, 1948), p. 362; Brown, *Scotland before 1700*, p. xv.

5 The most recent summary is J. F. D. Shrewsbury, *A History of the Bubonic Plague in the British Isles* (Cambridge, 1970).

6 I. F. Grant, *The Social and Economic Development of Scotland before 1603* (reprint, Westport Connecticut, 1971), pp. 39–40. The correct date of the act is 1458.

grassum, followed by a fixed annual rent, it had attractions for feudal superiors in an age when personal services might be difficult to enforce and when a forecastable cash income had obvious merits. The terms of the act of 1458 seem to encourage the crown both to set an example by feuing its own lands and to authorize church- and laymen to follow its lead, but though a few crown feus were immediately granted at Falkland and elsewhere,[7] it was not until the reign of James IV and especially after *c.* 1508 that the process became decisive and widespread. Clearly the faith of clerics and laymen in traditional tenures with the opportunity of periodic readjustments died hard. Their uncertainty is well illustrated in the supplication of the vicar of St Giles, Edinburgh, in 1430, that he might have the 'faculty to set an annual ferme in perpetuity . . . or to a fixed term of all houses land . . . pertaining to the said vicarage with whomsoever he can make the best conditions'.[8]

Though the trend in thought is significant, the impact of perpetual tenure on the typical practising farmer was probably less immediate and widespread than changes in nature and duration of the conventional type of lease. Again the intention of legislation was helpful: thus an act of 1450 provided that 'the Buyer of landis suld keepe the tackes set before the Bying',[9] in other words that he should honour existing leases. On crown lands in the latter part of the fifteenth century leases of three to five years, with exceptional cases of fifteen years, seem to have been general. On other lands the practice varied and the generalized condemnation of extortion on renewal of leases, for example in Dunbar's poems, cannot lightly be disregarded. Yet where detailed examination is possible over a significant number of instances, notably in the records relating to the abbey of Coupar Angus, a different impression emerges.[10] Perhaps Coupar Angus was exceptional, but in the second half of the fifteenth century the abbey seems to have shown a vigour and enterprise in estate management reminiscent of the early years of Roman monasticism in Scotland. Thus David Blair (*c.* 1470s) was clearly a specialist in marsh drainage and about the same time the abbey had a *studarius* (keeper?) of black cattle; even in 1463 its rotation of pasture and arable on a nine-year cycle was described as established practice, and its arable crop yields were as good as, sometimes indeed better than, those of Monymusk in the eighteenth century.[11] Probably as a result of labour shortages after

7 *APS* II, p. 49; *ER* XIII, p. cxvi.

8 *Calendar of Scottish Supplications to Rome, 1428–1432*, edited by Annie I. Dunlop and I. B. Cowan (SHS, 1970), p. 69.

9 *APS* II, p. 35.

10 *Coupar Angus Rental.*

11 Calculated in T. B. Franklin, *A History of Scottish Farming* (Edinburgh, 1952), p. 74.

c. 1350 the monks had let virtually all their lands, and consequently their rental book is a fair reflection of the straight relationship between owner and tenants on lands subject to effective and progressive estate management.

The first inference is that leases often incorporated conditions governing husbandry. Sometimes these simply reflected the terms of a statute: thus in 1473 the tenants of Coupargrange were to 'defend the toun fra the guld [marigold] onder the pane of the parliament' and parliament's interest in tree-planting is reflected in the requirement on the tenants of the grange of Kerso (1470s) to plant 'frote treis of the best kind ma be gottyng'; sometimes the conditions were simply those of sensible estate conservation, as one of 1473 dealing with the replacement of top soil after the cutting of peat.[12] But even more striking is the extent of security of tenure. An analysis of the first twenty leases granted in each of four periods spread over sixty years yields the following pattern:

Period	Length of lease		
	Fewer than 5 years	5–7 years	Life
1443–4	2	17	1
1467–8	1	19	0
1476–8	2	4	14
1499–1504	1	13	6

Furthermore the lapse of lease did not necessarily mean change of tenant. The grange of Airlie was held by members of the Spalding family for about a hundred years; the grange of Aberbothrie (52 acres) was relet to David Young on four occasions between 1448 and 1468 and finally, in 1473, for life, and it is hard to conceive of more favourable terms than those in a lease of 1495 to Robert Pery and his wife and their male heir for the life of whichever survived the longest.[13]

Perhaps this is too complacent an impression. For though the rural economy was not, so far as one can judge, subject to the pressures of rising prices and rising population which produced so much tension in later periods, there is nevertheless evidence of friction. The acts of parliament from 1400 onwards to 1491, designed to give a measure of protection to tenants, seem to have been of little worth to the

12 *Coupar Angus Rental* I, pp. 165, 171 and 189.
13 Both examples cited in Franklin, *Scottish Farming*, p. 87; *Coupar Angus Rental* I, p. 245.

majority.[14] Equally clearly the pattern of relationships was becoming more complex, for at Coupar Angus and elsewhere leases frequently authorized sub-letting; in other words a kind of embryo tacksman system was beginning to appear. Furthermore renewal of lease was a tempting opportunity for upward revision of either grassum or annual rent or both. Thus Tullyfergus was let in 1449 to the three sons of the old tenant on a rising rental – of twelve marks for the first and second years rising to £10 for the fifth, plus capons and services in all cases. But this device of graduated rents was old-established,[15] and may have been no more than a simple method for easing a new tenant into a run-down farm. Yet men who knew their Scotland at the end of the fifteenth century did not mince their words. 'The country people', wrote Major,[16] 'have no permanent holdings, but hire only . . . at the pleasure of the lord of the soil', and Dunbar's allegation that 'mailis and garsomes' were 'raisit ouir hie' cannot be dismissed as the licensed propaganda of a poet.

The study is inevitably limited by the prevalence of tenures involving no formal instrument but which might nevertheless involve some form of mutually respected understanding. All we can say is that such evidence as is available indicates changes, perhaps only marginal and localized, in conditions of tenure and of land management.

The wider problem is whether, in the country at large, there were any significant changes in the area devoted to systematic food production. The outfield, that is the land temporarily reclaimed from waste or rough pasture, represented a potentially flexible element in the farming system. It has been reckoned that on some estates outfield could exceed the area of permanent arable by a factor of four,[17] and as the yield on newly broken land was normally high in the first couple of years an increased demand for grain could be accommodated at fairly short notice by marginal adjustments of this kind. Official policy, as demonstrated in acts of parliament, seems more concerned with the efficiency than with the area of arable farming; indeed the acts encouraging tree-planting and the scattered evidences of establishment of orchards might suggest some sacrifice of arable acreage. In general, however, there seems little doubt that deforestation continued throughout the century. Though the history of Scottish 'forests' is notoriously difficult to interpret it is tolerably certain that in Ettrick, covering some five hundred square miles, the ancient administration appropriate to a hunting region was giving place to

14 *APS* I, p. 213; II, pp. 96 and 225; Grant, *Social and Economic Development*, p. 257.

15 *Coupar Angus Rental* I, p. 127. For an example in 1312 see Grant, *Social and Economic Development*, pp. 87–90.

16 John Major, *A History of Greater Britain* (SHS, 1892), p. 31.

17 J. A. Symon, *Scottish Farming, Past and Present* (Edinburgh, 1959), p. 31.

conventional lets, and by the 1480s some of these were openly classed as 'shepe stedis'.[18] Royal participation – James IV reputedly had 20,000 sheep – combined with the relative lull in English hostility to produce something of an economic revival in the Southern Uplands, especially in sheep farming. Elsewhere the evidence is inconclusive; timber was locally felled for shipbuilding, construction and the like at points as widespread as Loch Lomondside, Glen Lyon and up to Darnaway in Moray, but whether the cleared land was systematically used is unknown.

Though the Scotland of the fifteenth century housed, and was to house for generations yet to come, a predominantly rural society based on stockrearing, hunting and arable farming, the balance had nevertheless already changed with the founding and growth of chartered burghs. For however strong may have been the agricultural activities of burgesses, the burgh, by its very nature, was a separate organism, possessing rights and conducting activities which distinguished it from the mass of Scottish society. Setting aside the legal and fiscal privileges, the holding of courts, self-taxation and the like, the 'cheif libertie of ane fre burgh of royaltie', to quote the Edinburgh council of 1570, lay in 'two thingis, the ane in the using of marchandice, the uther in using of craftes'. It is very plain that the fifteenth century witnessed great tensions within the burghs and important changes in the balance between the exponents of these two principal economic functions. Down to the middle years at least of the previous century, craftsmen had featured prominently in burgh administration, but by the fifteenth century the merchant element, with statutory backing, had gained virtually complete control and craftsmen had sunk to the level of second-class citizens. The usually advanced reasons are not wholly conclusive. It may be that, as in England, the staple industry of clothmaking had tended to migrate to the countryside to the advantage of the merchants but to the detriment of urban craftsmen. It may be that heavier financial demands, illustrated by the levy for the ransom of David II, had thrown burdens on the burghs which the merchants were better able to shoulder and that this in turn led the crown and the Estates to give *de jure* authorization to a *de facto* situation. At all events legislation, especially the act of 1469,[19] established very clearly a sharp differentiation between merchant and craft functions, and ensured for the merchants something approaching a monopoly of government within the royal burghs.

But we must neither exaggerate nor oversimplify. Despite the stated intention of the acts, wide variations in urban constitutions

18 M. L. Anderson, *A History of Scottish Forests* (London, 1967) I, p. 170.

19 *APS* II, p. 95. R. G. Nicholson, *Scotland: The Later Middle Ages* (Edinburgh, 1974), pp. 447–51.

persisted; there is, for example, no indication that the act of 1469 was applied in Peebles until 1504.[20] Furthermore the crafts were by no means dead. In Aberdeen, for example, their pageantry was displayed on feast days, the dyers presenting the emperor, two doctors and 'alsmony Squiares as thai may', and so on through the smiths and hammermen, the websters and fullers and the rest of them.[21] This type of activity alone must have involved some element of craft organization and, whether elected or appointed, recognizable offices began to receive official notice. Thus, after vacillation in 1426 and 1427, the Estates determined in 1428 that each craft should be subject to a warden who would 'pryse the mater and the workmanschip of ilk craft and sett it to a certaine price'.[22] But in so far as consistency can be detected it looks as if the Estates were reluctant to delegate any real economic power to the crafts. In 1493, for example, they came down heavily against leaders of crafts who had been pressing for payment for holy days and three years later they specifically authorized bailies to oversee price control.[23] Nevertheless on a wider front it looks as if, by the last thirty years of the century, the crafts were beginning to stage a comeback in urban life. The act of 1469, for all its pro-merchant bias, provided also that 'ilka craft sall cheise a persone of the samyn craft that sall have a voice in the said electioune' that is, of burgh officers; in 1474 the skinners in Edinburgh pioneered corporate recognition by obtaining their seal of cause,[24] the prototype for several other incorporations there in the next twenty-five years and in burghs generally in the early 1500s; and, if Dunbar's poetry is any indication of the social thinking of the time, there was rising criticism of the pretentious strutting of the merchants. In 1500 the crafts still had a very long furrow to till before they achieved anything like equality, but they had survived what can only be regarded as a century of challenge and crisis.

Are we to assume that the bias of official opinion in favour of the merchants reflected a preference for commerce as against industry, or was it rather a sociopolitical preference for the solid merchant-burgess as against the less substantial craftsman and his riproaring apprentices? Certainly the merchants had a head start in the race for official favour. Upon their skill in foreign trade depended the yield of the Great Custom which, in a typical year, might provide one-fifth of the total royal revenue; it was largely their wealth which enabled the burghs to

20 Mackie, *James IV*, p. 140.

21 Brown, *Scotland before 1700*, p. 185.

22 *APS* ii, p. 15.

23 *ibid.* ii, pp. 234 and 238.

24 *Extracts from the Records of the Burgh of Edinburgh, 1403–1528* (SBRS, 1869), pp. 28–30.

meet a similar fraction of the exceptional 'aids' to the crown in the 1470s and 1480s; through the Court of the Four Burghs and, by the later years of the century, the more general meetings of burghs, they were able to exercise some sort of discipline in commercial and inter-burghal relationships; overseas, especially in France and the Low Countries, they could maintain continuity and intimacy of contact of real diplomatic value; and self-interest made them active custodians of law and order within their own towns. Against this list of virtues there was little the craftsmen could offer of immediate political or fiscal value to the crown.

The assessment of the economic contribution of industry, whether the product of these urban craftsmen or of their rural contemporaries, is fraught with difficulty. The comments of foreign writers on Scottish industry, at least around the beginning of our period, were almost universally unflattering. 'When the English invade', wrote Froissart, 'they have to take their provisions with them, for there is nothing to be found in the country. It is almost impossible to get iron to make horseshoes, or leather for harness. Everything comes ready-made from Flanders; and failing that there is nothing', and this can be complemented by Hakluyt's rhyme about half the ships from Flanders being laden with cartwheels and wheelbarrows.[25] It is perhaps significant that, in the considerable volume of fifteenth-century legislation on economic matters, acts for the 'promotion of industry' are remarkably lacking. The act of 1473 against the import of English cloth, was more concerned with the inbringing of bullion than with the well-being of Scottish weavers, and that of 1493, deploring the 'greit innumerable ryches' lost by the lack of ships and calling on all burghs to build and equip fishing vessels, was clearly deficient in a sense of realism.[26] If their acts fairly reflect their attitude, the Estates were obsessed with the import of precious metal so that the realm might be 'stuffit of Bulyeone';[27] this may have meant a restraint of the import of goods and so protected Scottish craftsmen, but nowhere is there any substantial evidence that this objective was other than incidental.

Nevertheless, the industrial record of fifteenth-century Scotland is by no means wholly negative, and certainly in the later years there are evidences of vitality. Lacking any basis for firm conclusions, we can at least suggest that the most conspicuous products were those of the masons and carpenters. A century which could undertake a fresh wave

25 *Froissart's Chronicles*, edited by J. Jolliffe (London, 1948), p. 265; R.Hakluyt, *The Principal Navigations, Voyages, Traffiques and Discoveries of the English Nation* (Edinburgh, 1885) II, p. 121.

26 *APS* II, pp. 105 and 235.

27 *ibid.* II, p. 118.

of ecclesiastical building with collegiate churches of the quality of Lincluden and Roslin, which could rebuild Crossraguel and the cathedrals at Elgin and Dunkeld, begin the palace at Linlithgow and create such classic pieces of defensive architecture as the curtain wall at Craigmillar, was not lacking in either the inspiration or the techniques or the resources for great building.

But much of the work of man is ephemeral, and little evidence of the staple industries, textiles and the like, survives either in material or documentary form. It is clear, however, that both linen and wool were manufactured in rural districts: Henryson's account of the gathering, steeping, heckling and spinning of flax is written in terms of a rural cottage rather than an urban craft,[28] and the references to country fulling mills indicate not only possible areas of concentration but also the penetration of technical change.[29] In the metal-using industries there seems reasonable justification for postulating an increase both in size and sophistication as the century went on, a development associated, at least in part, with the rearmament undertaken by the crown. It is tolerably certain, for example, that cannon were being cast in Scotland from the 1470s, and the presence in Moscow in 1507 of four Scottish metalworkers, specialists in artillery, would suggest more than a purely local reputation.[30] Shipbuilding, undertaken only intermittently through previous centuries, became relatively more regular while the size of ships, certainly those financed by the crown, increased greatly. The peak of naval rearmament, typified in the *Great St Michael*, came in the later years of James IV, but royal patronage of shipbuilding can be traced from the interest of James I in a shipyard at Leith to the fitting out of a ship for James III at Dumbarton in 1487.[31]

National defence could have other but less obvious consequences. The accounts of the lord high treasurer for 1498 recount how the king, having set up strongholds at Tarbert and elsewhere, sent a 'cole man' into Kintyre to discover whether 'colys might be wonnyn there' to provide fuel for the garrisons. It has been suggested that this prospector, 'one Davisone, colyer, in Dumbertane', must be the first named collier in Scottish history.[32] Coal had long been extracted from superficial workings; there are fifteenth-century evidences from Dysart in the east to Tarbolton in the west, and though some was used industrially, in smithy work or for evaporating sea water to produce salt, it

28 Quoted in Grant, *Social and Economic Development*, p. 320.

29 For example, *Coupar Angus Rental* I, pp. 133 and 141.

30 *TA* I, p. 292; J. W. Barnhill and P. Dukes, 'North-east Scots in Muscovy', *Northern Scotland* I (1972), p. 50.

31 *ER* IV, pp. cxii and 383; *TA* I, p. 125.

32 L. A. Barbé, *Sidelights on the Industrial and Social Life of Scotland* (Glasgow, 1919), p. 198.

seems that the main demand was for elementary space heating. Aeneas Sylvius claimed that it was doled out as charity so that the poor might warm their dwellings, and John Major, a century later, explained that coal was used domestically over much of the southern part of the country because of the lack of timber for fuel.[33]

But there is no suggestion anywhere that there was anything more than a scratching at the nation's mineral resources, either of coal or metals, and it is perhaps significant that, except for making precious metals a royal monopoly, the Estates devoted little attention to mining or minerals. In contrast the fisheries were clearly a matter of constant concern. Foreign observers, however critical of other aspects of Scotland, were at one in their enthusiasm about the quantity of fish both in the inland waters and in the neighbouring seas. In 1447 Loch Fyne was said to produce herring in 'mair plenti than ony seas of Albion', and fifty years later de Ayala, admittedly with pro-Scottish bias, claimed that the quantity of Scottish fish was 'so great that it suffices for Italy, France, Flanders and England' – 'Piscinata Scotia', he wrote, putting the whole situation in a nutshell.[34] Whatever the cause, whether for example there had already been a migration of the herring from the opposite side of the North Sea, Scotsmen of the later fifteenth century were in no doubt about the immense potential value of fisheries. But there was no simple means of establishing a firm hold, let alone a monopoly, of this rich harvest. Foreign fishermen, especially those from Holland and Bremen, were technically better equipped in catching, curing and marketing, and the Scottish legislation of the later years of the century is a clear reflection of the anxiety to meet this competition by more and better vessels and gear. And official interest in the herring was at least matched by that in the salmon. The miraculous (and, for her, fortunate) recovery of the queen of Cadzow's ring through the agency of St Kentigern and a salmon symbolizes the place of the salmon in the early history of the Clyde; likewise, though still in the realm of half-tradition, the emergence of Glasgow as a commercial centre is popularly dated from the traffic in cured salmon conducted by William Elphinstone in the middle decades of the fifteenth century.[35] In fact, it looks as if the salmon fishery was widespread in the still unpolluted rivers and firths on both sides of the country, though Aberdeen may well have been the main centre for the exports which

33 Major, *History*, p. 138.

34 The evidence is conveniently collected together in A. M. Samuel, *The Herring: its Effect on the History of Britain* (London, 1918). De Ayala's letter is printed in full in *Calendar of Letters etc. relating to the Negotiations between England and Spain*, edited by G. A. Bergenroth (London, 1862) I, pp. 160–61.

35 This story originated with John McUre. It is critically examined in R. Renwick, *History of Glasgow* (Glasgow, 1921) I, pp. 248–9.

were officially so highly esteemed as earners of bullion and foreign coin.

If we relied solely on Dunbar we might suppose that the king had many 'craftismen fyne glasing wrichts, goldsmythis and lapidaris, pryntouris, payntouris and potingaris' [apothecaries], yet when the same king married Margaret Tudor, though the crown was made of gold supplied by the treasurer, the major embellishments, plate, tapestries and the like, were bought at considerable expense in Flanders.[36] Similarly, fine textiles for aristocratic or ecclesiastical use were generally of foreign make, for instance, the 'sea gown' of tawney Rouen cloth provided at the king's command for Lady Catherine Gordon and the stole with a fillet of Liege cloth of gold in Glasgow Cathedral.[37] In a variety of ways the cultural environment of Scotland was beginning to respond to Renaissance influences, but the emergence of sophisticated native craftsmanship, except in building, was restrained by the limited effective demand. There were signs of vitality and enterprise in the later 1400s, from the dead-end pursuit of alchemy to the open-ended pursuit of printing but, in reality, they may often have been little more than praiseworthy aspirations.

'The fifteenth century', wrote Cochran Patrick, 'is singularly deficient in any notices of Scottish trade and commerce.'[38] Without doubt overseas trade represented only a small segment of the overall economic life of the nation. Nevertheless it was prized and guarded, and for two not easily reconcilable reasons. For while, on the one hand, the export of Scottish wares was the obvious means of building up the highly esteemed stocks of bullion, on the other hand it was only by importing goods that the limitations of Scottish domestic production could be overcome and Scotsmen could enjoy a standard of life even approximating to that of their European contemporaries. The ideal pattern was a stable trading relationship with a more advanced economy which, in exchange for Scottish skins, hides and fish, would provide either precious metals, or natural products which for climatic or other reasons could not be grown in Scotland, or the more sophisticated manufactured goods for which Scottish demand was too small to sustain native production. But economic forces were not the sole determinants of the geographical pattern of Scottish overseas trade; above all, commercial cooperation with England, obviously convenient because it involved merely an extension of overland or coastal trade, had been eroded by generations of bitter political hostility. Yet whenever that hostility eased economic advantage made for a restor-

36 *TA* II, pp. 206 and 228.
37 *ibid.* I, pp. 343–4; Renwick, *History of Glasgow* I, p. 310.
38 R. W. Cochran Patrick, *Mediaeval Scotland* (Glasgow, 1892), p. 134.

ation of the contact. It has been reckoned that between 1433 and 1453 ninety licences were issued for commercial access by Scotsmen to English markets, and a further twenty-four between 1464 and 1468.[39] Nor was Scotland without its commercial attractions even to Englishmen. It has been suggested that a concession in 1482 whereby Berwick and Carlisle became legal points of entry for Scottish goods and the merchants of Berwick were allowed to ship Scottish wool direct to the continent was, in fact, an English attempt to divert the wool trade of the Southern Uplands; equally there is clear implication in Scottish legislation that English cloth was likely to be sold in Scotland.[40] Nevertheless, substantial evidence of Scottish trade is very rare in English commercial records and the classic work on English trade in the fifteenth century is almost devoid of references to Scotsmen except as pirates,[41] while detailed studies of individual English ports are mostly equally barren. Whether, to cite one such instance, the very substantial volume of goods entered at Bristol as coming from Ireland included some of Scottish origin,[42] is a matter of guesswork; the frequent imports of fish, including 'haburden' fish might be evidence if we were certain that 'haburden' meant Aberdeen and was not simply a generic trade name.

If trade with England was unhealthy, that with the Baltic and the Low Countries almost certainly increased in the fifteenth century; perhaps it took up some of the slack. The Baltic was the scene of complicated politico-commercial rivalries involving the Hanse, the Scandinavian countries uneasily united under Denmark by the treaty of Calmar, the English and the Dutch. Within this context Scottish trade not surprisingly had its ups and downs. The commercial links with the Hanse, well established in the fourteenth century were so jeopardized by Scottish piracy that between 1412 and 1436 trade with the Hanse ports was either seriously curtailed or completely banned.[43] But as the century progressed relationships generally improved. From about 1470 the ascendent Danes controlled the Sound, and, because of her friendly associations with Denmark, Scotland was, within the narrow limits of her shipping capacity, able to take advantage of the opening thus created. In 1474–6 an annual average of eight Scottish

39 Grant, *Social and Economic Development*, p. 336, n.1.

40 W. S. Reid, *Skipper from Leith: the History of Robert Barton of Over Barmton* (Philadelphia, 1962), p. 21; *APS* II, p. 105.

41 *Studies in English Trade in the Fifteenth Century*, edited by Eileen E. Power and M.M. Postan (London, 1933).

42 *The Overseas Trade of Bristol*, edited by E. M. Carus-Wilson (Bristol Record Society, 1937), p. 254.

43 P. Dollinger, *La Hanse, xiie–xviie siècles* (Paris, 1964), p. 305; T. A. Fischer, *The Scots in Germany* (Edinburgh, 1902), pp. 13–14.

ships entered Danzig; in 1497 twenty-one were recorded as having passed through the Sound (that is, eleven passing through, ten returning) rising to forty-three in 1503.[44] By Baltic standards this was a mere trickle of commerce, but in Scottish terms it was a valuable foothold which could be exploited when, for political or other reasons, the giants of the Baltic trade were discommoded. In 1485, for example, because of a shortage of supply, Bay salt at Danzig had gone up to 40 marks a last, about six times the level of the 1470s. 'Local' Luneburg salt was 38 marks, Scottish was only 22.[45]

Valuable as this northern trade may have been both for the export of skins, cloth and salt and for the import of industrial raw materials plus, when necessary, grain,[46] it did not provide Scotland with access to a general emporium. The Low Countries, with their international trading links, possessed unique qualifications to fulfil this role, and in the fifteenth century commercial convenience was reinforced by dynastic links and institutional arrangements. Thus James II married Mary of Gueldres, niece of the duke of Burgundy, and his sister married a son of the lord of Vere – 'oure welebeloved cousinge' in their subsequent correspondence. From 1406, when William VI granted Scotsmen freedom to trade in Holland 'nullam molestationem',[47] the century is punctuated by similar expressions of good intentions between the rulers of the Low Countries and the kings of Scotland. Though the final evolution of the Scottish staple in the Low Countries belongs to the sixteenth century the seeds were being sown before 1400, and the interest of various towns, Middleburg, Vere, Antwerp and Bruges, in acquiring the monopolistic staple has been commonly regarded as indication of the value they placed on the Scottish commercial link. Very likely the specific attraction was Scottish wool, or perhaps wool from the north of England in Scottish ships. Though there was a background of fine wool production by some of the Scottish abbeys,[48] Scottish quality was generally no more than middling, but nevertheless, as we saw in relation to salt sales at Danzig, the alert Scottish shipper could exploit opportunities created by the default of normal major suppliers. In 1438, for example, the restrictive practices of the English wool staplers were said to have produced a rise in demand for

44 Grant, *Social and Economic Development*, p. 339; *Tabeller over Skibsfart og Varetransport gennem Øresund 1497–1660*, edited by Nina E. Bang and Knud Korst (Copenhagen, 1906–33).

45 Records of Caspar Weinreich of Danzig, quoted in Dollinger, *La Hanse*, p. 482.

46 For example, in 1478 a Friesland ship arrived at Leith with grain from Danzig; *Bronnen tot de geschiedenis van den Handel met Engeland, Schotland en Ierland*, edited by H. J. Smit (S-Gravenhage, 1928), doc. 1834.

47 *ibid.*, doc. 834.

48 'La practica della mercatura', printed in W. Cunningham, *Growth of English Industry and Commerce* (Cambridge, 1922) i, appendix D.

Scottish wool in Flanders, and again, at the end of the century, the export duties imposed by the English promoted the market for Scottish wool.[49] While quantification is impossible, it is plain from both Scottish and Dutch evidences that throughout the fifteenth century Scotland was a not inconsiderable supplier of wool, sheepskins, hides and goatskins.[50]

The Scots staple in the Low Countries had a disjointed and chequered history in the fifteenth century. After a spell at Middleburg it was settled at Bruges in 1407 in terms of a treaty with the duke of Burgundy which, without establishing any extraterritorial jurisdiction, gave the Scots the right to have commissioners to safeguard their trading interests. This did not last long. Perhaps, as has been suggested, Bruges was 'too great a centre for the Scots' and their custom would be more fully appreciated by a smaller port.[51] At all events they went back to Middleburg, then tried Bruges again, and then, in 1468, a letter from Archibald Napier conveyed to Middleburg the good news that all Scots ships were to 'pass to Scelande and los in Medylburch . . . for owr soveran lord . . . has raserwyt that stapell be maide'.[52] From 1492 to 1503 Andrew Halyburton was conservator (a sort of commercial consul) at Middleburg, and his account book provides a unique picture not simply of the nature of late fifteenth-century commerce but equally of the varied transactions which were conducted through commercial channels.[53] The Scottish products he recorded at Middleburg were predictable – wool, skins and fish; the items returning to Scotland were, by contrast, extremely varied – cloth, spices, wood, fruits, wine (other evidences suggest Rhenish) and a miscellany of small purchases ranging from embroidery thread to a tombstone. But equally Halyburton acted as a commission-earning agent for all manner of Scotsmen, merchants, noblemen and churchmen in particular. Thus he paid twenty ducats into the bank of Cornelius Altonatz for transmission to Rome to expedite the issue of a dispensation for Sir John Crawford, arranged for the making of a seal for the earl of Ross, and bought plate and floor-tiles for the archdeacon of St Andrews. In short, Halyburton's *Ledger* confirms the view that the real value to Scotland of a permanent foothold in the Low Countries lay in the ready access it gave to a unique and efficient supplier of goods and services.

49 Power and Postan, *Studies in English Trade*, p.83; Grant, *Social and Economic Development*, pp. 328–9.

50 For example *ER* III, p. 495; Smit, *Bronnen*, docs 896, 1008, 1448, 1758, 1764, 1871 and 1975.   51 Rosalind Mitchison, *A History of Scotland* (London, 1970), p. 66.

52 Smit, *Bronnen*, doc. 1585.

53 *The Ledger of Andrew Halyburton, Conservator of the Privileges of the Scotch Nation in the Netherlands*, edited by C. Innes (Edinburgh, 1867).

Basically the trade with France arose from the complementary nature of the two economies: God had given France warm sunshine to ripen grapes and evaporate salt water and, as Major pointed out, had compensated Scotland by great abundance of fish. But political alliance, and the personal associations which stemmed from it, put the French trade in a unique context. The migration of Scots, initially as mercenaries, led to permanent settlement and to intermarriage; there were Scots colonies in Dieppe and Rouen and a group of Scotsmen acquired property and the right to clear part of the forest of Haute-Brune.[54] France, indeed, dominates the story of the 'Scot abroad' in the fifteenth century. Not surprisingly, in this cordial context, commerce had official approbation. It may be correct, as Dr Grant argues, that despite the close political alliance 'the Scots do not seem to have enjoyed very valuable commercial privileges',[55] and certainly the major concessions in Normandy came only with the duke of Albany's negotiations in 1518. But further south, in the classic wine and salt regions, mutually agreeable commercial relationships were well established and reinforced by Scottish legislation. An act of 1467, for example, specifically listed Bordeaux and La Rochelle as legitimate markets for Scottish traders and, by an earlier act of 1436, the lieges had been forbidden to buy wine from Flemish importers to Scotland.[56] Because the available French port records are discontinuous and in any event include only those sailings which were the subject of some notarial act in France, the data they yield are inadequate for any statistical examination of the trade.[57] Its broad features are, nevertheless, clear. It was mainly concentrated in the autumn when the sun had done its annual work. Unlike the Baltic and Flanders trade it was more widely dispersed over all the main Scottish ports. Thus the freighting of the *Christofe* of Bordeaux in 1499 with 75 tuns of wine for Wigton or Kirkcudbright, at the master's discretion, supports Scottish domestic evidence of direct sailings to the west coast ports, a route which at least avoided the risky waters off the southeast of England.[58] In general, import cargoes were wholly of wine or of salt, though the *Marie* to Leith in 1499 carried both,[59] and some had smallish parcels of dyestuffs and the odd tun of vinegar. Without such imports Scotland's life

54 T. D. Cook, *The Story of Rouen* (London, 1928), p. 169; F. Michel, *Les Ecossais en France, les Français en Ecosse* (London, 1862) I, p. 145.

55 Grant, *Social and Economic Development*, p. 337.

56 *APS* II, 87 and 24.

57 For example, E. Trocmé and M. Delafosse, *Les Commerce Rochelais de la fin du xve siècle au début du xviie* (Paris, 1952), pp. 70–71.

58 J. Bernard, *Navires et Gens de Mer à Bordeaux, vers 1400–vers 1550* (Paris, 1968) III, appendix; Renwick, *History of Glasgow* I, p. 247.

59 Bernard, *Navires et Gens.*

would have been the poorer, for, in spite of domestic salt production, curers of fish and flesh depended upon supplies from Biscay, and certainly without the wine the social life of the better-off must have been impoverished in an age when whisky was still almost unknown.

Quantification is impossible, but the impression prevails that the dispute with the Hanse, followed by internal troubles in Scotland in the 1440s and 1450s, resulted in a decline in the level of Scottish exports and that recovery came with the fall of the house of Black Douglas and the restoration of royal authority. Even then, by the standards of the Dutch or the Hanse, the volume was trivial. But small as it was in relative terms, it represented a material link with more advanced societies and so acted as a catalyst within Scotland. The monopoly of the royal burghs confined its conduct to a small clique, but that group of relatively affluent merchants constituted the nearest approach to a middle class in Scottish society. The biographer of one of them has spoken of 'the alertness of the middle class' and has shown how they were entering into public service, deploying their maritime skill as naval commanders, and, by purchase or marriage, entering the rural landowning stratum.[60] Dunbar was bitter about the avarice of the merchants of Edinburgh:

> Your proffait daylie dois incres,
> Your godlie workis les and les,

but there was not much scope for moral posturing in the risky commercial world of King James IV.

Yet even if we accept this view of the dynamic effect of foreign trade we cannot present a balanced picture unless we revert to events and influences within Scotland itself. How far, for example, were conditions influenced by public policy? Can we, with any pretence to historical reasoning, speak of a national economic policy in fifteenth-century Scotland? Certainly a cursory reading of the statutes suggests a watchful paternal concern for the welfare of the community; anything from rewards for the slaughter of wolves (1427) to the crying down of football and golf (1458), from punitive action against 'masterful beggars' (1449) to sumptuary restrictions on elaborate dress (1430), or from encouragement of the planting of trees and hedges (1458) to provisions for the import of bullion (1431).

Even in a modern society there can be a gap between the intention and the application of laws. The repetition of enactments by fifteenth-century parliaments (for example the anti-wolf act of 1427 was repeated in 1458) itself suggests lack of enforcement. The extent to which any centrally issued edict might prevail was limited not

60 Reid, *Skipper from Leith,* pp. 30–32 and 67–9.

simply by the existence of semi-independent jurisdictions such as that of the Lordship of the Isles but also by periodic trouble from some of the magnates both to the north and to the south, and the impression of greater material and intellectual progress in the closing years of the century must be associated with the relative success of James IV in weakening these resistances to royal authority. A further question may well be interposed for the attention of a future researcher. By what mechanism, in this pre-printing age, was official information communicated? Proclamation in a burgh or interpretation by monastic officers could inform a few (hence, as we have seen, the echoes of statutes in leases at Coupar Angus) yet even a well-conducted abbey 'almost universally disregarded' the acts of 1427 and 1472 about the balance of crops.[61] Even more one may wonder whether the news that all stacks were to be threshed by 31 May and that game birds were not to be killed during the moulting season ever reached the ears of a tenant of Badenoch.

In short any realistic examination of the 'role of the state' must be conducted with all these limitations constantly in mind, and the conclusions are likely to be in terms of intentions rather than of achievements. Clearly one major element was, as Bacon said of English policy before Henry VII, consideration of plenty. The statutes about food supply, ranging from the planting of windbreaks to the encouragement of the import of victuals, though sometimes immediately associated with threats of dearth, reveal an underlying anxiety to safeguard at least one of the necessities of life. But the aim of conserving resources comes out most sharply in the policy on bullion and the precious metals.[62] Various possible devices were tried. The most obvious was a straight ban on the export of coin, but this immediately cut across the financial arrangements between Scottish churchmen and Rome; nevertheless an act of 1424 sought to check even this form of currency drain. A second device is reflected in a series of acts requiring merchants to bring back bullion in exchange for the fish or animal products they had sold abroad. For both administrative and economic reasons these devices were difficult to implement. It may be true that part of the nation's shortage of precious metals stemmed from the ransoms of David II and James I, but more fundamental was the country's inability to establish either a 'natural' inflow of precious metals by a favourable balance of trade or to produce any significant amount of gold or silver within her own bounds. The act on mines of 1424 set up a mechanism to channel any domestic production into

61 Franklin, *History of Scottish Farming*, p. 45.

62 The principal acts are summarized in Dickinson *et al.*, *Source Book of Scottish History*, II, pp. 233 ff., and will not be individually cited here.

royal custody 'as is usuale in uther realyms',[63] but there are few signs of any significant results until the closing years of James IV when Crawford Muir began to yield its golden harvest. In fact Scotland's bullion shortage differed only in degree from that of many another European nation and, like most similarly deficient, she resorted to the deceptively simple device of making each pound of silver spin out into more and more coins.[64] But we must be careful not to introduce modern concepts of depreciation into the context of fifteenth–century Scotland. Her domestic coinage provided only a part of the circulating money and virtually every coin hoard in Scotland has disclosed the presence of money of other national origin. Over wide sectors of the economy relationships were maintained with little or no resort to actual cash and it has been argued with reason that this was an age when commodity prices were relatively insensitive to the supply of money.[65] Nevertheless, this weakening of the quality of the coinage cannot have made for confident economic health, either internally or in external trading relationships.

Yet despite these difficulties the economy was sufficiently buoyant, at least in the second half of the century, to sustain a significant level of expenditure on 'public works' ranging from churches to instruments of war. Though it may be argued that the interest of the kings was primarily political, their expenditure had immediate implications and, even more, their policy of widespread effective government was an essential step towards the creation of an adequate infrastructure for long-term economic growth. Success depended, *inter alia*, upon their ability to maintain royal revenue at a level commensurate with the task, and from the return of James I in 1424 two broad objectives became clear – to improve financial administration and to broaden the range of sources of revenue. Hitherto formal exemptions, grants which were virtually bribes for good behaviour, and straight peculation, had made heavy inroads on the effective yield of the export duty levied in ports on staple goods and known as the Great Custom. Partly by administrative reform,[66] partly by the greater authority of the crown, James I went a long way towards reducing this wastage, but even so the yield from the Great Custom was never more than a secondary element in royal revenue. Indeed, apart from the proceeds of royal trading and farming, especially by James III, its really buoyant element was the yield from crown lands. By forfeiture, annexation or marriage, the first four Jameses achieved remarkable success in virtu-

63 *APS* ii, p. 5.

64 The figures are quoted in W. C. Dickinson, *Scotland from the Earliest Times to 1603* (Edinburgh, 1961), p. 231. See also I. H. Stewart, *The Scottish Coinage* (London, 1955).

65 A. E. Feaveryear, *The Pound Sterling* (London, 1931), p. 40.

66 A. L. Murray, 'The Comptroller, 1425–1488', *SHR* lii (1973), pp. 2–3.

ally recreating a chain of royal estates from the Borders up to Shetland and, by 1493, out west into the old Lordship of the Isles.

But the regrettable truth is that the history of fifteenth-century Scottish public finance is full of obscure corners. As Dr Murray has noted, in the early summer of 1488 such was the apparent state of royal penury that some of the plate was in pawn, yet 'James III carried with him to Sachieburn not only the sword of Robert the Bruce but also a box containing not less than £4,000 in gold coin.'[67] How, with his meagre revenue and considerable outlays, James III had accumulated his hoard, and indeed what subsequently happened to it, lies outside the evidence of any record available either to his immediate successor or to the modern historian.

The conclusion must be that though the rulers of fifteenth-century Scotland had emerging policies and aims, their ability to influence economic life was little more than marginal save in the broad sense of creating respect for law and order. They lacked the material resources to make any widespread direct impact; their administrative machinery was inadequate for the enforcement of sweeping reforms. But basically they were operating within a society which was still highly custom-bound and which, in general, was still conditioned by concern for immediate survival. Major economic change comes only when men are able to think beyond tomorrow. Changes, as we have seen, were afoot, for example in tenure and in the status of the mercantile middle class, and such changes could well be fostered by legislation or by royal patronage, but at most they affected only a minority of the community. For the mass of the people in 1500, as in 1400, happiness depended above all on safety of the person, safety of possessions, a tolerable winter and a kindly summer.

67 *ibid.*, p. 19.

5

Scotland's foreign relations

Scandinavia
Barbara E. Crawford

1

The fifteenth century was an important turning point in the history of relations between Scotland and Scandinavia. During this century the way was paved for Scotland's strong economic contacts with Denmark and Sweden which are so evident in the sixteenth century and later.[1] Although the origins of these contacts and their development during the fifteenth century have been considered to be obscure, yet the evidence shows that Scottish merchants were established in Denmark by the mid-fifteenth century, no doubt because of the commercial importance of the country on the route to the Baltic. The first formal political links between Denmark and Scotland were made soon after with the marriage of James III to King Christian's daughter, Margaret, in 1468. The Stewart kings were able to exploit the difficult situation of the kings of Denmark-Norway in order to further their own territorial ambitions, as in 1460 and 1468, and desire for standing in the international situation, as in 1472 and 1499. They appear to have been the dominant partner in the friendly relationship which resulted from the marriage alliance of 1468, as is shown by their attitude over the redemption of the islands of Orkney and Shetland, and their ability to provide the Danish king with military assistance as and when they wished.

The development of Scotland's political links with Denmark was the result of a directional change in the diplomatic sphere which itself resulted from the changed situation within Scandinavia after the union of the Danish and Norwegian crowns in 1380. Before then Norway

---

1 There is an excellent survey article of all relevant historiography by T. L. Christensen, 'Scoto-Danish Relations in the Sixteenth Century', *SHR* xlviii (1969), as well as his 'Scots in Denmark in the Sixteenth Century', *SHR* xlix (1970). See also the articles by James Dow, '*Skotter* in Sixteenth-century Scania', *SHR* xliv (1965), and 'Scottish Trade with Sweden, 1512–80', *SHR* xlviii (1969).

had been an independent sovereign state with its own crowned head, and the Scottish kings' previous diplomatic contacts across the North Sea had been with the kings of Norway. Since 1098 and Edgar of Scotland's treaty with Magnus Barelegs the two countries had had adjoining territorial boundaries divided only by narrow strips of water, such as the Pentland Firth and the sea lochs of the west coast. This had led to close political contacts – two formal treaties in 1266 and 1312; a marriage between the two ruling houses in 1281, which was followed up by Erik Magnusson's second marriage to Isabella Bruce; the inheritance of the Scottish crown for a brief period by the Maid of Norway in 1290; and the claim put forward by King Erik to the Scottish throne in 1292. There were economic links too, as can be seen from the complaints about reciprocal attacks on the merchants of both countries in 1312.[2] The islands of Orkney and Shetland in particular provided an entrepôt centre for the exchange of goods, and an area of cross-fertilization between the two peoples, with the earl of Orkney combining allegiance to both kings.

After 1380, and particularly after the union of Kalmar of 1397, Denmark was drawn into this picture as the most powerful partner in the Scandinavian political association. To begin with, Norwegian interests were left to the Norwegians. For instance, in 1426 the treaty between James I and Erik of Pomerania, king of Denmark and Norway, was treated essentially as a Norwegian matter; it was signed in Norway by Norwegians with a special mandate from King Erik.[3] The joint kings, however, took upon themselves the claims and rights of the former Norwegian kings, so that when king Christian I of the house of Oldenburg was in financial straits in the middle of the century, he pursued with enthusiasm the right of his Norwegian predecessors to the annual payment of 100 marks from the king of Scotland. Once this thorny problem had been settled, after protracted negotiations, by the marriage of his daughter Margaret to James III of Scotland in 1468, then direct links between Scotland and Denmark were forged. The year 1468 proved to be a very important milestone in the development of Scottish–Scandinavian relations.

2

Before 1468 the question of the 'annual' dominated the political scene. This was the payment of 100 marks which Scotland had pledged herself to pay to Norway in perpetuity for the transfer of the Western Isles in 1266, renewed in 1312.[4] After 1312 payments are no longer

---

2 *DN* ii, no. 114; see below, p. 94.
3 L. Hamre, *Norsk Historie frå omlag år 1400* (Oslo, 1968), p. 72.
4 *DN* viii, no. 9; *APS* i, pp. 78 (1266) and 101 (1312).

recorded in the central Scottish records, but the appearance of sums of 200 nobles[5] in Orkney records suggests that the payment may have continued through the fourteenth century.[6] One can assume that with the absence of the Scottish king in England during the first part of the fifteenth century, no payments were made, an assumption which is supported by the renewal of the 1266 and 1312 treaties between the Scottish and Norwegian kings in 1426 after James I had returned to Scotland. The treaty of 29 July 1426 with Norway fits into the pattern of adjustment and goodwill towards his neighbours on the part of the newly restored Scottish king, seen in the peaceful relations with England following the treaty of London of 1423, and the renewal of the Franco-Scottish alliance in 1428. The initiative for the treaty, however, probably came from the other side of the North Sea. The activity of Simon, herald of the king of Norway, in Scotland, in April–May 1426 shows that King Erik was taking advantage of the existence of a king in Scotland to make representations for the renewal of relationships. As at this date he was at war with both the Hansa and the count of Holstein, his financial situation was very precarious, which made the prospect of the renewal of an annual payment of 100 marks an attractive one. Besides this, Erik was a king who was very keen on his legal rights, as can be seen throughout his quarrel with the count of Holstein and with England over fishing rights in the North Sea. The whole purpose of the 1426 treaty was to stress the legal position of the king of Norway and his right to the annual payment.[7]

5 In 1426 after the renewal of the 1266 and 1312 treaties the bishop of Orkney promised King Erik to receive on his behalf the sum of 200 nobles which Scotland had agreed once more to pay; *DN* II, no. 689. The 'annual' was said to be 100 marks sterling or 200 English nobles by Arild Huitfeldt in the sixteenth century, when he wrote his chronicle of Danish history; *Historiske Bescriffuelse om hvis sig haffuer tildraget under Her Christiern den Første, etc.* (Copenhagen, 1599), p. 171. 1 noble = 6s. 8d. or half a mark.

6 In 1369 Håkon Jonsson, who had a grant of authority in Orkney and Shetland, was owed the sum of 200 nobles by the chapter of St Magnus's Cathedral, Kirkwall, which, according to the terms of the 1266 treaty, was responsible for receiving the sum and handing it over to the Norwegian authorities; *DN* I, p. 309, no. 404. When Henry Sinclair acknowledged his grant of the earldom of Orkney in 1379 he promised to pay King Håkon Magnusson 1000 nobles which he owed him as a 'just debt'; *ibid.* II, p. 356. This could represent a debt of five annual payments for which the earl of Orkney was held responsible on behalf of his other overlord, the king of Scotland (in 1313 the earl of Orkney had handed over to the royal commissioners in Kirkwall the annual payments for the preceding five years; *ibid.* II, no. 111). Thereafter Earl Henry owed the sum of 200 nobles to Håkon Jonsson in 1379 (*ibid.* I, no. 458), which was still owing in 1380 (*ibid.* I, no. 465) and in 1384 (*ibid.* III, no. 455); and he owed the sum of £140 Scots in 1389 (*ibid.* II, no. 515). These sums may represent a continuation of the annual debt to the man who had had authority in Orkney and who was perhaps still the royal official in Shetland.

7 The treaty is in *DN* VIII, no. 276. For the activity of the herald of the king of Norway see *ibid.* XX (i), nos. 762 and 763, and for the quarrel with the count of Holstein see Hamre, *Norsk Historie*, p. 66.

The fact that both the treaty and the charter of James I granting authority to his ambassadors were twice transcribed by the bishop and chapter of Bergen in the months following,[8] shows how important they were considered to be in Norway. Furthermore, on 3 October 1426 Bishop Thomas of Orkney, who had been a commissioner of Erik in the treaty negotiations with a special mandate to make oaths on the king's behalf, agreed that he would receive for the king the sum which Scotland had pledged afresh to pay, and promised to further the king's best interests in this matter.[9] There was therefore full expectation from the Norwegian side that the 'annual' would be paid, although there is no evidence at all that James I ever actually paid up (just as he showed himself reluctant to pay any of the £40,000 ransom owed to England). Nor is there any evidence that arrears were paid to the Norwegians in 1426.

When, therefore, a succeeding king of Denmark–Norway was in as difficult a financial situation in the 1450s and 1460s the insoluble problem of the annual payment once more became a central issue, and was responsible for bringing Scotland and Denmark–Norway together in a diplomatic relationship. It featured in the complex bargaining that went on through the 1450s and 1460s between France, Scotland and Denmark, and was finally remitted by Christian I in the marriage alliance of 1468 between his daughter Margaret and James III. Two factors help to explain why in these negotiations Christian came off worst, by having to pledge the islands of Orkney and Shetland to Scotland for part-payment of Margaret's dowry. The first was his real need of money, or else for a prestigious marriage alliance and treaty which would mask the ignominy of having to admit that he was no longer the recipient of the 'annual' and that he could not force the Scottish kings to continue paying it. Second and most obvious were the ambitions of James II and James III who actually utilized their apparently disadvantageous situation as defaulters to further their desire for territorial aggrandizement, and to get possession of the islands of Orkney and Shetland. In the end therefore the settlement of the intractable problem of the 'annual' resulted in the first Scandinavian queen for Scotland, a development which ensured very close political contacts between Scotland and Denmark for the rest of the century. It also resulted in the *de facto* permanent possession of Orkney and Shetland by Scotland, a situation which was going to be an important factor in Denmark's foreign policy during the next century and one which ensured further contacts between Scotland and Denmark, although ultimately not of the friendliest kind.[10]

8 *DN* VIII nos. 277 and 278.   9 *ibid.* II, no. 689.

10 For a detailed discussion of the events of 1468 see Barbara E. Crawford, 'The

The most notable result of this new relationship in the diplomatic sphere was the part played by the Scottish kings as intermediaries for the Danish kings in their negotiations with France. This happened first in 1472 when a treaty of friendship was arranged between Christian and Louis XI of France, including a marriage alliance for Prince Hans with Louis's daughter, Jeanne.[11] It would appear to have been mostly the work of James III, for he acted as host to the two embassies and, throughout the document containing the treaty, his mediating position is referred to (just as in 1460 it was the French king who had acted as intermediary between James II and Christian).[12] The Scottish king even appears to have provided the Danish ambassadors, who were William Tulloch, bishop of Orkney and a close adviser of James,[13] and John Hawden. Although it may have satisfied Stewart ambitions to play such a role in diplomatic relationships, the initiative for this treaty of 1472 came from Denmark. The whole purpose of the treaty and the marriage alliance was to ensure support for Christian in his struggle with the rebellious elements in his dominions. The clauses are all concerned with the provision of support, both physical and monetary, in the event of either king being faced with rebellion, and with the apprehending of any rebels who might seek refuge in the other country, or the punishment of subjects who might support such rebels.[14]

This treaty appears to have been totally non-productive, however, in terms of either the proposed marriage or French support for Christian. Twenty-seven years later the situation was repeated when the successors of all three kings involved in 1472 again drew up a treaty of friendship between France and Denmark. This was concluded on 30 April 1499, two years after Louis XII had come to the throne. It was again drawn up in Edinburgh, and this time James IV acted as procurator himself for his uncle, King Hans of Denmark and Norway.[15]

Pawning of Orkney and Shetland', *SHR* xlviii (1969), and K. Hørby, 'Christian I and the Pawning of Orkney', *ibid.*

11 *Diplomatarium Christierni Primi* (Copenhagen, 1856), no. 183; Huitfeldt, *Christiern den Første*, p. 227. This marriage never took place; Hans married Kristina, daughter of Ernest of Saxony, on 6 September 1478.

12 Crawford, 'The Pawning of Orkney and Shetland', p. 39.

13 Bishop Tulloch had been a trusted councillor of King Christian in the difficult years before the pledging of the islands. He was then used by the Scottish king as one of his ambassadors in the 1468 negotiations; Crawford, 'The Pawning of Orkney and Shetland', pp. 43 and 49. He appears from the evidence at present under discussion to have continued serving both masters, and in the same year, 1472, he was granted the tack of the lordships of Orkney and Shetland, giving him the complete authority in the islands which so many of his predecessors had striven so hard to get.

14 *Diplomatarium Christierni Primi*, pp. 269–71.

15 *RSS* i, no. 391; *Repertorium Diplomaticum Regni Danici Mediaevalis*, edited by K. Erslev, W. Christensen and A. Hude (Copenhagen, 1932), series 2, v, no. 8799. In Edinburgh Louis was represented by Vedastus Affleck or Auchinleck, his councillor

This tripartite alliance in fact remained effective for some time as each party stood to benefit from it, particularly in the period 1511–13, when France and Scotland wanted help from Hans in the planned anti-papal council of Pisa, as well as in the imminent war with England. The whole edifice collapsed however with the death of Hans and the battle of Flodden in 1513.

3

The reign of King Hans[16] was a very important one in the history of Scottish-Scandinavian relations, for he particularly encouraged close contacts with his 'amantissime nepos', James IV. The two were in correspondence even before the death of James III, notably on the occasion of the death of Queen Margaret, when Prince James informed his uncle that this had been brought about by the agency of James Ramsay who had poisoned her.[17] After James IV succeeded to the throne they corresponded and exchanged gifts, hawks and masts from Hans, clothes and precious stuffs from James.[18] The prime reason was as usual the Danish-Norwegian king's urgent need of finding a fruitful source of help in his struggles with the Swedes and the Hanseatic towns. The terms of a military and political alliance were evidently under discussion from the beginning of James's reign, for in 1489 ambassadors were to be sent to Denmark to renew treaties.[19] However, they did not go until 1492 when James Ogilvie of Airlie and John Liston, provost of St Andrews, concluded a treaty of defensive and offensive alliance with Hans in Copenhagen on 21 June. Military assistance was its *raison d'être* although a clause allowed for freedom of trading between the two countries, and five years later protection for Danish merchants in Scotland was assured by letters of conduct.[20]

and 'magister hospitii', evidently a Scot in the French king's service. There are many references in the Scottish records to diplomatic exchanges just before this treaty was drawn up. In 1506 James again acted for his uncle when he negotiated for a French marriage for King Hans's son and heir, Christian; Arild Huitfeldt, *Kong Hansis Krønicke* (Copenhagen, 1599), p. 245; *The Letters of James the Fourth, 1505–1513* (SHS, 1953), p. 29.

16 King of Denmark, 1481–1513; king of Norway, 1483–1513; king of Sweden, 1497–1502.

17 *Forty-sixth Annual Report of the Deputy Keeper of the Public Records* (London, 1886), p. 52; Thelma Jexlev, 'Scottish History in the Light of Records in the Danish National Archives', *SHR* XLVIII (1969), p. 102; A. Taranger, *Norges Historie* (Kristiania, 1917), pt 3 (II), p. 146.

18 F. Scheel, 'Orknøerne og Hjaltland i pantsaettelsestiden, 1468–1667', *Historisk Tidsskrift* (norsk) V (1912), p. 386; *TA* I, p. 179; II, p. 147.

19 *APS* II, p. 214.

20 The treaty is in Erslev *et al.*, *Repertorium* 2, IV, no. 7160; Ogilvy's and Liston's expenses appear in *TA* I, p. 200. Christensen, 'Scoto-Danish Relations', p. 93, stresses the lack of trading arrangements in this alliance, as compared with those made at this

As a result of the alliance of 1492 military aid was sent to Denmark, and the beginnings of a long history of Scottish mercenary activity in Scandinavia can be seen. Scottish mercenaries are first heard of in Denmark in 1497 although on what sort of basis is not entirely clear.[21] Five years later however there was an official expedition, very evidently in response to an appeal by Hans according to the terms of the 1492 arrangement, and it is with this expedition that the present survey of the political relationship between Scotland and Scandinavia will close.

Hans was not acknowledged as king in Sweden until 1497 and soon afterwards was faced with the same sort of disruption from the Swedes as his father had suffered. In 1501 Sten Sture once more stirred up disaffection against Danish officials there at a time when there had been similar risings against Danish officials in Norway. A member of the Norwegian aristocracy, Knut Alvsson, joined forces with the Swedes and there were local risings in Norway during the winter of 1501–2 when the royal castles of Akershus, Tunsberghus, Bergenhus and Båhus were seized from their Danish military commanders.[22] In April and May 1502 the Scottish records show that there was preparatory activity for an expedition to aid Hans. Firstly a levy was called out in Fife, Forfar and Perth, and the earls of Atholl and Crawford and the earl marschal, as well as the 'lordis in tha boundis', were summoned for the expedition.[23] It appears however that many of those summoned in this levy did not in the end go to Denmark, as a result of which compensation was claimed for the expense to which they had been put. The final total of foot soldiers was probably in the region of 2,000, and a later source mentions the raising of a tax of £12,000 Scots to equip this force.[24] In May there is evidence that two ships, the *Eagle* and the *Towaich*, were being prepared at Leith (while

time with England. But the purpose of the 1492 alliance was essentially military. There had not been the stormy relationship in the commercial sphere with Scotland that there had been with England; see E. M. Carus-Wilson, 'The Iceland Trade' in *Studies in English Trade in the Fifteenth Century*, edited by Eileen E. Power and M. M. Postan (London, 1933). For the 1497 protection see *Forty-sixth Annual Report*, p. 52.

21 Christensen, 'Scoto-Danish Relations', p. 92.

22 Taranger, *Norges Historie*, p. 221.

23 *TA* II, pp. 144–5. In June the squire of Cleish was also required to 'red him furth of Strivelin to pas in Denmark'; *TA* II, p. 150. The expedition was led by Lord Hamilton who received the earldom of Arran soon after (*Scots Peerage* IV, p. 355), although it does not appear that this was a direct result of his leadership of the Scottish force as Christensen suggests; 'Scoto-Danish Relations', p. 92.

24 For the claim of compensation see *Acts of Council (Public Affairs)*, p. lix. Huitfeldt, *Kong Hansis Krønicke*, p. 194, gives the number of troops as 2,000, whereas Bishop Lesley talks of 10,000; John Lesley, *The History of Scotland from the Death of King James I in the Year 1436 to the Year 1561* (Bannatyne Club, 1830), p. 72. The taxation sum of £12,000 was extracted by Sir John Skene from old registers *c.* 1600; *Laerde Brev fraa og til P. A. Munch*, edited by G. Indrebø and O. Kolsrud (Oslo, 1924) I, p. 35.

the *Trinity* is said to have returned from Denmark). Only the latter two sailed to Denmark as a few months later Lord Seton, who owned the *Eagle*, had some claims against him for money that had not been spent. The two ships were well equipped with guns and powder, spices and provisions, as well as trumpeters.[25] King Hans sent the Scottish force, along with Danes and Germans under the command of his son, Prince Christian, to Norway where they besieged Båhus followed by the Swedish fortress of Elvsborg, which capitulated on 17 July.[26] But this appears to have been the extent of the achievements of the Scottish expedition, despite the fact that claims have been made for its great success.[27] In a later letter James clearly expressed his dissatisfaction with the results.[28] In fact we learn from a contemporary report by Knut Alvsson that a good number of Scots who had joined one of the Danish commanders, Henry Krummedige, in attacking Akershus, near Oslo, at this time, were killed. Moreover, the rest fled by sea, and one lot are said to have deserted and gone back to Scotland. This ignominious conclusion to the 1502 Scottish expeditionary force was well known in Denmark.[29] Certainly one if not both Scottish ships was back in Edinburgh in August,[30] and the Danes succeeded in recovering control of the royal fortresses in Norway of their own accord, while Knut Alvsson was murdered on board Henry

25 *TA* II, pp. lxxxvi, 146–7, 157 and 340; *ER* XII, p. 92; Huitfeldt, *Kong Hansis Krønicke*, p. 194.

26 *ibid.*, pp. 195–6; *DN* VIII, no. 461.

27 Lesley, *History*, pp. 72–3; A. J. G. Mackay, 'Notes on the Relations between Scotland and Denmark, 1488–1513' in William Dunbar's *Poems* (STS, 1893) III, p. 391 (appendix), where it is said that the Scots assisted in releasing Queen Kristina from imprisonment in Stockholm. If the evidence for this is a letter written by James to Kristina in 1506 then it has been misinterpreted (see note 28 below). There is no evidence that the Scots were ever in eastern Sweden.

28   Written in July 1506 in reply to Kristina's letter of March 1506: *James IV Letters*, no. 37. He notes that the fleet which he sent to Copenhagen 'achieved less than it should have done and returned sooner than was expected. The ill-success would not have been tolerated had the news not been that she [Kristina] was safe.' But this in no way proves that the Scots had been involved in the siege of Stockholm where Kristina was holding out with a garrison. The castle capitulated to the rebels in May 1502 and the queen was put in a convent in Sweden; presumably it was this news which the Scots took back with them in the summer of 1502. The editor of James IV's letters assumed that these comments indicate that help had been sent to Denmark at a date nearer the exchange of letters between James and the queen, that is, in 1505; *ibid.*, p. xl. But the siege to which Kristina refers must have been the six-month siege of Stockholm in 1501–2, as there was no other siege in which she was involved.

29 Knut Alvsson's report is in *DN* VIII, no. 461; see also Taranger, *Norges Historie*, p. 227. A letter written in August 1502 by Henry Krummedige's mother-in-law tells of the desertion of the Scots; *DN* XVIII, no. 192. Prince Christian was forced to return to Denmark because of disputes among the mercenary soldiers; O. J. Benedictow, 'Drapet på Knut Alvsson og dommene over ham', *Historisk Tidskrift* (norsk) XLVIII (1969), p. 183.

30 *TA* II, p. 157.

Krummedige's ship in August. But Hans's problems were not at an end, and he continued to make many more requests for help from James.[31]

Despite the fact that Hans and James remained on good terms throughout their reigns, the problem of Orkney and Shetland can be seen lurking in the background, a problem that was going to be the cause of strained relations between Denmark and Scotland during the latter part of the sixteenth century. It was a result of Denmark's attempts to redeem the islands and the Scottish kings' refusal to let them go. Hans promised in his coronation oath, as all his successors were to do, that he would redeem the islands.[32] However, political necessity meant that he could not make an issue of it. His position was insecure enough without jeopardizing the friendship of the Scottish king. Nevertheless, he had the wishes of the Norwegian *riksråd* to consider and his cultivation of Sir David Sinclair (which is discussed later) may have been an attempt to promote the interests of the Dano-Norwegian crown in the islands. He acted as though he still possessed rights there, particularly in the sphere of church patronage and income, an aspect which had not been mentioned in the 1468 treaty. In 1491 he granted to Sir David Sinclair 'the crown's rents and rights over all the church servants in Orkney', which Bishop William Tulloch had had for life from King Christian.[33] This was interference which was unacceptable to a Stewart king and, a few years later (*c.* 1504), James IV made an identical grant to Sir David Sinclair of the skatts, rents and duties of the kirklands of Orkney which had been uplifted by William Tulloch during his lifetime. This grant asserts that these dues 'now pertenis to us be resson of the renunciation and ourgeving of our said grantschir of his richt and clame of the lordschip of Orkney to umquhile oure derrest fader'.[34] Further evidence of the hard line taken by James IV over this issue can be seen from a presentation of the archdeaconry of Shetland to Henry Phantouch in January 1502. The office had previously been purchased 'of temerarite

---

31 *James IV Letters*, pp. xl–xliii.

32 T. Torfaeus, *Orcades seu Rerum Orcadensium Historiae* (Copenhagen, 1715), book iii, p. 190. This section of his work is a history of the attempts to redeem the islands. See also G. Goudie, 'The Dano-Norwegian Claims upon Orkney and Shetland' in *The Celtic and Scandinavian Antiquities of Shetland* (Edinburgh, 1904), p. 216; and Scheel, 'Orknøerne og Hjaltland', pp. 410–20.

33 *Orkney and Shetland Records*, edited by A. W. Johnston (Viking Society, 1907–13), p. 56.

34 *RSS* I, no. 1031. The theory that Christian renounced his right to redeem the islands on the birth of his grandson James IV was current in the sixteenth century: Goudie, *Antiquities of Shetland*, p. 215. This theory may have been derived from the rather misleading statement in the above document, which probably, however, refers to the 1468 pledging of the islands. James considered that it had given him all royal rights over the church in Orkney.

and presumption' from the king of Denmark by Magnus Herwood.[35] The sheriffs, Henry, Lord Sinclair and Sir David Sinclair, were to charge him and others 'to haf na intrometting with the said archidenry or to purches ony presentation of the king of Denmarkis thairupon, under the pane of treson considering the presentation thairof concernys to our soveran lordis heretage'. Apart from the question of church patronage there were other spheres in which Hans acted as though he still had jurisdiction in the islands; in 1490 he granted Amsterdam and other Dutch towns freedom to trade in his kingdom and in Shetland and Iceland.[36] It is well known that Shetland land transactions continued to be dealt with by royal officials in Bergen throughout the sixteenth century.[37] This is hardly surprising, as it was only there that the Shetlanders could get justice according to their own laws, and many Norwegians continued to hold land in Shetland. In conclusion, therefore, it can be said that the arrangement of 1468 brought about close relationships between the ruling houses of Scotland and Denmark-Norway, but it also established a situation which was bound to cause strain, given the determination of the Scottish kings not to see the islands redeemed; and the aspects which were going to prove sensitive are fully in evidence by the end of the fifteenth century.

4

Moving from the field of political relationships to that of commercial intercourse, the area of real contact between Scotland and Scandinavia is reached. The evidence is thin compared with the sixteenth century when a flourishing trading situation is seen to be in existence. However, it is clear that this must have been based on growth throughout the fifteeenth century and there is evidence that Denmark was already a centre of established trading. Here again there had been a directional change. Trade between Scotland and Norway had existed for many centuries, and the islands of Orkney and Shetland had provided a meeting ground for the traders of both nations. Relationships in the area had not been always harmonious, as can be seen from the memorandum after the treaty of 1312 when a subject of the king of Scots, Patrick Mowat, had had his goods spoiled in Orkney, and some merchants of St Andrews had been attacked in Norway itself.[38] It is

35 *RSS* I, no. 755; see J. B. Craven, *History of the Church in Orkney* (Kirkwall, 1901), p. 121; Sir Magnus Harvod (not 'Harrod' as in the printed version of the will) was left two nobles and 'The Buk of Gud Maneris' by Sir David Sinclair in his will; *The Bannatyne Miscellany* (Bannatyne Club, 1827–55) III, p. 109.

36 Scheel, 'Orknøerne og Hjaltland', p. 407.

37 *ibid.*, p. 408; Goudie, *Antiquities of Shetland*, pp. 89 and 107–8; Johnston, *Orkney and Shetland Records*, p. 70.

38 *DN* II, no. 114.

evident that Scots like John Reid moved on to Norway via the islands of Orkney and Shetland, and became sufficiently settled in that country to become burgesses of Bergen, as Reid did in 1488. However, the absolute control of the Hansa made it difficult for any other nation to establish itself in that city.[39] Furthermore, once Denmark and Norway had been united, licences for trading had to be obtained from Copenhagen, which therefore became more of a centre for commercial contact, particularly as the sea route to the Baltic through the Sound replaced the land route across Jutland in the first half of the fifteenth century. Copenhagen must have been well known to the Scottish merchant because of this position, for the Scots had traded in the Baltic for a long time.[40] Around the middle of the fifteenth century there is evidence that Copenhagen was a base for Scottish merchants and shipowners, some of whom were already resident there. In 1440 eight Scottish merchants and shippers issued a declaration from Copenhagen concerning an incident when they had been stopped in the Sound by the fleet of King Christopher and the Hanseatic towns.[41] They were sailing to Scotland with a cargo of corn and other goods, which had probably been obtained at the Baltic ports. Copenhagen was evidently the usual place for such mercantile arrangements, as the capital of the Danish king who played an important role in Hanseatic policy, because of his control of the Sound. A few years later there is evidence that Scots were also using the city as a trading centre. In 1461, William Sinclair, the last earl of Orkney, asked King Christian for protection for a kinsman, Philip de Carribyr, 'de regno Scocie oriundum', who was trying to get back the value of certain goods which he had left twelve years previously in the care of John Welton 'etiam Scocie' who was apparently settled in Copenhagen.[42] The latter had died there and information had reached Philip that the deceased's goods had been impounded by royal officials. His natural son, Hector de Carribyr, had been sent to obtain the value of the goods, but nothing had been heard from him since. These two pieces of evidence show that the Scots were certainly active in Copenhagen, and resident there on a permanent or temporary basis, before the close political links established in 1468. By the end of the century the resident Scottish population in Copenhagen was numerous enough to have

39 For Reid, see *Records of the Earldom of Orkney* (SHS, 1914), p. 333. In 1523 there were riots between the Hanseatic merchants in Bergen, and Scottish traders who were resident, and some of them office-holders, in the city; H. Marwick, *Merchant Lairds of Long Ago* (Kirkwall, 1939) II,p. 46.

40 T. A. Fischer, *The Scots in Eastern and Western Prussia* (Edinburgh, 1903), pp. 7–13; P. Dollinger, *The German Hansa* (London, 1970), p. 192.

41 *Urkunden Buch der Stadt Lübeck* (Lübeck, 1885) VII, no. DCCCXL. There is a photocopy of this document in NLS, charter 56.

42 *DN* II, no. 840.

founded and supported St Ninian's altar in Our Lady's Kirk, which was administered by seven Scots custodians.[43] The 1492 alliance in which reciprocal trading is mentioned, and the safe conducts issued by James IV for Danish merchants in Scotland in 1497, merely indicate that the amount of commercial exchange was large enough to require general royal protection. From this same year come the oldest preserved accounts of Sound dues (that is, the tolls paid by ships passing through the Øresund), and they show eleven ships from Scotland passing through, ten of them returning the same year.[44] The development of trade with Denmark meant that Scots also settled in the Sound towns, and were there by the end of the fifteenth century, as well as at Ålborg in Jutland. The size of the Scottish community in Elsinore again led to the founding of an altar to St Ninian in the church of St Olaf there.[45]

5

Although the mass of material concerning Scots in Scandinavia and the Baltic comes from the sixteenth century and later, there is thus evidence that plenty of contacts existed in the fifteenth century; and while there are many biographies of Scots who established themselves in Denmark and Sweden in the sixteenth century, we have from the late fifteenth century the fascinating career of Sir David Sinclair of Swinburgh, which shows a Scot equally at home on either side of the North Sea in the service of both the king of Scotland and the king of Denmark-Norway. As a son of the last Norwegian earl of Orkney,[46] he was well placed to make his career in both countries, and was the only son to establish himself in Orkney, and particularly Shetland, where his main seat was Swinburgh (Sumburgh) from at least 1491. In 1498 he persuaded his brothers and sisters to resign to him their lands in Swinburgh and throughout Shetland which they had inherited from their father the last earl.[47] He made many more purchases of land

43 G. Hay, 'A Scottish Altarpiece in Copenhagen', *Innes Review* VII (1956), p. 5.

44 Jexlev, 'Records in the Danish National Archives', p. 103, citing *Tabeller over Skibsfart og Varetransport gennem Øresund 1497–1660*, edited by Nina E. Bang and Knud Korst (Copenhagen, 1906–33).

45 This was said in 1511 and 1513 to have been founded by the parents of Alexander Lyall and Ellen Davidson, who would appear to have been settled in Elsinore some time previously; Hay, 'A Scottish Altarpiece', p. 5.

46 He was apparently illegitimate (*Scots Peerage* II, pp. 335–6) and *not* therefore the son of Marjory Sutherland, second wife of Earl William, as stated in *Bannatyne Miscellany* III, p. 105.

47 Johnston, *Orkney and Shetland Records*, p. 58; A. Peterkin, *Notes on Orkney and Zetland* (Edinburgh, 1822), appendix 1.

in Orkney and Shetland, of which there is a nearly contemporary inventory, as well as some extant documents.[48]

David Sinclair is first in evidence in Orkney and Shetland during the 1480s, and he benefited from the family revival when in 1484 his nephew, Henry Sinclair, became the farmer of the bishop of Orkney who held the tack of the lordships of Orkney and Shetland. He is mentioned in the Orkney and Shetland accounts in 1486 in connection with some financial transaction with Henry Sinclair's factor.[49] By 1488 he was the 'foud' of Shetland. It seems most probable that this was a Scottish appointment, for the Scottish administration used the title of *foud, fowde* or *fold* for the royal administrator in Shetland, which derived from the Danish word for a local official, *foged*. The previous foud of Shetland under Scottish rule had been Thomas Inglis, factor of the bishops of Orkney from 1478 to 1482.[50] David Sinclair's rise to authority in Shetland would similarly appear to have been a result of his connection with the man who had control of the administration of the lordship after 1484. Both he and Henry, Lord Sinclair were called 'sheriffs in that part' in a royal letter of 1502 which concerned Shetland.[51] This position of power in the former Norwegian dominion evidently brought David Sinclair into close contact with Norwegian interests. By January 1491 he was in Hans's service to the extent that he had been knighted by him and was called 'our beloved man and servant' in the grant of rights over the church in Orkney which was made to him.[52] In 1496–7 he was governor of Bergen Castle,[53] a very powerful position in the kingdom of Norway. He was also at this time called 'landz høfdinghie i Hjaetland', which could indicate that he had received a duplicate grant of authority in Shetland from Hans, as he received the two grants of rights over the church in Orkney from both

48 *Records of the Earldom of Orkney*, pp. 422–5; Johnston, *Orkney and Shetland Records*, pp. 58 and 60.

49 *ER* IX, pp. 233 and 384. The identity of this David Sinclair with Sir David is not conclusive, as there was apparently another David Sinclair in Orkney at this time; *Records of the Earldom of Orkney*, p. 333.

50 *ibid.*, pp. 193 and 332; *ER* VIII, p. 483; IX, pp. 102 and 183.

51 *RSS* I, no. 755. In 1498 Sir David witnessed an important transaction between Henry Lord Sinclair and Henry's mother, in which she handed many lands over to her son: charter in private hands. The two remained in close partnership, for Henry, Lord Sinclair was the main beneficiary of Sir David's will; *Bannatyne Miscellany* III, p. 107.

52 Johnston, *Orkney and Shetland Records*, p. 56. His knighthood would appear to have been Norwegian, because it was first used in Norwegian documents, and Sir David was high in Norwegian official circles before he became closely connected with the Scottish king.

53 *DN* III, no. 999; *Bergens Historiske Forenings Skrifter* 33 (1927), p. 174. I am grateful to Dr O. J. Benedictow of the University of Oslo for this last reference. Sir David Sinclair had been active in Bergen before this, as can be seen from a lawsuit of 1491 when he represented a Shetlander before the royal council there; Johnston, *Orkney and Shetland Records*, p. 58.

Hans and James. This development in Sir David's career would appear to have been a result of deliberate policy on the part of the Dano-Norwegian king. Hans's attitude towards the exercise of certain rights in the islands has already been mentioned. There was certainly agitation from the Norwegian side during these years for the redemption of the islands to be effected, and in 1485 the Scottish exchequer rolls record exemptions on the Shetland account because of spoliation and plundering in the area by the 'lords of Norway' and their agents.[54] It was perhaps in an effort to gratify Norwegian demands that Hans cultivated Sir David Sinclair and provocatively gave him rights in Orkney and Shetland. By giving him office in both Shetland and Bergen he could be seen to be strengthening former ties and laying the foundation for redemption of the islands.[55]

For how long Sir David was governor of Bergen castle is not entirely clear. His presence in Edinburgh in December 1498 indicates that he then no longer held the office, which in 1499 was in Otte Matsson's hands once again. But this period saw the start of the unrest in Sweden and Norway in which Sir David was certainly involved. It might be expected that as a royal servant he would be active in support of Hans's authority. It is indeed stated in Scottish works that Sir David and Sir Oliver Sinclair sailed with the Scottish fleet in 1502 to suppress the insurgents.[56] But from the Scandinavian side it appears that Sir David was closely involved in the movement *against* King Hans. In 1501 he and Otte Matsson, 'rytters in Norwegen', were so closely in touch with the Swedish rebels and Knut Alvsson that they were present at Vadstena on the day that a confederation was declared there against Hans, and joined with the rebels in sending a letter to Danzig, requesting the city to join the rebel stand. Sir David and Otte Matsson, who had also been captain of Bergen Castle, may however have had some reservations about joining the confederates openly, for they did not seal the letter as did all the others named in it.[57] Indeed soon

54 *ER* ix, p. 306. The title 'lords of Norway' is always used in sixteenth-century sources for those Norwegian families who continued to hold land in Shetland under Scottish rule. The importance of these families in the islands, and their relationship with the Scottish settlers, has not yet been fully studied.

55 This interpretation of the reason for Sir David's powerful position in Norway is suggested by Bjørn Utne, 'Hovedsmanns-institusjonen i det nordafjelske Norge 1500–1524', *Bergens Historiske Forenings Skrifter* 72/3 (1972/3), p. 32.

56 I have been unable to trace this assertion further than Mackay's 'Notes on the Relations between Scotland and Denmark', p. 391. Sir David's participation may however have been assumed from the evidence that in 1502 he was granted 200 marks by James IV 'tempore sui passagii in Denmark' (*ER* xii, p. 31), though there is nothing to show precisely what this grant was for, nor to prove that he had been to Denmark as a member of the Scottish force. He had a half brother, Sir Oliver Sinclair of Roslin, but there appears to be no record that he accompanied the 1502 expedition either.

57 *Hanserecesse*, 3R, IV (Leipzig, 1876–1913), no. 347; O. J. Benedictow, *Henrik*

afterwards Otte Matsson was counselling the people of Voss to stand firm in support of the king.[58] Sir David, however, appears to have transferred his allegiance more permanently to Knut Alvsson's party, for a few months later, in December 1501, 'her david skotte af Norge' was at Elvsborg with three or four manned ships waiting for Knut to come over from eastern Sweden and lead the rebel forces.[59] The Danish royal official Henry Krummedige sent Sir David some fresh provisions and other goods, no doubt in an attempt to win him back into the royal service, but they were returned untouched, which must have been an indication of the firmness of the Scot's resolve to support the anti-Danish movement. There seems little doubt that someone from Norway known as 'David Skotte', who moreover had the title of 'Her', can be identified with Sir David Sinclair, and if so then his support of Knut Alvsson and the aristocratic party in Norway seems assured. The fact that after this date there is no evidence to suggest that he was ever in Denmark or Norway again certainly indicates that he was no longer in the service of Hans. There was time of course for him to have returned to Scotland to join the expedition of July 1502, but there is absolutely no evidence to support the statements that he did.

However there is no doubt about the fact that Sir David did return to Scotland and from the year 1502 pursued a very successful career in the service of James IV. Already in 1497 he had received letters from the Scottish king which were sent to him in Norway. Five years later, as well as the two hundred marks already mentioned, an annual pension of fifty marks was granted to him 'pro servicio impendendo',[60] indicating that he had been taken into the royal service on a permanent basis. In 1504 he was granted the offices and lands of chamberlain of the earldom of Ross and of the barony of Ardmannach. He was also keeper of Redcastle and Dingwall Castle from then until his death in 1506 or 1507 by which date he had got the account very much in arrears.[61] He remained a royal official in Shetland and at this time took the precaution of getting the parallel grant from King James of the church rights in Orkney which he had been given by Hans in

Krummedike, p. 102. (This reference is from the MS text of a biography of the Danish royal official, soon to be published.) Taranger, *Norges Historie*, p. 221, says that Sir David Sinclair supported an earlier declaration, of March 1501. The evidence for this cannot be traced.

58 *DN* xxi, no. 688.

59 This evidence comes from a report written by Erik Eriksson Gyllenstierna to Svante Nilsson on 12 December 1501; C. G. Styffe, *Bidrag til Skandinaviens Historia* iv (1875), pp. 297–9. He adds that Sir David was continuing to wait for Herr Knut off the coast of Norway.

60 *TA* i, p. 332; *RMS* ii, no. 2665, and the payments appear thereafter in *TA*.

61 *ER* xii, *passim*. In his will the pension of Dingwall and Redcastle for 1506–7 was granted to his executors; *Bannatyne Miscellany* iii, p. 107.

1491. Gifts were exchanged between him and James,[62] and Sir David Sinclair died at the height of a very successful career in the service of the king of Scots after a dramatic rise in the service of the king of Denmark-Norway.

His will, a copy of which is still extant, gives a fascinating picture of the contacts which he had built up in the North Sea area, the centre of which were his huge estates in Shetland and Orkney, inherited and acquired. His successful career had rested on mastery of the North Sea and this is reflected in the value placed on his ships; there was his English ship, his ship called the *Carvel*, the little ship, and the goods 'which come hame to me wyth my schipe out of Norroway'. Perhaps the most interesting of his personal effects was the golden chain which Hans had given to him, a symbol of the part which he had played in the political plans of that monarch, and which he left to St George's altar in Roskilde Cathedral, a place which he presumably knew well.[63] His most personal possession, his signet, he left to the provost of Bergen; and his closest servant, his chaplain and secretary, had been Dr Hans Ek, a canon of Uppsala, who received 'twelfe ellis of yper blak and twa rois nobillis . . . my sadell . . . and ane schort blak cote of wellous'.[64] Nearer home, in Orkney, he left his red velvet coat to the high altar of St Magnus's Cathedral, and two parts of his black velvet coat to Tingwall Kirk, and the third part to the Cross Kirk in Dunrossness.

The career of this illegitimate scion of the Sinclair family proves the ability of the fifteenth-century Scot to make his living in a foreign country and in the service of a foreign monarch, a phenomenon of which the Monypenny family's career in France is the most famous example. Sir David's life shows however that opportunities across the North Sea were evidently as productive for the enterprising Scot as were those in France. Continuing the traditions of his ancestors, the earls of Orkney, he foreshadows the remarkable growth of Scottish contacts with Scandinavia, a development which shows that many an ambitious Scot found in the Nordic countries the opportunities to make a living, as well as a fortune, which were not always available at home.[65]

62 Sir David received an 'albenat' from James; *TA* II, p. 228; and he presented the king with 'twa Orkney Trollis' (ponies) in 1505; *ibid.* III, p. 159.

63 *Bannatyne Miscellany* III, pp. 107–9. There is no evidence that he left a sword to Hans in his will as is said by Mackay, 'Notes on the Relations between Scotland and Denmark', p. 391.

64 *Bannatyne Miscellany* III, p. 109. For an account of this man's career see *Svenskt Biographiskt Lexicon* XII. I am grateful to Mr R. G. Cant for bringing this to my notice. Presumably Dr Ek joined Sir David's service when the latter was in Scandinavia. He attests a copy of the will (*Bannatyne Miscellany* III, p. 110) in which he also appears to have been left half of the island of Samfray in Yell Sound; *ibid.* III, pp. 191–5. In 1512 Dr Ek called himself vicar of Scatsta in Shetland and chaplain to king James IV; *ibid.* III, p. 193.

65 I wish to thank Dr Kai Hørby of the University of Copenhagen and Professor Knut Helle of the University of Bergen for much patient help in the checking of sources and information not readily available in Scotland.

England and France
Norman A. T. Macdougall

At first sight, Scotland's diplomatic relations with England and France during the fifteenth century appear to provide a less fruitful source of study than those with Scandinavia, and little evidence of change or development. The familiar pattern of endless truces with England, frequently ignored by both sides on the borders and at sea, is paralleled by the constant renewal of the Franco-Scottish alliance on terms which occasionally seem advantageous to individual Scots, but rarely to Scotland as a nation. Thus the overall picture would appear to be one of considerable, but on the whole pointless, diplomatic activity, a dreary succession of safe conducts, meetings of conservators of truces, and truce-breaking without adequate or any redress – in fact an interminable cold war, enlivened occasionally in the south of Scotland by major English invasions such as that of 1482.

A closer look, however, reveals much more consistency than the diplomatic chaos of the official records would seem to suggest, and we may for convenience identify two principal periods of development. First, Scottish foreign policy was profoundly affected by the recovery of France in the Anglo-French struggle after 1429, and by the contemporary weakness of the English central government during the minority of Henry VI. In the circumstances it was inevitable that the Scots should exploit this weakness through alliance with France in an effort to recover lost territory on the borders, especially Roxburgh and Berwick. Secondly, when this aim had been achieved by 1461, and the Yorkists had emerged as the victors in the English civil wars, a change of policy in Scotland was urgently needed if she was to live at peace with her more powerful southern neighbour; and this was eventually provided by the Anglo-Scottish alliance of 1474, a major turning point in the diplomatic history of Scotland.

Half a century earlier, a lasting alliance of this kind seemed neither desirable nor possible, and Scottish commitment to the French remained strong both before and after James I's release from eighteen years' captivity in England in 1424. As early as 1419 a Scots force of 6,000 men led by John, earl of Buchan, and Archibald, earl of Douglas, had been sent to defend the valley of the Loire for Charles VII of

France[66] and, despite heavy defeats at Cravant in 1423 and Verneuil in 1424, the Scots were still committed to the French cause in 1428, when Charles VII's position seemed hopeless. The Franco-Scottish alliance was renewed, James I promising his eldest daughter Margaret to the dauphin Louis, to be married when both reached lawful age. At the same time, he offered the French king 6,000 Scots to fight in France, in return for which Charles would confer on him the county of Saintonge.[67] From a Scots viewpoint, such an agreement may be regarded as understandable but ill advised. James I, faced with the constant problem of raising cash since his return to Scotland in 1424, seems to have believed that Charles VII might assist him financially, though in fact Charles was himself heavily in debt and his very survival was in question. At length, as part of a further treaty in 1436, James's daughter Margaret married the dauphin;[68] but by that time, Charles VII had been saved not by the Scots, but by Joan of Arc.

Two events in 1435, however, seemed to make a Franco-Scottish alliance a more profitable proposition for Scotland. First, a conference at Arras led to a Franco-Burgundian alliance against England, and secondly, following within a few weeks, John, duke of Bedford, royal lieutenant in France and the mainstay of the English government there, died.[69] This double blow to England provided the Scots with a consistent policy for almost thirty years – the exploitation of English weakness at home and the maintenance of ties with France and Burgundy for political and commercial reasons. Thus, although Anglo-Scottish truces were an almost constant feature of the period, in practice they meant little, especially on the borders, where the sizable battles of Piperden in 1435 and Sark in 1448 were fought during periods of truce.[70] At sea, piracy disrupted commerce on both sides regardless of truces. The English official records contain frequent references to attacks by Scots pirates on Bristol shipping, especially in the Irish Channel; while Scots merchant ships engaged in the French or Spanish trade, whether using the east or west coast route, and even when protected by English safe conducts, always ran a considerable risk of seizure by English pirates.[71]

66 Gaston du Fresne de Beaucourt, *Histoire de Charles VII* (Paris, 1881–91) I, pp. 320–21.

67 Paris, Archives Nationales, Treaties J687.27; printed in *Bannatyne Miscellany* II, pp. 181–6.

68 L. A. Barbé, *Margaret of Scotland and the Dauphin Louis* (London, 1917), pp. 87–96.

69 Beaucourt, Charles VII I, pp. 509, 538 and 546–7.

70 E. W. M. Balfour–Melville, *James I, King of Scots* (London, 1936), p. 221; 'Ane schort memoriale of the Scottis corniklis for addicoune' in *Asloan Manuscript* I, pp. 227–8.

71 Power and Postan, *Studies in English Trade*, pp. 175, 179 and 242; for examples of English piracy, see Annie I. Dunlop, *The Life and Times of James Kennedy,*

Thus there appeared to be good reasons for Scotland's maintenance of a continental alliance and an attitude of hostility towards England during James II's reign, and this seems to have been a nationally popular policy. It suited the king, who wished to recover Roxburgh and Berwick; it suited the traditionally minded Scottish clergy, above all James Kennedy, bishop of St Andrews; and it was clearly popular in the 1440s with many of the southern nobility like the earls of Douglas and Angus, who were able to take advantage of breaches of the truce on the English side to retaliate with profitable looting in Northumberland.[72] Trade with the Hanseatic towns, with Burgundy and with France made Scottish merchants incline to the traditional alliance, while important ecclesiastics, such as the bishops of St Andrews and Galloway, and the king himself, often had a stake in continental commercial ventures.[73] Finally, the alliance brought French territorial rewards to individuals, expatriate Scots like Sir William Monypenny, lord of Concressault, and James II still hoped to obtain sasine of the French county of Saintonge as late as 1458.[74]

Politically, however, such a policy involved major drawbacks for Scotland. The French king was a fickle ally, interested only in using the Scots to relieve English pressure on himself and, as early as 1448, the Scots had become apprehensive that Charles VII was about to conclude an Anglo-French peace from which Scotland would be excluded.[75] Furthermore, in the 1450s the challenge to the Lancastrian dynasty in England by the ambitious duke of York and his sons, culminating in the outbreak of war in 1455, forced the Scottish king to take sides in a complex international diplomatic struggle. By 1459 Scotland's allies, Burgundy and France, backed different sides in the English civil war, the duke of Burgundy supporting the Yorkists, the king of France the ruling Lancastrian dynasty represented by Henry VI and Margaret of Anjou.

James II's response to the challenge was to embark on a complex series of diplomatic manouevres with all the principal parties involved. Thus he attempted to reconcile Burgundy and France, interceding with Charles VII, together with the king of Castile, for the French king's rebellious son Louis, who had fled for protection to Burgundy; and the kings of Scotland and Castile were able to join in 1458 in condemning the English for attacking their shipping in the Channel. In the following year, James II was prepared to send his son's

Bishop of St Andrews (Edinburgh, 1950), pp. 350–51; and also *Cal. Docs. Scot.* IV, no. 1287.

72 *Asloan Manuscript* I, p. 237.

73 *Cal. Docs Scot.* IV, no. 1287; Dunlop, *Bishop Kennedy*, p. 350.

74 *RMS* II, no. 647.

75 BN, MS. Lat. 10187, no. 10.

tutor, Archibald Whitelaw, to Ireland to attempt to conclude a treaty with the Yorkist claimant to the throne, Richard, duke of York. All these schemes conveniently obscured the Scottish king's real interest, namely schemes of territorial aggrandizement at England's expense on the borders and in the Isle of Man.[76] James's accidental death at the siege of Roxburgh on 3 August 1460 left his successors the task of evolving a coherent and politically advantageous foreign policy.

In effect, the Scottish government, dominated at first by the queen mother, Mary of Gueldres, and subsequently by James Kennedy, bishop of St Andrews,[77] inclined to the Franco-Lancastrian axis. It was never a happy arrangement. Kennedy was pro-French by conviction, and had in fact been lying ill at Bruges when he was exhorted by Charles VII of France to return to Scotland and use his influence on the Scottish council in support of Henry VI.[78] Mary of Gueldres, on the other hand, was the niece of the duke of Burgundy, and seems to have been very reluctant to commit herself to the English Lancastrian cause. In the long run, her attitude was much more realistic than that of Kennedy, for the Yorkists emerged as the victors in the English civil war as early as the spring of 1461. Thereafter Henry VI and Margaret of Anjou became mere refugees with many sympathizers but few supporters; in the event, neither Charles VII of France nor his successor, Louis XI, would give the Lancastrian couple any practical assistance. Their presence in Scotland therefore became a source of embarrassment to the royal council, and provoked an invasion of southern Scotland by the leading Yorkist magnate, Richard, earl of Warwick. The one material gain by the Scots was Berwick, ceded by Margaret of Anjou on 25 April 1461 in return for Scottish support against the Yorkists.[79]

Thereafter the Scottish royal council split into Yorkist and Lancastrian factions, with the queen mother dominating the former. She was quite prepared to grant substantial loans to Margaret of Anjou in order to be rid of her, and in April 1462 the Lancastrian queen sailed from Scotland to France to plead her husband's cause with Louis XI. As soon as she had departed, Mary of Gueldres entered into negotiations with the earl of Warwick with a view to achieving a long truce and

76 A full account of James's international diplomacy at this time is to be found in Dunlop, *Bishop Kennedy*, pp. 195–207; *ER* vi, pp. 204 and 349; *The Apostolic Camera and Scottish Benefices, 1418—88*, edited by Annie I. Cameron (Oxford, 1934), pp. 45–6, 48–9 and 273.

77 John Major, *A History of Greater Britain* (SHS, 1892), p. 387.

78 Jehan de Waurin, *Anchiennes Cronicques d'Engleterre*, edited by M. Dupont (Société de l'Histoire de France, 1858–63) iii, pp. 165–6; Cora L. Scofield, *Edward IV* (London, 1923) i, p. 114.

79 *ER* vii, pp. xxxvi–vii.

Anglo–Scottish marriage alliances.[80] This effort was frustrated by Bishop Kennedy, who remained persistently loyal to the house of Lancaster, although by the end of 1462, as Scofield points out, 'no–one who did not wilfully shut his eyes to the truth could fail to see both that the king of France had practically abandoned Henry and Margaret to their fate and that there was slight prospect of them receiving aid from any other source.' Yet Scottish adherence to the Lancastians persisted throughout 1463; a futile seizure of Alnwick, Bamburgh and Dunstanburgh, and an ineffective siege of Norham in the summer, led to Yorkist retaliation in the east Marches and the south-west.[81]

In the late autumn of 1463, Mary of Gueldres died, leaving Kennedy apparently free to pursue the policy of his choice. However, the Scottish Lancastrian effort had already been sabotaged by Louis XI of France, who concluded a truce with Edward IV in October 1463, thus effectively deserting his Scottish allies.[82] Kennedy was now forced to send envoys to England to attempt to negotiate a long truce – a total reversal of his former policy. Either because he was ill, or perhaps because he could not accept his failure with a good grace, Kennedy was not among the seven Scots commissioners who negotiated the truce of York, a fifteen years' truce ratified on 1 June 1464.[83]

However, an atmosphere of mutual suspicion prevailed, and the truce was violated almost immediately. About the time of the York negotiations, and certainly before 8 July 1464, the young duke of Albany and Thomas Spens, bishop of Aberdeen, were seized by an English barge while returning to Scotland from abroad, despite the fact that both held an English safe conduct.[84] Negotiations for their release went on for more than a year, and in fact Kennedy died in July 1465 before the matter had been settled. Before his death Kennedy, like Spens, had become Edward IV's pensioner,[85] perhaps as a belated effort to save something from the Lancastrian wreck. There was certainly an urgent need for the Scots to become better informed about Yorkist foreign policy, and in 1464 the rumour was already current that Louis XI might join forces with Edward IV to conquer Scotland – an unlikely scheme, but one which emphasized Scotland's vulnerability when deserted by her cynical ally. From 1465 until 1469, there-

---

80 *ibid.* III, pp. xl and 80; Scofield, *Edward IV*, I, p. 247.
81 *ibid.* I, pp. 274, 287 and 291; *ER* VII, pp. 289 and 495.
82 Scofield, *Edward IV* I, pp. 306–7.
83 *Foedera, Conventiones, Litterae et Cuiuscunque Generis Acta Publica*, edited by T. Rymer (Record Commission, 1816–19) XI, p. 525.
84 *ibid.* XI, p. 520.
85 *Cal. Docs Scot.* IV, no. 1360.

fore, the Scots were working towards a closer understanding with the Yorkists, negotiating for a lengthy extension of the truce.[86]

The emergence of James III as an adult sovereign after 1469, however, created an entirely new situation. Confidently aggressive in the manner of his father, the king proposed between 1471 and 1473 a number of continental ventures which were undoubtedly inspired by the worsening of relations between England and France in 1470–71. Louis XI made a bad tactical error when he actively supported Margaret of Anjou in her last effort to thrust her feeble husband back on to the English throne; and the final triumph of the Yorkists in April–May 1471 left the French king without any reliable ally and the imminent prospect of an Anglo–Burgundian invasion of France. At this point, therefore, the renewal of the alliance with Scotland, and the frustration of any Anglo–Scottish understanding, became even more important to the French.

In the autumn of 1471 Louis XI offered James III part of Brittany in exchange for the services of a Scottish army;[87] and in parliament on 20 February of the following year, the Scottish king alarmed the Estates by proposing to lead an army of six thousand abroad in person. The duke of Brittany treated this threat seriously, appealing successfully to Edward IV for aid against the Scots. In fact the Scottish expedition never took place, mainly because the clergy in parliament protested with some justification that the king should not leave his realm open to English attack, he had no issue to succeed him, and he should avoid levying taxation on the Estates.[88]

The Scottish king's ambitions were not, however, confined to Brittany. In May 1473 he opened negotiations with Charles of Burgundy in an effort to secure the duchy of Gueldres, in which he had an interest as the son of Mary of Gueldres; but this scheme came to nothing because Charles had already determined to add Gueldres to his own territories.[89] An equally ambitious project in 1473 was James III's demand that Louis XI should surrender Saintonge to the Scots. An embassy had gone out to France to negotiate the cession of Saintonge in 1465, but without success, and James III was simply renewing the optimistic efforts of his father and grandfather in this direction.[90] At the same time, he seems to have been prepared to settle with the French king for hard cash. On 12 May 1473, Christoforo di Bollati,

---

86 Rymer, *Foedera* XI, pp. 549 and 556–9. The rumour of 1464 is mentioned in Scofield, *Edward IV* I, pp. 349–50.

87 A. Dupuy, *Histoire de la Réunion de la Bretagne à la France* (Paris, 1880) I, p. 302.

88 *APS* II, p. 102; Scofield, *Edward IV* II, p. 31.

89 M. Napier, *Memoirs of John Napier of Merchiston* (Edinburgh, 1834), pp. 33 and 512–14.

90 BN, Legrand, MS. français 6972, ff. 234–9; *APS* II, p.104.

Milanese ambassador at the French court, reported to his master, the duke of Milan: 'The ambassadors of the king of Scotland have been here some time, with offers to wage active war on the king of England, if he chooses to land in this Kingdom, and they promise his Majesty [Louis XI] that they will adhere to their ancient league and confederation, but that they must have . . . a pension of some 60,000 crowns a year, so that they may be able to oppose the king of England in favour of his Majesty.'[91]

Thus the most urgent business facing the Scottish parliament of July 1473 was the king's determination to go abroad. Parliament advised strongly against this course, pointing out that James could not afford it, suggesting instead that if the king was 'uterly determyt to pas in vthir countreis', the most useful role he could perform would be to act as mediator between the duke of Burgundy and Louis XI of France. This would mean great saving of Christian blood, and might eventually result in a crusade against the Turk. The respect which James would thus gain throughout Christian Europe, according to his parliament, would enable him to press more effectively for the cession of Gueldres and Saintonge. The message was clear. As in 1472, parliament was opposed to the king's desire to squander money on dubious continental adventures, and yet wished to provide him with a formula whereby he could intervene abroad more safely and cheaply. James does not appear to have accepted this advice; yet he was forced to abandon his foreign schemes since the July parliament clearly suspected him of carrying on urgent negotiations with Louis XI without even consulting the privy council.[92] Foreign ventures could hardly be successful without the grant of a tax from the Estates, an unpopular and infrequent method of raising money in Scotland, to avoid which parliament had passed the act of annexation of August 1455.[93] Since James III had apparently imposed such a tax in 1472, it is hardly surprising that parliament should protest at his effort to repeat the device the following year.

The eighth clause of the acts of the same parliament, however, indicates the logical alternative to James's foreign adventures – peace and alliance with England, a policy which the king initially accepted with reluctance. He may have been influenced in favour of such a policy by Bishop Thomas Spens of Aberdeen, who sat on the Committee of the Articles until his death, was constantly employed on embassies to England, and was himself a pensioner of Edward IV.[94]

91 *Cal. State Papers (Milan)* I, pp. 174–5.

92 *APS* II, pp. 103 and 104.

93 *ibid.* II, p. 42.

94 That is, in 1469, 1471, 1474, 1475, 1478 and March and October 1479; *ibid.* II, pp. 93, 98, 106, 111, 117, 121 and 124. Spens died in 1480, probably in April: *Hectoris Boetii*

With the Yorkists once more securely in control of the English government, the advantages of an Anglo-Scottish alliance were rapidly becoming more apparent for the Scots; and there was the added fact that Edward IV, engrossed in schemes for a joint invasion of France with the Burgundians, was also anxious for a permanent Scottish settlement. Two outstanding grievances which had resulted in mutual suspicion were settled by 1474. It became clear to Edward IV that the Lancastrian earl of Oxford, whom the English king had expected to sail from France to Scotland, had not in fact done so, and was not receiving James III's active support.[95] More important, the Scots, after repeated protests and the sending of an embassy to England, received compensation of 500 marks from Edward IV for the looting of the *Salvator*, Bishop Kennedy's barge, at Bamburgh in March 1473.[96]

The way was finally clear for the firm alliance between Scotland and England which Louis XI had feared for three years but not really laboured convincingly enough to prevent. Yet the French king should have had ample warning of James III's intentions. Some time before the spring of 1474, James sent John Murray as his ambassador to Louis to tell him plainly that Edward IV of England was pressing him to break the Franco-Scottish alliance and instead negotiate a treaty with England, but that he was resisting the English king's offers; and also that he intended to visit the shrines of St Peter and St Paul in Rome, passing through France on his way.[97] Louis replied by sending Alexander Monypenny, son of William, first Lord Monypenny, lord of Concressault, to Scotland to persuade James to stay at home. As a sop he offered the Scottish king 10,000 crowns if he could launch an attack on Edward IV and so divert him from his intended invasion of France; and Louis also made Lord Monypenny seneschal of Saintonge.[98]

This was not enough. James III, whose embassy to Louis had probably been sent with the object of bringing pressure to bear on the French king in the hope that he would surrender Saintonge, was not now prepared to be used by Louis in an Anglo-French war. In view of his own parlous condition, threatened by both Burgundy and England, it is worth considering why Louis XI adopted a high-handed and unhelpful manner towards the Scottish king in 1474. The answer

Murthlacensium et Aberdonensium Episcoporum Vitae (New Spalding Club, 1894), p. 53. For embassies to England and the pension see *Rot. Scot.* II, pp. 432, 436, 439, 441, 443 and 444; *Cal. Docs Scot.* IV, nos. 1360 and 1383.

95 *Cal. State Papers (Milan)* I, p. 175; *Paston Letters*, edited by J. Gairdner (London, 1904) V, pp. 186 and 188.

96 *Cal. Docs Scot.* IV, nos. 1416 and 1424. For the probable date of the wreck see Lesley, *History*, p. 39.

97 BN, MS. Lat. 10187, ff. 59–62r.

98 BN, MS. français 6981, f. 217r; *Lettres de Louis XI, roi de France*, edited by J. Vaesen *and others* (Paris, 1883–1909) III, p. 157.

probably lies in Louis' belief that Scotland and England were in any case on the brink of war. In April 1474, the duke of Gloucester was expected to invade southeast Scotland.[99] Although nothing came of this, rumours of Anglo-Scottish conflict had reached the French court by 17 June, when the Milanese ambassador reported that 'this year the king of Scotland and the king of England are preparing to have war together, and it has already been declared and the first of July next appointed as the day of battle.'[100]

Some time in the late summer of 1474, however, Louis XI must have learned that his embassy to Scotland had failed, and that far from being on the brink of war, Edward IV and James III were about to conclude an alliance. In desperation, Louis made an eleventh-hour effort to interest the duke of Milan in a marriage alliance between one of his daughters and the prince of Scotland;[101] but the duke caustically replied that though he was willing to oblige the French king by opening negotiations, Louis knew well enough that his eldest daughter was already married, and that in any case he would not wish to marry any of his daughters 'so far off as Scotland would be'. In this he was only echoing his ambassador, who on 27 September described Scotland as 'in finibus orbis'.[102] Less than a month later, England and Scotland concluded the first firm alliance of the century.

Among other advantages, the English treaty of October 1474 brought James III the prospect of immediate financial gain. Edward IV's daughter, Cecilia, was to marry the Scottish king's eldest son, Prince James (born in 1473) when both reached marriageable age; but her dowry, fixed at 20,000 marks of English money, was to be paid in annual instalments from February 1475. Despite the fact that the marriage never took place, James III was to receive 8,000 marks from Edward IV, none of which was ever returned. More directly, the alliance was rapidly followed by substantial restitution on Edward IV's part for the capture of James III's own ship *Yellow Carvel* by the duke of Gloucester's *Mayflower*, and also for the seizure of one of Sir James Colquhoun's ships by an English vessel belonging to Lord Grey.[103]

The 1474 alliance may be regarded as the forerunner of the much more famous treaty of perpetual peace of 1502, and it marks a distinct advance on the earlier treaty of London of 1423. This was concerned

99 *TA* I, p. 49.

100 *Cal. State Papers (Milan)* I, p. 180.

101 Prince James (the future James IV) born March 1473.

102 *Cal. State Papers (Milan)* I, pp. 186–8.

103 The last instalment of Cecilia's dowry paid by Edward IV was delivered to the Scots before 4 March 1479: *Cal. Docs Scot.* IV, no. 1456; BM, Cotton MS. Vespasian C xvi, ff. 118–20.

primarily with ensuring that the Scots paid for James I's costs and expenses during his eighteen years' captivity in England; truces and a marriage alliance had to be negotiated quite separately,[104] and there was no real slackening of Scottish aid to France as a result. The treaty of 1474 involved far greater commitment to friendship with England, and sees an important shift of emphasis in Scottish foreign policy. In future Scottish economic ties with Burgundy and France would be maintained, and there would be occasional, and invariably disastrous, military support for the schemes of the latter until the 1550s. But the idea of a realistic alternative, the maintenance of peace and an alliance with her powerful southern neighbour – a political necessity for Scotland by the late fifteenth century – was established in 1474, and it remained a feature of James III's foreign policy from 1474 until his death in 1488. Thus in 1479, there were protracted negotiations for a marriage between James's sister Margaret and Anthony, Lord Rivers, Edward IV's brother-in-law. Even after the disastrous interlude of 1480–82, when James III only just survived a combination of internal political crisis and English invasion and seizure of Berwick, the same policy was adopted towards England in much less favourable circumstances. In 1484 James negotiated a three year truce with his old enemy, Richard of Gloucester, now Richard III, based on a marriage alliance between Anne de la Pole, Richard's niece, and the Scottish king's eldest son, James, duke of Rothesay. The marriage was to be solemnized within the period of the truce, and it was hoped that it would lead to a firm peace and alliance.

Nor did Richard III's death at Bosworth in August 1485 affect the tenacity with which James III pursued peace negotiations with his successor, Henry VII, throughout 1486 and 1487. Thus in July 1486, a three years' truce between Scotland and England was, if possible, to be converted into a firm alliance through the marriage of James's second son, the marquis of Ormonde, to Katharine, Edward IV's fourth surviving daughter. This scheme was a forerunner of the much more elaborate marriage proposals of November 1487, by which James III himself was to marry Elizabeth Woodville, Edward IV's widow, while his eldest son, James, duke of Rothesay, would wed an unspecified daughter of Edward IV, and the marquis of Ormonde, in terms of the truce of the previous year, remained contracted to Edward IV's daughter Katharine. The truce of 1486, however, was only extended by three months, to expire in September instead of July 1489, and a firm alliance was probably impossible so long as the English retained Berwick, captured together with Dunbar in August 1482. The Scots had recovered Dunbar by the spring of 1486, and

104 Rymer, *Foedera* x, pp. 302–8. The marriage alliance is in *Rot. Scot.* II, pp. 245–6.

James III clearly regarded the cession of Berwick as the necessary preliminary to a lasting alliance. Thus in May 1488, English and Scottish commissioners were to meet to discuss 'the appeasing of the said mater of Berwik', and in July, the two kings were to meet.[105] However, on 11 June 1488 James III was killed at Sauchieburn.

Not surprisingly, the new policy of peace and alliance with England did not produce immediately beneficial results in Scotland generally. In particular, border warfare continued largely unchecked until the creation of an effective border police force in the reign of James VI. It was probably also from the Borders that immediate opposition to the idea of permanent peace with England came. Thus 'Blind Hary', author of the epic poem *The Wallace*, which probably dates from this period and which is full of savage vituperation against the English, seems to have found his patrons among members of the southern nobility and their supporters.[106] It may also be that later animosity between James III and his brother Alexander, duke of Albany, greatest of the southern magnates, was the result of Albany's opposition to the treaty of 1474. As early as July 1475, the Milanese ambassador at the duke of Burgundy's court reported a rumour circulating there that Albany had poisoned James III, driven out his family, and made himself king in order to assist Louis XI against the English.[107]

After the death of James III in 1488, the victorious rebels, a combination mainly of southern nobility and ambitious clergy, were to declare that the king had been guilty of 'the inbringing of Inglissmen to the perpetuale subieccione of the realm'.[108] This piece of guilty self-justification and blatant hypocrisy illustrates that verbal attacks on the English remained good government propaganda in Scotland; and the policy of 1474, James III's policy of peace and alliance with England, was discarded in favour of a reversion to dubious foreign adventures by the young James IV. These were, however, shortlived. The Anglo-Scottish alliance of 1502 established the revival of James III's pro-English policy, vindicated his struggles in the 1470s and 1480s, and confirmed the vital change of emphasis in Scottish foreign relations introduced by the treaty of 1474.

105 *Cal. Docs Scot.* IV, no. 1455 (for proposed marriage of 1479); Rymer, *Foedera* XII, pp. 242–4 (for 1484); *Rot. Scot.* II, pp. 473–7 (for 1486); *Cal. Docs Scot.* IV, no. 1530 (for 1487). The proposal for a personal meeting between James III and Henry VII is in *Rot. Scot.* II, p. 481.

106 M. P. McDiarmid, 'The Date of the "Wallace"', *SHR* XXXIV (1955), pp. 26–31. Two authorities cited by 'Blind Hary', Sir William Wallace of Craigie and Sir James Liddale of Halkerston, were southern knights; and the latter was steward of the duke of Albany; *Actis and Deidis of Schir William Wallace*, edited by W. A. Craigie (STS, 1940), book xi, lines 1443–6; SRO, Yester Writs, GD 28/170.

107 *Cal. State Papers (Milan)* I, p. 198.

108 *APS* II, p. 210.

6

Church and society
Ian B. Cowan

By the fifteenth century the church in Scotland was a well organized institution with a clearly defined structure. In the course of the century, the anomaly of Scottish sees directly subject to the pope was ended by the erection of St Andrews as a metropolitan see with an archbishop in 1472, and twenty years later similar status was conferred upon Glasgow; but in practice this meant little change for the existing Scottish sees which after this date formally included Galloway and the Isles and also the recently acquired diocese of Orkney. Elsewhere stability is equally evident and although existing cathedral chapters continued to acquire new prebends, most chapters had come close to their final form by mid-century. At a parochial level, fluctuation was again slight with a few new parish churches emerging while some in the face of population and other changes appear to have decayed, a process which in itself reveals a healthy vitality. On the organizational side so much is clear and well attested.[1] What is less certain, however, is how the church affected men's lives. In theory the relationship should have been close as the concept of an integrated society was one of the basic principles of political theorists throughout the middle ages. The presupposition that there was no sharp division between the life of the laity on the one hand and the life of the church on the other was, however, questionable in practice. Lay participation in the church was minimal and restricted to the exercise of lay patronage, the election of parish clerks by local landowners and the appearance of the occasional clerk or lawyer engaged in his professional duties in synods and other ecclesiastical bodies. Nevertheless, the converse was not the case as the church everywhere impinged on the lives of the laity.[2]

1 L. J. MacFarlane, 'The Primacy of the Scottish Church, 172–1521', *Innes Review* xx (1969), pp. 111–29; J. A. F. Thomson, 'Innocent VIII and the Scottish Church', *Innes Review* xix (1968), pp. 23–31; I. B. Cowan, 'The Organisation of Scottish Secular Cathedral Chapters', *Recs Scot. Church Hist. Soc.* xiv (1962), pp. 19–47; and 'The Development of the Parochial System in Medieval Scotland', *SHR* xl (1961), pp. 43–55.

2 A. P. D'Entrèves, *Aquinas: Selected Political Writings* (Oxford, 1948), p. xxi; D. McKay, 'Parish Life in Scotland, 1500–1560' in *Essays on the Scottish Reformation,*

An evaluation of how the church affected men's lives is not an easy task, but in the light of available evidence some assessment is possible. Before examining the multifarious aspects of church activity, however, it is important to stress that the fundamental duty of the church lay in the exercise of its spiritual duties. In this respect the church fulfilled its role in a variety of ways. Services could be magnificent occasions and the Aberdeen breviary compiled under the supervision of William Elphinstone, bishop of Aberdeen (1483–1514) gives not only an indication of the complicated nature of certain services and the wide variety of saints who were honoured but also illustrates that music was an integral part of such services.[3] Nevertheless, only cathedrals, collegiate churches and large burgh churches had the resources for the most impressive celebrations, and services in ordinary parish churches and chapels were much more down to earth, and often left much to be desired in the way in which worship was conducted. Sixteenth-century ecclesiastical statutes reveal that priests could be languid and listless in their delivery and 'stumble in mid-course of reading' while parishioners for their part are accused 'of hearing mass irreverently and impiously'. Even violence was not unknown during services, and in the fifteenth century churches are frequently described as violated by the effusion of blood. The bishop of Brechin was attacked in his cathedral by his archdeacon when he was saying the hours in 1438, a treasurer of Moray and his kinsmen were attacked by rivals in the cemetery of Elgin Cathedral and on another occasion the treasurer of Ross struck and wounded a woman in a church in the diocese of Caithness.[4] Such incidents however may have made little impact upon popular devotion which is most strikingly illustrated in the popularity of pilgrimages.

In the course of the century Scottish pilgrims visited Compostella and the Holy Land, but the most popular was undoubtedly Rome. The papal jubilee of 1450 took a large number of Scots there, but others, including a certain Thomas Clerk who atoned in 1458 for the killing of his brother-in-law by having masses celebrated in the Scala Celi while in Rome, were drawn there throughout the century. Among the most popular of the Scottish shrines were those at Tain, Whithorn, St Andrews and Glasgow, whose cathedral was described in 1449 as 'the most stately among cathedrals in Scotland in which the bodies of

edited by D. McRoberts (Glasgow, 1962), p. 85; D. Shaw, *The General Assemblies of the Church of Scotland* (Edinburgh, 1964), pp. 21 and 95.

3 *Breviarium Aberdonense* (Bannatyne Club, 1854), Pars Estiva, pp. iii–xxvii; A. Oldham, 'Scottish Polyphonic Music', *Innes Review* xiii (1962), pp. 54–61; D. McRoberts, 'The Scottish Church and Nationalism', *Innes Review* xix (1968), pp. 8–9.

4 *Statutes of the Scottish Church*, edited by D. Patrick (SHS, 1907), pp. 139 and 146; Reg. Supp. 347, f. 96; 416, f.213v; 394, f.79v.

many saints especially St Kentigern repose', and to which a great multitude of people flowed on saints' days. Smaller pilgrimage centres were no less favoured and the chapel of the Holy Cross, venerated because of its cross which had been found on the sea shore, and the chapel of St Catherine the Maiden in Moorhall to which a multitude of people often resorted 'for sake of pilgrimage' were only two of a vast number of such offertory chapels.[5] If the relics exhibited at some of these shrines were less than authentic few of the more blatant frauds which were perpetrated both in England and Europe appear to have been attempted in Scotland. The bogus miracle of the herd boy who was cured of blindness, for example, associated with the Loretto chapel of Musselburgh, appears to be a seventeenth-century invention. The pardoner with his collection of false relics, so vividly portrayed by Sir David Lindsay in his sixteenth-century *Satire of the Three Estates*, is not entirely a literary fiction, as the conviction in Aberdeen burgh court on 27 May 1496 of John Red, pardoner, for molesting Friar John Arnot, master of the Trinitarian priory, attests; but this is the only known case of a pardoner in pre-Reformation Scotland. In general, it is significant that Protestant historians such as Knox are remarkably silent about any such activities which would almost certainly have been seized upon with relish.[6]

Spiritual services were not confined to the saying of the mass, however, and the sacraments which accompanied birth, marriage and death were all of extreme importance as was the hearing of confession and the granting of dispensations of all kinds. In these respects churchmen fulfilled their role in many different ways with the commitment of the clergy varying between bishop and parish priest and from individual to individual. Bishops were not only spiritual leaders within their diocese but also statesmen who might sit on the king's council or otherwise serve in the royal administration, and for this reason could not devote themselves entirely to diocesan business. Nevertheless, it is clear that, with the possible exception of confirmation which would have entailed extensive travelling throughout his diocese, even the busiest fifteenth-century bishop, such as James Kennedy, bishop of St Andrews (1440–65), managed, by judicious delegation of his functions and by acting personally when appropriate, to fulfil his expected episcopal duties within the framework of the standards of a society which clearly accepted the duality of episcopal

5 D. McRoberts, 'Scottish Pilgrims to the Holy Land', *Innes Review* xx (1969), pp. 80–106; McKay, 'Parish Life in Scotland', pp. 108–9; Annie I. Dunlop, *The Life and Times of James Kennedy, Bishop of St Andrews* (Edinburgh, 1950), pp. 410–14; Reg. Supp. 514, f. 151; 433, f. 43v; 413, ff. 293v and 299v; 410, f. 84.

6 D. McRoberts, 'Hermits in Medieval Scotland', *Innes Review* xvi (1965), pp. 209–12; *Aberdeen Friars*, edited by P. J. Anderson (Aberdeen, 1909), p. 56.

functions.[7] The same is true for the lesser clergy; it is undeniable that by modern standards there were abuses, allowing parsonages and even vicarages to be held by non-resident pluralists who in turn engaged underpaid curates to carry out parochial functions, while the vicars who otherwise performed this task increasingly had no share in the teinds; but these weaknesses may have been more than offset by close contact between layman and priest. No doubt this contact was at times imperfect, in more remote parishes, for example, and also in Gaelic-speaking areas such as Argyll in which a request was made in 1466 that no one should have a benefice in that diocese unless he spoke the idiom which the greater part of the people used. But normally the rural parish priest who farmed his glebe would be integrated both socially and economically with the populace which he served. Likewise in urban areas the clergy and in particular chaplains in burgh churches were in constant contact with the guilds and fraternities whose altars they served. Even the most modest landowners, moreover, maintained at least one chaplain to say mass in the lord's chapel and act as tutor to his children.[8] This bond may have weakened by the sixteenth century as increased rapacity by both vicar and curate, brought about by the inflationary spiral of the period, led to the incumbent's right to mortuaries and offerings being pushed to their utmost. But until secular attitudes among churchmen became more widespread towards the end of the fifteenth century, such trends were almost imperceptible and the church and its servants were admirably poised to serve the society in which they lived and worked.[9]

The impact of the church was dependent, however, upon its own vitality as an institution and as the fifteenth century has frequently been treated as a period of decline in the fortunes of the Scottish church, the continuing contributions of the church have often been overlooked. It is open to question whether the church in this period was faltering in its purpose. Monasticism was certainly out of favour, and several of the smaller houses such as Saddell which was suppressed in the early sixteenth century and Urquhart which was united to Pluscarden in 1454 because only the prior and two other monks were then living there, were in very obvious difficulties. At the larger

7 J. Dowden, *The Medieval Church in Scotland* (Glasgow, 1910), pp. 48–50 and 139–48; Dunlop, *Bishop Kennedy*, pp. 211–58; G. Donaldson, 'The Church Courts' in *An Introduction to Scottish Legal History* (Stair Society, 1958), p. 364.

8 I. B. Cowan, 'Vicarages and the Cure of Souls in Medieval Scotland', *Recs Scot. Church Hist. Soc.* xvi (1968), pp. 111–27; Reg. Supp. 592, f. 127; *The Hammermen of Edinburgh and their Altar in St Giles*, edited by J. Smith (Edinburgh, 1906), pp. xxxviii–xlvii; McKay, 'Parish Life in Scotland', p. 88.

9 I. B. Cowan, 'Some Aspects of the Appropriation of Parish Churches in Medieval Scotland', *Recs Scot. Church Hist. Soc.* xiii (1959), pp. 220–21; McKay, 'Parish Life in Scotland', pp. 85–115.

houses the number of religious had likewise fallen and, by the end of the century, lay commendators were gradually acquiring control over them as the crown exploited to the full the 1487 indult which entitled the sovereign to recommend nominees of his own choosing to the pope for provision to elective benefices worth more than 200 florins.[10] Nevertheless the situation was not wholly black. Extensive rebuilding took place at many monasteries such as Cambuskenneth, St Andrews and Jedburgh during this century. And if corporate life had been weakened by the allocation of individual portions and private quarters to monks and canons some of whom may have enjoyed a worldly life within the security of the cloisters, others equally remained faithful to their vocation; thus the plea of one canon of Holyrood to be allowed to return from serving an appropriated parish church because he could not live there as a good Catholic and religious could have been echoed by others. Many monasteries apparently had adequate libraries and the *scriptorium* at Culross was capable of producing a very fine psalter in the second half of the fifteenth century. Yet ideas had clearly changed. Men still demonstrated their interest in the religious ideal, and their continuous belief in the strength and efficacy of prayer for the dead. But only James I, probably following the example of Henry V, expressed this in the older fashion of establishing a monastic foundation, and it is significant that this was a house of the strict order of Carthusians.[11] For the rest, the meaningful form of expression is seen in the foundation and endowment of the collegiate church.

Over twenty such institutions, with colleges of clerks for saying votive masses for the dead, were founded in Scotland during the course of the fifteenth century. Two of these – Holy Trinity, Edinburgh, and Restalrig – were founded by the crown, but the majority owed their creation to the piety of nobles, lairds and bishops. The zeal of the founders which was strengthened by this outward demonstration of their worldly success was however, more considerable than their resources; even at Trinity College, founded in 1460 by Mary of

10 A. R. McEwan, *A History of the Church of Scotland* (London, 1913–18) I, pp. 358–99, presents a particularly gloomy picture of the church in this period; A. L. Brown, 'The Cistercian Abbey of Saddell, Kintyre', *Innes Review* xx (1969), pp. 130–37; *CPL* x, pp. 23–4; for the text of the indult see J. Herkless and R. K. Hannay, *The Archbishops of St Andrews* (Edinburgh, 1907–17) I, pp. 157–8; for a discussion of its effects see M. Mahoney, 'The Scottish Hierarchy, 1513–1565' in McRoberts, *Essays on the Scottish Reformation*, pp. 39–84.

11 RCAHMS, *Inventory of Stirling* (1963) I, pp. 120–29; *Inventory of Fife, Kinross and Clackmannan* (1933), pp. 230–37; *Inventory of Roxburghshire* (1956), pp. 194–209; G. Donaldson, *The Scottish Reformation* (Cambridge, 1960), pp. 2–8; *Protocol Book of James Young 1485–1515* (SRS, 1952), no. 859; A. Ross, 'Notes on the Religious Orders in Pre-Reformation Scotland' in McRoberts, *Essays on the Scottish Reformation*, pp. 215–17. For Henry's foundation at Twickenham see D. Knowles and R. N. Hadcock, *Medieval Religious Houses England and Wales* (London, 1971), p. 202; I. B. Cowan and D. E. Easson, *Medieval Religious Houses in Scotland* (London, 1976), p. 86–7.

Gueldres, the choir and transepts were all that existed when building operations came to an end in 1531. A similar fate befell the most ornate, and for that reason the most untypical of all Scottish collegiate churches, that of Roslin which, although founded in the mid-fifteenth century, possessed only its elaborately decorated choir one hundred years later. Most frequently, however, the college was erected in an existing parish church or chapel which was thereafter reconstructed, although here again, as at Crichton founded by William, Lord Crichton in 1449, where the nave was left unfinished, completion was seldom achieved. On the other hand, it is clear that the foundation of these colleges stimulated ecclesiastical architecture throughout the fifteenth century.[12] Rebuilding sometimes preceded collegiate status, moreover, and one of the most magnificent churches, St Giles, Edinburgh, which was virtually rebuilt in the first quarter of that century, did not achieve collegiate status until 1468 when the magistrates and community successfully revived an earlier proposal for the erection of their parish church. In their petition to the pope for confirmation of this act, stress is laid on the fact that the king and his nobles often reside in Edinburgh which is described as among the most populous, famous and splendid towns of the realm. In other Scottish towns the same factors were at work, and there are many churches which became collegiate in the sixteenth century and which exhibit the same close links between the parish church and the burgh community, for example, Holy Rude, Stirling which was rebuilt after fire in the early fifteenth century, the church of St Andrew, Peebles and St Mary, Haddington whose choir was reconstructed in mid-century.[13]

If collegiate churches reveal a continuing vitality in the church it is equally important to note that their growth in status and wealth added little to the parochial services available. Although prebends and altars continued to be added to the original foundation at St Giles, Edinburgh, all these were devoted to the saying of votive masses for the dead, the parochial work and the cure of souls being entrusted in spite of the magnificence of the church to a vicar pensioner. Moreover, as the foundation of such colleges meant an upsurge in the appropriation of parish churches, the revenues of which were diverted to the college from the parish which was thereafter invariably served by a vicar pensioner, the erection of a collegiate church could vitiate service over

12 Cowan and Easson, *Religious Houses*, pp. 213–28; RCAHMS, *Inventory of Edinburgh* (1951), pp. 25–34 and 36–40; *Inventory of Midlothian and West Lothian* (1929), pp. 44–7 and 98–106.

13 Reg. Supp. 620, f. 229; *Inventory of Edinburgh*, pp. 25–34; *Inventory of Stirling* I, pp. 139–40; *Inventory of Peebles* (1967) II, pp. 209–11; *Inventory of East Lothian* (1924), pp. 38–43.

quite a considerable area.[14] Doubts as to the advantages of the erection of such colleges arose from time to time and although Bothans, erected in 1421, claimed four local lords as its founders, one of these, Robert Boyd, had evidently zealously opposed the foundation and his son in 1440 was still trying to reverse the process on the grounds that the patrons had not fittingly endowed the college. Further examples such as Methven, erected into a collegiate church in 1433, where the provost paid thereafter only twelve merks to a vicar pensioner from the not inconsiderable parochial revenues which accrued to his provostship, lend force to the argument that parochial incumbents in these cures and in churches appropriated to monasteries and cathedrals in an earlier period, were suffering financial hardship as other clerics prospered. In this respect prebends of cathedrals and collegiate churches which did not entail the cure of souls, and were thus free from the restriction placed by canon law on the holding of only one benefice to which the cure of souls was attached, were particularly attractive to pluralists.[15]

Nevertheless in the burghs in particular a collegiate church in which the pride of the burgesses could be reflected, and in which their participation in its devotions could be further effected by the foundation of altars by the guilds and individuals, demonstrates to the full the integral part still played by the church in the life of a medieval burgh. This association was most evident in the religious processions and other celebrations occasioned by holy days which were frequently held in honour of the particular patron saint of a craft guild within a burgh. These were specially associated with the religious life of the citizens, but the secular side was also provided for by the holding of wappinschaws and sports. The major processions took place at Candlemas and Corpus Christi and both at Aberdeen where all the guilds of the town went in procession before the blessed sacrament and at Edinburgh where a band of musicians led the way, the spectacle must have been imposing. Religious objects or relics were frequently carried in such processions and at Edinburgh on 1 September each year, St Giles's day, a statue of the saint led by 'tabors and trumpets, banners and bagpipes' was borne through the burgh. How far such manifestations encouraged popular religious fervour is uncertain, but the efforts made later by the reformed church to ensure their suppression would indicate that the enthusiasm engendered was not

14 I. B. Cowan, 'The Early Ecclesiastical History of Edinburgh', *Innes Review* xxiii (1972), pp. 20–21; *Inventory of Edinburgh*, pp. 25–34; D. E. Easson, 'The Collegiate Churches of Scotland', *Recs Scot. Church Hist. Soc.* vi (1938), pp. 193–215; *ibid.* vii (1939), pp. 30–47.

15 Cowan and Easson, *Religious Houses*, pp. 215–16 and 224; Reg. Supp. 366, f. 77; 368, f. 214v; *CPL* viii, pp. 460–61; Patrick, *Statutes*, p. 113; Donaldson, *Scottish Reformation*, p. 16.

inconsiderable.[16] Closely associated with these processions were the plays and pageants; little is known about them but they represented in dramatic form a variety of scriptural subjects which were at first acted in churches and afterwards in the streets on a movable stage. Taking themes such as the creation and the fall of man, these plays were enacted annually at Perth from the late fifteenth century to the Reformation, while in Edinburgh the play produced by the hammermen for over a decade after 1505 had King Herod as its subject. The canonical parts of scripture appear to have provided most of the themes which provided further contributions to the social and religious life of the burgh communities.[17]

In other burghs in which the churches did not acquire collegiate status the same traits are discernible. A proposal in 1430 that the parish church of Linlithgow which was being rebuilt after a fire in 1424, should be erected into a collegiate church with a provost and twelve prebendaries came to nothing, but this fine burgh church with a fifteenth-century nave and tower became the centre of an active ecclesiastical community. Likewise, the burgesses of Cupar in Fife shortly before 1429 had rebuilt the parish church, formerly outside the town, within their burgh in order to enhance its dignity. In all these cases it is possible that the zeal displayed was a demonstration of social aggrandizement as much as a truly devotional manifestation. Nevertheless, other evidence also points towards a continuing concern for religious ministrations. As at Cupar this was frequently exhibited by the building of new churches in more convenient centres or by the upgrading of a chapel to full parochial status. Thus the parish church of Abdie which is described in 1473 as sited in an almost uninhabited place was to be rebuilt in the neighbouring new town of Newburgh in which the parishioners commonly assembled. In Aberdeenshire the chapel of Glenbuchat was granted full parochial rights in 1470 and three years later, arrangements were made for the sustenance of a chaplain, later styled vicar, who was to serve the parish.[18] But in other cases, the apparent religious motivation is less certain. The

16 Anna J. Mill, *Medieval Plays in Scotland* (Edinburgh, 1927), pp. 247–53; *Extracts From the Council Register of the Burgh of Aberdeen* (Spalding Club, 1846–8) I, pp. 448–51; Smith, *Edinburgh Hammermen*, pp. 18–19; John Knox's *History of the Reformation in Scotland*, edited by W. C. Dickinson (Edinburgh, 1949) I, p. 127; W. McMillan, 'Festivals and Saints' Days in Scotland after the Reformation', *Recs Scot. Church Hist. Soc.* III (1927), pp. lxv–lxxi.

17 Anna J. Mill, 'The Perth Hammermen's Play', *SHR* XLIX (1970), pp. 146–53, supplements information contained in her general study *Medieval Plays in Scotland*; Smith, *Edinburgh Hammermen*, pp. lxv–lxxii.

18 *Calendar of Scottish Supplications to Rome, 1428–32*, edited by Annie I. Dunlop and I. B. Cowan (SHS 1970), pp. 27, 140 and 176; Reg. Supp. 691, f. 273; I. B. Cowan, *The Parishes of Medieval Scotland* (SRS, 1967), pp. 74–5.

collegiate church of Dalkeith which became parochial in 1467, ostensibly because the inhabitants of the town could not attend their parish church of Lasswade, may have been granted this status simply to add to the college's dignity or in the unrealized hope that certain teinds might be retained, rather then for the convenience of its new parishioners. Similarly, the inhabitants of the Bass Rock may not have been able to attend the parish church of North Berwick 'at certain times of the year, especially in high seas', but the erection in 1477 of the chapel in the castle of Robert Lauder, lord of the Bass into a parish church was not entirely altruistic; Lauder's real concern was not for the inhabitants' souls but for the teinds of the solan geese which he apparently obtained thereafter.[19]

A similar duality is found in the repair of parish churches, which was a joint responsibility shouldered by 'rectors', who were often the monastic house to which the church had been appropriated, and vicars with their parishioners. Neglect was frequent. The parish church of Dalry was said to be 'badly collapsed in its structures, roof and other buildings' in 1428 while the church of the Three Holy Brethren of Lochgoilhead lacked not only its roof, but ornaments, books and other trappings in 1441. In southern Scotland, parish churches suffered from the devastation of war and in 1476 the church of Wester Upsetlington was reported completely razed, a fate which had befallen the church of Ednam some twenty years earlier. In such circumstances repair was almost completely impossible, particularly in cures such as that of the rector of Dornock who could not lift his teinds in time of war. Most to be pitied, however, was the vicar of Berwick who in times of English occupation was paid £20 sterling but complained bitterly in 1466 that after the capture of the town by the Scots he was receiving his stipend at the value of money of that kingdom which was only one third part of its English equivalent. In these circumstances it is scarcely surprising that twenty-two churches were reported as ruinous in the deanery of the Merse in 1556.[20] However, that report is not entirely typical. The mensal churches of the bishop of Dunkeld were well looked after during the episcopate of Bishop George Brown (1483–1515), and the abbey of Arbroath employed a carpenter in 1474 to repair its appropriated churches, although only eleven years previously the abbey had been accused of neglecting to repair its churches in the diocese of Aberdeen. The evidence is inconclusive, but the extent of neglect of parish churches may well have been exaggerated, except in the case of

19 Reg. Supp. 635, f. 107v; 691, f. 273; Cowan, *Parishes*, pp. 15 and 48.

20 Patrick, *Statutes*, p. 168; Reg. Supp. 377, f. 43v; 473, f. 49; 476, f. 141; 596, f. 127v; 740, ff. 25v–26; *A Source Book of Scottish History*, edited by W. C. Dickinson, G. Donaldson and I. A. Milne (Edinburgh, 1958) II, pp. 151–2.

chapels which probably lacked adequate endowment in the first place.[21]

The need to make churches not only functional but also beautiful meant the encouragement of many of the usual arts including stone-carving, wood-carving and painting; the major inspiration for these was undoubtedly of French and Flemish origin. As previously noted the fifteenth century saw extensive ecclesiastical reconstruction. Stylistically, late medieval Scottish Gothic developed to its most elaborate form in the abbey of Melrose, the collegiate church of Roslin, in the heraldic motifs at the college of Lincluden and in certain carved work in Glasgow Cathedral. In the latter the Blacader aisle is a late fifteenth-century production, but even finer is the set of mid-century carvings on the front of the choir screen. These are probably the work of John Morrow, a French master mason born in Paris. Scottish masons undoubtedly worked under his direction, and he was certainly responsible for the completion of the transepts and five bays at the western end of the church of Melrose in which Morrow left a panel recording the various churches including those two, and the high kirk of St Andrews and the abbey of Paisley, all of which were under his surveyance.[22] In the case of wood-carving also, the earliest surviving examples are late fifteenth-century and all show indications of French or Flemish influence. Among the best examples of these are 'The Ochiltree Stalls' in Dunblane Cathedral, the remains of the stalls of Lincluden College and the rood screen with its magnificent oak door in the parish church of Foulis Easter. This church also contains four large pre-Reformation paintings on oak panels, surpassed only by the superb panels, attributed to the Flemish artist Hugo van der Goes, which were painted for the collegiate church of the Holy Trinity shortly after 1469.[23] Similar paintings must have been evident in other large Scottish churches and in this respect the patronage of the church must have played an important part in the creation of an artistic tradition in fifteenth-century Scotland. As in England where Flemish artists were prominent, so in Scotland most of the artists came from Flanders, but one of the most distinguished Flemish miniaturists, Alexander Bening, who first appears in Ghent in 1468–9, was almost

21 *Dunkeld Rentale*, pp. 91–2, 109, 148, 231, 259 and 266; *Liber S. Thome de Aberbrothoc* (Bannatyne Club, 1848–56) II, no. 192; *CPL* XI, pp. 643–4 and 665–8.

22 J. S. Richardson, *The Medieval Stone Carver in Scotland* (Edinburgh, 1964), pp. 35–47 and 51–2; *Eccles. Arch.* II, pp. 331–4, 361–82 and 386–94.

23 J. S. Richardson, 'Unrecorded Scottish Wood Carvings', *PSAS* LX (1925–6), pp. 384–408; J. H. Cockburn, 'The Ochiltree Stalls and other Medieval Carvings in Dunblane Cathedral', *The Society of Friends of Dunblane Cathedral* VIII (1961), pp. 102–8 and 142–5; *Eccles. Arch.* III, pp. 195–7; M. R. Apted and W. N. Robertson, 'Late Fifteenth-Century Church Paintings from Guthrie and Foulis Easter', *PSAS* XCV (1961–2), pp. 262–79; *Inventory of Edinburgh*, pp. 38–40.

certainly of Scottish origin. Much of Bening's work was associated with the illumination of manuscripts and in this respect also, Scotland was far from being an intellectual and artistic backwater in this period. The Yester Book of Hours written about 1480 has illuminations of the Image of Pity and the Mass of St Gregory, an illumination of the latter also appearing in the Arbuthnot Book of Hours which was compiled about the same period. Art of a different character was provided by ecclesiastical embroidery and it is clear that in fifteenth century Edinburgh 'broderers' both native and foreign were supplying the embroidered vestments and hangings which the church's ritual demanded. In these ways the church not only added dignity to its services, but also by its patronage encouraged the development of the visual arts.[24]

Of all the arts fostered by the church, music, forming an integral part of its devotions, was one of the most favoured and the flowering of the art of composition which followed the erection of the Chapel Royal at Stirling in 1501 clearly derived its main inspiration from the church music of an earlier era. Little of the repertoire has survived the Reformation but sufficient is still extant to demonstrate that a rich store of polyphonic music existed in Scotland before that event. Most of the surviving pieces are by sixteenth-century composers but their antecedents clearly lie in the previous century in which the foundation of collegiate churches and the song schools associated with them undoubtedly stimulated musical studies. Thus at Restalrig, founded by James III in 1487, particular emphasis was placed on a canon's skill in plain singing and descant and a sixpenny fine was to be levied on any canon who performed below standard in singing the antiphonies, responses, psalms and other parts of the choir service. At the cathedrals too music was encouraged and in the course of the century existing song schools were frequently expanded; at Dunkeld, for instance, Bishop Bruce endowed four additional vicars' choral in 1446, and Bishop Lauder instituted six choir boys (1452–75). These endowments apparently had the desired effect; in the early sixteenth century members of the choir could be described in one case as 'highly trained in the theory of music as well as the art of singing', in another as 'steady in the chant', and in yet another as 'sublime in musical theory and in organ playing'. This latter accomplishment was very important as the organ occupied a central part in church music, and masses and motets frequently incorporated a solo voice for the organ which in turn blended with the singers.[25] Nevertheless, it cannot be assumed from this example that

24 D. McRoberts, 'Notes on Scots-Flemish Artistic Contacts', *Innes Review* x (1959), pp. 91–6; 'The Fetternear Banner', *ibid.* vii (1956), pp. 74–5 and 85–6; and 'Scottish Medieval Chalice Veils', *ibid.* xv (1964), pp. 103–16.
25 Oldham, 'Scottish Polyphonic Music', pp. 54–61; *Charters of the Hospital of Soltre,*

all cathedrals were as fortunate; in 1454 the bishop of Moray complained that whereas six marks had previously sustained a vicar choral, a sum of ten marks was now required and, as many of the canons refused to pay the increase, for every two persons at one time singing in the choir only one was now to be found. Parsimony is evident elsewhere. At Glasgow in 1480 owing to a wastage among choristers who were leaving for more remunerative posts, the stipend of vicars choral was doubled.[26]

Much of the music was not Scottish in origin, the Low Countries in particular being a source of many compositions, and it was to this region that Scottish musicians such as John Fethy and Thomas Inglis, both of whom left Scotland in 1498, turned their attention in order to study music. Among other musicians of the period, William Roger deserves to be remembered not as one of the legendary favourites of James III, but as an accomplished performer who settled at the Scottish court and trained several sixteenth-century musicians. It is unfortunate that nothing survives of the compositions of native musicians such as Fethy, Inglis or John Broune, lutanist, who was sent to Bruges in 1473 'to lere his craft'.[27]

In its encouragement of music and the visual arts the church was fulfilling both the spiritual and temporal aspirations of contemporary society. This same duality is evident in the church's interest in education, where theoretical concern for knowledge in its own right is matched with the very practical need for an educated priesthood. Education was primarily the concern of the church. Universities were founded by bishops and, if by the fifteenth century the foundation and patronage of schools was no longer exclusively an ecclesiastical function, teachers almost without exception were churchmen. Schools fell into two categories, at an elementary level the song schools and reading schools which can be corporately termed little schools and at a more advanced level grammar or high schools. The principal concern of such institutions, attached to several of the cathedrals and other important churches including those with collegiate status, was to train choristers in music and at least the rudiments of Latin in order that the services of the choir could be fittingly maintained. Thus at Brechin

of Trinity College, Edinburgh, and other Collegiate Churches in Midlothian (Bannatyne Club, 1861), p. 287; A. Myln, *Vitae Dunkeldensis Ecclesiae Episcoporum* (Bannatyne Club, 1831), pp. 19–20 and 24; a translation of this work covering the years 1483–1516 is printed in *Dunkeld Rentale*, pp. 302–34; Reg. Supp. 423, f. 186; 473, ff. 207v–208; *Dunkeld Rentale*, pp. 329–30.

26 Reg. Supp. 473, ff. 207v–208; *Registrum Episcopatus Glasguensis* (Bannatyne Club, 1843) II, p. 443.

27 Oldham, 'Scottish Polyphonic Music', p. 56; *TA* I, p. 43; *History of the Chapel Royal of Scotland*, edited by C. Rogers (Grampian Club, 1882), pp. xiii–xix and xxvi–xxx.

where there was a college of choristers with a residence of their own, two chaplains were attached to the college in 1429, one to teach in the song school and the other in the grammar school. Other scholars may have joined the endowed choristers from time to time, but this was probably the exception rather than the rule. Similarly, at most of the smaller collegiate churches, all of which necessarily possessed song schools, the number of scholars would normally be restricted to the choristers. Education in such cases was strictly functional and the impact upon society other than in terms of the resultant music and singing must have been slight.[28]

At some centres, however, the education provided by such schools reached a wider circle of pupils and even though many of these students may in turn have been destined for an ecclesiastical career, others were not. The cathedral school founded at Elgin by the chapter of Moray in 1489 was a 'general school' for the burgh and was to provide instruction in music and reading for all who came to it, and in the parish of Aberdeen-St Nicholas Robert Hutchison, songster, in 1496 took charge of the song school specially designed for burgesses' sons. Such steps were not uncommon for by this period many of the schools which had originated as church schools had become the concern of the burgh. Thus at Peebles the baillies appointed Sir William Blaklok in 1464 'to haf the scule and to be sculemaster and tyll teche the chylder' and two years later when Master John Doby was appointed to the same school it was enacted that 'quha that put ony bairnis tyll him suld pay him a yeris payment'. At Aberdeen also it was the burgh council which in 1483 ordained that 'Richard Boyl sal haf and bruke the song scule of Aberdene as principale maister of the samyn, with help and supple of his old maister Sir Andro Thomson.' These teachers were churchmen, however, and the rapid turnover in schoolmasters underlines the point that these schoolmasters were generally poorly paid hirelings who but for the addition of a chaplaincy or some other living could not have subsisted. Thus the schoolmaster of the grammer school at Glasgow in 1494 was also chaplain of the leper hospital of St Ninian beyond Glasgow bridge. He lived at the hospital and so also did twenty-four poor scholars who attended the school. Provision for poor scholars was fairly common although how far such schemes were effected is more difficult to judge, but in theory at any rate no one was to be denied an opportunity of serving in the church because of poverty.[29]

28 J. Durkan, 'Education in the Century of the Reformation' in McRoberts, *Essays on the Scottish Reformation*, pp. 145–68, presents a more optimistic picture than D. E. Easson 'The Medieval Church in Scotland and Education', *Recs Scot. Church Hist. Soc.* VI (1936), pp. 13–26; *Registrum Episcopatus Brechinensis* (Bannatyne Club, 1856) II, p. 26.

29 *Moray Registrum* , pp. 262–3; *Cartularum Ecclesiae Sancti Nicholai Aberdonensis* (New

Such schooling was essentially urban. Little is known of rural education, and the only positive provision for it on record appears to be the endowment of a chaplaincy at Carmyllie in Angus in 1500 when in addition to the normal religious stipulations the chaplain was instructed to hold at the chapel 'a school for the instruction of the young'. It would be hazardous to argue from this single piece of evidence that a system of rural schools existed in fifteenth-century Scotland, and it seems much more likely that education in such areas was effected either by boarding pupils in burgh grammar schools, a practice for which there is ample evidence in the early sixteenth century, or by utilizing the services of the many private chaplains attached to even the smallest households.[30] The results of such an education might go no further than acquiring the ability to read and write, and if so might justify the opinion of John Major that the gentry educated their children neither in letters nor in morals – though this was a scholarly criticism of the standard of education of the nobility and gentry which was not confined to Scotland. It was partially to meet this lack of education and in more practical terms to provide the country with competent administrators of justice that an act of parliament in 1496 ordained that all barons and freeholders should send their eldest sons to grammar schools at eight or nine years of age, and to keep them there till they have 'perfyte latyne'. This act was largely abortive insofar as the penalties for non-compliance were concerned, but it may reflect a growing tendency to board pupils in burgh grammar schools. If in all this there was no concept of universal education, if the system fostered by the church, aided and abetted by the municipalities, was to subserve the church's ends, nevertheless a service was provided for some part of society and its natural extension was a higher form of education through the universities.[31]

No less than three Scottish universities – St Andrews in 1412, Glasgow in 1451 and Aberdeen in 1495 – were founded in the course of this century when the intellectual stimulation brought about by the revival of learning was reflected in the foundation of many European universities. The founders, Henry Wardlaw, William Turnbull and William Elphinstone, in each case situated the university in the city in which their cathedral lay and in whose schools the nascent universities had their origins. At each of these universities the nucleus was pro-

Spalding Club, 1888–92) II, pp. 335 and 339; *Extracts from the Records of the Burgh of Peebles* (SBRS, 1910), pp. 152 and 155; Durkan, 'Education in the Century of the Reformation', pp. 158–9, citing NLS, Advocates MS. 9A. 1.2, f. 1451.

30 *Registrum de Panmure*, edited by J. Stuart (Edinburgh, 1874) II, p. 266; Durkan 'Education in the Century of the Reformation', p. 158; John Major, *A History of Greater Britain* (SHS, 1892), p. 30.

31 Major, *History*, p. 48; *APS* II, p. 238.

vided by the faculty of arts; at St Andrews this was strengthened by the addition of the college of St Salvator, founded by Bishop Kennedy in 1450 and in which the arts predominated, while at Aberdeen, King's College erected by Bishop Elphinstone at the very end of the century became the focal institution within his university.[32] Within these faculties the teaching of logic and rhetoric was accorded pre-eminence although the standard of tuition even in these subjects was never high. Course requirements were not being fulfilled at St Andrews in 1478 and this was still the case fifteen years later. A similar decline in standards, reflected in a falling away of numbers, can also be observed at Glasgow during the same period. The provision of a grammarian for the teaching of Latin at Aberdeen was undoubtedly an attempt to raise standards, and was paralleled at St Andrews in 1495 when the faculty of arts raised its entrance requirements in grammar. Part of the difficulty stemmed from the limitation of the arts curriculum which resulted in the arts courses being viewed either as only a preliminary to further vocational study or as an extension of a general education which might be terminated long before graduation. This latter category included the sons of the nobility, lairds and burgesses who are found in attendance in small but increasing numbers during the course of the century. These few may not have quite measured up to the hopes of the 1496 education act, stating that the eldest sons of barons and freeholders having mastered Latin at their grammar school should be sent to study arts and law at the university, but it no doubt ensured a higher measure of efficiency in some local courts.[33]

In this way the church through its teaching (and all university teachers were churchmen) provided a service for the community at large, and in theory at least the other faculties within the universities strove to do the same. In practice, however, the return to society was less than it might have been. Medicine, if it was taught at all before the appointment of a mediciner at Aberdeen shortly after 1505, was not regarded as a serious vocational study, and although a doctor of medicine, Andrew Gorleth, was received as a member of both Glasgow and St Andrews universities in 1469, this was clearly in an honorary rather than in a professional capacity.[34] Exponents of civil

32 H. Rashdall, *The Universities of Europe in the Middle Ages*, edited by F. M. Powicke and A. B. Emden (Oxford, 1936); R. G. Cant, *The University of St Andrews* (Edinburgh, 1970); J. Durkan, 'William Turnbull, Bishop of Glasgow', *Innes Review* II, (1951), pp. 5–61; L. J. Macfarlane, 'William Elphinstone, Founder of the University of Aberdeen', *Aberdeen University Review* XXXIX (1961–2), pp. 1–18; R. G. Cant, *The College of St Salvator* (St Andrews, 1950).

33 *St Andrews Acta* I, pp. lxxi, cv–cvi and cliii; II, pp. 201–2 and 243–4; J. D. Mackie, *The University of Glasgow 1451–1951* (Glasgow, 1954), pp. 37, 41 and 53–5; R. S. Rait *The Universities of Aberdeen* (Aberdeen, 1895), pp. 34–5; *APS* II, p. 238.

34 *St Andrews Acta* I, p. clvii; Rait, *Universities of Aberdeen*, pp. 33–4; *Officers and Graduates of University and King's College, Aberdeen* (New Spalding Club, 1893), p. 35.

law were received in very much the same manner and in neither of the two older universities is there much indication of the teaching of civil law. At Glasgow, lectures in civil law are not recorded until 1460 and at best were intermittent while it had been earlier admitted at St Andrews in 1432 that 'few if any, betake themselves to the study of civil law, on account of which there are found few experts in civil law by whom justice can be duly administered in civil business.' This concern became greater as the century proceeded but not until the appointment of a civilist at Aberdeen and movements towards revival at St Andrews following the education act of 1496 were attempts made to remedy this situation.[35] In theology, the scarcity of students is more explicable. Stress was laid upon theological studies in the foundation of St Salvator's College and Glasgow University. But as the requirements for even the baccalaureate in theology were stringent in terms of both age of the entrant and the years of study required, only advanced scholars of considerable ability were likely to embark on such a course. Consequently while there was some theological teaching at Glasgow, students were few and far between. Equally at St Andrews, the emphasis must always have been on quality rather than quantity and many of the students appear to have come from religious houses, including the Augustinian priory of St Andrews which in turn also provided many of the teachers.[36] In career terms, theology was not in any case the most important subject an ambitious secular clerk could pursue; canon law provided a much more attractive prospect and this may explain why of all the faculties other than arts, that of canon law proved to be be the most successful. While at Glasgow this success proved transitory, and the buildings in which canon law was taught were in disrepair in 1483 and few graduates appeared thereafter, at St Andrews the faculty was firmly established by 1415, and although the study of law was ignored in the foundation of St Salvator's, the faculty continued to be well organized during the fifteenth century and produced many distinguished graduates who later found service as advisers and secretaries to kings and magnates or practised as lawyers in ecclesiastical and possibly even in civil courts.[37]

When to this small number of home-produced graduates is added the considerable number of Scots who continued to study abroad, particularly at Bologna and Paris, the trained reserve of personnel for all types of professional employment in Scotland, to which a very high percentage of them returned, is sizably increased. In their studies abroad a similar pattern emerges. Canon law provided the major

35 *St Andrews Acta* I, p. cliii; *APS* II, p. 238; Durkan, 'Bishop Turnbull', p. 55.
36 *St Andrews Acta* I, pp. cxxxix–cxlix; Durkan, 'Bishop Turnbull', pp. 53–5.
37 Mackie, *University of Glasgow*, pp. 27–8; Durkan, 'Bishop Turnbull', p. 55; Rait, *Universities of Aberdeen*, pp. 33–4.

attraction and may even have supplanted arts as the principal subject of study, for increasingly a first degree was acquired at a home university and was followed by more specialized studies abroad. A mere handful of students appear to have studied civil law either separately or in conjunction with canon law and only a small elite turned to theology.[38] The services which such men rendered thereafter were varied. In the academic world Laurence of Lindores, who had studied at Paris and became first rector of St Andrews, composed works of a scientific nature which were utilized by continental universities such as Prague and Leipzig for much of the fifteenth century;[39] in the literary field Glasgow can claim Robert Henryson, later schoolmaster at Dunfermline, who received membership of the university in 1462 and was to produce such masterpieces as the *Testament of Cresseid* and the *Morall Fabillis*, while St Andrews can counter with two other accomplished poets, William Dunbar, a skilled versifier and priest who graduated in 1479, and Gavin Douglas, who graduated in 1494, became bishop of Dunkeld in 1515, but is best remembered for his translation of the *Aeneid*. The first principal of Aberdeen university, Hector Boece, a humanist of repute, produced his *History of Scotland* in the early sixteenth century, which also saw the appearance of a *History of Greater Britain* by John Major – 'the last of the schoolmen' – who had been educated at Cambridge and Paris, but whose achievements like those of Boece were firmly rooted in the preceding century.[40] In educational circles William Turnbull, the founder of Glasgow University, was initially a graduate of St Andrews and later studied at Louvain and Pavia where he graduated in canon law. William Elphinstone, founder of Aberdeen University, had a similar career; having read law at Paris and Orleans he was made an honorary doctor of laws at Glasgow in 1474. In the field of statesmanship and diplomacy, educated churchmen rendered public services at home and also abroad as royal ambassadors; thus Elphinstone and others such as John Cameron, bishop of Glasgow, and James Kennedy, bishop of St Andrews, successively served the Scottish kings and in 1475 John Edwardson had been at the papal curia for a long time on the king's business. These qualifications

38 D. E. R. Watt, 'University Graduates in Scottish Benefices before 1410', *Recs Scot. Church Hist. Soc.* xv (1964), pp. 77–88; *St Andrews Acta* I, pp. cxlix–clvii.

39 J. D. Baxter, 'Scottish Students at Louvain University, 1425–1484', *SHR* xxv (1928), pp. 327–34; D. Shaw, 'Laurence of Lindores', *Recs Scot. Church Hist. Soc.* xii (1954), pp. 47–62.

40 *The Poems and Fables of Robert Henryson*, edited by H. Harvey Wood (Edinburgh, 1958); *The Poems of William Dunbar*, edited by W. M. MacKenzie (London, 1966); J. W. Baxter, *William Dunbar, a Biographical Study* (Edinburgh, 1952); *The Poetical Works of Gavin Douglas*, edited by J. Small (Edinburgh, 1874) I, pp. i–clxvii; A. A. M. Duncan, 'Hector Boece and the Medieval Tradition', *Abertay Historical Society Publications* no. 16 (1972), pp. 1–11; J. Durkan, 'John Major: after 400 years', *Innes Review* I (1950), pp. 131–9.

were not restricted to bishops and a narrow elite, however, and most positions of importance in cathedrals and collegiate churches were invariably held by clerks with a variety of degrees. If the possession of a degree alone could not guarantee preferment which was frequently dependent upon ties of blood or service, in the fifteenth century academic qualifications were still an essential requirement for any place seeker.[41]

With a sufficient body of qualified lawyers within its ranks, it is clear that one of the major services which the church could offer to the community at large was its legal expertise. As an institution the church's jurisdiction covered many fields. Out of its responsibility for faith and morals arose the competence of its courts in cases of matrimony which included actions for annulment and disputes over dowries and legitimacy. The confirmation of testaments also fell under its aegis as did any transaction whether spiritual or secular which had been made binding upon oath. Suits involving churchmen alone, especially those concerned with benefices and their revenues, were invariably dealt with by church courts, but churchmen dealing in litigation outside the strict purview of these courts frequently succeeded in having their cases heard in an ecclesiastical court which, because of its efficiency, was often preferred to the civil courts even by the laity. The constitution of such courts varied. Sometimes cases and appeals from lesser courts would be heard by judges delegate, usually three in number, who were appointed by the pope to decide the merits of a particular case. More commonly, however, the ecclesiastical jurisdiction vested in a bishop of a diocese was delegated to a principal judicial officer called the official who might have lesser officials under him. From the mid-fifteenth century onwards, moreover, commissaries of varying nomenclatures and competence, begin to appear with their courts as a complementary part of the ecclesiastical judicial system centred upon the diocese.[42]

The type of cases heard before these courts varied greatly and the only extant native records, which date from the sixteenth century, suggest that executry cases, followed by cases arising from failure to fulfil a contract under oath together with court orders to pay ecclesiastical dues, predominated over a lesser volume of business relating to matrimony, defamation and disputes over benefices. But as most benefice disputes went to Rome before one of the supreme tribunals of

41 Durkan, 'William Turnbull', pp. 5–18 and 55; J. Dowden, *Scottish Bishops* (Glasgow, 1912), pp. 31–2, 129–35 and 319–22; Reg. Supp. 734, f. 243v; *St Andrews Acta* I, p. clii. A survey of fifteenth-century petitions reveals that the pattern of university graduates in cathedral benefices noted by Watt, 'University Graduates in Scottish Benefices', pp. 81–2, is maintained for the remainder of the century.

42 Donaldson, 'The Church Courts', pp. 363–6.

the papal curia – the Rota – sometimes on appeal but more often as a case of first instance, the small number of such cases heard in Scotland is obviously misleading as to the total number of such disputes. The papal records also give some early insight into the type of litigation sometimes held initially in Scotland and thereafter on appeal to Rome. Not unnaturally the bulk of the actions are ecclesiastical as the rules of provision and reservation gave endless opportunities for place seekers to obtain at least sufficient legal rights in a benefice to initiate litigation against the actual possessor who might find it advantageous and less costly to secure the intruder's resignation by means of a pension or some similar concession.[43] Nevertheless, the laity appear at fairly regular intervals. A typical case is that of Christine Heriot, wife of Patrick Blackadder, who in 1478 is found trying to recover her dowry from a layman who was retaining it. It was frequently claimed that marriages were designed to preserve bonds of friendship between the families of the contracting parties and, while on occasion this may have been little more than common form, one marriage celebrated in 1443 was apparently brought about to ease the enmity caused by the slaying of the groom's father by the father of the bride. Likewise in 1451 it was claimed that the feud between the Kirkpatricks and Maxwells had been allayed by a marriage which had followed wars and dissensions in which 'as many as one hundred men were miserably killed in one day.' Disputes over leases and feus also appear and one in 1469, alleging that a layman who had obtained land on lease from the abbey of Dryburgh had subsequently 'built some sumptuous buildings', extended the original lease and had obtained further land on lease, was being contested as harmful to the abbey. Such complaints were becoming fairly frequent during the course of the century and as early as 1441 the charge was made that the ambition of certain people in Scotland had proceeded so far that not content with their own limits they were trying to acquire and snatch goods pertaining to the church.[44]

Such cases touched only a tiny majority of the population, but at a lesser level each diocesan archdeacon possessed his court in which breaches of discipline by clergy and laity alike could be dealt with, while beneath him in station the dean of Christianity could take cognizance of moral offences and also confirm minor testaments of under £40 in value. No records of such courts are extant, but glimpses of the type of jurisdiction exercised by these courts can be obtained

43 An examination of the archives of the Rota (for which see L. E. Boyle, *A Survey of the Vatican Archives and of its Medieval Holdings* (Toronto, 1972), pp. 90–92) is at present being conducted on behalf of the universities of Dundee and Glasgow and is the source of this information. For native cases, see Donaldson, 'Church Courts', pp. 365–6.
44 Reg. Supp. 377, ff. 121–2; 391, f. 223v; 448, f. 158; 636, f. 249; 769, ff. 58–58v.

through the eyes of Alexander Myln, official of Dunkeld, who in his *Lives of the Bishops of Dunkeld* gives a pen portrait of his diocesan colleagues of the early sixteenth century; of Walter Brown, official of Dunkeld in the late fifteenth century, and for whom Myln acted as clerk and notary in his court for three years, he notes that he possessed a 'remarkable knowledge of canon law and strong sense of justice'. David Abercrombie, commissary of Dunkeld in the same period, is credited with punishing the 'excesses and crimes of highland folks', while Thomas Greig, dean of Atholl and Drumalban, punished 'judiciously all public offenders whether they be clergy or country folk'. Not only members of the chapter practised in a judicial capacity, however, and of the vicars choral one acted as an advocate in the consistorial court, while another who wrote in 'a very good style' was clerk to the same court.[45]

Because of their training such priests were able to perform a variety of legal functions, one of the most important of these undoubtedly being that of notary public, a position held exclusively by priests during the fifteenth century. Notaries who usually held a chaplaincy or some other ecclesiastical benefice in addition to their legal office, were enrolled by a protonotary apostolic and were then authorized to authenticate legal acts, which were engrossed in their protocol books, or register of deeds, by the addition of their docquet and sign manual.[46] The vast majority of these deeds were evidences of title, many of them recording the leasing and feuing of church lands. In this respect it is clear that many church tenants possessed continuity of tenure and security of possession as early as the fifteenth century, a fact which redounds to the credit of the churchmen in question. Leases were sometimes granted for life and nearly always were of at least five years duration. Furthermore, evictions at the end of such a period were uncommon, the tenants themselves frequently changing their lands, not under pressure, but of their own free will. The spread of feu–ferm tenure during this century also brought for some tenants a heritable tenure of their holdings, although to others it simply meant a new landlord. The record of the church in this respect was at its best paternalistic, an attitude which was only slowly eroded in the following century. In addition to recording such land transactions, notaries also made out instruments on indentures, marriages, admissions of parish clergy and protests against various actions. Such duties performed by a priest for members of the laity cemented the bond between them, and this affinity was frequently strengthened by the

45 Myln, *Vitae*; *Dunkeld Rentale*, pp. 324, 326, 328 and 330.
46 McKay, 'Parish Life in Scotland', p. 93; W. Angus, 'Notarial Protocol Books, 1469–1700' in *Sources and Literature of Scots Law* (Stair Society, 1936), pp. 289–300.

clergy acting as agents for the people in a burgh court, witnessing their wills and deputizing as their scribes.[47]

Such legal actions could also be characterized as acts of social welfare and in this respect the fifteenth-century church could still demonstrate its concern, even though disquieting elements of a contrary disposition were becoming more prominent towards the end of the century. Of the social services provided by the church some were institutionalized, others of a more individual nature. Of the former, hospitals which often could be more accurately described as almshouses, even though founded in many cases by laymen, were ecclesiastical institutions. Of the early foundations many had certainly fallen into decay or were on their way to becoming secularized. Thus two small hospitals at Lauder and Smailholm may have had their activities curtailed or terminated by the annexation of their revenues in 1429 to the monastery of Dryburgh, while at St Germains in East Lothian the rector was charged with having given over the hospital to laymen, their wives and families whom he allowed to dwell at the hospital as though it were his private house.[48] Concern for the poor was by no means at an end, however, and at least twenty new hospitals were founded in the course of the century. A few of these were in rural areas, such as Covington in Lanarkshire, founded before 1468 for a certain number of poor who were to be helped in their need, but the great majority were in the burghs; thus at Edinburgh in 1438 the provost and burgesses founded a hospital because 'many of the poor and weak die on account of the severe colds in these parts and lack of hospitals there.' The lack of understanding of hygiene is seen in the enactment that in each of the hospital's twenty-four beds 'two can be sufficiently put up', although by contemporary standards this was by no means bad, and social concern was certainly to the fore. Some hospitals also dealt with disease; St Anthony's in Leith founded for the poor and sufferers from erysipelas, and leper houses such as those at Dundee, Edinburgh, Glasgow and Haddington which were still active in the fifteenth century, dealt with specific ailments, while others founded at Lasswade in 1478 and Perth in 1434 were more generally for the poor and infirm.[49] Leprosy was still an active disease and no respecter of persons, and the parson of Libberton in Lanarkshire who had contracted it in 1449 not surprisingly feared deprivation. Those

47 Margaret Sanderson, 'Kirkmen and their Tenants in the Era of the Reformation', *Recs Scot. Church Hist. Soc.* XVIII (1972), pp. 26–42; McKay, 'Parish Life in Scotland', pp. 92–3.

48 J. Durkan, 'Care of the Poor: Pre-Reformation Hospitals' in McRoberts, *Essays on the Scottish Reformation*, pp. 116–28; Dunlop and Cowan, *Calendar of Scottish Supplications*, pp. 67–8 and 243; Reg. Supp. 755, ff. 10v–11.

49 Cowan and Easson, *Medieval Religious Houses*, pp. 162–94; Reg. Supp. 348, f. 28v; 633, f. 222.

who suffered from disease of any kind were likely to be treated as outcasts, as two scholars discovered in 1475 when, travelling from a plague-stricken part of Scotland, they were accepted contrary to a royal edict as guests by a friendly layman. A deputation of parishioners led by their priest urged the ejection of the scholars by their host, who refused, and in the heat of the argument was stabbed to death by the priest. In this case ecclesiastical charity was totally lacking, but not all individual churchmen showed lack of concern for the afflicted. In 1441 it was claimed to be customary for the vicar of Soroby in Tiree to 'hold hospitality towards the poor and other comers', and although this may be viewed with suspicion, the action of George Hepburn, dean of Dunkeld in the late fifteenth century in supplying daily alms and a weekly bowl of meal for 'certain decrepit poor folk' in Dunkeld and a daily supply of porridge when there was a dearth in the country, rings a truer note. Institutions do however seem to have become less assiduous in this part of their duties and friaries in particular appear in the face of increasing wealth to have reduced their charity to a routine in which 'one penny or one peice of breade anis in the oulk' was deemed sufficient concern for the poor.[50]

If, however, the poor were often neglected by the church – and it is significant that almshouses increasingly became the concern of the burghs – a section of the populace which continued to obtain solace and comfort at the hands of the church were travellers who, unlike the poor, might be expected to contribute as much in return for the services which they obtained. The comfort offered was occasionally spiritual and chapels were frequently situated near bridges like the bridge of Balgownie over the Don; in other cases hospitals, such as that of St James near Stirling bridge or the hospice and almshouse of St Leonard on the Tweed near Peebles, could offer more material comfort for the weary. From a description of the hospice of Soutra in 1444 which was built at the top of a hill 'very near a public way where there are often fierce winds and frequent cold spells' such shelter must have been very welcome.[51]

The provision of better communications could also aid travellers and here again the church made a significant contribution, sometimes to allow parishioners to attend their parish church more easily, but in other instances as a direct social service. The problem in certain areas such as the Highlands and Islands was acute, but Aberdeenshire could also be described as 'an area beyond the mountains in which the distance between churches is long and there are many impediments of

50 Reg. Supp. 375, f. 147v; 438, f. 255v; 728, f. 4v; *Dunkeld Rentale*, p. 320; 'The Beggars' Summons' in Dickinson *et al.*, *Source Book of Scottish History* II, pp. 168–9.
51 Dunlop, *Bishop Kennedy*, p. 407; Cowan and Easson, *Medieval Religious Houses*, pp. 187 and 193; Reg. Supp. 400, f. 34.

floods and mountains which often cut the inhabitants off from their devotions.' In this respect the church could provide a remedy, and bridge building was often initiated by churchmen such as the abbot of Kilwinning who proposed to erect a bridge over the River Garnock in Ayrshire in 1439. In similar spirit Thomas Lauder, bishop of Dunkeld, laid the foundations of a bridge over the Tay in July 1461. Even where the benefactor was lay the church played its part as the pope could be petitioned to grant an indulgence to those who gave alms for the building or repair of bridges; this was the case with the bridge built by Margaret, countess of Douglas, over the river Bladenoch in Galloway in 1441, or that about to be constructed over the Dee by the inhabitants of Aberdeen in 1446. Where there was no bridge hermits appear to have acted as ferrymen as at Ardclach near the river Findhorn, while others may have provided the means of crossing the Forth and its tributaries. Religious hermits indeed appear to have performed a variety of services for travellers, maintaining not only inland routes but also providing sea marks and lighting beacons along the coasts for shipping.[52]

The benefits conferred by the church on the society which it served and with which it apparently so successfully identified itself are seemingly inexhaustible. Unfortunately for the future role of the church, however, the service which was increasingly overlooked amid its myriad of interests was the necessity of preaching and administering the sacraments to the people. The venal sins of the rich pluralists increasingly brought about an acceptance of more secular attitudes throughout the structure of the church. By the early sixteenth century, even household chaplains could be described by one writer as men who in war were 'not inferior to others that are laymen'. This was clearly a well founded description as petitions from such chaplains for indulgences attest. Thus in 1453 Patrick Black describes his active participation in a battle to which he had accompanied his lord to hear confessions, and in 1476 Alexander Piot, chaplain to the lord of Glamis, who had hastened from preparing to say mass, relates how he had killed an opponent with a lance in a fracas over the revenues of the hospital of Balgownie in Angus. These were not isolated incidents, and in these and similar cases churchmen had too clearly identified themselves with a society whose way of life should have been alien to them.[53] Churchmen who had integrated with society to such an extent that their behaviour and standard of values corresponded with that of

52 Dunlop, *Bishop Kennedy*, pp. 406–7; Reg. Supp. 359, f. 139; 371, f. 53; 410, f. 90; 544, f. 24v; Myln, *Vitae*, p. 23; McRoberts, 'Hermits in Medieval Scotland', pp. 199–216.

53 Major, *History*, p. 30; Reg. Supp. 470, f. 183; 734, f. 252; Dunlop, *Bishop Kennedy*, pp. 399–400.

the laity whom they were expected to inculcate with more charitable virtues were not unnaturally increasingly measured by secular standards. Moreover, as the spiritual role of many churchmen diminished and as their increased rapacity came to threaten many of the services which they had previously provided, society began to take measures to make similar provision for itself. Already in the fifteenth century, education and provision for the poor was being increasingly undertaken by burgh councils and although priests might still be appointed to oversee such schools and almshouses, a breach in the exclusive position of the church had been achieved. Likewise in legal matters, if churchmen were to retain their exclusive right to act as notaries public until after 1540 when the first lay notaries begin to appear, lay advocates were becoming increasingly conspicuous in the late fifteenth century as royal courts became more efficient in their administration of justice. Moreover, as the church ceased to be the only institution in which an ambitious youth could expect preferment, the consequent removal of the necessity of entering holy orders accelerated the movement towards a society in which the laity would increasingly supplant churchmen as lawyers, teachers and statesmen. Even culturally the church had ceased to be the sole patron of the arts by the end of the century, and crown and nobility were poised to accept a major share of patronage as secular architecture became increasingly important.[54] Faced with this challenge to its role in society the bulwark of the church's strength should have been its religious ministrations for these alone of the church's many contributions to society could not be performed by the laity. In the last instance, however, the secular attitudes which had been bred within the church coupled with even stronger manifestations of secularism outside its ranks proved too strong for survival. These factors even more than incipient Protestantism led to the Reformation, but it is noteworthy that the reformers, whatever their theological views, had no quarrel with their predecessors' concept of the church's place in society.[55] It was a noble ideal, and if in certain respects it could not be maintained, the struggle for its realization which continued for most of the fifteenth century contributed greatly to the development of Scottish society.

54 J. Grant, *History of the Burgh and Parish Schools of Scotland* (Glasgow, 1876), pp. 30–31; *Cast. and Dom. Arch.* I, pp. 222–6; S. H. Cruden, *The Scottish Castle* (Edinburgh, 1960), pp. 127–43.
55 I. B. Cowan, 'Church and Society in Post-Reformation Scotland', *Recs Scot. Church Hist. Soc.* XVII (1971), pp. 185–201.

7

The development of the law
James J. Robertson

In a collection of essays on the society of fifteenth-century Scotland, it
is appropriate that there should be a contribution on the law or laws
which regulated that society, a survey of the legal history of the
period. But what is legal history and, in particular, Scottish legal
history? This problem of definition can be illustrated from the writings of two modern English legal historians. Thus Professor S. F. C.
Milsom states:

> Legal history means different things to different people. To historians it
> is usually a branch either of administrative or of social history; and legal
> thinking is not considered for its own sake. Lawyers are interested in
> legal thinking. But to them the subject usually appears as law read
> backwards, the inevitable unfolding of things as they came to be; and the
> thinking is seen as a fumbling for the result eventually reached. In this
> gulf between the disciplines there is lost the interest of a story and
> perhaps the measure of an achievement.[1]

Dr J. H. Baker writes in a similar manner:

> Legal history is a fascinating and intricate study in itself, and it continues
> to attract the attentions of researchers and scholars. But perhaps by its
> seeming to fall between the two disciplines of law and history, its basic
> relevance to both is sometimes overlooked.[2]

Perhaps the two most notable publications in the past century in
English legal history are Pollock and Maitland's *The History of English
Law before the time of Edward I*, first published in 1895, and Sir William
Holdsworth's monumental *A History of English Law*, published between 1903 and 1966. There is also a wealth of modern material, much
of it on particular subjects. But even though the study of English legal
history is now established on an academic and scholarly foundation,
especially in the universities of Oxford, Cambridge and London, there
is still much scope for improvement as the comments above indicate.

1 S. F. C. Milsom, *Historical Foundations of the Common Law* (London, 1969), p. ix.
2 J. H. Baker, *An Introduction to English Legal History* (London, 1971), p. v.

It is an understatement to say the same about Scotland. It is perhaps not too extreme to suggest that, compared to the study of English legal history, there is, as yet, no real study of Scottish legal history. There has been pioneering work, much of which is valuable and should not be underestimated, but it must also be remembered that the bulk has been done by amateur legal historians who, through no fault of their own, have not had adequate facilities, especially time, for sustained research and writing. This is not to belittle the important work of men like Thomas Thomson, Cosmo Innes, George Neilson, David Murray, David Baird Smith and Lord President Cooper. Yet it must be admitted that Scotland has not yet produced a legal historian of the calibre of a Maitland or a Holdsworth.

The prospect for future development is not, however, unpromising. The professional study of Scottish history in Scottish universities has advanced greatly in this century, especially over the past thirty years. Indeed, it could be maintained that the bulk of original research and writing, much of which can be regarded as Scottish legal history, has been carried out by the professional historian. Professor G. W. S. Barrow's works on the acts of the kings of Scots and the Scottish justiciar are an example.[3] The contribution of Scottish historians is important but it does also illustrate Milsom's comment that the historian is more concerned with the development of the administration of a kingdom than with the particular study of law connected with the administration. It is here, as Baker states, that legal history falls between the two disciplines of law and history. Ideally the legal historian should be qualified in both, and a much closer collaboration is needed between academic lawyer and academic historian. While Scotland is far from achieving this ideal state, there is at least the beginning of such collaboration.

What has been written so far may seem to have little relevance to the title of this essay, but it is necessary to illustrate the present state of study in Scottish legal history and the difficulties yet to be overcome.

This essay will therefore attempt to suggest two things. First, there should be an appreciation of certain phases of social development. The point is that the laws of a society will reflect that phase through which it is passing. For instance, in what is termed feudal society, the legal system will show certain characteristics peculiar to that society and likewise in the case of a mature legal society.

Secondly, the characteristics of the legal system of fifteenth-century Scotland suggest that the country was emerging into a legal maturity. The arguments and evidence to support this suggestion are tentative

3 *Regesta Regum Scottorum*, edited by G. W. S. Barrow, I (Edinburgh, 1960), II (Edinburgh, 1971); Barrow, 'The Scottish Justiciar in the Twelfth and Thirteenth Centuries', *Juridical Review* 16 (1971), pp. 97–148.

and exposed to criticism and there has been so little research into legal development in the fifteenth century that much of what follows is, of necessity, speculation. But speculation can promote further enquiry and, if this is achieved, will not have been in vain.

The opening paragraph refers to the law of a society. What is meant by law? An answer must include a statement that the law is the body of rules which is created within a society to enable the members of a society to live in harmony. These rules will also discourage antisocial behaviour. In a primitive society the rules tend to be usage or custom. The study of primitive law is important to a legal historian but much of the work in this field may be classified as social anthropology and more satisfactorily studied by the social anthropologist.

In a mature society the law tends to be the creation of a legislature. There is also authority for the enforcement of law and machinery for the settlement of disputes between members of the society, and there will generally be professional lawyers. Here the work of the legal historian is more clearly defined for in a mature legal society there are legal ideas and concepts whose development can be studied. Similarly, the system for the administration of law is more clearly defined and is a proper study for the administrative historian.

It has been observed that a society may develop from what has been termed a primitive state to a mature state and there may be various intervening states.[4] The first grade, food-gatherers and hunters, develops into a society of agriculturalists and from this emerges a mercantile and industrial society. This process reflects an economic progression and, at the same time, rules for the ordering of society develop within each grade. Although local or unique influences may affect the development of any particular society, all societies tend to emerge in the same way and to pass through the various grades between a primitive and an industrialized state. It follows from this that all societies tend to go through the same stages in the development of their laws.

A brief illustration is the emergence of feudalism. What is termed a feudal society results when a society is mainly composed of agricul-turalists established in one area. The society has a ruler or paramount chief. The economic and governmental needs of the society are most adequately met by a system of delegation of the control of land through a series of grants from the ruler to sub-rulers with the appro-priate supplies being made as a return on each sub-delegation of authority. Feudalism is not confined to Europe but is found through-out the world when societies go through a certain stage of economic development. Moreover, on the nature of feudalism, Marc Bloch

4 For a general account of the development of law in society, see A. S. Diamond, *The Evolution of Law and Order* (London, 1951), pp. 180–87.

suggests that 'it is a question of the deepest interest whether there have been other societies, in other times and in other parts of the world, whose social structures in their fundamental characteristics have sufficiently resembled that of our western feudalism to justify us in applying the term "feudal" to them as well.'[5]

The link between the development of law and the various stages through which society passes can be illustrated in Scotland. It can be maintained that there are only three types of law which reveal clearly distinguishable aspects – primitive, archaic and mature law.[6] Primitive law represents the customs or usages of those preliterate peoples who have not developed courts but possess recognized social rules and have discovered means of coping with social conflicts. This group includes food-gatherers and people who are mainly hunters and herdsmen. Primitive law would only have existed in Scotland at the very latest in the period prior to the commencement of Anglo-Norman influence in the eleventh century. Even in the era between the withdrawal of Roman influence from Scotland and the eleventh century it is possible that primitive law was being replaced by archaic law.[7]

Archaic law is the law of those preliterate peoples who have court organizations and officialdoms. The concept of archaic law is based not upon the use of writing, although this may be beginning in such a society, but upon the appearance of courts, the basic institution of every legal system. Archaic law includes the laws of agriculturalists and, in general, of feudal societies and in Scotland clearly emerged between 1100 and 1400. In this period there was the creation of an hierarchic system of courts, staffed by officials rather than by professional lawyers; the law in this period still tended to be customary. There are, however, signs of literacy and professionalism. Thus, from the twelfth century charters were increasingly used in relation to grants of land; *Regiam Majestatem*, a quasi-professional treatise on the law in Scotland, was compiled, probably no later than the early fourteenth century.

By the fifteenth century, the beginnings of mature law in Scotland can be discerned. This is a law which is 'not only officialized but which

5 M. Bloch, *Feudal Society*, translated by L. A. Manyon (London, 1962) pp. xviii and xix, and II, chapter 32, 'Feudalism as a Type of Society'.

6 For an elaboration of this, see W. Seagle, *The History of Law* (New York, 1946), pp. xiv and xv.

7 While there is not enough evidence to allow definite comparison, it is not unlikely that Scottish society, particularly in the west, was similar in many respects to that of Ireland, at least before the period of the Viking invasions. This might strengthen the assumption that Scottish law was developing from primitive to archaic, for Irish law was certainly archaic. See Kathleen Hughes, *Early Christian Ireland: Introduction to the Sources* (London, 1972), pp. 43–64; D. A. Binchy, 'The Linguistic and Historical Value of the Irish Law Tracts', *Proceedings of the British Academy* XXIX (1943), pp. 195–228.

is professionalized. It is the creation primarily not of court officials but of a class of professional men.'[8] Thus, mature law belongs to mercantile and industrial societies and its main characteristic is professionalism. Moreover, it is only in such a legal system, containing a class of professional lawyers, that jurisprudential concepts can emerge. These require facilities for contemplation and concrete expression, which are found only in a literate society with centres such as universities. If the criteria for a mature legal society are accepted, all the available evidence shows that the foundations of a mature legal system in Scotland were established in the fifteenth century. Although the three stages of legal development are useful as a way of putting the development of the law into a truer context, they are only general categories and have no clear-cut division. There may be elements of primitive and archaic law in a mature legal system; one stage gives way to another when the characteristic elements of the first are no longer predominant but receding before the characteristic elements of the next stage. However, the situation in Scotland and in western Europe was not a simple progression from primitive to mature law: western Europe had already seen in Roman law the emergence of a mature legal system which had itself developed from a primitive stage; and the archaic law of the barbarian peoples who settled in Europe and in Britain after the decline of the Roman empire was underlaid with many elements of mature Roman law which also survived in the canon law of the church, developing throughout the archaic period of European and Scottish law.[9]

This analysis of Scotland emerging in the fifteenth century from archaic law into the beginnings of legal maturity, differs from what can be regarded as established opinion. The current view is that the period between the Wars of Independence in the early fourteenth century and the establishment of the Court of Session in 1532 was the 'Dark Age' of Scottish legal history. Lord President Cooper, followed by Dr G. C. H. Paton, maintains that after an auspicious beginning in the twelfth and thirteenth centuries, Scottish legal development was minimal until the seventeenth century.[10] Cooper refers to the period as a 'prolonged eclipse'. He detects 'ominous symptoms of decline and decay . . . in Scots law . . . during the later fourteenth, the fifteenth and the early sixteenth centuries, and nowhere more notably than in

---

8 Seagle, *History of Law*, p. xv.

9 P. Stein, 'Roman Law in Scotland' in *Ius Romanum Medii Aevi, Pars V, 13b* (Milan, 1968), p. 13.

10 Lord Cooper, 'The Dark Age of Scottish Legal History, 1350–1650' in *Selected Papers, 1922–1954* (Edinburgh, 1957), pp. 219–36; G. C. H. Paton, 'The Dark Age, 1329–1532' in *An Introduction to Scottish Legal History* (Stair Society, 20, Edinburgh, 1958), pp. 18–24.

legal procedure' and 'reversion to patriarchal method and archaic ideas'. Cooper summarizes his opinions when he states that 'this was unquestionably the period when Scots law . . . reached its low-water mark.'[11]

Although the conclusions of Cooper and Paton concerning the period are, in general, negative, both writers admit, somewhat paradoxically, that the 'Dark Age' was not 'so dark as it has been painted'.[12] Cooper instances the Scottish statute book of the fifteenth century as containing evidence of 'pivotal' reforms and sees much ingenuity in the development of the conveyancing system. He also questions how Scottish churchmen who administered an efficient and mature system of canon law could sit in civil courts and there 'rest content with methods so jejune, so informal and so relatively immature'.[13]

Cooper and Paton both overstress the effects on legal development of the political difficulties which emerged in Scotland after the Wars of Independence and of the apparent weakness of the central authority in the fifteenth century. They consider the period prior to the wars as a 'Golden Age' of legal development followed by retrogression and decline which was only reversed in the seventeenth century.

A truer perspective is perhaps given if the so-called 'Golden Age' is regarded as the full flowering of archaic law in a predominantly archaic feudal society. The feudal courts and officialdoms which developed between 1100 and 1300 were Anglo-Norman feudal importations, already in an advanced state of development when they were introduced into Scotland. In general this system of archaic law worked well and rightly attracts the admiration of Cooper. During this period the organs typical of Anglo-Norman feudal government were firmly established in Scotland – the king at the top, advised by a council, and a royal bureaucracy in the offices of the chancellor and chamberlain. Justice was administered through a series of courts, that of the justiciar, the sheriff and the baron. The nature of feudal society meant that government and the dispensation of justice were to a great extent, decentralized and delegated, administered locally by local officials for this was the most efficient, indeed, the only, way in which a feudal society could operate. At the same time, centralized organs of government were developing and by the end of the thirteenth century there are signs of a parliament in Scotland. Throughout the fourteenth century the feudal structure of government continued to exist and, although the upheavals caused by the Wars of Independence and their

11 Cooper, 'Dark Age', pp. 220, 228–30.
12 *ibid.*, p. 235, and Paton, 'Dark Age', p. 24.
13 Cooper, 'Dark Age', pp. 230, 231 and 235.

aftermath should not be minimized, they were not the cataclysmic event in Scottish legal history portrayed by Cooper and Paton. There are indications, moreover, of change and development. Parliament, although still in a rudimentary form, was beginning to assert itself as a legislative body and, from the end of the fourteenth century, there was a 'quickening' of legal development. While there was no break with the past and a sudden influx of Romano-canonic legal concepts, the emergent professionalism in the law no doubt gave scope for their influence, but there is no evidence of any wholesale reception of these. The archaic society of the 'Golden Age', therefore, had reached its peak and was already developing into a mature society – a fact which apparently has not been appreciated to any extent. By the fifteenth century, the roots of legal maturity had been established in Scotland.

This can be examined from three aspects – first, the central organs of government for the creation of law and the hearing of cases, that is, the emergence both of parliament as a legislative body and of a supreme court; secondly, the growth of professional lawyers, especially notaries public, to which is related the development of what may be termed 'lawyers' law', involving the development of legal procedures, techniques and concepts; thirdly, the significance of the influence of ecclesiastical law and courts on the development of law in Scotland.

From the return of James I to Scotland in 1424 and, generally, throughout the fifteenth century, it is accepted that important attempts were made to establish parliament as an effective and su-preme legislative body.[14] However, the general conclusion on this development is that it was to a great extent ineffective. Rait considers that any 'superstructure of parliamentary government' which may have been laid in the second half of the fourteenth century 'was a foundation upon which no man built. . . . Administration continued to be inefficient and expensive, and reform was always for tomorrow.'[15] It is true that throughout the fifteenth century many of the enactments of parliament may have been ineffective. But from the standpoint of the legal historian it is of more importance to consider what parlia-ment was attempting to do and to assess the significance of these attempts in terms of legal development.

It must be remembered that in 1424 parliament, as such, had been in existence for only a little more than a hundred years and throughout the fourteenth century its functions were not clearly defined and the political exigencies of the time hindered anything other than rudimen-tary constitutional development.[16] After 1424, however, there appears

14 Robert S. Rait, *The Parliaments of Scotland* (Glasgow, 1924), pp. 30–39.
15 *ibid.*, p. 30.
16 *ibid.*, pp. 19–30.

to be an acceleration which, while it may be more obvious because the records of parliament are more extensive after this date, does also indicate a growing vitality in parliament. This new maturity can be illustrated in several ways.

The parliaments of James I, II and III provide evidence of a continuous desire for the improvement of justice, both in its substance and dispensation. First, there was recurrent concern to establish a supreme court, which was promoted, under James I and James II, in the acts of 11 March 1426 and 6 March 1458.[17] In 1426 parliament ordained that the chancellor and certain 'discreet personis of the thre estatis' be chosen to sit three times a year at a place determined by the king to 'knaw examyn conclude and finally determyn all and sindry complayntis causis and querellis that may be determynit befor the kingis consal'. While this act is in general terms, that of 1458 is much more specific. It states that the sessions shall be in Edinburgh, Perth and Aberdeen, each of forty days' duration, and also specifies that there shall be three members from each estate along with the clerk of the registers in each session; the names of those persons nominated to sit on the next three sessions are then given. The inclusion of the clerk of the registers would seem to indicate a concern for the recording of the activities of the sessions. Ancillary to these acts are many acts throughout the reigns of James I, II and III regulating the jurisdiction and procedure of the 'sessions', and most of the acts of the parliament of 1468 can be cited as examples.[18]

Secondly, there is shown throughout the three reigns a desire for the general improvement of the dispensation of justice both in the reform of the law and in legal procedure. Several acts can be cited as evidence of proposals for law reform, those of 11 March 1426 – 'Of persons to be chosen to examyn and mend the bukis of law', 19 January 1450 – 'Persons chosyn of the thre estatis til examyn the actis of parliamentis and general counsallis', 27 November 1469 – 'The personis to quhom the thre estatis has committit ful power to avise commone and refer to the next parliament . . . the reductione of the kingis lawis' and 2 August 1473 – 'Anentis the mending of the lawis'.[19]

Concerning legal procedure many acts can be cited. In the parliament of 6 March 1430, ten of the twenty-two acts deal with some aspect of procedure such as summonses, exceptions and appeals.[20] The first two acts cover procedure before the local courts of sheriff and baron by defining more clearly the power of the mair or sheriff officer

17 *APS* II, p. 11 c. 19; p. 47 c. 1.
18 *ibid.*, II, p. 92 cc. 2, 4, 6 and 7.
19 *ibid.* II, p. 10 c. 10; p. 36 c. 10; p. 97 c. 20; p. 105 c. 14.
20 *ibid.* II, p. 17–18 cc. 1–7, 16, 18 and 21.

and the method of summonsing parties to court. In the following two acts, technical grounds for taking exception to a royal brief are removed. Likewise a person who pleads an exception may now only be able to do so with special leave. The remainder of the acts all show some aspect of improvement in court procedure. There is a detailed procedure for the falsing of a doom, the making of an appeal, the form of the oath to be taken by an advocate before a temporal court and the form for the making of inquests. Of the eleven acts of the parliament of 20 November 1475, five acts deal with procedure both criminal and civil.[21] The first act states that justice ayres for the administration of criminal law should be held twice a year throughout the kingdom. The next two acts concern the sheriff court. The first ordains that parties in civil causes should proceed in the first instance before their local court before going to the council. The second is again concerned with the 'reformacione of . . . criminale accions befor oure Soverane lordis Justice sherifs or uther officiaris'. The last two deal with the brieve of idiotry and further reform of sheriff court procedure. These are random examples and there are similar ones in most of the parliaments of all the three reigns.

Thirdly, many acts throughout the fifteenth century show development and reform in particular aspects of the substantive law. Two examples can be given. The first concerns the development of the law of leases. In the early fifteenth century, a tenant had only a personal right to his tenancy which meant that he had no security of tenure when the landlord transferred his lands. Three acts reformed this situation and changed a personal right into a real right. These acts give evidence of deliberate legal evolution in that there are three phases to the change. The first phase is seen in the parliament of 16 April 1429 where an act was passed which gives tenants security for a year unless the landowners want the land for their own use.[22] The second phase was the creation of the tenant's real right to possession, found in the act of 19 January 1450 which permits tenants to stay in their lands until the end of their leases irrespective of changes in the ownership of the lands.[23] The final stage was in the act of 20 November 1469,[24] which gives protection to a tenant against distraint by a landlord's creditor; a creditor could not do diligence for the landlord's debts against the possessions or tenancy of the tenant. These acts are evidence of a deliberate policy of law reform in a particular legal field. Perhaps it is worthy of note that an analogous development concerning

21 *ibid.* II, p. 111 cc. 2–4, 8 and 11.

22 *ibid.* II, p. 17 c. 2.

23 *ibid.* II, p. 35 c. 6. Lawyers refer to this under its Old Style dating, as the Leases Act, 1449.

24 *ibid.* II, p. 96 c. 12.

security of tenure was taking place in England in the fifteenth century.[25]

Another example of the development of a particular law is in the prescription of obligations. This is the situation where an obligation becomes of no value to the creditor in the obligation if he does not take steps to enforce it within a certain period of time. The act of 27 November 1469 introduces a prescriptive period of forty years. In the act of 9 May 1474 there is further clarification of the law of prescription, with reference made to the earlier act.[26]

The tendency in the past to minimize the effect of the fifteenth-century statutes overlooks the fact that they reflected a continuous movement for the improvement of the administration of justice. But they also raise questions, to which answers are not at present possible or, at least, can only be tentative. Who was responsible for the introduction of the legislation and the drafting of the acts? The Scottish kings in the fifteenth century no doubt influenced the course of legislation and it has been suggested that James I personally sponsored many of the reforms proposed in his parliaments. However, it is much more probable that the legislation was the work of professional lawyers and draftsmen and this is reflected in the acts on security of tenure, for example. Rait observes that 'between the return of James I in 1424 and the accession of James VI in 1567, there are distinct indications of the development of rules for the drafting of parliamentary enactments', further evidence of a growing professionalism in legal matters.[27]

A second question arises concerning the legal content of the acts. What are the sources of the law? Many show the influence of canonical procedure.[28] In the parliament of 1 July 1427, provision was made for reducing the expenses of litigation by the introduction of a more expeditious method for citing clerical witnesses in civil causes. In addition, this parliament provided general rules for the process of arbitration. The reference of a dispute to arbiters is in itself evidence of a desire to reduce the time and expense of litigation, while the process of arbitration was derived from canon law and was also much resorted to in cases which came before the Roman Rota. It will later be shown that, in the fifteenth century, Scottish canon lawyers were in close contact with the Rota and its procedure which involved the frequent referral of Scottish cases from Rome to arbiters in Scotland. The influence of Roman law is also seen in the acts concerning prescription

25 Baker, *Introduction to English Legal History*, pp. 165–6.
26 *APS* II, p. 95 c. 4; p. 107 c. 9.
27 Rait, *Parliaments*, p. 423.
28 For example, *APS* II, p. 14 cc. 5 and 6.

and again provides evidence of a developing professionalism in law-making. What is now required is a legal analysis of the acts of the fifteenth-century Scottish parliaments.

This general survey demonstrates that parliament was seriously concerned with the improvement and reform of law and that there was an increasing professionalism in law-making throughout the fifteenth century to achieve better standards of justice – both features characteristic of legal maturity.

Closely linked with the emergence of parliament as a legislative body was the development of a supreme court. To a certain extent this may be evidence of dissatisfaction with the localized feudal jurisdictions but, taking everything into account, the local courts on the whole carried out their functions satisfactorily; they were run by men of the locality for men of the locality, and their justice, although simple, was probably fairly administered. Such administration of justice can normally be expected in an archaic legal society. But society was changing in the fifteenth century. The archaic feudal courts were not necessarily inefficient within their own limited jurisdictions but, rather, inadequate to deal with the legal problems of an emergent commercial society. Thus the desire to establish a centralized and professional judicature more likely reflected this inability of the feudal courts.

It is not proposed to examine in detail the beginnings of a centralized supreme court. It is enough to state that these are found in the auditors appointed by parliament and latterly in the causes heard by the lords of council. Throughout the fifteenth century there was a sustained movement for the creation of a permanent supreme court and by the end of the fifteenth century such a court did in fact exist in Scotland. Its historical development and the problems connected with it have been clearly outlined by Professor A. A. M. Duncan.[29] What is of importance to the legal historian is the assessment of the significance of the establishment of a supreme court. Cooper paints a distorted picture in dismissing 'the court which sat on 19 March 1482-3 as an oddly constituted tribunal, capable of dispensing rough justice, but quite incapable (especially in the absence of reports) of making any coherent contribution to the orderly exposition and development of Common Law'.[30] Moreover, he laments the paucity of Scottish decisions before 1500 when, in fact, the 'decisions' of the lords of council in civil causes exist from 1478. These contain a wealth of legal material which has not yet been analysed. It is true that these 'decisions' are not decisions in the modern sense, which give a detailed account of legal reasoning

29 A. A. M. Duncan, 'The Central Courts before 1532' in *Introduction to Scottish Legal History*, pp. 329–39.
30 Cooper, 'Dark Age', pp. 220 and 227.

leading to a final decision, but they are the council's interlocutors on the causes heard by them, providing a narrative account of the action. Nevertheless they contain valuable evidence on the state of the civil law of the time. Indeed, to this day the record of many actions before the court of session is left in interlocutory form without any full decision and it would be absurd to suggest that the modern court is therefore primitive in some way. Similarly, the acts of the lords of council are often in a terse form, but this does not mean that the procedure followed by the court in reaching its decision is rudimentary. As will be shown later, it is now possible to suggest that the procedure of the lords of council was modelled on that of the Roman Rota which could in no way be regarded as a court with homespun procedure.

Cooper is also in error in his views on the constitution of the court. On examination, the sederunts of the court are always found to have a strong ecclesiastical element. There has been no analysis in print of the composition and qualifications of the members of the court but, in view of the high proportion of churchmen, it is probable that many of the members were qualified in both civil and canon law. Bishop William Elphinstone, for example, was a frequent member of the court. It is almost inconceivable that a body comprising men of such calibre would have dispensed, as Cooper suggests, 'rough justice'.[31]

Again, as in the case of parliament, this is a field for further legal research. As George Neilson and Henry Paton have observed, 'strangely enough, it does not seem that the legal content of even the published volumes of the Acts of Auditors and Lords of Council has ever received systematic consideration. . . which may one day repay a detailed constructive investigation'.[32] But even on this cursory view, the court established as a supreme court in the fifteenth century was clearly staffed, or at least influenced, to a great extent by professional lawyers and was far from incoherent in the dispensing of justice.

The professional practice of law appears to have become well established in fifteenth-century Scotland and is another subject requiring

---

31 A statistical analysis of the sederunts of the court (printed in *ADC* and *ADA*) in the reign of James III and the early part of James IV's reign, was made by Professor A. L. Brown, in the Balfour Melville Memorial Lecture given in Glasgow in April 1975; 'The Scottish "Establishment" in the Later Fifteenth century'. This showed that the same small group of people turned up again and again. There were two earls who came frequently, and a number of lords; and there was the small group of 'statesmen' bishops and lesser clerics in royal service, like Archibald Whitelaw, the king's secretary, who were no doubt hoping for a bishopric – though in this case disappointed.

32 *Acts of the Lords of Council in Civil Causes*, edited by G. Neilson and H. Paton (Edinburgh, 1918) ii, p. lvi.

full investigation.[33] Here it is proposed to offer only tentative comments on the emergence of a professional class of lawyers in Scotland and certain consequences of this.

An archaic legal community provides little scope for the professional lawyer. There is a court structure and parties came before such courts but they usually appear for themselves. The law in such a community also tends to be simple, observed and applied, rather than interpreted and the subject matter of professional litigation. In an archaic community where society is relatively static, there is little extensive mercantile activity to engender legal activity in the form of contracts and the transfer of property.

As already stated, Scotland can be regarded as being in a state of legal archaism between the twelfth and fourteenth centuries. While the activities of the ecclesiastical courts, in particular, qualify this over-simplification,[34] the lack of professionalism at this period is the normal situation in legal matters.

By the end of the fourteenth century a change is apparent with evidence of increasing professionalism throughout the fifteenth century. This is exemplified in the emergence of the notary public, an office with a long history which can in fact be traced back to the imperial notaries of the Roman empire. In Europe, especially from the eleventh century, a professional class of notaries emerged, licensed either by the emperor or by the pope. Their main function was the preparation of instruments recording facts. The privilege accorded to such instruments was that they required no further proof and therefore formed the basis of public records and registers which were held *pro veritate*.[35]

The notary public first appeared in Scotland towards the end of the thirteenth century,[36] when his work was mainly connected with ecclesiastical matters, but the office really emerged at the beginning of the fifteenth century. From that time there is abundant evidence of notarial instruments, particularly the instrument of sasine. The exact date of its first appearance is controversial, but there can be little doubt that it was in common use after 1430.[37] It is interesting to note that in almost all the surviving chartularies the first references to notarial

33 R. D. Carswell, 'The Origins of the Legal Profession in Scotland', *American Journal of Legal History* xi (1967), pp. 41–55, provides a useful introduction, but cannot be regarded as more.

34 Lord Cooper, *Select Scottish Cases of the Thirteenth Century* (Edinburgh, 1944).

35 C. R. Cheney, *Notaries Public in England in the Thirteenth and Fourteenth Centuries* (Oxford, 1972). This is an excellent study of the history of the notary public. A comparable study could and should be made of the Scottish notary public.

36 *ibid.*, pp. 33 and 34.

37 W. Rodger, *The Feudal Forms of Scotland Viewed Historically* (Edinburgh, 1857), pp. 133–57.

instruments are in the fifteenth century. Taking three as an example, at Inchaffray the first reference is in 1454, at Inchcolm in 1420 and at Coupar Angus in 1404.[38] The sudden proliferation of instruments of sasine after about 1430 suggests a deliberate introduction of a new technique for the preservation of records relating to the transference of land. An instrument of sasine recording the giving of sasine was indisputable evidence of the fact of sasine, whereas a charter which relied on witnesses and seals for its authenticity could give no such evidence and was not proof of a conveyance. The significance of the instrument of sasine is seen when Balfour, referring to the case of Gibsone *contra* Monypenie decided in 1488, stated that a 'persoun, to preive him . . . to be, in heritabill state and fie of ony landis, he . . . sould preive the samin be writ, and not be witnessis; because nathing concerning fie and heritage may be provin be witnessis.'[39] The writ referred to here must be an instrument of sasine since a charter could only be proved by witnesses. By the end of the century the instrument of sasine had become an essential element in obtaining heritable title.

The emergence of the instrument of sasine also reflected an increasing commercialism in society. By the process of feu farming, formally encouraged in the act of 6 March 1458, land was becoming the subject of commerce.[40] New techniques, which still need to be studied, were evolving to overcome the feudal restraints on alienation of land and devices like the wadset and reversions were being developed to create securities over land.[41]

At the same time, the growing commercialism in society necessitated the reduction of transactions to writing. The notaries fulfilled these needs and also kept records of the transactions in their protocol books. Again, these books commence in the fifteenth century but they still await a detailed analysis.

Another aspect requiring further examination and clearly linked with commercialism is the increasing use in the fifteenth century of the disposal by will of moveable property. It is significant that the provincial synod and general council of 1420 restated the procedure for the confirmation of testaments.[42] This suggests that the legal machinery for the confirmation of an executor to administer a deceased person's

38 *Charters of Inchaffray Abbey*, edited by W. A. Lindsay and J. Dowden (SHS, 1908), p. 147; *Charters of the Abbey of Inchcolm*, edited by D. E. Easson and A. Macdonald (SHS, 1938), p. 46; *Charters of the Abbey of Coupar Angus*, edited by D. E. Easson (SHS, 1947–8) II, p. 5.

39 *The Practicks of Sir James Balfour of Pittendreich* (Stair Society, 21 and 22, Edinburgh, 1962–3) II, p. 363.

40 *APS* II, p. 49 c. 15.

41 *ibid.* II, p. 94 c. 3 and p. 95 c. 12; and see generally R. G. Nicholson, 'Feudal Developments in Late Medieval Scotland', *Juridical Review* 18 (1973), pp. 1–20.

42 *Statutes of the Scottish Church*, edited by D. Patrick (SHS, 1907), p. 80.

moveable estate required to be improved, possibly as a result of the increase in moveable wealth and will-making.

The activities of the notaries, therefore, brought a new professionalism into legal affairs. A further aspect of this is the appearance of professional pleaders before the courts. Acts of the parliaments of James I refer to advocates,[43] and that of 4 August 1455 clearly envisaged the existence of a professional body of pleaders when it decreed that 'forespeakers' should wear green tunics with the sleeves open like a tabard.[44]

A legal profession demands provision for the education and instruction of its intrants, but little is known about the methods used for the notaries. That there was some form of examination is evident from the act of 20 November 1469 which refers to the examination and certification of notaries by their bishops.[45]

The universities of St Andrews, Glasgow and Aberdeen were all founded in the fifteenth century. The influence of their teaching of law on the emergence of a legal profession has not been examined and it would be interesting to ascertain from the number of known notaries and advocates in fifteenth-century Scotland, how many were graduates either of arts or law in the Scottish universities. The appearance at this time of many collections of treatises on legal practice suggests that there was some formal instruction being given either in the universities or elsewhere.[46]

Similarly, the extent to which teaching of law in the universities disseminated new legal concepts is a matter of conjecture. The evidence indicates that the law faculties were not firmly established, and that teaching was not extensive;[47] even so, this must have promoted to some extent the latest ideas in canon and civil law. In this context it is worth noting that the majority of the Scottish collegiate churches were established in the fifteenth century. Is this evidence of the development of the canonical and juridical concept of the *collegium*, regarded as a novelty in France in the twelfth century?[48] Did the faculties of canon law give any impetus to its progress in Scotland?

As far as ecclesiastical influence on general legal development in Scotland is concerned, it seems probable that in the fifteenth century much can be attributed either directly or indirectly to it. Since at least the twelfth century in Scotland there had been a developing profes-

43 *APS* ii, p. 8 c. 24; p. 18 c. 6; p. 19 c. 16.

44 *ibid.* ii, p. 43 c. 12.

45 *ibid.* ii, p. 95 c. 6.

46 J. J. Robertson, 'De Composicione Cartarum' in *Miscellany* i (Stair Society, 26, Edinburgh, 1971), pp. 78–85.

47 Stein, 'Roman Law in Scotland', pp. 42–5.

48 *Dictionnaire de Droit Canonique*, edited by R. Naz (Paris, 1935–65) v, p. 233.

sional system within the church for the administration of the canon law. This involved a system of diocesan courts staffed by trained canon lawyers who were in contact with the main streams of canon law on the continent.

As already mentioned, many of the members of the lords of council were ecclesiastical lawyers disciplined in the canon law and some of the decisions of the lords of council must have been, at least indirectly, the result of legal reasoning based on canon law. Moreover, any attempt to determine who was responsible for the legislation of the fifteenth century should consider the probable influence of canon lawyers, especially in the acts which dealt with court procedure. The ecclesiastical influence also underlies the emergence of the legal profession, especially the development of the notary public which was based on the notarial practice of the church.

Although not sufficiently researched, these influences are well known, but information now available on the appeals from Scotland to the Roman Rota introduces a new dimension, both to the effect of canon law on Scottish legal development and to Scottish ecclesiastical history in general. The Rota was, and is, one of the supreme tribunals of the Roman church established permanently in Rome. Work has only recently commenced on the recovery and examination of these appeals.[49] Although appeals were probably made before 1464, the record survives only from that date, showing a continuous traffic between Scotland and Rome of litigants, procurators, witnesses and evidentiary instruments. Between 1464 and 1500 at least 104 cases have been identified;[50] their average length was one year but several continued for two or more years. Apart from two cases on illegitimacy from St Andrews and Aberdeen and one on testamentary succession from Brechin, all the cases concern disputed provisions to benefices. The procedure before the Rota was to lodge written submissions with written replies although witnesses were frequently heard in person. If witnesses could not appear personally, their evidence, taken by a notary in Scotland, was presented in an instrument lodged with the process. The striking feature of the procedure before the Rota is that in the majority of the cases the pleadings were made in Rome by Scottish procurators. The various interim decisions leading to the final decision were recorded in interlocutory form. These interlocutors contain much information on procedure and also on the

49 The writer has been privileged to initiate this research which is being conducted under the auspices of the Department of Scottish History, University of Glasgow. The Scottish records of the Rota are in the custody of the department, and are being classified and indexed by the writer.

50 The distribution of the cases is as follows – from the diocese of Aberdeen 8, Lismore 1, Brechin 6, Caithness 3, Dunblane 8, Dunkeld 7, Galloway 5, Glasgow 24, Moray 3, Ross 7, St. Andrews 32.

witnesses and their evidence. Preliminary work on these records and comparison with the acts of the lords of council in civil causes reveals similarities in the styles of the interlocutors, which is hardly surprising since many lawyers in Scotland must of necessity have been well versed in the procedure of the Roman Rota. Thus it is possible that the procedures of the Scottish supreme court have been modelled on the procedures of the supreme court of Christendom.

   This short commentary on aspects of the legal history of fifteenth-century Scotland has sought to provide a framework on which to build a more detailed study. The main object has been to demonstrate that the period under consideration, far from being a 'Dark Age', heralded the beginnings of a legal maturity. A truer perspective of legal developments has been veiled by ignorance of the facts. It is hoped that this essay has to a little extent raised the veil or has, at least, indicated paths for future exploration.

Plate 1   Affleck Castle, Angus, from the southwest: late fifteenth-century tower-house of L-plan form (Crown Copyright, reproduced by permission of the Department of the Environment).

Plate 2 Affleck Castle: second-floor hall or great chamber showing (centre) arched entrance to small oratory contained in the wing of the tower (Crown Copyright, reproduced by permission of the Department of the Environment).

Plate 3 Doune Castle, Perthshire, from the northwest (Copyright J. D. Keggie).

Plate 4   Balgonie Castle, Fife, from the southwest: tower-house and late fifteenth-century hall (left centre background) (Crown Copyright, Royal Commission on Ancient Monuments, Scotland).

Plate 6   Linlithgow Parish Church, West Lothian, from the northwest (Crown Copyright, Royal Commission on Ancient Monuments, Scotland).

Plate 5 Ravenscraig Castle, Fife, from the northeast (Crown Copyright, reproduced by permission of the Department of the Environment).

Plate 7 Fowlis Easter Parish Church, Angus, from the southwest (Copyright J. D. Keggie).

Plate 8 Trinity College Church, Edinburgh: sketch of interior of choir and apse by R. W. Billings, (from R. W. Billings, *The Baronial and Ecclesiastical Antiquities of Scotland* (1845–52) II, plate 29).

Plate 9 Lincluden Collegiate Church, Dumfries: monument to Princess Margaret, countess of Douglas, in the north wall of the choir (Crown Copyright, reproduced by permission of the Department of the Environment).

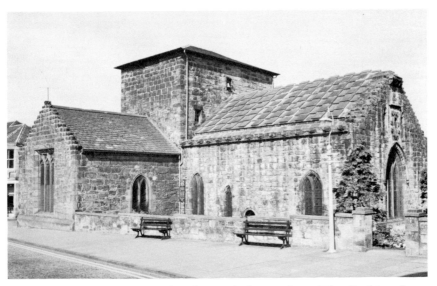

Plate 10   Carmelite Friary-Church, South Queensferry, West Lothian, from the southeast (Copyright J. D. Keggie).

Plate 11   Melrose Abbey-Church, Roxburghshire, from the southeast (Crown Copyright, reproduced by permission of the Department of the Environment).

Plate 12 Cathedral-Church, Old Aberdeen, from the southwest. Spires added to west towers in the sixteenth century (Copyright J. D. Keggie).

8

Architecture: the changing needs of society
Geoffrey Stell

From the viewpoint of the architectural historian, there appears to have been a general increase in the total amount of building activity in Scotland during the last quarter of the fourteenth century. To this period can be ascribed the commencement or completion of increasing numbers of buildings such as tower-houses, courtyard castles, collegiate churches and large burgh churches, all of which are directly relevant to a study of fifteenth-century architecture. So far as it can be measured, this activity was generally sustained throughout the greater part of the century, but a noticeable slowing down in the progress of several building operations towards the end of the century was followed by an almost complete cessation of activity, except for royal and some secular works, by the early years of the sixteenth century. The aim of this brief essay is to bring together some of the abundant architectural evidence from the period between about 1380 and the year 1500, and to consider aspects of this architecture as a reflection of the changing wealth and demands of society.[1]

The evidence for this period is derived from documentary sources and from the physical remains of the buildings themselves. There are, however, special problems involved in the use and interpretation of this material, even in such a fundamental matter as that of dating the architectural fabric. Building contracts between patrons and craftsmen, reliable narrative accounts of building operations, and the issue of royal licences to erect fortified structures provide direct historical evidence of *terminus post quem* dates, but are few in number for this

1 Detailed architectural and historical descriptions of the buildings mentioned in this essay will be found, except where otherwise stated, in the standard works by D. Macgibbon and T. Ross, *The Castellated and Domestic Architecture of Scotland* and *The Ecclesiastical Architecture of Scotland*, and in the published regional and county *Inventories* of the Royal Commission on the Ancient and Historical Monuments of Scotland. Accounts of a number of fifteenth-century buildings and architectural features are also contained in periodical literature, especially in the *Proceedings of the Society of Antiquaries of Scotland*. Buildings mentioned in this chapter are identified according to the old shire divisions in existence prior to 1975.

period.[2] And, although accounts for the administration of expenses for royal building works have been recorded in relative abundance,[3] there is seldom an indisputable correlation between these entries and surviving architectural remains. Documentary evidence for the great majority of fifteenth-century buildings in Scotland is in fact indirect; in most cases the approximate date of building or the identity of a builder is obtained by inference from any known changes in, for example, ownership, tenure, economic circumstances or status that correspond most closely in date to the architectural evidence. So far as the buildings themselves are concerned, few inscribed date-stones commemorating in either Arabic or Roman numerals a pre-sixteenth century date can be regarded as above suspicion, although they may enshrine fairly accurate local tradition. The only reliable non-scientific physical evidence for absolute dating purposes is heraldic. Carved stone armorials, which usually contain the arms of the builder or patron, are found in association with architecture of the early fifteenth century, and the fashion continued throughout this period.[4] In the absence of heraldry, a comparison of architectural plan-forms and details with those of buildings of known or ascertainable date helps to establish a relative chronology and typology. Some account, however, has to be taken of the possibilities of a time-lag in the occurrence of certain architectural features, owing to reasons not necessarily of geography only, but equally to the hierarchical nature of society and the pace of fashion. Finally, it should be borne in mind that the numerous structures which still survive above ground represent only a proportion of fifteenth-century building activity, and that for certain classes of late medieval building such as urban domestic architecture and rural dwellings the problems of identification and dating now rest very largely on the results of archaeological excavations.

2 A few of the known Scottish building contracts for this period are printed in L. F. Salzman, *Building in England down to 1540* (Oxford, 1967), pp. 466–7 and 471, and in *Edinburgh St Giles Registrum*, pp. 24–6, no. 18. See also *Coupar Angus Rental* I, pp. 304–10. Other entries and agreements, usually relating to church building operations, also occur in contemporary burgh records and ecclesiastical cartularies and registers, for example: *Extracts from the Council Register of the Burgh of Aberdeen* (Spalding Club, 1844–8) I, pp. 18 and 32–3; *Dunfermline Registrum*, pp. 299–301, no. 417. Chronicle accounts, usually terse, are contained in, for example: A. Myln, *Vitae Dunkeldensis Ecclesiae Episcoporum* (Bannatyne Club, 1831), pp. 16ff.; *Hectoris Boetii Murthlacensium et Aberdonensium Episcoporum Vitae* (New Spalding Club, 1894), pp. 24, 34–7 and 97–8; *Ferrerii Historia Abbatum de Kynlos* (Bannatyne Club, 1839), pp. 28, 30–32 and 74; and 'Ane schort memoriale of the Scottis corniklis for addicoune' in *Asloan Manuscript* I, pp. 228–9. Many of the known royal licences granting permission to strengthen a tower or fortalice have been collected and discussed by W. Mackay Mackenzie, *The Mediaeval Castle in Scotland* (London, 1927), pp. 215–29.

3 *ER* III–XI; *TA* I.

4 J. S. Richardson, *The Medieval Stone Carver in Scotland* (Edinburgh, 1964), pp. 38 and 52–6.

In view of these problems it is perhaps not surprising that the dating and precise significance of much of the secular architecture of this period has in the past excited debate among architectural historians. It has been suggested, for instance, that the hundred and forty years after 1400 were characterized by the emergence in increasing numbers of courtyard castles of quadrangular plan-form, which by degrees appear more domestic in purpose and generally of a more regular lay-out.[5] Particular attention was paid by a later writer to the feature of the hall within this type of courtyard castle, to which he applied the term *palatium*.[6] On the other hand, a paramilitary explanation has been put forward for a keep-gatehouse type of enclosure-castle which, dating mainly from the fourteenth century in England and Scotland, has been regarded as a specialized product of a martial and anarchical society based upon a system of so-called 'bastard feudalism'.[7] More recently, however, the numerical superiority of fifteenth-century tower-houses over surviving examples of any other kind of contemporary secular building has been re-emphasized.[8] There can, in fact, be little doubt that the stone-built tower, whether surviving as the principal element of a small enclosure or barmkin, which in many cases has disappeared, or whether forming part of a larger courtyard lay-out, is the most ubiquitous type of surviving secular building of fifteenth-century date. But, except in terms of original architectural design, the distinction between an enclosure-castle and developed tower-house in this period becomes exceedingly blurred, especially when one considers the ways in which castles of earlier date were adapted for use in the changing conditions of the fifteenth century. Moreover, building types classified on purely architectural grounds are not necessarily exclusive of each other in a wider social context. Seen not merely as architectural types but as the residences of the crown, the nobility and the greater lairds, the buildings may thus reflect some of the social, political and tenurial complexities of contemporary society. In order to detect any changes in this society, therefore, it is necessary to group together all types of secular architecture and to examine briefly some of the changes in their planning, that is, in the disposition and number of apartments and, where appropriate, in the overall lay-out of buildings; in their defensive equipment; in the features indicative of a concern for domestic comfort and amenity; and in the building materials used.

5 *Cast. and Dom. Arch.* I, pp. 222–6; III, pp. 161–2.

6 Mackenzie, *Mediaeval Castle*, pp. 137ff.; and see also *The Stones of Scotland*, ed. G. Scott-Moncrieff (London, 1938), pp. 50–76.

7 W. Douglas Simpson, '"Bastard Feudalism" and the Later Castles', *Antiquaries Journal* XXVI (1946), pp. 145–71.

8 S. H. Cruden, *The Scottish Castle* (Edinburgh, 1960), pp. 127–43.

A late fourteenth- or fifteenth-century tower-house of simple oblong plan-form[9] usually consists of a series of main apartments which are arranged vertically, one above the other, rising to a height of at least three or four principal storeys. The ground floor, which is often vaulted, is normally set aside as cellarage, and may have independent access from outside, the only means of internal communication with the floor above being a hatch in the vaulted ceiling. The first floor, which is sometimes provided with its own external entrance doorway, usually served as the principal domestic and public reception room – the laird's hall – and several features attest its relatively grand purpose. From the hall mural stairs give access to the upper chambers which are frequently subdivided and were probably designed as the laird's master bedroom, or solar, guest rooms and other private bedrooms. In addition to mural garderobes and, in a number of cases, purpose-built pit-prisons, sizable chambers which probably served as bedrooms or retiring rooms are often contrived within the thickness of substantial external walls; but because of the gradual reduction in wall thicknesses towards the end of this period the practice of intramural construction was increasingly confined to small chambers and passages. Additional space could also be provided within the main structural shell of the tower by entresols and galleries, usually introduced beneath the stone vaulted ceilings of the lower floors. Considerable domestic advantages could also be gained by the erection of a wing or turret either as an integral part of an original design or as an addition to an existing tower.[10] Stair-turrets of modest projection are characteristic of a number of late fifteenth-century tower-houses, and usually contain the principal stair at the lower floor levels with small chambers above (plates 1 and 2). Larger wings, or 'jambs', could provide not only increased accommodation but also more convenient service facilities by the positioning of a kitchen within the wing usually at first-floor level adjacent to the service end of the hall in the main block. Moreover, the kitchen fireplace flue was often of a size and shape sufficient to provide heating for many of the upper chambers without the need for separate fireplaces. Examples of what might be termed 'kitchen-wings' dating from this period are by no means rare, but whether it was housed in a projecting wing, contained in the entresol of a ground-floor vault, or even built within the screens area of a hall, the kitchen, sometimes in the guise of a mere cooking-stance, appears with increasing frequency from the late four-

9 See the list in *PSAS* LVII (1922–3), p. 92.

10 For towers of L-plan, U-plan (Borthwick Castle) and those such as Crookston Castle, Renfrewshire, and Hermitage Castle, Roxburghshire, which incorporate angle-towers, see *Cast. and Dom. Arch.* I, pp. 314–58 and 523–37; III, pp. 138–55 and 256–92.

teenth century onwards as a more closely integrated feature in the domestic lay-out of Scottish castles and towers.[11] In many cases, however, cooking must still have been done on the hall fireplace or in a temporary outbuilding, but where special provision for cooking and baking is still to be seen, the size and position of the kitchen probably reflect quite accurately the domestic priorities and the scale of the catering needs of the household.

The service facilities and the precise amount of accommodation afforded by these types of tower-house cannot be calculated exactly. There are, however, noticeable variations in size and sophistication that provide some indication of the domestic and public needs of their owners, families, servants and guests. Some social significance may also attach to the fact that proportionately fewer of the towers of small or intermediate size appear to date from the period before about 1450. Moreover, it is unlikely that few towers, however large or small, served as completely self-contained domestic units, and ancillary buildings where they still survive often provide some measure of the changing needs of the owner. In this respect, particular reference should be made to the presence of a separate hall block either as a developed adjunct of a tower-house (figure 1) or within a courtyard castle of earlier date.

The hall or *aula* was by no means a new feature in castle planning in the British Isles and its occurrence in the Scottish enclosure-castle from at least the thirteenth century has been demonstrated either through surface remains, archaeological excavations or documentary sources.[12] As with the kitchen, however, a series of more complete and generally stone-built specimens of this kind of structure appear to date from the later fourteenth century onwards. An impressive number of late medieval great halls that survive wholly or in part are ascribable to the period between the erection of the quasi-royal castle of Doune (Perthshire) (plate 3) and James IV's magnificent great hall of *c*. 1500 in Stirling Castle. They include the great hall at the royal palace of Linlithgow (West Lothian) and other halls of lesser scale, such as those within the castles of Balgonie (Fife) (plate 4), Balvenie (Banffshire), Bothwell (Lanarkshire), Crichton (Midlothian), Darnaway (Moray),

---

11 Mackenzie, *Mediaeval Castle*, pp. 122–4. Examples of kitchen-wings added during this period can be seen at Clackmannan Tower, Dundas Castle (West Lothian) and Hermitage Castle.

12 J. G. Dunbar, *The Historic Architecture of Scotland* (London, 1966), p. 35. Examples chosen at random include the remains of a stone-built late thirteenth-century hall at Kildrummy Castle, Aberdeenshire; W. Douglas Simpson, 'A New Survey of Kildrummy Castle', *PSAS* LXII (1927–8), pp. 59–61; and halls apparently of timber-framed construction which were formerly associated with, among others, the castles of Tarbert, Kintyre, Argyll and Roxburgh; *ER* I, pp. 52–8; see also W. R. Cunningham, 'A Survey of Roxburgh Castle', *SHR* xx (1923), pp. 81–3.

Dean (Ayrshire), Dirleton (East Lothian) and Innis Chonnell (Argyll). A number of the known or probable builders of these halls, like many of the builders of the larger fifteenth-century towers, were, if not actually royal officials, often firm political supporters of the crown, men like Sir Duncan Campbell of Lochawe and Sir Robert Lundy of Balgonie. Equally striking, however, is the physical evidence which these halls provide for the political importance and pretension of men

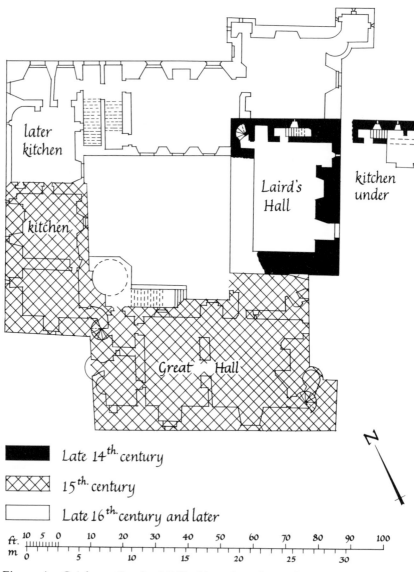

Figure 1   Crichton Castle, Midlothian: first-floor plan.

such as Robert, first Lord Boyd, Sir William Crichton and the earls of Douglas.

Architecturally, the halls were usually of an elongated rectangular plan and contained a spacious apartment which was generally, but by no means invariably, set at first-floor level above vaulted cellarage. The internal lay-out of screens, dais and sometimes galleries, followed the usual medieval domestic plan. The erection of a hall of this kind, however, required provision of service facilities on a scale quite beyond the capacity of those designed for a tower or other smaller unit, hence the need to construct or adapt chambers for use as butteries, pantries, bakehouses and kitchens. Practical considerations demanded that these ancillary chambers should have convenient access to the service end of the hall, but the position of the hall in relation to other buildings of the castle follows no precise pattern, its situation within structures of earlier date being to some extent predetermined by the existing lay-out. The hall could intercommunicate with, simply adjoin, or even be physically detached from the principal tower or *donjon*. Whatever their relative positions, however, it would seem reasonable to suppose that the arrangement would gradually create a separation of function between the domestic privacy of the solar tower and the use of the hall for ceremonies and other public affairs.

Few, if any, of the changes in the planning of castles and towers described above can be related directly to the needs of defence, and it is questionable to what degree the predilection for such features as thick walls, stone vaults and narrow newel stairs can be attributed to those needs rather than simply to current ideas of building practice. That is not to deny, however, that these buildings, often serving as centres of royal, noble or ecclesiastical authority, were in essence defensible residences, and one of the reasons for the popularity of the tower-house in Scotland, as well as in parts of Ireland and northern England, was its adaptability both for domestic use and as a place of strength. It offered protection equally against hostile human incursions, animal intruders and even, one might be tempted to think, the climate. The erection of buildings on naturally defensible and often isolated sites, and the rebuilding or continued occupation of sites with a previous history of fortification, certainly argues a demand for defensive strongholds. The choice of a site might, however, be tempered by other, more pacific considerations, such as proximity to valuable and fertile estates, and convenient access by sea or land. Whether serving political, administrative or military purposes, there are also indications that the siting or occupation of secular buildings was, in certain areas, positively or tacitly encouraged by the crown, but a concern for defence on anything wider than a local scale only begins to emerge, in architectural terms at least, towards the end of the fifteenth century, the best example perhaps being the strategic disposition of strong-holds such as Inchgarvie, Ravenscraig and Largo on the shores of the Forth estuary.[13]

Apart from demonstrating the crown's direct concern for matters of local and national defence, the few known royal licences granting permission to fortify a tower in this period also provide some indica-tions of contemporary notions of defence. At least two of these licences demonstrate that certain elements of defence, whether sym-bols of prestige or of real martial intent, had become standard in the better-endowed fortifications in the first half of the fifteenth century.[14] Specific mention is made of those features associated with the wall-head of the tower, and with the outer enclosure; and from architectural evidence it is clear that special concern was also naturally shown for the protection of all entrances.

The late fourteenth century or the early years of the fifteenth cen-tury witnessed the introduction of machicolations in Scotland.[15] These slots, through which missiles could be dropped, were formed either by corbelling out a parapet wall-walk or were housed within a special box-like projection usually above an entry. Machicolations of these kinds, however, simply represent a completely stone-built ver-sion of the older form of timber hourd or *bretasche*,[16] and their useful-ness diminished with the advent of artillery defences later in the century. But the tradition of corbelled wall-walks continued, and the corbelling began to provide some scope for decorative stone-carving. Adherence to established practice can also be seen in the nature of the outer defences. The effectiveness of fifteenth-century curtain-walls generally appears to have been dependent still on sheer height rather than thickness, and they are often distinguishable from their thirteenth-century predecessors only by the provision of angle- or drum-towers of bolder projection, stone machicolations, or the occurrence of contemporary windows of domestic character. Special measures continued to be taken for the protection of the entry to the courtyard enclosure, and this period saw the erection of a number of impressive gatehouses.[17] These were provided with the usual draw-bridge and portcullis apparatus, and were sometimes structurally combined with the laird's principal residence immediately above. At

13 Mackenzie, *Mediaeval Castle*, pp. 138–41 and 225–6.

14 *RMS* II, no. 1 (Dundas Castle, 1424) and *The Book of the Thanes of Cawdor* (Spalding Club, 1859), pp. 20–21 (Cawdor Castle, 1454), the former to be erected 'iuxta modum regni Scotie'.

15 Mackenzie, *Mediaeval Castle*, pp. 89–91.

16 *ibid.*, pp. 86–8.

17 At, for example, Dalhousie Castle, Midlothian, and Spynie Palace, Moray.

the entrance to the tower some protection might also be afforded by a double door arrangement incorporating an inner iron gate or yett, and a principal doorway at an upper floor level might have been associated with a retractable timber stair or ladder.

Such relatively passive forms of defence for use with and against arms of traditional kinds do not represent a significant departure from conservative principles of military fortification. Even the increasing use of artillery, especially by royal armies, in the fifteenth century is reflected only to a limited degree in contemporary architectural design.[18] By the end of the century, it is true, gun-loops, which were mainly of the 'inverted keyhole' type and apparently intended for use with breech-loading handguns, had become a recognized feature of many buildings and they could, of course, be improvised from slit windows in older structures. Whether or not gun-loops in the fifteenth-century curtain-wall of Craigmillar Castle, Edinburgh, represent the earliest appearance of this feature in Scotland very much depends upon the authenticity of a 1427 date-stone, which has now disappeared, and upon proof of the contemporaneity of the loops and the wall in which they are built. Similar problems of dating surround the gun-looped curtain-wall of Threave Castle (Kircudbright) where recent archaeological excavations have tended to suggest that the wall may have been in existence prior to the famous siege of 1455. Whatever the dates of the gun-loops at Craigmillar and Threave, Ravenscraig Castle (Fife) (plate 5) is generally regarded as the earliest comprehensive scheme of artillery fortification in Scotland.[19] There may, however, be grounds for questioning the assumption that the greater part of what is seen today is the result of documented building operations carried out on behalf of James II's queen, Mary of Gueldres, after March 1460. Especially in view of the strategic importance of the stronghold at the end of the century, the Lords Sinclair, possessors of the castle from 1470, may in fact have been responsible for far more than the adaptation of the upper part of the central block as a gun platform.

Also by the end of the century, certain domestic features had apparently become more widespread, at least in the eyes of one observer. In 1498 Pedro de Ayala, the Spanish ambassador to the court of James IV, commented on the fact that 'the houses [of Scotland] are good, all built of hewn stone and provided with excellent doors, glass windows, and

18 Early artillery fortifications in Scotland are discussed by Cruden, *Scottish Castle*, pp.198 ff., especially pp. 212–18, and by Dunbar, *Historic Architecture*, pp. 56–7. See also A. M. T. Maxwell-Irving, 'Early Firearms and their Influence on the Military and Domestic Architecture of the Borders', *PSAS* ciii (1970–71), pp. 192–223. Contemporary developments in England are described by B. H. St J. O'Neil, *Castles and Cannon* (London, 1960), pp. 22–40.

19 W. Douglas Simpson, *Ravenscraig Castle* (Aberdeen, 1938), pp. 7–8 and 29–30.

a great number of chimneys.'[20] Ayala's observations are probably biased and restricted to the dwellings of proprietors of substantial means. Nevertheless, the remarks of a foreign visitor have some relevance in distinguishing aspects of what might be termed the Scottishness of contemporary better-class Scottish building – the practice of glazing windows; the more widespread provision of chimneyed fireplaces in a climate considerably different from that of Spain; and the use of stone for building purposes.

One of the earliest documentary references for the use of glass in place of hangings or shutters for the windows of a secular building in Scotland appears in a record of 1329 relating to work in the erstwhile King's Chamber at Cardross.[21] Glass, although still regarded as a precious and perhaps portable luxury, is, however, more frequently mentioned in the royal building accounts of the second quarter of the fifteenth century,[22] and especially from the last decades of the century. It is to this latter period that much of the surviving architectural evidence of glazing can probably be ascribed. Incised grooves, designed to receive iron or lead glazing frames, are usually confined to the upper halves of the window openings, the lower halves having had wooden shutters. Glazed windows, even if half shuttered, however, probably rendered the already popular use of window bench seats more consistently pleasant and convenient.

Advances in domestic amenity and comfort, and to some extent in constructional ingenuity, can also be measured by the more generous provision of fireplaces with stone-built flues which served both public and private chambers alike. Borthwick Castle (Midlothian), to take an admirable but perhaps rather exceptional example, was heated by about a dozen fireplaces, whose flues are grouped into six chimney-stacks, and two upper chambers gained sufficient warmth from the sloping hood of the cavernous kitchen fireplace to obviate the need for separate fireplaces. Sloping chimney-hoods of stone carried on boldly projecting jambs and lintels are characteristic of the fireplaces in this and other structures of the first half of the fifteenth century, but subsequent trends in fireplace design are marked by the gradual disappearance of the hood and by the closer integration of jambs and lintel with the vertical plane of the wall or chimney-breast.[23] Of whatever design, the importance of the hall fireplace (and sometimes of that serving the principal chamber) was reflected in its great size and in the

20 P. Hume Brown, *Early Travellers in Scotland* (Edinburgh, 1891), p. 47.

21 *ER* I, p. 125. References to the early use of glass in secular building operations are noted in *TA* I, pp. ccii–iii.

22 *ER* IV, pp. 533, 619 and 621; V, p. 274. Cf. RCAHMS, *Inventory of Stirlingshire* (1963) I, p. 182.

23 Mackenzie, *Mediaeval Castle*, pp. 117–19.

decorative carved treatment of its stone surround, or its associated cornice or proto-mantel, and of the nearby mural buffet or dresser which was probably designed for the display of plate. The development of mural fireplaces is by no means a constant theme of this period, however, for the absence of surviving flues and chimneys in a number of halls may suggest a preference for open hearths or braziers in buildings of this type. Original mural fireplaces are also absent from the remains of at least three major fifteenth-century castles of the Western Isles, one of which, Moy Castle, Lochbuie, on the island of Mull, shares with Balgonie Castle in Fife the distinction of possessing what appear to be vents in the walls for the dispersal of smoke from an open hearth.[24]

The comment of the Spanish ambassador regarding the use of 'hewn stone' acquires greater architectural and social significance in view of the fact that all surviving standing buildings of fifteenth-century date in Scotland are of stone-and-lime construction. The durability of these materials as compared with clay or turf partly accounts for their survival, but there is a noticeable lack of brick-built or timber-framed structures. Scraps of evidence from historical sources and archaeological excavation suggest that buildings of timber construction which were associated with enclosure-castles, or on a lesser social scale with moated homesteads or manors, remained in use well into this period, and special mention of stone-built structures within burghs would indicate that urban domestic residences of timber represented the accepted norm in at least the first half of the fifteenth century.[25] The available evidence for contemporary rural houses of peasants and tenant farmers permits few generalizations, but timber, probably in association with other less permanent materials, may have been much utilized in the construction of walls and roofs in many parts of Scotland.[26]

The building practices of the lower ranks of society may not necessarily have been related simply to the convenient availability of materials for, as John Major trenchantly observed of the condition of rural

24 Kisimul Castle, Barra, Inverness-shire, Breachacha Castle, Coll, and Moy Castle, Lochbuie, Argyll. The results of the most recent investigations at Breachacha are contained in D. J. Turner and J. G. Dunbar, 'Breachacha Castle, Coll: Excavations and Field Survey, 1965–8', *PSAS* cii (1969–70), pp. 155–87. Cf. H. G. Leask, *Irish Castles* (Dundalk, 1964), p. 93.

25 For example, *Edinburgh St Giles Registrum*, p. 57, no. 42; and for evidence from an earlier period, *Early Records of the Burgh of Aberdeen, 1317, 1398–1407*, edited by W. C. Dickinson (SHS, 1957), pp. 14 and lix–lx, n. For castle buildings of timber, see above, note 12; and for moated homesteads, RCAHMS, *Inventory of Roxburghshire* (1956) i, pp. 47–8.

26 J. G. Dunbar, 'The Peasant-House' (The Study of Deserted Mediaeval Settlements in Scotland (to 1968)) in *Deserted Mediaeval Villages*, edited by M. W. Beresford and J. G. Hurst (London, 1971), pp. 241–4; Brown, *Early Travellers*, pp. 12 and 26–7.

tenants in 1521, 'they have no permanent holdings, but hired only, or in lease for four or five years, at the pleasure of the lord of the soil; therefore do they not dare to build good homes, though stone abound.'[27] Conversely, a correlation has been noted between the construction of small stone-built tower-houses and the more wide-spread practice of feuing of crown lands in the later fifteenth century.[28] The degree of security enjoyed by a tenant or landholder, whether based on leases, burgage tenure or heritable feu-ferme tenure, may thus have had a profound effect on secular building practice in terms not only of house types but also of building materials. When, for economic and tenurial reasons, a fifteenth-century laird was in a position to erect a more permanent dwelling for himself, his choice would presumably be conditioned by several factors – contemporary fashions, considerations of finance , and the need to employ craftsmen who had had some experience in the winning and working of readily available materials.

Contemporary masonry techniques, although differing in some respects from those of an earlier period, cannot be regarded as debased, and at its best fifteenth-century coursed rubble or ashlar walling is outstanding, exhibiting considerable skill and facility on the part of the mason-craftsmen. Moreover, some constructional techniques, although not necessarily proof of a lack of timber for floors and roofs, at least demonstrate a preference for the use of stone for building purposes. A type of all-stone roof structure, for example, which usually consists of a pointed barrel-vault covered with overlapping slabs, made its first recorded appearance at the very end of the fourteenth century and came into fairly widespread usage during the following century.[29] The local origins of rubble and freestone for some major fifteenth-century building operations are either known or can be surmised, and in these cases regional variations in the geology of Scottish building stone become rather more apparent.[30] Little information is yet available on the general organization of the quarrying and building industries in this period, and particularly concerning the ways in which masons met the demands placed upon them in various parts of the country.[31] Nevertheless, there are slight indica-

27 John Major, *A History of Greater Britain* (SHS, 1892), pp. 30–31.

28 RCAHMS, *Inventory of Peeblesshire* (1967) I, p. 42.

29 *Eccles. Arch.* II, pp. 333–4. Cf. I. C. Hannah, 'A Half-Scottish Building on English Soil. Bolton Church, Cumberland', *Transactions of the Scottish Ecclesiological Society* X, part 1 (1930–31), pp. 33–7.

30 Myln, *Vitae*, p. 20, for the source of some of the building stone used in the rebuilding of the nave of Dunkeld Cathedral. It is interesting to note that granite was extensively used in the fifteenth-century rebuilding of St Machar's Cathedral, Old Aberdeen.

31 *Cast. and Dom. Arch.* v, pp. 525–45; D. Knoop and G. P. Jones, *The Scottish Mason*

tions of a gradual emergence of local schools of stone-building throughout most of Scotland, extending by degrees to a widening circle of patrons.

However, numerous timber buildings were in the towns in the earlier part of this period, the few urban dwellings of the late fifteenth or early sixteenth century of which some architectural record has been made, although probably atypical and in some cases much rebuilt, appear to have been mainly of stone-and-lime construction.[32] Undoubtedly the most impressive of these and, at the time of its demolition in the late nineteenth century, probably also the least altered, was the so-called 'Mint' or town-house of the Knights Hospitallers in Linlithgow. The lay-out of this house, which incorporated a two-storeyed hall wing extending along one side of an inner courtyard, can best be appreciated by reference to the accompanying drawing (figure 2).[33] The hall, which was set above vaulted cellars, was open to a braced timber roof structure of some interest, and was provided with a carved stone fireplace of superior quality. Adjoining the southeast end of the hall block there was a self-contained and lofty five-storeyed tower-house, the upper chambers of which were evidently for domestic functions. Unfortunately, little can now be learnt of the original purposes served by the other apartments, especially in the block fronting the street, where there may have been booths (or shops) and additional chambers.[34]

The overall size of certain burghs and the nature of their domestic architecture would no doubt be affected by the need to erect residences for the accommodation of increasing numbers of prosperous burgesses, or of staffs of growing cathedral chapters, or of nobility and officials in centres of more frequent royal presence.[35] Apart from the evidence of a few structures standing above ground,[36] a fairly accurate architectural barometer of changes in the social, economic and politi-

and the Mason Word (Manchester, 1939); and Richardson, *Medieval Stone Carver*, pp. 13–15 and 56–8.

32 *Cast. and Dom. Arch.* I, pp. 508–14; v, pp. 1–4; F. C. Mears, 'Notes on a Mediaeval Burgess's House at Inverkeithing', *PSAS* XLVII (1912–13), pp. 343–8; and R. G. Cant, *The College of St Salvator* (Edinburgh, 1950), pp. 82–3.

33 Based on measured drawings deposited in the archive of the National Monuments Record of Scotland (cf. *Cast. and Dom. Arch.* I, figures 436–42).

34 See *Protocol Book of John Foular 1501–28* (SRS, 1930–53), p. xii and nos. 25 and 64, for early sixteenth-century descriptions of comparable properties in Edinburgh.

35 For example, Edinburgh and Canongate; see *Calendar of Scottish Supplications to Rome 1418–22*, edited by E. R. Lindsay and Annie I. Cameron (SHS, 1934), p. 94. For town houses in general, see also Annie I. Dunlop, *The Life and Times of James Kennedy, Bishop of St Andrews* (Edinburgh, 1950), p. 386 and references cited.

36 Much altered domestic buildings of possible fifteenth-century origin in St Andrews, Fife, and mercat crosses of fifteenth-century date which survive wholly or in part in, for instance, Peebles, Banff and Edinburgh.

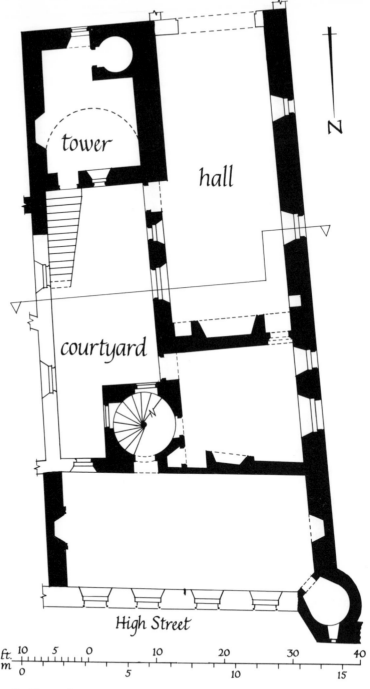

tower

hall

courtyard

N

High Street

ft. 10   5   0   10   20   30   40
m 0   5   10   15

Figure 2   Town house, Linlithgow: 'The Mint'.
            First-floor plan (above)
            Section (opposite)

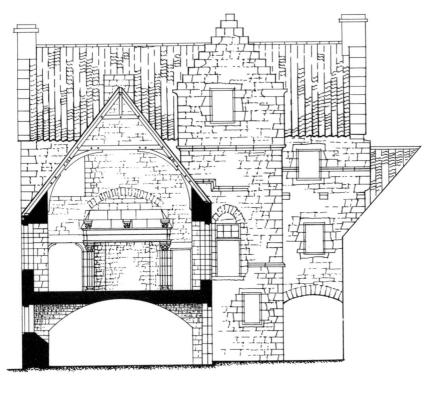

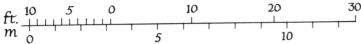

cal fortunes of a fifteenth-century burghal community is generally provided by changes in the character of the local parish church.

The spiritual needs of some burghs could of course be served by the parochial functions of local cathedral or monastic churches. But a group of sizable burgh parish churches bear evidence of having been newly erected or substantially rebuilt and enlarged during the period from the second half of the fourteenth century onwards (plate 6).[37] The funding of building operations in most of these cases appears to have been largely the corporate responsibility of burgh magistrates and community, occasionally with royal or episcopal aid. But before

37 For example, Aberdeen, Dundee, St Vigeans (Angus), Cupar (Fife), St Andrews, Perth, Stirling, Linlithgow, Edinburgh and Haddington (East Lothian). There is also evidence of sizable late medieval churches in other centres such as Dysart and Kilrenny, Fife, and possibly Falkirk, Stirlingshire.

major rebuilding projects of this kind could be undertaken some agreement had to be reached with those monasteries and cathedrals that had, under a system of appropriations, become accustomed to the enjoyment of considerable rights over the majority of parish churches in Scotland. Within the completed church numerous altars and chantries were founded either by trade and craft gilds, wealthy burgesses or members of noble families. The more substantial of these endowments frequently took a permanent architectural form in the shape of lateral, stone-built chapels.

The majority of these burgh churches in Scotland are more than 45 m. in internal length, and the largest attained lengths of over 60 m. They are either of cruciform lay-out with a tower over the crossing, or incorporate a west tower, transeptal chapels and no structural crossing; the principal distinguishing feature of the planning of these churches, however, is the existence of both an aisled nave and an aisled choir. The naves tend to be of a fairly standard five-bay length, capacious enough to accommodate a preaching hall and as many altars as were necessary. Except for occasional clues provided by the survival of piscinae, the marks of a reredos or by heraldic devices carved on piers or roof-bosses, all traces of these altars in the nave-aisles and transepts have generally been swept away. Happily, the shells of a number of the chapels or chantries, which usually project from the side walls, have survived later changes, and nowhere in Scotland do they remain in greater profusion than at the church of St Giles, Edinburgh.[38] Here, the construction of a large aisled church of cruciform plan was probably scarcely completed by 1387 when a contract for the erection of five chapels, the first in a series of substantial additions to the structure, was agreed upon by the laird of Nether Liberton, the provost and community of Edinburgh, and three masons. The more important later foundations include an early fifteenth-century chapel, which adjoins the north nave-aisle and bears the arms of the duke of Albany and earl of Douglas, and the Preston Aisle, a large three-bay chapel which was added after 1455 by the magistrates and community of Edinburgh to commemorate the acquisition of the arm-bone of the patron saint by Sir William Preston of Gourton, who had unconditionally bequeathed it to the 'mother kirke'. The organic growth of the church as a result of these and other fifteenth- and sixteenth-century foundations is shown in schematic

---

38 Lists of altars are contained in, for example, *Cartularium Ecclesiae Sancti Nicholai Aberdonensis* (New Spalding Club, 1888–92) II, pp. lv–vi; D. Peacock, *Perth: its Annals and Archives* (Perth, 1849), pp. 589–96; J. Ferguson, *Ecclesia Antiqua: the history of an Ancient Church (St Michael's, Linlithgow)* (Edinburgh, 1905), pp. 281–328; and *Edinburgh St Giles Registrum*, pp. xciv–v, the foundations of some of the chapels noted in figure 3 in this article being documented in *ibid.*, pp. lxviii–ix, n. 3; and pp. 24–6, 106–7, 199–203 and 203–7.

form in figure 3, and this dramatic expansion can be regarded as physical testimony to the growing wealth and importance of Edinburgh during this period.

Increases in the staff of chaplains and priests required for the service of altars and the performance of other divine offices probably rendered the erection of a larger choir both a matter of practical necessity as well as of prestige. The rebuilding of the east limb, usually with an associated sacristy and a polygonal or square-ended apse, thus appears in most of these cases to have followed, rather than preceded, the reconstruction of the nave from which it would ordinarily be divided by a choir screen. Much importance and pride was attached to the building operations at the east end of the church which, in contrast to those of the nave, are the subject of most direct historical references.[39] The enlargement or extension of the choir often marked a prelude to a request for collegiate status, the ultimate symbol of prestige which, in the case of the burgh church of St Giles, was finally achieved by the magistrates and community of Edinburgh in 1468 after an unsuccessful attempt earlier in the century.

Out of a total of more than forty collegiate churches known to have been in Scotland at the time of the Reformation over twenty were founded between 1380 and 1500.[40] Considering that only three incorporations of secular canons existed in Scotland before 1380, this figure is an impressive reflection of fashionable trend towards the endowment of fairly small, non-monastic foundations of this kind. This figure does not, however, take into account those several churches that were developing a quasi-collegiate organization in this period, and it represents only the successful applications for collegiate status; even an unsuccessful attempt at the establishment of a college was usually preceded by building operations of some kind in order to ensure that the fabric of the church would match up to its proposed functions and enhanced dignity (plate 7).[41] Moreover, the architecture of a parish church or chapel, to which chantry priests or canons were attached but were

39 For example, *Aberdeen Council Register* I, pp. 35–6; *Dunfermline Registrum*, pp. 299–301; and *Charters and other Documents relating to the Royal Burgh of Stirling*, edited by R. Renwick (Glasgow, 1884), no. 37.

40 I. B. Cowan and D. E. Easson, *Medieval Religious Houses in Scotland* (London, 1976), pp. 213–36, distinguishes those churches which preserve physical remains. The most recent review of the architectural evidence is by G. Hay, 'The Architecture of Scottish Collegiate Churches' in *The Scottish Tradition: Essays in Honour of Ronald Gordon Cant*, edited by G. W. S. Barrow (Edinburgh, 1974), pp. 56–70.

41 Much of the surviving architecture of Fowlis Easter parish church, Angus (plate 7), seems to fit more happily with the attempt to erect a college here in the mid-fifteenth century rather than with its appearance as a fully-developed collegiate organization in 1538: Cowan and Easson, *Religious Houses*, p. 221 and references cited; see also M. R. Apted and W. N. Robertson, 'Late Fifteenth-century Church Paintings from Guthrie and Foulis Easter', *PSAS* XCV (1961–2), pp. 262–79.

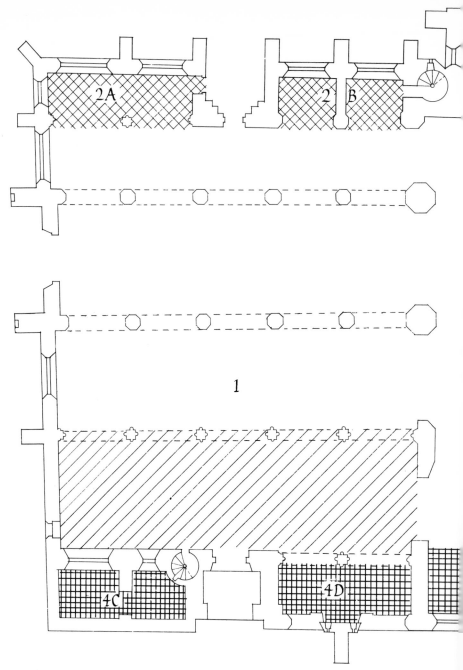

Figure 3   St Giles' Church, Edinburgh: block plan (partly reconstructed)
showing some probable additions to the church in the period
1387–1560:

1	1387	Five chapels
2	*c*.1401–*c*.1420	A Albany Aisle
		B Two chapels

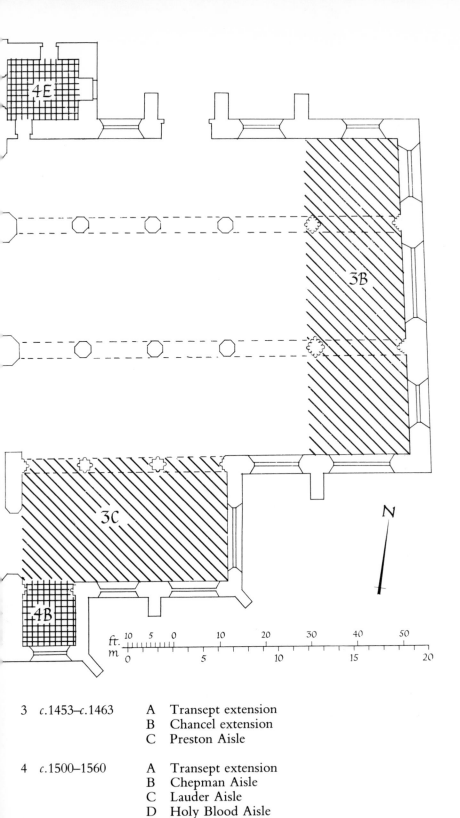

N

| | ft. | 10 | 5 | 0 | 10 | 20 | 30 | 40 | 50 |
| m | 0 | | | 5 | | 10 | | 15 | | 20 |

3   c.1453–c.1463   A   Transept extension
                       B   Chancel extension
                       C   Preston Aisle

4   c.1500–1560   A   Transept extension
                       B   Chepman Aisle
                       C   Lauder Aisle
                       D   Holy Blood Aisle
                       E   Revestry or sacristy

never intended to constitute a governing body, might bear remarkable affinities to contemporary collegiate churches, and this type is perhaps best exemplified by Tullibardine Chapel (Perthshire), which was possibly a pendicle of Muthill parish church. [42]

Until about the middle of the fifteenth century the founders of these churches appear to have been mainly members of the greater nobility and more substantial lairds. In southwest Scotland, for example, the munificent piety of the powerful earls of Douglas and, incidentally, their patronage of mason craftsmen, is reflected in their establishment of colleges in the former Benedictine nunnery of Lincluden, near Dumfries, in the parish church of St Bride, Bothwell (Lanarkshire), and in their subsequent ineffective efforts to raise St Bride's, Douglas (Lanarkshire) to the same rank. [43] King James I made a similarly abortive attempt to erect a college in Linlithgow parish church in 1430, [44] a few years after rebuilding operations had commenced there, but the first collegiate church of successful royal foundation was in fact that of the splendid Trinity College, Edinburgh (plate 8), established by Mary of Gueldres before 1460. It was followed in 1487 by James III's endowment of colleges at Restalrig, Edinburgh, and Tain (Ross and Cromarty), the former still preserving the lower part of a remarkable and possibly unique two-storeyed chapel royal of hexagonal plan. [45] Episcopal foundations are best represented by the academic colleges of St Salvator at St Andrews, which was endowed by James Kennedy, bishop of St Andrews, in 1450 and completed in 1460, and King's College, Aberdeen, founded by William Elphinstone, bishop of Aberdeen, in 1505. [46] The royal and the major episcopal colleges are thus relatively late in date and comparatively few in number; some of them are distinguishable from many of the other collegiate churches in their overall size and superiority of treatment, but remarkably few represent completely new edifices erected on previously unconsecrated sites.

The converted monastery of Lincluden is one of the most patent

42 *HMC, Seventh Report*, appendix, p. 708a, no. 43. Cf. *Eccles. Arch.* III, pp. 330–37.

43 Cowan and Easson, *Religious Houses*, p. 228 and references cited.

44 Cowan, *Medieval Parishes*, p. 133.

45 I. MacIvor, 'The King's Chapel at Restalrig and St Triduana's Aisle: a Hexagonal Two-storied Chapel of the Fifteenth Century', *PSAS* xcvi (1962–3), pp. 247–63.

46 Cant, *College of St Salvator*, pp. 49–53 and 81–105. For architectural and historical descriptions of King's College, Aberdeen, see N. Macpherson, *Notes on the Chapel, Crown and Other Ancient Buildings of King's College, Aberdeen* (Aberdeen, 1890); *William Kelly: a Tribute Offered by the University of Aberdeen*, edited by W. Douglas Simpson (Aberdeen, 1949); and F. C. Eeles, *King's College Chapel, Aberdeen* (Edinburgh, 1956).

47 For example, Trinity College, Edinburgh, which appears to have occupied the site of a former chapel of St Ninian.

examples of a collegiate church which was adapted from an existing structure and rebuilt in more elaborate style; and the conventual buildings of the nunnery continued in use as domestic residences for the staff of the newly instituted college. The majority of the colleges of baronial foundation were founded within parish churches or chapels that were usually rebuilt for the purpose. The erection of an enlarged choir with associated sacristy and transeptal chapels was a matter of priority, but rebuilding operations at a remarkably high proportion of these churches seem to have stopped short of the reconstruction of the nave.[48] Since many of the colleges still needed to retain some provision for the parochial cure of souls, an altar may have been placed in the crossing or transept of a parish church which had been converted into a naveless collegiate church.

The incompleteness of these colleges probably reflects a disinclination on the part of patrons and canons alike to disburse funds on the work of reconstruction beyond what they considered to be the primary functions of the church. The endowments usually made provision for a small number of prebendaries, generally about a dozen or less.[49] Even though they were frequently augmented by numerous chaplains and other officers, the overall staffing requirements of most, especially rural, collegiate churches may have been of a fairly modest order, and their domestic and ecclesiastical buildings are of a correspondingly small scale. But, even in their present, frequently denuded state, the churches retain much evidence of lavish, and no doubt costly, architectural treatment, the exotic sculptural detail of Sir William Sinclair's fantastic chapel at Roslin (Midlothian) being the most conspicuous example. More typical perhaps of the better-quality craftsmanship in these churches is the tomb of Princess Margaret, who died *c.* 1440, daughter of Robert III and wife of Archibald, fourth earl of Douglas, erected in the choir of Lincluden College (plate 9); the tomb surround is decorated with a crocketted and ogival hood-mould, traces of soffit cusping, and heraldic devices – all features of the stone-carver's art in the fifteenth century.[50]

The patronage of most landholders did not extend exclusively towards collegiate churches, but also, to a lesser degree, towards the endowment of a number of houses of friars. Considerably fewer of

48 The foundations west of the crossing of Seton collegiate church, East Lothian, for example, represent the remains of an un-rebuilt nave of a church of earlier date on that site; S. H. Cruden, 'Seton Collegiate Church', *PSAS* lxxxix (1955–6), pp. 417–37, especially pp. 424–5.

49 By contrast, larger numbers of clergy were attached to St Giles, Edinburgh, the college of St Salvator, St Andrews, and King's College, Aberdeen.

50 Richardson, *Medieval Stone Carver*, pp. 35 ff. Cf. the late medieval monumental sculpture of distinctive character produced by different schools of stone carving in the West Highlands and Islands: RCAHMS, *Inventory of Argyll* (1971) I (Kintyre), p. 24.

these houses have survived, however, and the architectural evidence is somewhat random. Of those late medieval friaries which were adapted from existing churches a few traces can still be seen of the conventual buildings which were added to the thirteenth-century pilgrimage church of Cross Kirk at Peebles after it had been formally raised to a house of Trinitarian friars by James III in 1474. But it is not entirely clear how much of the architecture of the present parish church of St Monance (Fife) represents a remodelling of David II's royal chapel following its refounding by James III as a house of Friars Preacher, and there is no confirmation that the claustral buildings for which papal authorization was granted in 1477 were ever built. The evidence from the surviving friary-churches in Elgin (Moray) and South Queensferry (West Lothian), however, is less enigmatic. The restored friary-church of the house of Reformed Franciscans founded in Elgin by John Innes of Innes some time before 1494 is the sole standing reminder of the nine houses of that order established in Scottish burghs from the second half of the fifteenth century,[51] and a house of Carmelite friars, one of a small number of late medieval foundations of that order in Scotland, was erected on a site in South Queensferry, bestowed by James Dundas of Dundas in 1441 (plate 10). A roofed cloister walk appears to have adjoined both these churches, but recent archaeological excavations at South Queensferry failed to reveal any foundations of a claustral lay-out.[52] At Elgin, the unaisled, rectangular plan of the friary-church was apparently divided by a rood-screen and loft into a large nave, or preaching house, and a smaller chancel, or private chapel of the friars. The plan of the unaisled church at South Queensferry, on the other hand, consisted of a lengthy chancel and a relatively short nave which has unfortunately been demolished; the nave and chancel were formerly separated by a low stone cross-wall and a vaulted passage, which constitutes the lowest floor of a three-storeyed tower of domestic character, and was extended on one side to form a transeptal chapel. Although constructed from about the middle of the fifteenth entury in a wholly vernacular idiom and incorporating a lateral chapel, the lay-out of this friary-church otherwise retains some of the features characteristic of the planning of churches of the Carmelite order from their earliest foundations in England in the thirteenth century.[53]

   A subsequent destructive fate similar to that experienced by many

51 Cowan and Easson, *Religious Houses*, pp. 129–33; W. Moir Bryce, *The Scottish Grey Friars* (Edinburgh, 1909) I, pp. 361–5; II, pp. 176–7.

52 J. C. Wallace, typescript report and plan (University of Edinburgh, 1971). For references to the foundation and history of the friary, see Cowan and Easson, *Religious Houses*, pp. 137–8.

53 For example, the friary-church of Hulne Priory, Alnwick, Northumberland.

of the houses of friars has also befallen the only sizable new monastic foundation of this period, the house of Carthusian monks established by James I in Perth in 1429. All the other larger Scottish monasteries were already in existence by 1380, but only a very small proportion do not exhibit some architectural evidence of work undertaken during the course of the late fourteenth and fifteenth centuries.[54] These operations were generally occasioned by the need to carry out repairs to those monasteries which had allegedly suffered depredations at the hands of private or, especially in the Border counties, English armies, and probably more frequently, to those which were decaying either through chance misfortune, poverty, sheer neglect or the effects of bad design. The surviving architectural fabric of some monasteries might suggest that contemporary or near-contemporary statements concerning their ruinous or ravaged condition frequently contain more than a slight element of exaggeration, and that the damage caused by hostile forces was perhaps more often confined to fittings and combustible structural features.

Whatever the cause of damage or decay, the extent to which the fabric of the monastery was made good, altered or extended depended, of course, on the funds available for this purpose. Larger monastic communities of the majority of the orders seem to have been capable of financing the necessary rebuilding operations, at least in the earlier part of the period; this is evidenced by the remains of late medieval work in most of the Scottish houses of the regular canons of the Augustinian order, both Cluniac foundations of Paisley (Renfrewshire) and Crossraguel (Ayrshire) and several of the Cistercian monasteries, especially Melrose Abbey in Roxburghshire. A comparative lack of surviving fifteenth-century evidence from the wealthy monasteries of Dunfermline (Fife) and Kelso (Roxburghshire) does not necessarily bespeak any lack of activity, but building operations at the larger Benedictine and Tironensian foundations during this period are best represented by some portions of the abbeys of Iona (Argyll) and Arbroath (Angus) respectively. Notwithstanding the fortunate position in which most monasteries found themselves as a result of earlier endowments and appropriations, there are indications that some of the more substantial works of rebuilding were not undertaken without a degree of aid or favour, mainly from royal and episcopal sources, or other wealthy patrons.[55] The special royal esteem and benevolence

54 See also the documentary evidence for those monasteries such as Coupar Angus, Perthshire, and Kinloss, Moray, both Cistercian, where the surviving physical remains are slight: *Coupar Angus Rental* I, pp. 304–10; Ferrerius, *Historia*, pp. 28, 30–32 and 74.

55 J. C. Lees, *The Abbey of Paisley* (Paisley, 1878), pp. 110–45; *Registrum Monasterii de Passelet* (Maitland Club, 1832), pp. 257–8; *Charters of the Abbey of Crossraguel* (Ayr-Galloway Collections, 1886) I, pp. 37–40, no. 22, and pp. xxxii–iii and 45–6.

traditionally reserved for Melrose Abbey (plate 11) was supplemented by generous acts of contrition on the part of Richard II, king of England, and no doubt materially assisted in the reconstruction of the abbey-church along more ambitiously conceived and magnificently executed lines than any other church building programme of the later middle ages in Scotland.

The work of reconstruction at Melrose, which was probably begun soon after 1385, failed to reach completion because of the impoverishment of the community by the first decade of the sixteenth century. Although incomplete, subsequently modified and now in ruins, the rebuilt abbey-church with its richly carved detail, its vaulting and flying buttresses, and its window tracery wrought in both Decorated and Perpendicular Gothic styles, is of quite exceptional interest to the architectural historian and of a conscious splendour far removed from the austere strictures which governed the designs of the earliest Cistercian foundations. The plan of the rebuilt church also represents a considerable enlargement of its twelfth-century predecessor, especially in the areas of the presbytery and aisled transepts; and a large choir, which was partly contained within three screened bays of the nave, was probably capable of accommodating an increased number of choir monks. A significant departure from the earlier Cistercian lay-out was the addition of a chapel-aisle on the south side of the nave, but of the ten chapels envisaged only five were apparently completed.[56] Some part of the ritual nave of the enlarged church, contrary to earlier Cistercian (and Premonstratensian) practice, may also have been set aside for an altar for parochial purposes, as well as possibly serving as a choir for the *fratres conversi*, or lay brothers. There is insufficient evidence, however, to determine the precise extent of the structural nave when work came to a halt in the early years of the sixteenth century. Whatever measures were taken for its parochial responsibilities, it seems that the monastery's possession of a notable collection of relics attracted an increasing number of pilgrims and, unlike earlier, more isolationist attitudes, the lucrative effects of this traffic were recognized and encouraged.

No other monastic church was so thoroughly altered in character and lay-out as that of Melrose, and its architecture therefore illustrates more clearly than most the changing needs of a monastic community and the demands placed upon that community by lay society in general. Elsewhere, rebuilding operations, although executed in contemporary architectural styles, tended to adhere more closely to existing lay-outs. Where radical alterations occurred, they usually reflected the use of the chancel, and often took the shape of an eastward

56 Cf. F. Bond, *An Introduction to English Church Architecture* (London, 1913) I, pp. 158–63.

extension of the presbytery, the addition of a choir-aisle or lady chapel, and sometimes the erection or rebuilding of a sacristy.[57] Those claustral and extra-claustral buildings that bear evidence of reconstruction in this period may also afford some clues as to the priorities of contemporary monastic communities, a point illustrated perhaps by the survival of a small number of vaulted chapter houses which were substantially and, in many cases, elaborately rebuilt in the fifteenth century.[58] Partly because their useful existence in the post-Reformation period was often more assured than many of the other monastic buildings, abbots' and priors' domestic lodgings and contemporary gatehouses survive either wholly or in part in even greater numbers, and perhaps most impressively of all at the abbey of Arbroath.[59] By this period abbots and priors had in general come to be housed in a building which was detached from the common dorter. Like its purely secular equivalents in town and country, it appears to have been sufficiently well appointed with fireplaces and other amenities to serve as a comfortable and relatively secure domestic residence that was also capable of providing accommodation for the guests of the monastery.

As in the case of the monasteries, the cathedrals and those churches which were to become the centres of Scottish dioceses and archbishoprics created during the course of the fifteenth century were already in being or at least nearing completion by the end of the fourteenth century. Such building works as were carried out in the fifteenth century, therefore, again mainly constitute repairs, reconstruction or the remodelling of existing structures, and the surviving remains of most of the cathedral-churches, however exiguous, show signs of having been altered or repaired in some manner. Especially in the case of the foremost cathedral-priory of St Andrews, the architectural evidence supports what is known of the extensive refurbishing of structure and fittings executed over a period of about sixty years following a serious fire in the nave in 1378. The burning of Elgin Cathedral by Alexander Stewart, 'Wolf of Badenoch', in 1390 evoked loud complaints from the bishop of Moray, and payments for its repair were aided by royal annuities and the revenues of the vacant see in the early fifteenth century; but the damage to the actual structure of the church, while no doubt fairly serious, may not have been quite so

57 For example, at the abbeys of Crossraguel, Ayrshire, and Inchcolm, Fife (choir and apse); Iona, Argyll (choir-aisle); and Arbroath, Angus (sacristy).

58 For example, at the abbeys of Balmerino, Fife, Crossraguel, Glenluce, Wigtownshire, and Pluscarden Priory, Moray.

59 For example, at the abbeys of Arbroath and Crossraguel (domestic buildings and gatehouse); Inchcolm (domestic buildings); and Pittenweem Priory, Fife (gatehouse).

catastrophic as has been assumed.[60] Despite later calamities such as the fall of the central tower, much thirteenth-century architecture still survives, and it is improbable that all portions of fifteenth-century work can be directly attributed to the fire of 1390; the reconstruction of the chapter house, for example, is datable on the evidence of heraldic inscriptions to the second half of the fifteenth century. Apart from repairs to fire-damaged structures, rebuilding operations may also have been motivated at Elgin and elsewhere by reason of prosperity and prestige, often corresponding with increases in the size and responsibilities of the cathedral chapters. At the cathedral-church of St Machar, Old Aberdeen, for instance, the increase in the number of canons from thirteen in about the middle of the thirteenth century to twenty-eight by the beginning of the sixteenth was matched by a reconstruction of the church along enlarged lines from the second half of the fourteenth century onwards. And at Glasgow, although the principal architectural components were more or less completed by about 1400 when the number of prebendaries stood at twenty-three, further increases in staff probably led to the erection of manses and the reconstruction of the chapter house.[61]

The importance of the cathedral chapter house in this period is attested by the size and grandeur of the magnificently reconstructed polygonal edifice at Elgin; by the two-storeyed building at Glasgow whose upper stage was also utilized as a congregation-house for the university upon its foundation in 1451; and, to a lesser degree, by the two-storeyed structure at Dunkeld which was either wholly rebuilt or simply heightened in the fifteenth century. Although much attention was devoted to the problems of erecting crossing-towers and steeples, the only serious attempt at a thorough-going reconstruction or enlargement of the chancel of a cathedral-church appears to have been that made by Bishop Elphinstone at Old Aberdeen towards the close of this period. The choir ceremonial and seating at most Scottish cathedrals and colleges of secular canons appear to have continued to follow the Use of Sarum or its English variants,[62] but only a few cathedrals preserve any architectural evidence for the arrangements of

60 *Moray Registrum*, pp. 204–5; *ER* III, pp. 276, 316, 348, 376, 403 and 430 (1391–7); IV, pp. 68–9 and 173.

61 *Registrum Episcopatus Aberdonensis* (Spalding and Maitland Clubs, 1845) II, pp. 39–40 and 254–5; Boece, *Vitae*, p. 24; *Registrum Episcopatus Glasguensis* (Bannatyne and Maitland Clubs, 1843) I, pp. 298–300; II, pp. 340–41. Much of the reconstruction at Glasgow may also have constituted repairs to fire-damaged portions of the building: J. Durkan, 'The Great Fire at Glasgow Cathedral', *Innes Review* XXVI (1975), pp. 89–92.

62 The significance of the Aberdeen Breviary of 1509–10 in this connection is discussed by Eeles, *King's College Chapel*, pp. 120–33, and D. McRoberts, 'The Scottish Church and Nationalism in the Fifteenth Century', *Innes Review* XIX (1968), pp. 7 ff.

the ritual choir as it may have existed in the fifteenth century.[63] At Glasgow, some time after the completion of the nave, the lower end of the canons' choir was demarcated by a stone *pulpitum* which still stands immediately east of the crossing. The high altar may originally have occupied a position in the third bay of the chancel, and to the east of the high altar probably stood the feretory containing the relics of St Kentigern. A petition of 1420 requesting the translation of these relics may reflect disruption caused by an eastwards shift of the high altar, perhaps due to the removal of the ritual choir entirely into the east limb of the church. An upper floor of an extended transeptal aisle which was begun before 1508 by Robert Blackadder, the first archbishop of Glasgow, may have been intended as the ultimate repository of this important shrine, but the aisle was never completed above the level of a vaulted undercroft.[64]

The arrangements of the choir and nave of Glasgow Cathedral can in some measure be inferred from references to altar dedications, a number of which appear on record from about the second quarter of the fifteenth century.[65] A concern for the provision of a parochial or semi-parochial nave furnished with altars for the laity is also evinced by the major works of reconstruction carried out at the cathedrals of Dunkeld and Old Aberdeen.[66] As rebuilt in the fifteenth century, the naves of each of these churches, although differing in overall sizes and in their use of local building materials, were laid out on similar seven-bay aisled plans. The larger nave of St Machar's and its associated west towers were completed by about the middle of the fifteenth century (plate 12), and appear to represent a continuation of a scheme for an enlarged church of cruciform plan conceived in the second half of the fourteenth century. The reconstruction of the nave of Dunkeld Cathedral, which was probably begun after about 1406, may have followed the lines of an existing lay-out with the addition of a lofty west tower, but these substantial works of improvement in the nave were not accompanied by any changes in the planning of the chancel to which the chapter house was attached. In the case of Dunkeld several altar dedications are known and the probable sites of chapels in the nave-aisles can be located; further evidence of fifteenth-

63 See plans of choir arrangements in *Dunkeld Rentale*, p. xli, and *Epistolare in Usum Ecclesiae Cathedralis Aberdonensis*, edited by B. McEwen (Edinburgh, 1924), p. xx.

64 McRoberts, 'The Scottish Church and Nationalism', pp. 9–10. For a probable source of the disruption see Durkan, 'The Great Fire at Glasgow Cathedral', pp. 89–92.

65 List of altars in *The Book of Glasgow Cathedral*, edited by G. Eyre-Todd (Glasgow, 1898), pp. 303–23, revised by J. Durkan, 'Notes on Glasgow Cathedral', *Innes Review* XXI (1970), pp. 51–69.

66 Myln, *Vitae*, p. 20, and see also *Dunkeld Rentale*, pp. xxxiii–xl; Boece, *Vitae*, pp. 34–7.

century chapels of this kind within a cathedral of secular canons can also be found in the outer south nave-aisle of Elgin Cathedral.

Although the physical condition of the small cathedral-church of Lismore (Argyll) may not have been quite so parlous as a historical record of 1512 would suggest,[67] its architecture, like that of some of the smaller or more isolated monasteries, might at least indicate that it did not develop to the same extent as the larger and more prosperous churches in the fifteenth century. The same may be substantially true of a fairly considerable number of appropriated parish churches and chapels, which either did not possess special value to compensate for their use as mensal or prebendal churches or were not fortunate enough to enjoy the initiative and patronage of prosperous burgesses and influential lairds in attaining collegiate or quasi-collegiate status. Of the rest, some developed in a modest way by the addition of a stone-built chapel or sacristy, and a very small number of pendicles were enlarged as a result of promotion to parochial status.[68] Equally few achieved growth in other ways; a considerable and well-endowed pilgrimage traffic, for example, largely accounts for the modestly spectacular growth of the church of Whitekirk (East Lothian) in this period. The number of small rural parish churches and chapels that were newly erected in this period is more difficult to calculate. Especially in the Highlands and Islands a few either first come on record in the fifteenth century or can be tentatively ascribed to the later middle ages. But in many cases their architectural remains are not closely datable and are sometimes scarcely distinguishable from those which are known to be of an earlier period.[69] The structural fabrics of the majority of parish churches and chapels appear at best to have been kept in no more than a state of repair, and their arrested development contrasts with the growth of many of their rural counterparts in late medieval England.

Several aspects of fifteenth-century Scottish architecture do indeed compare unfavourably with the contemporary, and perhaps rather

67 In a letter by James IV to Julius II, *The Letters of James the Fourth, 1505–1513* (SHS, 1953), pp. 245–6.

68 Lateral chapels at, for example, Killean, Argyll; Edrom, Berwickshire; Arbuthnott, Kincardineshire; Borthwick, Midlothian; Tullibardine, Perthshire; and the Old Parish Church, Airth, Stirlingshire. Cf. architecture of the burial-aisles of the post-Reformation period, in G. Hay, *The Architecture of Scottish Post-Reformation Churches, 1560–1843* (Oxford, 1957), pp. 29–31. The architectural evidence for the few chapels that achieved parochial status is not altogether conclusive. During the course of the fifteenth century an aisled nave may have been erected at the chapel of St Nicholas, Dalkeith, Midlothian, which became collegiate in 1406 and a parish church in 1467, but subsequent reconstructions of the nave have removed much of the dating evidence.

69 RCAHMS, *Inventory of Argyll* I (Kintyre), nos. 268 and 301; *Inventory of the Outer Hebrides, Skye and the Small Isles* (1928), pp. xlvii–viii.

remarkable developments that were taking place south of the Border. But aesthetic considerations should not be allowed to distort unduly the general similarities in fundamental social requirements and fashions that are implied in the planning and function of certain building types in both kingdoms. Although Scottish examples frequently tend to be either comparatively limited in numbers, small in scale, or late in date, large burgh churches, collegiate churches and the chantry movement are features of late medieval ecclesiastical architecture in Britain as a whole, and the requirements governing the design of the domestic component units of secular residences in fifteenth-century Scotland are not totally alien from those in many parts of England, especially in the north.[70] Despite similarities of purpose, differences in the general evolution of architectural styles in the two countries during this period make the use of terms which are conventionally applied to English period styles less appropriate to a chronology and understanding of the structural systems employed in the late phases of medieval Scots Gothic.[71] Moreover, an increasing and fashionable preference for the use of stone in the erection of secular buildings of importance distinguishes much of the Scottish architecture of this period from the timber building traditions and the more exclusive use of brick found in many parts of England, even including some of those areas which had an abundance of good building stone.[72]

The use of stone for secular building purposes in fifteenth-century Scotland to a large extent represented a mark of social and tenurial rank. The scale and development of some of these stone-built residences and the results of the patronage exercised by their owners on church architecture may also be interpreted as crude measures of status or ambition within the hierarchy of contemporary society. In these

70 Cf. English tower-houses, especially those erected in Northumberland in the fourteenth century; W. Douglas Simpson, 'Belsay Castle and the Scottish Tower-houses', *Archaeologia Aeliana* 4th series XVII (1940), pp. 75–84, and Margaret Wood, *The English Medieval House* (London, 1965), pp. 166–76; and late fourteenth-century English courtyard castles; P. A. Faulkner, 'Castle Planning in the Fourteenth Century', *Archaeological Journal* CXX (1963), pp. 215–35. Parallels for some features of the construction and planning of fifteenth-century towers, particularly in west and southwest Scotland, can also be found in Ireland where there was a general revival of building activity from about 1440 onwards; Leask, *Irish Castles*, pp. 75–112, and *An Archaeological Survey of County Down* (HMSO, Belfast, 1966), pp. 120–27.

71 I. C. Hannah, 'The Penetration into Scotland of English Late Gothic Forms', *PSAS* LXIV (1929–30), pp. 149–55. Cf. *Eccles. Arch.* I, pp. 50–63; II, pp. 331–4; and III, pp. 1–7, in which the late medieval ecclesiastical architecture of Scotland is classified, not without some difficulty, into periods of Decorated (*c.* 1350–*c.* 1460) and Perpendicular (*c.* 1460–*c.* 1560) styles. Arguably the only convincing examples of each of these styles occur in the abbey-church of Melrose where they appear to be roughly contemporary and to represent the work, or at least the influence, of different schools of craftsmanship and design in northern France and northern England respectively.

72 A. Clifton-Taylor, *The Pattern of English Building* (London, 1972), pp. 213–17 and 301–2.

ways the architectural evidence provides confirmation of the social and political importance of such major baronial families as the earls of Douglas, and some indication of the prominence of royal building works which was reaffirmed during the reigns of James I and II and became almost total by the later decades of the century. However, the continuous occupation and consequent rebuilding in the sixteenth century of a number of royal castles and palaces which came to be so much favoured during the course of the fifteenth century has largely obscured, with one or two exceptions, the magnitude and character of the royal works in the earlier period.[73] Doune Castle, on the other hand, which was probably begun by Robert, duke of Albany, regent of Scotland, and was quickly taken into royal custody in 1425, has remained incomplete and relatively undeveloped. How this undoubtedly large and impressive structure compared at the time of its erection with the neighbouring royal castle of Stirling (which, of course, also came to be occupied by Duke Robert) is now largely a matter of conjecture, but the late fourteenth-century remains at Stirling, fragmentary though they are, suggest the existence at that date of buildings and lay-out of no mean scale. The residences of the crown tended to dictate fashions in secular architecture from about the last quarter of the fifteenth century, and may in some cases have furnished models from which lesser owners consciously copied. Even if, on the basis of current knowledge, the features of some royal edifices erected in the first half of the century appear to be slightly later in date than those of the nobility, they are generally of a much greater size and grandeur, as a comparison between the halls of the Douglas castle at Bothwell and that of the royal palace at Linlithgow will illustrate. Moreover, the influence of the crown on building activity in this period extended far beyond its direct patronage of royal works; numerous secular or ecclesiastical building operations were carried out with its sanction or assistance.

The amount of construction work undertaken by all ranks of landholding society has not been precisely assessed in financial or economic terms, but a few general trends can be deduced from a broad conspectus of the historical and architectural evidence. The total quantity of building activity compares favourably with that which appears to have been undertaken in the half century of warfare immediately preceding 1380, and in several decades following the year 1500. Especially in relation to church architecture, however, the beginnings of a recession in the building industry can be detected in the deceleration in the progress of building works in about the last quarter of the fifteenth century. Royal building operations are a notable exception to this

73 For example, the castles of Edinburgh and Stirling, and the palaces of Falkland (Fife) and Linlithgow.

general trend, and tower-houses in several parts of Scotland, which on the evidence of their architectural features are approximately datable to the turn of the sixteenth century, are sufficiently numerous to suggest that many lairds could still afford at this late date to erect fairly sizable residences for their own use.[74] Cardoness Castle is one of a group of towers of this date in Kirkcudbrightshire, and its impressive bulk shows little sign of having been affected by stringent economic circumstances. Even allowing for vicissitudes in family fortunes and changing historical circumstances, there are also some indications that the builders of these late fifteenth- and early sixteenth-century towers were drawn from a wider social group than those of a century earlier, thus perhaps implying a slightly more widespread distribution of wealth. So far as ecclesiastical architecture is concerned, however, the distribution of funds within a worsening economic situation appears to have been increasingly restricted to the larger houses of regular or secular clergy at the expense of those appropriated churches and chapels which could not depend on wealthy lay patrons for the development or even upkeep of their fabrics. The burgh churches and collegiate churches which successfully overcame this disadvantage in the fifteenth century have a markedly eastern and central geographical distribution, and, especially in areas such as the Lothians, coincide with the distribution pattern of a number of fine examples of contemporary secular architecture. But very few regions of Scotland are without some physical reminder of the wide-ranging economic, social and political changes that took place in this important period of its history.

74 Cf. Cruden, *Scottish Castle*, pp. 1445.

9

The literature of fifteenth-century Scotland
John MacQueen

1

Fifteenth-century Scottish poetry and, to a lesser extent, prose, has a threefold significance. First is the level of artistic achievement, for the period saw the production of a number of masterpieces, and many of the lesser works show at least considerable literary accomplishment. Secondly, the poetry often comments on social and political life in such a way as to interest the historian, and of course the mere fact that so much good poetry was written has in itself a social and intellectual significance; a good deal of evidence survives to show under what circumstances, and to satisfy what audiences, the literature was composed. Thirdly, patterns of literary utterance were established which continued to be developed during the sixteenth century, and were still of some importance even during the Scottish Enlightenment; indeed, one is sometimes tempted to see twentieth-century Scottish letters as still in some measure developing the philosophic and historical traditions established half a millennium earlier.

The first major figures, Andrew of Wyntoun (*c.* 1350–*c.* 1425),[1] prior of St Serf's Isle in Loch Leven, Fife, and James I (1394–1437)[2] illustrate complementary aspects of the developing tradition. One is the historical. The Celtic peoples of the British Isles shared an awareness of their individual remoteness from the European centre, and partly as a counterbalance, tended to elaborate and systematize their own legendary and historical traditions. The most familiar, indeed notorious, example, is the *History of the Kings of Britain* produced about 1136 by Geoffrey of Monmouth, but Geoffrey's work at least partially derives from earlier Welsh compilation of a type which in turn may readily be paralleled in Gaelic and Pictish annalistic and narrative sources. Resistance to Anglo-Norman expansion everywhere encouraged this tendency, especially perhaps in Scotland, when the War of

---

1 *Chron. Wyntoun.*

2 The most recent editions of the *Kingis Quair* are by M. P. McDiarmid (London, 1973), J. Norton-Smith (Oxford, 1971), J. R. Simon (Paris, 1967), and W. M. Mackenzie (London, 1939). All quotations are from McDiarmid's edition.

Independence had been brought to a successful conclusion. The treaty of Northampton, however, did not alter the geographical position of Scotland, or finally remove external pressure, and it is typical of Scottish literature as a whole that Wyntoun's central concern is the history of his own country. If we may judge by the nine surviving manuscripts, his work was more popular than anything other than the Latin *Scotichronicon* of Walter Bower (*c.* 1385–1449), abbot of Inchcolm in the Firth of Forth,[3] which survives in twenty-one manuscripts. Wyntoun was encyclopaedic in the manner developed by late classical antiquity from the fusion of the Graeco-Roman and Hebrew traditions under the influence of the Christian church. His 'cornykkillis callit Originall' follows the pattern established in the fourth century by the *World Chronicle* of Eusebius of Caesarea, and later elaborated by St Jerome, Prosper of Aquitaine, and their successors.[4] Wyntoun aimed to set the history of Scotland firmly within the framework of the Christian world-picture, and by so doing to demonstrate the links joining the Scottish monarchy and people to the overall providential scheme. His first intention was to complete the work in seven books, corresponding to the seven ages of the world; later he found his formal purpose better suited by nine books corresponding to the nine orders of angels. He was not, as has already been indicated, the first to set the Scots in such a frame. His predecessors included the so-called Irish synthetic historians, who compiled the *Lebor Gabàla Érenn* (*Book of Invasions*),[5] the mainly anonymous authors of Pictish and Scottish chronicles,[6] and John of Fordun, whose Latin *Chronica Gentis Scotorum*, later included bodily in *Scotichronicon*, had been completed about 1385.[7] Wyntoun, however, was more concerned than any of his predecessors to show the detailed interconnection of Scottish with world history; this is most obvious in his treatment of earlier ages, but remains to some extent true when he comes to later centuries. In some ways he continued and developed the narrative style of John Barbour (*c.* 1320–95), who had treated Robert I as a figure comparable to the heroes of biblical, classical and romance antiquity.[8] But Wyntoun is not concerned with a single figure or small group, and it is the entire, albeit often legendary, course of Scottish history which he sees as possessing a general importance. Interestingly enough, St Andrews, the first Scottish university, was establishing itself when Wyntoun

3 *Chron. Bower.*

4 J. MacQueen, *Allegory* (London, 1970), pp. 39–40.

5 Edited by R. A. S. Macalister, xxxi–xxxv (Irish Texts Society, 1938–42).

6 *Chronicles of the Picts and Scots*, edited by W. F. Skene (Edinburgh, 1867); A. O. Anderson, *Early Sources of Scottish History* (Edinburgh and London, 1922).

7 *Chron. Fordun.*

8 *The Bruce*, edited by W. W. Skeat (STS, 1894).

was working on his poem; poem and university alike indicate the sense, characteristic of the new century, that Scotland held a place, politically and intellectually, in the general scheme of Christendom. At the very end of the century, Gavin Douglas included Scots in a list of the great poets of the world:

> Of this natioun I knew also anone
> Gret Kennedy and Dunbar yit vndede
> And Quyntyne with ane huttok on his hede.
> *(Palace of Honour,* 922–4)[9]

Wyntoun remains unmentioned, but the realization that Scottish poetry mattered in a European context has developed from Wyntoun's demonstration that Scottish history mattered in a world context.

During the sixteenth century Wyntoun's literary form was adapted to a more clearly didactic purpose by Sir David Lindsay in the *Monarche* (*c.* 1550).[10] It is possible that the world–historical *schema* of James Thomson's *Liberty*[11] (1735–6) stems from the *Monarche*, which long retained its popularity in Scotland, and so indirectly from Wyntoun. Wyntoun's approach to history was also developed and distorted for their own purposes by such men as Bower, Boece, Buchanan, and in the eighteenth century by James Macpherson, the translator of Ossian.

Wyntoun is commonly dismissed as a mechanical chronicler in verse, an opinion which does him less than justice. As is shown by his laudatory defence of the mysterious Huchone of the Auld Ryall, he was well aware of the stylistic possibilities open to the medieval poet:

> Men of gud discretioun
> Suld excuss and loif Huchoun,
> That cunnand wes in litterature,
> He maid the gret Gest of Arthure,
> And the Anteris of Gawane,
> The Epistill als of Suete Susane.
> He wes curyouss in his stile,
> Faire and facund and subtile,
> And aye to plesance and delite,
> Maid in meit metyre his dite,
> Litill or ellis nocht be gess
> Waverand fra the suthfastnes

9 *The Shorter Poems of Gavin Douglas*, edited by P. J. Bawcutt (STS, 1967), pp. 62–3. Quyntyne is unknown, although he is also mentioned by Dunbar and Lindsay.

10 *The Works of Sir David Lindsay*, edited by D. Hamer (STS, 1931–6) I, pp. 197–386.

11 *James Thomson: Poetical Works*, edited by J. Logie Robertson (London, 1908), pp. 309–413.

> Had he callit Lucyus procuratour,
> Quhare he callit him emperour,
> It had mare grevit the cadens
> Than had relevit the sentens.
> (Wemyss text, 4329–44)

A 'curious' style to give pleasure by its complexities, a metre appropriate to the subject, an eye for truth which nevertheless within reason was subordinated to the cadence of the verse – these are the qualities singled out by Wyntoun as characterizing the good narrative or historical poet, and he is obviously writing for an audience prepared to discuss and accept such distinctions. But he is not himself an innovator, or given to technical display, which no doubt, he would have regarded as inappropriate for the plain style of history. Nowhere else but in this passage does he approach the style of the literary manifesto, and he is clearly setting out what he takes to be self-evident truths rather than instituting any kind of programme.

2

Temperamentally James I was a different kind of poet, and as king he was in a position to extend patronage to poets who wrote in the more elaborate styles, of which he, as much as Wyntoun, heartily approved. His only certain surviving work, the *Kingis Quair*, written probably at some time between his return to Scotland in 1424 and his death in 1437, belongs to the more ornate tradition:

> Vnto the impnis of my maisteris dere,
> Gowere and Chaucere, that on the steppis satt
> Of rethorike quhill thai were lyvand here,
> Superlatiue as poetis laureate,
> In moralitee and eloquence ornate,
> I recommend my buk in lynis seven,
> And eke thair saulis vnto the blisse of hevin.
> (1373–9)

Notably and curiously, James gives Gower precedence over Chaucer, while his own older English contemporary, John Lydgate (1370–1450), as a model considerably more important than Gower, remains unmentioned, probably because he was alive when the *Quair* was composed. The long captivity in England and France, which gave the king the experience on which he based the poem, no doubt also gave him some acquaintance with the vernacular literature of the southern courts, and with a rhetoric more complex than anything that had yet been produced in Scots. It is certainly poetry of this general kind, emerging from a courtly life resembling that of England and

France, which he recommends, through the *persona* of Venus, to the Scottish nation:

> Say on than, quhare is becummyn, for schame,
> The songis new, the fresch carolis and dance,
> The lusty lyf, the mony change of game,
> The fresche array, the lusty contenance,
> The besy awayte, the hertly obseruance,
> That quhilum was amongis thame so ryf?
> Bid thame repent in tyme and mend thaire lyf.
>
> (841–7)

C. S. Lewis long ago noted that the prologue to the *Kingis Quair* is in effect a literary manifesto, which lays strong emphasis on personal experience as the basis for courtly philosophical poetry.[12] Although at first it may appear an excrescence, the stanza just quoted adds a new dimension to the manifesto. What has the complaint of Venus, or indeed the court of Venus, to do with the poet's personal development, or with the development in terms of the poem of a philosophic theme? The answer lies in the highest developments of the poetry of *amour courtois* exemplified, say, by the *Vita Nuova* of Dante, or the *Troilus and Criseyde* of Chaucer. Love, the operation of Venus, was central to the operation of the medieval universe. But as the universe was a complex work of art, so the celebrations of the central power of the universe must themselves be complex works of art, and the product of a complex and ornate society. The philosophic subject which emerges from the personal experience of the *Kingis Quair*, is the part played by Fortune in

> luffis ordinance,
> That has so mony in his goldin cheyne
> (1277–8)

The service of Venus was a courtly play, a serious make-believe, philosophically worked out in terms of literature and music, and vitally related to the experience of every intelligent man and woman. The complaint of Venus is that the Scottish court has omitted this kind of observance; the remedy urged is that the court should adopt a philosophy, a way of life, and a literature embracing the kinds exemplified in the *Kingis Quair*. This is not merely to say extended dream vision. The poem incidentally contains specimens of other kinds, most notably the songs which punctuate the first autobiographical episode – stanzas 34, 52, 63 and 64–5. In my book, *Ballattis of Lufe*, I have tried to show how the Scottish courtly lyric developed, in part at least, accord-

---

12 C. S. Lewis, *The Allegory of Love* (London, 1936), pp. 235–6.

ing to James's example, an example which had not entirely lost its power when Alexander Scott (*c*. 1515–*c*. 1583) was writing for Mary of Guise and her daughter Mary, nor when Alexander Montgomerie (*c*. 1545–97) was James VI's master poet.[13]

The *Kingis Quair* is the earliest Scottish poem which we can describe with reasonable certainty as intended for the court, and intended to set an example, which others could follow, of the art appropriate for such poetry. It has long been recognized that this last appears, partly in the elaborate stanza used, partly in the level of diction, imagery and thematic development.[14] Less well recognized, indeed scarcely recognized at all, is the importance of the formal structure – the Boethian prologue in 13 stanzas, the 59 (but possibly rather 57 or 58, see below) stanzas of the first autobiographical section, the 101 (possibly 99 or 100) stanzas of the dream-vision, the 11 stanzas of the second autobiographical section, the 13-stanza epilogue, and the single stanza of dedication. The individual stanza forms the operative unit of the poem, and it has not, I think, previously been noticed that the total structure has a numerological basis, involving not only the arithmetical position of individual stanzas, but also the chronology of events. The poem, to begin with, is circular; the first line, 'Heigh in the hevynnis figure circulere', returns on itself as the conclusion of the 196th and penultimate stanza. The additional stanza of dedication emphasizes, among other things, the seven lines of the stanzaic unit, and the final word is 'hevin'. Numbers, especially 1, 3, 4, 5, 7, 9 and 13, with their derivatives, play a significant part throughout the poem. The 13 stanzas of the prologue and epilogue have already been mentioned, and the reader should recollect that to the medieval mind 13 in general was not an unlucky, but rather a powerful, even holy, number, made up as it is of 10, signifying the return to divine unity after the complexities of the eight intermediate integers, and 3, the masculine, finite and god-like first of the odd numbers. The number 13 in itself is also prime, and 9 as the square of 3 and 1 short of 10 shares many of the properties of the other two numbers. Stanza 19 is an invocation of the 9 muses, 3 of whom are named (one in apparent misunderstanding). In stanza 22 the age of James at the time of his capture is given as 7 plus 3 years. The presence of 3, and the fact that his total age at the time was 10, is enough to give the figure significance, but 7 is also emphasized,

13 *Ballattis of Lufe*, edited by J. MacQueen (Edinburgh, 1970).

14 See especially Lewis, *The Allegory of Love*; J. Preston 'Fortunys Exiltree: a Study of the *Kingis Quair*', *RES* VII (1956), pp. 339–45; M. Markland, 'The Structure of the *Kingis Quair*', *Research Studies of the State College of Washington* XXV (1957), pp. 273–86; J. MacQueen, 'Tradition and the Interpretation of the *Kingis Quair*', *RES* XII (1961), pp. 117–31. Despite protestations to the contrary, the interpretation offered in McDiarmid, *Kingis Quair*, pp. 48–77, does not significantly differ from others previously advanced.

not only because the first seven years of life form the age of innocence, but also because 7 is primarily the number of the universe and man, 'signifying the creature as opposed to the Creator'.[15] In particular, 7 is the number of the body, in contrast with 9, the number of the mind. The poem demonstrates how a youth, 'of nature indegest' and 'of wit wayke and unstable', progressed by way of his captivity to a philosophical balance of mind and body. Stanza 25 emphasizes the twice 9 years of his captivity, at the end of which he was 28 years old. The number 28 is the second perfect (and therefore powerful and benevolent) number, the factors of which (1, 2, 4, 7, 14) themselves add up to a total of 28. The central problem of the poem:

> The bird, the beste, the fisch eke in the see,
> They lyve in fredome, everich in his kynd,
> And I, a man, and lakkith libertee!
> Quhat schall I seyne, quhat resouns may I fynd
> That fortune suld do so?
>
> (183–7)

is posed in the 27th stanza. The number 27 is the first odd, or masculine, cube (3^3), and the more comprehensive of the two generative cubes of the world-soul in Plato's *Timaeus* 35. The first hint of an answer appears 7 stanzas later in the 'Cantus', the first of the songs which mark crucial developments in the first part of the poem. The poet's prayer in stanza 39 (3 × 13) is immediately followed by the revelation in stanza 40 of 'the fairest or the freschest ʒong floure' – the poet's lady. The number 40, in turn, is 'a sort of glorified tetraktys. For if each of the first four numbers be multiplied in turn by 4 and the 4 products added, the result will be found to be 40' (1 × 4 + 2 × 4 + 3 × 4 + 4 × 4 = 40).[16] 'These 4 terms, of which 40 is the sum, combine to produce all the principal harmonic proportions. Moreover, 40 is the sum of the first two quadrates and the first two cubes (1 + 4 + 8 + 27 = 40); and it is also the sum of the uneven *lambda* series (1 + 3 + 9 + 27 = 40). In short, it is a number of great generative and harmonic properties'[17] – and as such absolutely appropriate to the central generative and harmonic moment of the poem.

In stanza 45 (5 × 3^2) occurs the first reference to the transforming power of 'lufis dance' – a circular dance, one presumes, to which corresponds the overall circular scheme of the poem. Seven stanzas later comes the second song, one of thanks and praise to Venus. It is

15 V. F. Hopper, *Medieval Number Symbolism* (New York, 1938), p. 84.

16 *ibid.*, p. 45, referring to Plutarch, *De animae procreatione*, xii–xiii.

17 Alastair Fowler, *Spenser and the Numbers of Time* (London, 1964) p. 189 – also referring to Plutarch.

introduced in stanza 51 by a reference to the 7-line stanza form of the poem. The second song, however, is preceded by another important numerological point, the first or bodily climacteric, 49, the square of the body's number, 7. Correspondingly, in stanza 49 the lady for the first and only time becomes recognizably, in however refined a way, a desirable and partially naked bodily presence:

> And for to walk that freschë mayes morowe
> Ane huke sche had vpon hir tissew quhite,
> That gudeliar had nought bene sene toforowe
> As I suppose, and girt sche was alyte.
> Thus halflyng louse for haste, to suich delyte
> It was to see hir ȝouth in gudelihed,
> That for rudeness to speke thereof I drede
>
> (337–43)

The number 63 is the second or median climacteric, the product of 7, the number of the body, and 9, the number of the mind, and the 63rd stanza begins the third song, linking body and mind, but emphasizing the superior heavenly power of the latter:

> Bot, hert, quhere as the body may nought throu,
> Folow thy hevin.
>
> (438–9)

The birds continue this song through the next two stanzas. The final climactic celebration (distantly related to Petrarch's Sonnet LXI, *In vita*, 'Benedetto sia 'l giorno') begins with the 189th stanza (189 = 63 × 3) and occupies 3 stanzas. The total number of stanzas, 196, apart from the dedication, is 4 times the bodily climacteric, 49.

Properly speaking, the third or intellectual climacteric is 9 or 81, but in the poem its function seems to have been assumed by the 181st stanza, which details the intellectual advancement of the poet as his mind achieves the paradox of liberty with his sovereign:

> The quhich treuly efter, day by day,
> That all my wittis maistrit had tofore,
> From hennesferth the paynis did away;
> And schortly, so wele Fortune has hir bore
> To quikin treuly day by day my lore,
> To my larges that I am cumyn agayn,
> To bliss with hir that is my souirane.
>
> (1261–7)

The medieval scholar would have found no particular difficulty in allowing 181 to act as the equivalent of 81, but it should perhaps be added that if the number of stanzas in the dream-vision is taken to be

100, stanza 181 is in fact stanza 81 of the main narrative, and occupies the precise position of the third climacteric.

The dream-vision itself seems less imaginatively involved with numerology. The number 100 has much the same properties as its square root, 10, 99 is closely related to 9 and 3, and 101 is a prime number. During the vision, the dreamer meets 3 goddesses, Venus, Minerva and Fortune. The court of Venus contains 4 companies, 3 of fortunate and 1 of unfortunate lovers. Cupid is armed with 3 arrows. Three stanzas (155–7) are devoted to the beasts in the domain of Fortune; the first and second each name 9 species, the third 12. These, however, are little more than decorative flourishes. More exciting is the fact that part of the first and last line of the entire circular poem, 'Heigh in the hevin', appears in the 75th stanza of the vision, the 146th of the poem, as part of Minerva's discussion of freewill, and at a point almost exactly threequarters of the way through vision and poem alike. The dream-vision itself begins at a point almost exactly three quarters of the way through the poem *apart* from the dream-vision. These ratios, I suspect, form part of the symbolic structure of the poem, but the precise significance I am not at the moment able to interpret.

3

It is sometimes claimed that the *Kingis Quair* remained virtually unknown during the fifteenth and sixteenth centuries.[18] This seems improbable, even if one ignores the apparent verbal reminiscences which occur in later poets, the direct reference made by Walter Bower, John Major, John Bale, George Buchanan and Thomas Dempster,[19] and the fact that the manuscript was for a time in the mid-sixteenth century apparently in the possession of a MacDonald chieftain, Donald Gorm of Sleat in Skye.[20] The poem, as has been illustrated, is programmatic, and even if this last point is disputed, all fifteenth-century poetry was a public rather than a private art, and it is not intrinsically likely that a king of James's accomplishments would have written for the benefit of a few intimates only. It seems fairly certain that Henryson, Dunbar, Douglas and Lindsay knew and made use of the *Kingis Quair*. A considerable gap, however, separates them from James; they were subject to other influences, some of which will be

18 For instance, Norton-Smith, *Kingis Quair*, p. xiii.

19 *Chron. Bower* XVI xxx; *Historia Majoris Britanniae* VI xiv (Paris, 1521), most readily consulted in *A History of Greater Britain*, translated by A. Constable, with Life by A. J. G. Mackay (SHS, 1892); *Scriptorum Illustrium Majoris Britanniae Catalogus* XIV lvi (Basle, 1557–9); *Rerum Scoticarum Historia* X lvii (Edinburgh, 1582); *Historia Ecclesiastica Gentis Scotorum* (Bologna, 1627; Bannatyne Club, 1829) II, p. 381.

20 Mackenzie, *Kingis Quair*, pp. 12, 137.

noted below, and of course each was himself an original and accomplished artist. To judge from his poetry, James himself had a literary programme, but his own pursuit of it was interrupted by his murder, and insofar as it was immediately carried out, it was by lesser men, translators, no doubt for the most part under royal patronage, who continued the process of naturalizing courtly concepts to the Scottish language. For these men, as for most significant writers of the century, patronage made a substantial contribution to the continuance and success of their work.

First is the author of the work now known as *The Buik of the Most Noble and Valiant Conquerour Alexander the Grit*,[21] completed in 1438, one year after James's death, and derived from parts of the second and third branches of the French *Roman d'Alixandre*, 'Li Fuerres de Gadres' ('The Forray of Gadderis'), and 'Les Voeux du Paon' ('The Avowis of Alexander' and 'The Great Battell of Effesoun'). Second is the author of *Lancelot of the Laik*,[22] a poem based on parts of the anonymous thirteenth-century French prose *Lancelot del Lac*, and apparently composed during the reign of James III (1460–88), in all probability for the queen, or another lady of the court. The figures of Alexander and Lancelot were both central to the courtly tradition. Each translator claims to have written only to assuage the pangs of a love which is obviously courtly. Both, in other words, write on the assumption of a Scottish audience which itself could appreciate the skilled handling of such themes.

James III resembled his grandfather in being a patron of literature and the arts. His character is difficult to assess, but it is clear that he was more to the liking of the artists, craftsmen, scholars and writers among his subjects than to that of many among his nobility. One of his favourites was William Rogers, an English doctor of music, under whose influence, perhaps, James became the effective founder of the musical tradition at the Chapel Royal of Stirling. There is also some evidence that James collected books – how extensively the records do not indicate, though they make his interest clear. 'A fine manuscript of Virgil in the Edinburgh University Library (no. 195 in Miss Borland's catalogue), written in a beautiful Italian hand by a French scribe, Florius Infortunatus, and bearing the arms of Scotland, probably of James III, testified to the ambition of a Scottish prince to follow in the footsteps of the French collectors of the Renaissance' (plate 13).[23] James also commissioned a manuscript of *The Travels of Sir John Mandeville*,[24]

21 Edited by R. L. Graeme Ritchie (STS, 1925–9).

22 Edited by M. M. Gray (STS, 1912).

23 *The Works of William Fowler*, edited by H. W. Meikle, J. Craigie and J. Purves (STS, 1914–40) III, p. lxxxvi. I am told by my former colleague, Professor D. A. Bullough, that Florius was in fact an Italian.   24 *ER* VII, p. 500.

for the making of which the royal chaplain, John Blair, in 1467 received payment of £4 16s. He commissioned Hugo van der Goes to paint the fine portraits of himself with his son, the future James IV, and of his queen, which originally formed part of the altar piece of the collegiate church of the Holy Trinity in Edinburgh, and which now hang in the National Gallery of Scotland. His coinage is the first in western Europe to have an authentic portrait-bust with the monarch in half- or three-quarter profile, on the obverse.

James probably and significantly owed much to his former tutor, Archibald Whitelaw, archdeacon of Lothian and sub-dean of Glasgow, who held the office of royal secretary for the greater part of his reign. Whitelaw had graduated in arts from St Andrews in 1439, and taught at St Andrews and Cologne before he entered the king's service. The secretary's office may already have been, to some extent, a centre of humanistic influence; in James II's reign it had been occupied by William Turnbull, who afterwards as bishop of Glasgow became the founder of Glasgow University, and who had also been one of Whitelaw's predecessors as archdeacon of Lothian. Whitelaw belonged to the tradition of Turnbull. Several of his books have survived: they include a *Lucan*, printed at Louvain *c.* 1475 and annotated in Whitelaw's own hand, an *Appian*, printed at Venice in 1477, a *Horace*, printed at Venice in 1478, a *Sallust*, printed at Venice in 1481, and Asconius' *Commentaries* on the speeches of Cicero, printed at Venice in 1477. Whitelaw also owned an Italian (or French) manuscript (Aberdeen University 214), containing Florus, Orosius and Dares Phrygius. As secretary, he composed a Latin oration, delivered in 1484 at Nottingham to Richard III of England, which seems to be the earliest extant piece of extended humanistic prose to be composed by a Scot. The Latinity is that of a Christian humanist, modelled on Cicero, to whom in the course of eight pages he refers four times. In addition, he quotes Statius three times, Virgil five times, Seneca, Sallust and Livy once each. On one occasion he gives the etymology of a Greek word, *amnesia*, which he uses. Other specimens of his Latinity are in all probability preserved in the limited extant Latin correspondence of James III. Whitelaw died in 1498.[25]

A colleague, whose interests may have run parallel to those of Whitelaw, was John Reid of Stobo, the 'gud gentill Stobo' of Dunbar's 'Quhen he wes sek'. It has been suggested that Stobo was the author of *The Three Priests of Peebles*, an anonymous poem composed in James III's reign; whether or not this is so, he was certainly a vernacular poet of some reputation. But he was also described by the king as 'familiari

25 See my 'Some Aspects of the Early Renaissance in Scotland', *FMLS* III (1967), pp. 206–7; and *Robert Henryson* (Oxford, 1967), pp. 13–15. The *Oratio Scotorum ad Regem Ricardum Tertium* is to be found in *Bannatyne Miscellany* II (Edinburgh, 1836), pp. 41–8.

Plate 13 'Arrival of Aeneas at Carthage', Edinburgh University Library MS. 195 (reproduced by permission of the Edinburgh University Library).

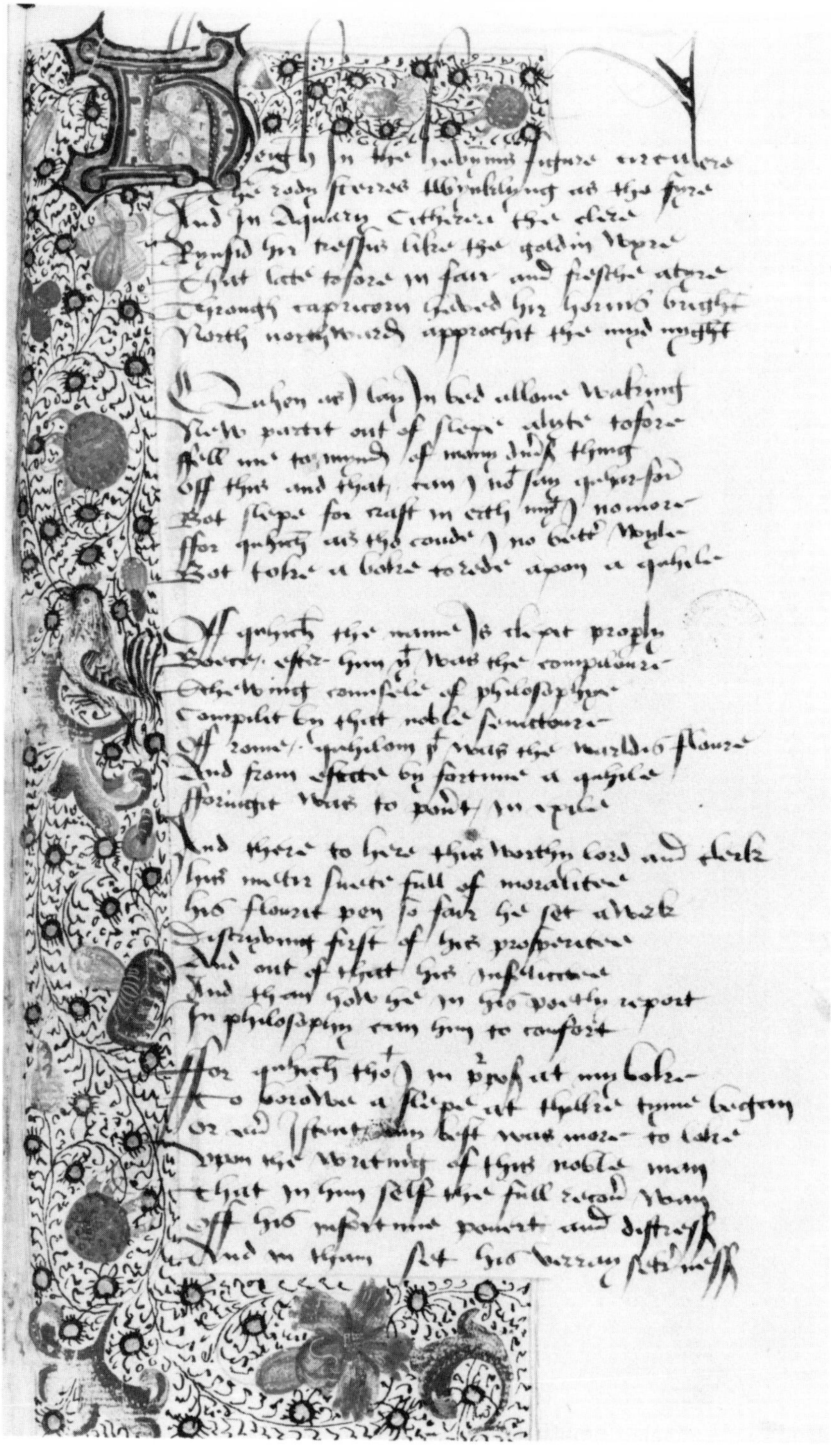

Heigh in the hevynnis figure circulere
The rody sterres twynklyng as the fyre
And in Aquary Citherea the clere
Rynsid hir tressis like the goldin wyre
That late tofore in fair and fresche atyre
Through capricorn heved hir hornis bright
North northward approchit the myd nyght

Quhen as I lay in bed allone waking
New partit out of slepe a lyte tofore
Fell me to mynd of mony diverse thing
Off this and that, can I noght say quharfore
Bot slepe for craft in erth myght I no more
For quhich as tho coude I no better wyle
Bot toke a boke to rede apon a quhile

Off quhich the name is clepit properly
Boece, eftir him that was the compiloure
Schewing counsele of philosophye
Compilit by that noble senatoure
Off Rome, quhilom that was the warldis floure
And from estate by fortune a quhile
Foriugit was to povert in exile

And there to here this worthy lord and clerk
His metir suete full of moralitee
His flourit pen so fair he set awerk
Discryving first of his prosperitee
And out of that his infelicitee
And than how he in his poetly report
In philosophy can him to confort

For quhich thogh I in purpose at my boke
To borowe a slepe at thilke tyme began
Or ever I stent my best was more to loke
Upon the writing of this noble man
That in him self the full recover wan
Off his infortune povert and distresse
And in tham set his verray sekernesse

Plate 14 *Kingis Quair*, Bodleian MS. Arch. Selden B. 24 (reproduced by permission of the Bodleian Library, Oxford).

servitori suo et scribe' when in 1478 he was awarded a pension for life in return for services to the king and his predecessors as a writer of letters to the pope and diverse kings, princes and magnates outside the kingdom. In 1497 there is record of a payment to Stobo and Walter Chepman (the associate of Andrew Myllar in the establishment of printing in Scotland) 'for thare lawboris in lettrez writing the tyme the king past in Ingland'. Stobo died in 1505.[26]

The importance of royal patronage is better documented for the reign of James IV. Between 1490 and 1492 five payments to Blind Hary, the author of the *Wallace*, are mentioned in the treasurer's accounts.[27] The close, if sometimes ambiguous relation between the king and William Dunbar is illustrated by the poet's New Year prayer for the king:

> God gif the blis quharevir thow bownes,
> And send the many Fraunce crownes,
> Hie liberall heart and handis not sweir – –
> ('A New Year's Gift to the King', 17–19)

No less than fifteen (the number might easily be extended) of Dunbar's extant poems are classified by W. Mackay Mackenzie as petitions[28] – wry, witty poems written in the confidence, for the most part, rather than the hope, that a well-turned stanza would ultimately bring its own reward. 'Of the Warldis Instabilitie', for instance, brings the adventurous and profitable voyages of the later fifteenth century into unexpected conjunction with the Scottish coinage ('unicornis and crowns of wecht') and the poet's needs. The benefice which he deserves is a cargo of treasure which seems to be coming from the back of beyond:

> It cumis be king, it cumis be quene,
> But ay sic space is us betwene,
> That nane can schut it with ane flane;
> Quhilk to considder is ane pane.

> It micht have cumin in schortar quhyll
> Fra Calyecot and the new fund Yle,
> The partis of Transmeridiane;
> Quhilk to considder is ane pane.

---

26 MacQueen, 'Aspects of the Early Renaissance', pp. 205–7. *The Three Priests of Peebles* was edited by T. D. Robb (STS, 1920).

27 *TA* I, pp. 133, 174, 176, 181 and 184.

28 *The Poems of William Dunbar*, edited by W. M. Mackenzie (London, 1932), pp. 27–51. In line 70 I have ventured to amend *Paris* to *Pers* (Persia).

It micht, be this, had it bein kynd,
Cumin out of the desertis of Ynde,
Our all the grit se occeane;
   Quhilk to considder is ane pane.

It micht have cumin out of all ayrtis,
Fra Pers, and the Orient partis,
And fra the Ylis of Aphrycane,
   Quhilk to considder is ane pane . . .

Upon the heid of it is hecht
Baith unicornis and crowns of wecht,
Quhen it dois cum all men dois frane;
   Quhilk to considder is ane pane.
                    (57–72; 77–80)

Even when he wrote this poem (from the reference to the queen, presumably after James's marriage in 1503), Dunbar's position was comfortable. In August 1500 he had received an annual pension of £10 for life, or until he should be provided with a benefice worth £40 a year – a pension which the king more than once increased in the latter years of his reign. Dunbar's grievance was simply that he had never been provided with a benefice.

4

The royal court was not the only possible source of literary patronage. During the reign of James I, Wyntoun's patron was Sir John Wemyss of Leuchars and Kincaldrum (1372–1428):[29]

A worthy knycht and of gud fame,
Albeid his lordschip be nocht like
To gretare lordis in the kinrik,
He mone of neid be personer
Off quhat kin blame sa ever I beire;
Syne through his bidding and counsaill
Off det I spendit my travale.
                    (Wemyss text, 58–64)

The *Scotichronicon* of Walter Bower (*c.* 1385–1449), abbot of Inchcolm, was compiled at the instigation of Sir David Stewart of Rosyth, who died in 1444. Sir Richard Holland (*c.* 1420–*c.* 1490), priest successively in the dioceses of Caithness, Moray and Orkney, wrote

29 *Chron. Wyntoun* I, pp. xli–ii; II, pp. 6–7.

the *Buke of the Howlat*[30] under the patronage of Elizabeth Dunbar, countess of Moray, the wife of Archibald Douglas, earl of Moray. The Gaelic poetry, collected early in the sixteenth century by the dean of Lismore,[31] was mostly composed for the courts of the major highland chiefs, notably those of the Lords of the Isles, the earls of Argyll, and the chiefs of Clan Gregor, the clan to which the dean himself belonged. James I's literary policy was most consistently furthered by the Sinclair family. The only surviving manuscript of the *Kingis Quair* (Bodleian, MS. Arch Selden B 24; plate 14) was copied by James Gray and another for Henry, third Lord Sinclair, at whose suggestion Gavin Douglas later undertook the translation of the *Aeneid* which he completed in 1513.[32] Henry's maternal grandmother had been Margaret, eldest daughter of Robert III, and so elder sister of James himself. This relationship may help to explain the inclusion of the poem in the manuscript[33] (although this scarcely suggests that the poem was in any sense uniquely the property of the Sinclair family). The Sinclair family long maintained a tradition of patronage and scholarship. Henry himself is described by Gavin Douglas as 'fader of bukis'.[34] His grandfather William, first Lord Sinclair, owned a library to which he is reported to have been passionately devoted;[35] in 1446 he founded the celebrated and beautiful collegiate kirk of St Matthew at Roslin near Edinburgh. He requested Sir Gilbert Haye, 'maister in arte and bachilere in decreis', a former chamberlain to Charles VII of France (1422–61) to translate from the French the *Arbre des Batailles (Buke of the Law of Armys)* of Honoré Bonet (*c.* 1340–*c.* 1410), the anonymous fourteenth-century *Le Livre de l'Ordre de Chevalerie (Buke of the Ordre of Knychthede)*, later translated by Caxton, and the *Buke of the Governaunce of Princis*, based on a French rendering of the Latin *Secreta Secretorum*, usually in the middle ages attributed to Aristotle. These were completed in 1456.[36]

The third Lord Sinclair's cousins, the brothers Henry Sinclair, bishop of Ross (ob. 1565) and John Sinclair, bishop of Brechin (ob.

30 *Scottish Alliterative Poems in Riming Stanzas*, edited by F. J. Amours (STS, 1897), pp. xx–xxxiv, 47–81.

31 *Scottish Verse from the Book of the Dean of Lismore*, edited by W. J. Watson (SGTS, 1937).

32 *Virgil's Aeneid Translated into Scottish Verse by Gavin Douglas Bishop of Dunkeld*, edited by D. F. C. Coldwell (STS, 1957–64).

33 Norton–Smith, *Kingis Quair*, p. xxxiv.

34 Coldwell, *Virgil's Aeneid*, Prologue to Book 1, line 85.

35 *Gilbert of the Haye's Prose Manuscript (AD 1456)* 1 The *Buke of the Law of Armys or Buke of Bataillis*, edited by J. H. Stevenson (STS, 1901), p. xxxvi.

36 J. H. Stevenson edited *The Buke of Knychthede* and *The Buke of the Governaunce of Princis* as the second volume of *Gilbert of the Haye's Prose Manuscript* (STS, 1914).

1566), were patrons of literature at least to the extent of becoming notable collectors of books. Durkan and Ross list 102 books which are known to have belonged to the first, and thirty-one which belonged to the second.[37]

Sir Gilbert Haye afterwards received the patronage of the Erskine family; it was for Lord Erskine that he made *The Buik of Alexander the Conqueror*, to distinguish it from the one previously mentioned, now generally known as the *Taymouth Alexander*.[38] As is illustrated by the career of the musician and poet Alexander Scott (*c*. 1515–*c*. 1583), the Erskine family maintained the custom of patronage well into the sixteenth century.[39]

In a rather different way, the merchants and craftsmen of the Scottish burghs were also patrons. Dr Anna J. Mill has brought together the evidence for local medieval drama.[40] Fifteenth-century records are sparse, but Aberdeen is relatively well documented, and there is clear evidence for Perth and Lanark. Patrick Johnson, one of Dunbar's *makaris*, is on record as a writer of plays, who seems to have had particularly close connections with Linlithgow. It seems probable that most Scottish burghs maintained regular dramatic performances, but no texts have survived the Reformation. The burghs may also on occasion have commissioned panegyric verse. Dunbar's 'Blyth Aberdein, thow beriall of all tounis' directly parallels his 'London, thou art the flour of Cities all' and, more distantly, 'To speik of science, craft or sapience', which in the Maitland folio manuscript is entitled 'Dunbar at Oxinfurde'. The denunciatory, but vividly realistic, 'To the Merchantis of Edinburgh' seems less likely to have been the result of a commission.

In comparison with aristocratic patronage, that of the burgesses remained relatively unimportant. But their importance as an audience for literature, with the lesser clergy and professional men, should not be forgotten. The work of James I and Dunbar is clearly intended primarily for court circles, and with Dunbar we often know some details of the person to whom a given poem was addressed or at whom it was aimed. With an intermediate figure, Robert Henryson (*c*. 1420–*c*. 1490), it is different. In the *Prolog* to the *Morall Fabillis*, for instance, he makes a gesture towards the convention that literary works were written only at the request of noble patrons:

37 J. Durkan and A. Ross, *Early Scottish Libraries* (Glasgow, 1961).

38 *The Taymouth Alexander* has not yet been edited or published. It is preserved in two MSS., BM Add. MS 40732 and SRO GD 112/71/90. A. Hermann's *The Taymouth Castle Manuscript of Sir Gilbert Hay's 'Buik of King Alexander the Conqueror'* (Berlin, 1898), is a brief monograph, based on the manuscript now in the British Museum.

39 MacQueen, *Ballattis of Luve*, pp. xxxviii–ix.

40 A. J. Mill, *Mediaeval Plays in Scotland* (Edinburgh and London, 1927).

I wald preif
To mak a maner of translatiowne;
Nocht of myself, for vayne presumptioune,
Bot be request & precep of ane lord,
Of quhome the name it nedis nocht record.
(Makculloch MS. 31–5)[41]

If such a lord ever existed, Henryson subjected him to fairly cavalier treatment. One suspects that he is as fictitious as the *uther quair* on which Henryson said he had based his *Testament of Cresseid*.[42] The very stanza in which he mentions the lord begins with an address to 'my maisteris', and such parallel phrases as 'worthie folk', 'freindis', once even 'My Brother', occur time and again in the *Fabillis*. This is not the language of the court but rather, I suggest, of one professional man, reasonably well placed on the social scale, addressing a group of his peers. Throughout the *Fabillis* the vocabulary is similarly professional rather than courtly. Henryson's extensive and precise use of legal language is well known. 'Lords' are directly addressed in the *moralitates* of *The Lion and the Mouse* and *The Wolf and the Lamb*,[43] but not in a courtly manner; the poet speaks as the representative of ordinary people who suffer under the conduct of their superiors. The *Fabillis* are not courtly poetry and seem intended for private reading rather than the public performance which all court poetry to a certain extent demands. Their market was the new non-courtly reading public of the fifteenth century, the public which in its English manifestations has been discussed by H. S. Bennett,[44] and whose demands were in part satisfied by Caxton. Lesser Scottish works which seem likely to have been written for a similar market are the alliterative *Rauf Coilyear*,[45] *The Three Priests of Peebles*, *The Talis of the Fyve Bestis*,[46] and *The Freiris of Berwick*;[47] Hary's *Wallace*, based as it is ultimately on the popular *Scotichronicon*, and centred on a hero who belonged more to the folk than the nobility, may well have been primarily intended for the same audience.

41 *Pieces from the Makculloch and the Gray MSS, together with the Chepman and Myllar Prints*, edited by G. Stevenson (STS, 1918), p. 4.

42 *The Poems and Fables of Robert Henryson*, edited by H. Harvey Wood (second edition, Edinburgh and London, 1958), p. 107.

43 *ibid.*, pp. 56, 94–5.

44 H. S. Bennett, *English Books and Readers, 1475–1557* (Cambridge, 1952). Compare also 'The Author and his Public', chapter 5 of his *Chaucer and the Fifteenth Century* (Oxford, 1947).

45 Amours, *Scottish Alliterative Poems*, pp. 84–114; facsimile of the edition by Robert Lekpreuik (St Andrews, 1572), edited by W. Beattie (Edinburgh, 1966).

46 *Select Remains of the Ancient Popular and Romance Poetry of Scotland*, edited by D. Laing, re-edited by J. Small (Edinburgh and London, 1885), pp. 278–93.

47 Mackenzie, *Dunbar*, pp. 182–95.

5

Beyond doubt, the possibility of patronage and the relative certainty of an audience affected the production of new poetry and prose. But other factors were involved. Elsewhere I have commented on the fact that the majority of the Scottish writers of the fifteenth and early sixteenth centuries were graduates, and more were graduates of St Andrews than of any other university.[48] The foundation of the three oldest Scottish universities (St Andrews, 1412, Glasgow, 1451, Aberdeen, 1495) was a factor which affected the literary ambitions and methods of the writers themselves and also, as has already been suggested, helped to provide an audience for their work. The medieval custom of oral recitation certainly continued throughout the fifteenth century and beyond, but at least by the latter part of the century, an appreciable demand for manuscript and printed books had grown up in Scotland, not least, one presumes, among university graduates. Henryson, for instance, certainly made use of the productions of Caxton's press at Westminster.[49] English and continental presses, however, were not appropriate vehicles for the production and circulation of vernacular Scottish poetry and prose, which essentially depended on native resources. So far as is known, no press was established in Scotland before 1507, but the nature of the market then already in existence is indicated by the fact that so many of the pieces first printed were vernacular poetry and prose;[50] there were three poems of Dunbar, including what are still his best-known pieces, *The Goldyn Targe* and *The Twa Mariit Wemen and the Wedo*, *The Flyting of Dunbar and Kennedy*, Hary's *Wallace*, Henryson's *Orpheus and Eurydice*, the anonymous *Golagros and Gawane*, and the prose *Porteous of Noblenes*. Before this, the audience for such works depended on the copying of manuscript texts. Within the fairly narrow limits of the surviving evidence, we have minimal details of at least eight scribes who produced one or more substantial literary manuscripts in the course of the fifteenth century.

As has already been mentioned, John Blair, a licentiate (1461) of Glasgow University and by 1472 vicar of Maybole, in 1467 transcribed a copy of Mandeville's *Travels* for the young king. He died after 1488. His manuscript does not appear to have survived. John Gibson junior, canon of Glasgow and rector of Renfrew (who may have been

48 MacQueen, 'Aspects of the Early Renaissance', pp. 201–2; MacQueen, *Henryson*, pp. 17–19.

49 MacQueen, *Henryson*, p. 191, n. 1, pp. 209–15, 218–20. Denton Fox in 'Henryson and Caxton', *JEGP* LXVII (1968), pp. 586–93, attempts to prove that Henryson was unacquainted with Caxton's work. His arguments do not bear detailed examination.

50 See especially *The Chepman and Myllar Prints: a Facsimile*, edited by W. Beattie (Edinburgh, 1950).

archdeacon of Glasgow in 1495) in 1502 made extracts (MS. NLS Advocates' 35.6.8) from the *Scotichronicon* in the *Black Book of Paisley* (MS. Royal Library, BM, 13 E.x.), itself a product of a Scottish scriptorium.[51] During the second half of the fifteenth century, a scribe known only by his initials, V de F, made copies of *Ratis Raving* and *Lancelot of the Laik* (MS. CUL Kk 1.5, nos. 6 and 7).[52]

More important than any of these is James Gray, master of arts, notary public, priest of the diocese of Dunblane, and secretary to William Schevez (ob. 1497) and James Stewart (ob. 1504), successive archbishops of St Andrews. Gray may have been chancellor of St Andrew's diocese in 1460; he was vicar of Hailes in 1490. In 1481 he illuminated the Panmure manuscript (SRO GD 45/26/48) of Bower's *Scotichronicon*, which had been copied by Magnus Makculloch. Somewhere between 1485 and 1490 it seems likely that he wrote the manuscript (Abbotsford Library, 2, 1), which has preserved Sir Gilbert Haye's translations, mentioned above.[53] Between 1488 and his death (*c.* 1505) he wrote part of the manuscript (Bodleian, Arch. Selden B24) which contains the *Kingis Quair* as well as *The Quare of Jelusy, Troilus and Criseyde, The Parlement of Foules, The Legend of Good Women*, and a number of lesser Scottish and English poems.[54] (The second hand is that of V de F, or of another scribe trained in the same scriptorium.) Both these latter manuscripts were written for members of the Sinclair family. Gray also wrote the manuscript (MS. NLS Advocates' 34.7.3), which contains the earliest extant text of a poem by Robert Henryson, that generally known as 'The Annunciation'.[55] Gray, it is fairly clear, was a professional scribe who worked for a number of patrons, and was something of a specialist in vernacular works.

Somewhat similar is the figure of Magnus Makculloch, who graduated in Louvain, was a cleric of the diocese of Ross, and for a time *familiaris clericus* of Archbishop Schevez. In 1477, during his studies at Louvain, he wrote the Makculloch manuscript (Edinburgh University, Laing, no. 149).[56] This is no more, essentially, than a student's notebook. Texts of a number of vernacular poems, which include the *Prolog* and *The Cock and the Jasp* from Henryson's *Fabillis*, as well as

51 Descriptions of MSS of *Scotichronicon* are based primarily on *Chron. Fordun* I, pp. xv–xxx. Some seem to have disappeared since Skene's work was published.

52 *Ratis Raving and Other Early Scots Poems on Morals*, edited by R. Girvan (STS, 1939). For *Lancelot of the Laik*, see above, note 22.

53 See above, notes 35 and 36.

54 McDiarmid, *Kingis Quair*, pp. 2–7.

55 Stevenson, *Makculloch and Gray MSS*, pp. 43–5; Harvey Wood, *Henryson*, pp. 199–201.

56 Stevenson, *Makculloch and Gray MSS*, pp. 3–37.

two other poems attributed to Henryson are in a second later hand of the very late fifteenth or early sixteenth century. As has already been noted, Makculloch in 1481 wrote the Panmure manuscript of *Scotichronicon*, which Gray illuminated. In 1483 he wrote the manuscript (BM, Harleian 712) of *Scotichronicon* for Archbishop Schevez.

J de R, *capellanus*, in 1487 wrote MS. St John's College, Cambridge, G23, which contains Barbour's *Bruce*, 'Documenta Matris ad Filiam', and Lydgate's 'A Dietary'.[57] John Ramsay in 1488 wrote the copy of the *Wallace* and in 1489 that of the *Bruce* (combined to form MS. NLS Advocates' 19.2.2). The *Bruce* was copied for Sir Symon Lochmalony, vicar of Auchtermoonzie in Fife.

Richard Striveling, *notarius publicus*, in 1497 wrote part of the *Scotichronicon* (to be found in MS. BM Harleian 4764) for George Broun, who was bishop of Dunkeld from 1483 to 1515, and was the predecessor in office of Gavin Douglas. The manuscript was one of many commissioned for the cathedral by the bishop in 1497.

The activities of a single fifteenth-century monastic scriptorium are well illustrated, within a comparatively narrow range, by the manuscripts of the abridged version of *Scotichronicon* usually entitled *Liber Pluscardensis*.[58] The title is derived from references in Book X of George Buchanan's *Rerum Scoticarum Historia*, first published in 1582, and suggests that the work was compiled at the Benedictine priory of Pluscarden in Moray, originally a Valliscaulian foundation, which in 1453–4 had become dependent on the great Benedictine abbey of Dunfermline. The abridgement, whether or not it actually took place at Pluscarden, seems to have been made in 1461 at the request of Richard Bothwell, abbot of Dunfermline from 1445 to 1470 (who may also have been responsible for the transfer of Robert Henryson from Glasgow University to the grammar school of Dunfermline), and perhaps to have been the work of one Maurice Buchanan. The original manuscript has been lost, but all the extant copies of fifteenth-century date have a Dunfermline provenance.

MS. Marchmont AC 15 was written at Dunfermline by a scribe who had personal knowledge of Joan of Arc (1412–31). The same scribe apparently wrote part of MS. Bibliothèque Royale, Brussels, no. 7396. Between 1478 and 1496 MS. Glasgow UL BE 7.b.8[s] was written for Archbishop Schevez on the instructions of Dominus Thomas Monymelle, monk and sacrist of Dunfermline. MS. Bodleian Fairfax 8 seems also to have originated at Dunfermline. This last manuscript has an undefined traditional association with William

---

57 Skeat, *The Bruce*, pp. lxvii–lxxi. John Ramsay's MS is described, pp. lxxi–lxxv. Skeat erroneously concluded that J de R and John Ramsay were the same.

58 *Liber Pluscardensis*, edited by F. J. H. Skene (Edinburgh, 1877) i, pp. x–xvi. This supplements the account in *Chron. Fordun* i, pp. xv–xxx.

Elphinstone, bishop of Aberdeen from 1483 to 1514, and founder of Aberdeen University.

The *Liber Pluscardensis* is rendered doubly interesting by the inclusion in it of two vernacular Scottish poems.[59] The first is a translation of the Latin epitaph for the dauphiness Margaret, wife of the future Louis XI of France, and daughter of James I. She died in 1444, and the translation was commissioned by her brother, James II, at some time before his death in 1460. The stanza is the same as that in Henryson's 'Complaint of Orpheus' from *Orpheus and Eurydice*. The second, which concludes the book, is 'A morality representing the state of a kingdom by the figure of a harp'. Fairly obviously, it refers to the reign of James III and, given the connection with Dunfermline, there must, I suppose, be a reasonable possibility that it is Henryson's work – style, versification and subject matter come very close to the *moralitates* of the *Morall Fabillis*. Indeed it is not inconceivable that both poems are Henryson's. Their inclusion in *Liber Pluscardensis* certainly indicates the awareness of vernacular literature which characterized Dunfermline in the second half of the fifteenth century.

To complete the survey of fifteenth-century Scottish reading requirements, we have instances, finally, of the purchase of literary manuscripts by individuals. Some have already been mentioned. The Donibristle MS. of *Scotichronicon* (now in the library of Darnaway Castle, Moray) was written for Dominus Symon Fynlay, chaplain of the altar of St Michael in St Giles, Edinburgh. MS. BM Cotton Vitellius E XI of *Scotichronicon* is yet another which belonged to Archbishop Schevez. The first hand here resembles that of MS. Trinity College, Cambridge, Gale O ix 9 (yet again a *Scotichronicon*), which was presented to King's College, Aberdeen by Hector Boece, first principal. The Royal Manuscript of Wyntoun (BM, Royal 18 D xx) belonged to George Barclay of Achrody; the second Edinburgh manuscript (NLS, Advocates' 12.2.4) and manuscript BM, Lansdowne 197, belonged to Henry Sinclair (perhaps Henry, third Lord Sinclair rather than the bishop of Ross). The first Edinburgh manuscript (NLS, Advocates' 19.2.3) belonged to John Ærskine, and may have been written by John Feiller. Manuscript St Andrews University TT 6 6 belonged to Patrick Lermontht of Dersy (Dairsie, between Cupar and St Andrews in Fife).

6

The central literary figure of the later fifteenth century is Robert Henryson. It is true that he does not exemplify the tradition in every feature. Historical narrative, as practised in different ways by Barbour,

59 Book xi, caps viii and xi; i, pp. 382–8, 392–400.

Wyntoun, Bower and Hary, seems not to have interested him, because at least partly, as the *Fabillis* indicate, his first concern was with the Scotland of his own day. Almost everything else may be illustrated from his career or from his verse.[60] He was a university graduate in arts and law, probably of one or more continental universities, who in 1462 was incorporated in Glasgow University, perhaps to give lectures in law. He was thus a man of some learning, which was not confined to legal studies. It is possible that even before his Glasgow appointment he had made some reputation as a poet. If in fact he made the translation of the Latin epitaph on the dauphiness Margaret, it must have preceded the death of James II in 1460. During his residence in Glasgow, it seems probable that he wrote his *Orpheus and Eurydice*, drawing much of his material from the manuscript copy of Boethius's *De Consolatione* with the gloss of Nicholas Trevet, which in 1432 is on record among the books held by Glasgow Cathedral.[61] He also made notable use of two other works by Boethius, *De Musica* and *De Arithmetica*, and of Boccaccio's *De Genealogia Deorum*. About 1468 he seems to have moved from Glasgow to Dunfermline to become master of the grammar school attached to the abbey. Although during his period in Dunfermline he is on record (in 1477 and 1478) as a notary public, the change implies the abandonment of a legal in favour of a humanistic career. The importance of Dunfermline as a cultural centre has already been noted, and it was there that he wrote most of his major poetry. The *Fabillis*, or at least those among them based on books printed by Caxton, probably belong to the 1480s; the *Testament*, with its hints of a Dunfermline background and reference to the poet's old age, may well be a work of the same decade. Nothing suggests that Henryson, was still active during the reign of James IV, and it seems likely that he was dead by 1490 at latest. His reputation among his near contemporaries is shown by the inclusion in *Liber Plusʳ ᵢrdensis* of two poems which may tentatively be ascribed to him, by the inclusion of two more certain poems in manuscripts probably connected with St Andrews and Archbishop Schevez, by the presence of *Orpheus and Eurydice* among the Chepman and Myllar prints, and by the references in Dunbar and Douglas.[62]

60 MacQueen, *Henryson, passim*, but especially chapter 1 and the appendices. It seems likely that numerology plays some part in his poetry, but details have not yet been established. *Orpheus and Eurydice* almost certainly has a numerological basis in the Platonic formula for the *Anima Mundi* (*Timaeus* 35–6). Numerological elements are present in the *Testament of Criseyde* and the *Preiching of the Swallow*.

61 *Registrum Episcopatus Glasguensis* (Edinburgh, 1843) ii, pp. 334–9. The *liber Boetii cum glossa Trevet* may well have included the *De Musica* and *De Arithmetica*. See also N. R. Ker, *Medieval Libraries of Great Britain* (second edition, London, 1964), p. 90.

62 'Quhen he was seik', Mackenzie, *Dunbar*, pp. 20–23. The reference to Henryson occurs in lines 81–2. See also Douglas's gloss on Virgil's *Musa, mihi causas memora;*

Henryson's subsequent standing as a poet has always in some degree been lessened by the pre-eminence accorded in the eighteenth century to Gavin Douglas and more recently to Dunbar. Henryson has nothing to compare with the translation of the *Aeneid*; in terms of Douglas's original work, however, there can be no question which poet has the greater range and body of achievement. Dunbar's metrical and linguistic virtuosity, the total effectiveness of his best poems, has to some extent hidden his emotional and intellectual limitations. He misses the two great literary kinds – tragedy and the form of comedy which depends on interplay of personality and social and stylistic level – partly at least because he possesses no extensive coherent body of general principles and ideas from which his poetry may grow. Henryson's virtuosity with language and metre is less ostentatious than Dunbar's, and so to some extent has passed unnoticed. His greatness is most plainly to be seen in the range of general principles and ideas which informs his verse and allows it to encompass tragedy and comedy alike. Henryson is more Shakespearian than Dunbar.

As was suggested above, the *Fabillis*, his great achievement in comedy of the kind I have described, were written for a middle-class professional audience of private readers, much interested in the state of contemporary Scotland, an audience which we may assume to have been predominantly masculine. By contrast, his tragedy, *The Testament of Cresseid*, is written in the more public high style, for recitation to a more courtly audience with more feminine interests and weaknesses. The central figure is a woman, and twice Henryson addresses the women in his audience. Once he does so obliquely through the mouth of Cresseid:

> O Ladyis fair of Troy and Grece, attend,
> My miserie, quhilk nane may comprehend,
> My frivoll Fourtoun, my Infelicitie
> (452–4)

(It is worth remembering that in the pseudo-historical tradition all the people of Britain were regarded as descended either from Greeks – the Scots, or Trojans – the Welsh and English.) A second time he speaks to the women in his own *persona* as narrator:

> Now, worthie Wemen, in this Ballet schort,
> Made for your worschip and Instructioun
> (610–11)

'Musa in Grew signifeis an inventryce or invention in our langgage, and of the ix Musis sum thing in my Palyce of Honour and be Mastir Robert Hendirson in New Orpheus'; Coldwell, *Virgil's Aeneid* II, p. 19 n. 13. Douglas here treats Henryson as a scholar and poet of like status with himself. The gloss is interesting also as indicating the probable original title of Henryson's *Orpheus and Eurydice*.

The *Testament*, his greatest poem, and one of the great poems in any variety of the English language, is also his most Chaucerian in that it presupposes in the reader a knowledge of Chaucer's *Troilus and Criseyde* and, for the most part, employs the *Troilus* stanza. But that is not to say that it is simply derivative. Chaucer is by no means the only *auctor* to influence the poem. More important is the way in which Henryson's imitation (in the rhetorical sense) conveys an implicit criticism and correction, as well as appreciation, of Chaucer's master-piece.[63] Henryson, in other words, follows the great masters by 'improving' as well as 'imitating' his predecessor, and in the process achieves a work which is uniquely his own.

The *Testament* exhibits the stylistic virtuosity appropriate to a poet of the school established in Scotland by James I. The assembly of the planets, for instance, is a masterly variation on the dream-vision convention so familiar in court poetry. Even so, the morality and humanity alike of the poem belongs more to the middle classes and some of the original courtly audience must have been startled, even shocked, by his powerful realism. None of Henryson's poetry pre-dominantly belongs to the court, and, perhaps as a consequence, with the southern courtly style he combines a strong element derived from the more northerly alliterative verse; in poems such as *Golagros and Gawane*, *The Buke of the Howlat* and even *Rauf Coílyear* this still retained something of a courtly cast, but was tending more and more to the provincial, the rustic and the popular. Both effects were later brilliantly combined by Dunbar in *The Twa Mariit Wemen and the Wedo*. Dunbar here wrote entirely in the alliterative long line; by contrast Henryson combines the measured rhyme-royal of Chaucer and James I with the formal sound-patterning characteristic of allitera-tive verse, to achieve an almost infinite range of tonal effects. This is as true of the *Fabillis* as of the *Testament*. In the *Testament* these lines may serve to illustrate:

> And I fra luifferis left and all forlane
> (140)
> Felterit unfair, ouirfret with Froistis hoir
> (164)
> Setting sangis and singand merilie
> (243)
> Under this stane lait Lipper lyis deid
> (609)

The lower style of *The Tod*, usually grouped among the *Fabillis*,

---

63 J. MacQueen, 'The Case for Early Scottish Literature', *Edinburgh Studies in English and Scots*, edited by A. J. Aitken, A. McIntosh and H. Pálsson (London, 1971), pp. 240–42.

opens quite different possibilities.[64] The hypocritical Fox, for instance, dissimulates to the Cock:

> Your fader oft fulfillit hes my wame
> And send me mete fra middingis to the muiris . . .
> Syne at the last that swete swelt in my arme.
> (45–6; 49)

Later the farm-house dogs pursue the Fox:

> With that but bade thay breddit our the bent,
> As fire of flint that our the feildis flaw.
> (155–6)

In the third episode, the lion summons a parliament on a spring morning:

> The ground was grene and as the gold it glemys
> With gresis growand gudely grete and gay.
> The spice than spred to spring on every spray.
> The lark, the mavis and the merle so hee
> Swetlye can sing, trippand fra tree to tree.
> (472–6)

With this, contrast the winter passage in *The Preiching of the Swallow*:

> Thir dailis deip with dubbis drownit is,
> Baith hill and holt heilit with frostis hair,
> And bewis bene ar bethit bare of blis
> Be wikkit windis of the wintare wair.
> All wyild beistis than fra the bentis bair
> Drawis for dreid unto thair dennis deip,
> Couchand for cauld in cowis thame to keip.
> (78–84)

All these examples are drawn from poems in rhyme-royal, but any complete analysis of Henryson's versification would have to include the beautiful chiming stanza of 'The Annunciation', the coarser rhyming alliterative verse of 'Sum Practysis of Medecyne', the use of ballad-like forms in 'The Garmont of Gud Ladeis', 'The Bludy Serk'

---

64 See the text in *A Choice of Scottish Verse*, edited by J. and W. MacQueen (London, 1972), pp. 55–85. The collection, generally known as the *Morall Fabillis*, in fact consists of the *Morall Fabillis* proper (the *Prolog*, the *Cok and the Jasp*, the *Uponlandis Mous and the Burges Mous*, the *Scheip and the Doig*, the *Wolf and the Lamb*, and the *Paddok and the Mous*); the more elaborate and independent *The Preiching of the Swallow*, linked by means of a prologue to its sequel, *The Lyoun and the Mous*; a beast-epic in three cantos, *The Tod*, and three independent beast tales, (a) *The Wolf that gat the Nekhering throw the Wrinkis of the Foxe that begylit the Cadgear*, (b) *The Foxe that begylit the Wolf in the Schadow of the Mone*, and (c) *The Wolf and the Wedder*.

and 'Robene and Makyne', and the elaborate stanzaic structures in the 'Complaint of Orpheus' and the 'Complaint of Cresseid'. Henryson was indeed a virtuoso of language, a superb master of his instrument.

7

In 'Quhen he was seik', generally known as 'Lament for the Makaris', Dunbar lists twenty-two Scottish poets from Barbour to Walter Kennedy, who died in 1507 or 1508. Virtually all the poets whose names have been mentioned in this essay are included, but for many nothing has survived, or no more than a few, perhaps quite unrepresentative, lines. Under such circumstances of loss and destruction no conceivable account of fifteenth-century literature can be more than tentative. Yet the evidence which has survived is reasonably consistent and forms a convincing pattern of social, philosophical and artistic development. The reality must have differed in at least one respect: it was richer than any reconstruction now open to scholarship and criticism.

10

The Lordship of the Isles
John Bannerman

The guidelines for an examination of the social organization and culture of the Lordship of the Isles in the fifteenth century are the same as those laid down for the country as a whole in the remainder of this book. In other words, a province of Scotland is being considered here, in so far as the available evidence allows, on the same basis as the nation itself. In many ways the Lordship of the Isles was, by the fifteenth century, unlike other comparable areas of Scotland. But it merits attention because of the abundance of evidence it provides for such an areal study, and even more because of the variety of that evidence. Nowhere else in Scotland is it possible to find a similar body of material to illuminate the contemporary social scene at the level of a province. Having said that, however, it is necessary to emphasize that what follows can only be a survey. Much detailed research remains to be done.[1]

An important factor in the availability of relevant source material is the continuity of tradition in the Lordship, particularly in terms of language. The Lordship had not seen the replacement of Gaelic by Scots already experienced in some other parts of Scotland, so that not only had fifteenth-century society there a relatively unobscured view of its own past but we too are thereby enabled to make direct comparisons with pre-twelfth century social conditions in both Scotland and Ireland, and with contemporary society in Ireland, particularly those parts which remained outside direct English control. This included in the fifteenth century the province of Ulster which neighboured the Lordship of the Isles and a part of which, the Glens of Antrim, had come into the possession of the Clan Donald towards the end of the fourteenth century.

It is this same continuity of tradition that often permits the use of incidental evidence gleaned from post-fifteenth century sources to illuminate the life and culture of that century, and an inherent rever-

1 Statements that depend on discussion in K. A. Steer and J. W. M. Bannerman, *Late Medieval Monumental Sculpture in the West Highlands* (Edinburgh, 1977) are not referenced.

ence for the past makes accounts bearing directly on the Lordship of the Isles by Gaelic-speaking authors of later centuries a much richer quarry for the historian of the period than might otherwise be expected. Donald Monro, archdeacon of the Isles, who wrote his description of the Western Isles in Scots *c.* 1550, was a near contemporary.[2] But it is surprising how often the narrative of the Clan Donald historians of the seventeenth century is confirmed by contemporary documentary evidence, and this despite the bias inherent in the fact that Hugh MacDonald, the Sleat *seanchaidh*, and the MacMhuirich authors of the *Book of Clanranald* were in the employ of MacDonalds. Moreover, by their own admission, their accounts, the one in more or less standard seventeenth-century English and the other in the classical Gaelic of the learned orders, were partly written in answer to what they considered to be George Buchanan's uncharitable treatment of Gaelic-speaking Scots, especially those of the Clan Donald, which was all the more reprehensible in Hugh MacDonald's opinion because 'it is well known that he himself was a Highlander',[3] by which he meant a Gaelic speaker.[4] The MacMhuirichs, Cathal and Niall, whose ancestors, as we shall see, were poets to the Lords of the Isles in the fifteenth century, clearly had access to an annalistic record of events associated with the Lordship. Some of these same events were recorded in contemporary Irish annals, which also provide a running commentary on the activities of the inhabitants of the Lordship and their descendants in Ireland itself; the *Annals of Ulster* are especially full in this respect.[5]

Another native source is the *Book of the Dean of Lismore*, a collection of Gaelic poetry, compiled by James MacGregor, dean of Lismore (died 1551), and his poet brother Duncan in the first quarter of the sixteenth century. It is written in a phonetic spelling based on Scots and contains many thousands of lines of poetry composed by Scottish and Irish poets.[6] Much of the poetry attributed to Scottish authors,

2 *Monro's Western Isles of Scotland and Genealogies of the Clans 1549*, edited by R. W. Munro (Edinburgh, 1961), pp 11–25. For Monro's knowledge of Gaelic, see A. Matheson, review *SHR* xlii (1963), p. 50.

3 *The Book of Clanranald*, edited by A. Cameron in *Reliquiae Celticae*, edited by A. MacBain and J. Kennedy (Inverness, 1892–4), p. 170; H. Macdonald, 'History of the Macdonalds' in *Highland Papers*, edited by J. R. N. Macphail (SHS, 1914–34) i, pp. 10–11 and 30–31.

4 Gaelic was Buchanan's mother tongue according to his contemporary Ninian Winzet, *Velitatio in Georgium Buchananum* (Ingolstadt, 1582), p. 197. I am indebted to Dr A. Williams for this reference.

5 *AU.*

6 NLS, Advocates' MS. 72.1.37. *Scottish Verse from the Book of the Dean of Lismore*, edited by W. J. Watson (SGTS, 1937), pp. xiv–xxi; D.MacKinnon, *A Descriptive Catalogue of Gaelic Manuscripts in the Advocates' Library Edinburgh, and Elsewhere in Scotland* (Edinburgh, 1912), pp. 225–46.

only one of whom is demonstrably from outside the area culturally dominated by the Lordship of the Isles, was composed in the fifteenth and early sixteenth centuries and gives us a unique insight into the culture of the contemporary kin-based society. Also in the *Book of the Dean of Lismore* is a MacGregor pedigree copied in 1512 by Duncan 'from the history books of the kings and great men'. A history book of the Lords of the Isles themselves was probably the source of the surviving rather untidy and now partly illegible copy, apparently made in 1467, of genealogies of the important clan chiefs who recognized the authority of the Lords of the Isles *c*. 1400.[7] Inscriptions, mainly in Latin, on crosses and funerary monuments throughout the area, of which more than a hundred are still legible in whole or in part, can be dated to the period *c*. 1350–1560 and give, besides further valuable genealogical information, some indication of the religious attitudes and aspirations of the people, while the style of carving is itself an expression of their culture on stone.

Finally, the official affairs of church and state, at both central and local level, are documented in Latin and, increasingly towards the end of our period, in Scots, in a manner common to the rest of the country, the one exception being a record in Gaelic of a grant of lands in Islay by Donald, Lord of the Isles, in 1408. It was signed by Donald himself and by Fergus MacBeth who probably drew it up, and as such it seems to be the earliest known deed in Scotland to bear the signatures of laymen.[8]

In terms of territory and manpower the Lordship of the Isles was by far the largest and most powerful province of Scotland in the fifteenth century. By the opening of this century it probably included all the Western Isles and such mainland territories as Kintyre, Knapdale, Morvern, Ardgour, Ardnamurchan, Moidart, Knoydart and Lochaber, while its ruling family, ever since the time of their ancestor Somerled (died 1164), had also possessed the neighbouring province of Argyll, or what was left of it. That there were once two provinces is exemplified in the titles *Rí Innse Gall*, 'king of the Hebrides', and *Rí Airir Goídel*, 'king of Argyll', sometimes borne by different members of this family at the same time. The disappearance of the second title in the first half of the fourteenth century is a measure of the effective leadership of John, son of Angus Óg, who died in 1387,[9] and who can be seen for much of his long life pursuing a consistent policy of consolidation which included the perpetuation of the leadership in the

7 For the pedigree, see the *Book of the Dean of Lismore*, p. 144. MS. 1467 is NLS, Advocates' MS. 72.1.1. See MacKinnon, *Catalogue*, pp. 72 and 106.

8 W. J. Watson, *Rosg Gaidhlig* (Inverness, 1915), pp. 182–3. See G. G. Simpson, *Scottish Handwriting 1150–1650* (Edinburgh, 1973), pp. 8–11.

9 *AU*.

hands of the ruling family of his own kindred, the Clan Donald, to the exclusion of other descendants of Somerled. It was probably he who extended the influence of the Lordship in a cultural, if not also in a political, context into the earldom of Atholl and it may have been during his rule that the west coast district of Lochalsh in the earldom of Ross was annexed to the Lordship.

At the opening of the fifteenth century we find the Lordship and the territories subordinate to it under the leadership of John's sons, Donald as Lord of the Isles and John Mór as the latter's designated successor, and progenitor of that section of the Clan Donald which became known as the MacDonalds of Dunivaig and the Glens. It was these two men and their descendants who were to control the destiny of the Lordship for the next century and a half. In the eyes of central government it became a crown possession after the final forfeiture in 1493, but not until 1545, with the death of Donald Dubh,[10] great great grandson of Donald, did the inhabitants thereof finally accept the crown as their immediate superior.

For much of the fifteenth century the Lord of the Isles was also earl of Ross, although this title only meant anything when he was able to impose his authority by force of arms on the kindreds of that earldom, especially on the MacKenzies who, after some initial support for the Lord of the Isles at the beginning of the century, then consistently contested possession of the earldom. The preoccupation of the Lords of the Isles with establishing their authority over this earldom probably contributed to their gradual loss of political influence over the province of Argyll. This becomes evident towards the end of the fifteenth century with the growing power of the Campbells in that area. The title of earl of Argyll conferred on Colin Campbell by the crown in 1457 was no more than recognition of the position towards which the Campbells were working in a kin-based context, namely, that of *Rí Airir Goídel*.[11] Once their position was secure in that province it was their turn to attempt to impose their political will on the neighbouring province of the Lordship of the Isles. The fluctuation in the fortunes of provinces at this level was endemic in the kin-based society, and in the end the crown itself had to act in accordance with its own position therein. For much of the time its role was to hold or attempt to hold the balance between rulers of provinces whose position did not depend upon the crown so much as upon the power and influence of the kindred groupings that they represented. In these circumstances the crown could only bide its time. So the forfeiture of

10 *RMS* II, no. 2172, and see C. M. MacDonald, *The History of Argyll* (Glasgow, 1950), pp. 274–5; *Calendar of Letters and Papers, Foreign and Domestic, Henry VIII* (London, 1864–1932) XXI, part 1, nos. 114, 275 and 815.
11 *Scots Peerage* I, p. 332; MacDonald, *Argyll*, p. 228.

1493 was implemented at a time when the ruling family of the Lordship, which had frequently flouted the authority of the crown in the past, more or less with impunity, was at its weakest, largely through the by now ineffective leadership of the contemporary ruler, John, Lord of the Isles. The real measure of his ineffectiveness as a leader is that he was deposed as *Rí Innse Gall*, probably in the following year, and replaced by John Mór of Dunivaig who was or had once been his designated successor. Equally this event is a measure of the ineffectiveness of a pronouncement of forfeiture over a ruler whose power depended on his position within the kin-based society rather than on any relationship with the crown. Not until the crown backed up its pronouncement with military and political pressure did it achieve its aim but this took more than fifty years, and even then the event which tipped the balance in its favour was the untimely death of Donald Dubh, grandson of the forfeited John. Not only was he recognized as *Rí Innse Gall* or Lord of the Isles by the inhabitants of the Lordship but there are indications that he was beginning to be recognized as such by society at large, a possible pointer, if he had lived, towards action by the crown sometime in the future to rescind the forfeiture.[12]

Consequent upon the weakening of the ruling family a province becomes wide open either to a takeover by the kindred within its bounds that profits most from the decline of the ruling family or to inroads by powerful neighbours. During the sixteenth century we can watch intermittent attempts by the MacLeans to extend their power and influence at the expense of the Clan Donald, particularly in Islay, but in the end the encroaching Campbells of the neighbouring province of Argyll won the race and the result was the annexation of the South Isles, including Islay and Mull, the base of MacLean power, in the seventeenth century.[13] At the beginning of the same century the MacKenzies of the earldom of Ross swallowed up Lewis. In 1623 their leader was made earl of Seaforth which like the earlier grant of the title, earl of Argyll, to the Campbells, was no more than formal recognition by the crown of the position of power that they had already won for themselves in the province of Ross in a kin-based context.[14] In other words, they were earls of Ross in all but name.

Only the rump of the Lordship remained in the possession of the crown, namely, Harris and the Uists, Skye and the Small Isles with the

12 *Henry VIII Letters* xix, part 2, appendix, no. 12; xx, part 1, nos. 382 and 463.

13 See D. Gregory, *History of the Western Highlands and Isles of Scotland from AD 1493 to AD 1625* (Edinburgh, 1881), pp. 191–2, 218, 230–44, 283–6, 289, 310–13 and 354–90; A. M. Sinclair, *The Clan Gillean* (Charlottetown, 1899), pp. 179–81, 192–3, 200–13 and 223–4.

14 *RMS* VIII, no. 539; Gregory, *Western Highlands*, pp. 290–92, 297–9, 309–10 and 334–8.

adjacent mainland districts. Nor was the crown reponsible for maintaining the status quo even here, but rather the power and influence of
the indigenous kindreds which included the Clan Donald of Sleat, the
Clan Ranald, and the MacLeods of Dunvegan and Harris.

The relationship between the Lordship and the crown takes on an
added complexity in our period, if it is true that the campaign by
Donald, Lord of the Isles, culminating in the battle of Harlaw in 1411,
was directed not only towards securing possession of the earldom of
Ross but also of the kingship of the Scots.[15] As far as is known there is
no concrete contemporary evidence to support such a theory but
Donald was a son of a daughter of Robert II and he was no doubt well
aware that his grandfather's accession to the kingship had come about
in exactly similar circumstances. It is therefore worth noting that
Donald had, in terms of the kin-based system of succession, which is
how after all he himself had succeeded to the Lordship of the Isles, a
perfectly good claim to be king of Scots providing that he could
muster the necessary support in the country. Strictly speaking this
would have been the case even if James I had not been a minor and a
captive in English hands. But the latter's circumstances in 1411 pre-
cluded even his consideration as a possible contender in the eyes of the
kin-based society. It is significant that only when Donald Dubh was at
liberty was he recognized as Lord of the Isles by the inhabitants of the
Lordship. It is just possible therefore that the concept of a MacDonald
king of Scots may also lie behind the grandiose scheme to carve up the
kingdom of Scotland envisaged in the so-called Westminster-
Ardtornish treaty of February 1462 between Donald's grandson, John,
Lord of the Isles, and James, earl of Douglas, on the one hand and
Edward IV of England on the other.[16] Even Donald Dubh, desperate
though his position was in comparison with that of Donald of Harlaw,
may have harboured similar dreams when treating with Henry VIII in
1545, especially if this is the construction that we ought to put on a
statement made late in the previous year in an English report to the
effect that there was 'risen a new king in Scotland out of the Scottyshe
Irysshe'.[17] In 1462 and 1545, just as at the time of Harlaw, the Stewart
incumbents, the one a minor and the other at once a minor and female,
were not acceptable in terms of a strictly legal interpretation of the
kin-based system of succession.

What we should not do is to infer from this series of events that the
Lords of the Isles were intent on establishing a separatist state in the

---

15 MacDonald, *Argyll*, p. 188; A. and A. MacDonald, *The Clan Donald* (Inverness,
1896–1904) I, p. 150. But see also R. Nicholson, *Scotland: The Later Middle Ages*
(Edinburgh, 1974), pp. 236–7.

16 *Rot. Scot.* II, pp. 405–7.

17 *Henry VIII Letters* XIX, part 2, no. 795.

west. Such a concept is alien to the kin-based society which looked upon the king of Scots as its patriarchal head. The Lords of the Isles and their supporters were very well aware of their identity as Scots and nowhere is this more clearly demonstrated than by the collection of clan pedigrees in MS. 1467 which begins with the genealogies of David I and MacBeth, and from whose ancestors many of the contemporary clan chiefs derived their own descent. However, their recognition of their identity as Scots did not prevent them, when it suited their book, from making such statements as the one to Henry VIII's council in Ireland by the commissioners of the Lordship in 1545, which reads in paraphrase:

> to show that no suspicion is to be had of us that is callit the Wyld Ilis of Scotland, it is to be remembered that we have always been enemies to the realm of Scotland, who, when we were at peace with the king, hangit, hedit, presoned, and destroyed many of our kyn, freindis and forbears.[18]

The interesting feature from our point of view is that they were careful to make a distinction between king and state, claiming that their enmity in the past had been directed at the state not at the king of Scots. Nor, indeed, had their archetypal role in the foundation of Scotland been forgotten elsewhere in the country. Thus, a royal letter of 1529 to the pope stresses the urgency of making an appointment to the vacant bishopric of the Isles, pointing out that this area had in the beginning formed the largest part of the kingdom of the Scots, while Hector Boece, in his lives of the bishops of Aberdeen published in 1522, tells us that William Elphinstone, bishop of Aberdeen (1483–1514), was concerned to search out 'the antiquities of the Scottish people, especially in the Hebrides, where are preserved the sepulchres of our ancient kings and the ancient monuments of our race'.[19]

Whatever the wider aspirations of the Lords of the Isles in the fifteenth and early sixteenth centuries, there is no doubt that one of their objectives in the short term was English gold. This is written into the Westminster-Ardtornish treaty, and money figured largely in the negotiations with Henry VIII in 1545.[20] However, repeated trafficking with England and its kings may have been prompted in some degree by the memory of pre-1266 conditions when the ambivalent position of the ruling family in the area vis-a-vis Scotland and Norway seemed

18 *ibid.* xx, part 2, no 294. Text in *State Papers during the Reign of Henry VIII* (London, 1830–52) v, p. 503.
19 *The Letters of James V*, edited by R. K. Hannay and D. Hay (Edinburgh, 1954), p. 162; *Hectoris Boetii Murthlacensium et Aberdonensium Episcoporum Vitae* (New Spalding Club, 1894), p. 99.
20 *Rot. Scot.* ii, p. 406; *Henry VIII Letters* xx, part 2, nos. 198 and 294–5.

to give them a certain freedom of action which they might otherwise not have had.[21]

The relationship of the Lordship of the Isles with Ireland was a constant factor and present at many levels. In a purely political context, Ireland was useful as a place of refuge. To avoid possible retribution for his victory as leader of the forces of the Lordship over a government army at the battle of Inverlochy, Donald Balloch, son of John Mór of Dunivaig, retired there in 1431, as did Alexander of the same family after the apprehension and execution of his father and grandfather in 1499.[22] But Ireland's main role was as an outlet for the surplus military potential of the Lordship. Ever since the thirteenth century mercenary soldiers from this part of Scotland had taken a considerable part in the unceasing strife in that country, not only between the English and Irish but also between rival groupings of Irish kindreds. Many of these mercenaries, termed *gall-óglaigh* or galloglasses by the Irish, settled as a more or less permanent military caste in Ireland before 1400,[23] but the annals are witness to the constant traffic across the North Channel throughout the fifteenth century and later. One result of this was that, potentially at any rate, the Lords of the Isles had an enormous reservoir of experienced fighting men on which to draw. This may explain, in part at least, their ability to put on the field of battle armies which, in terms of numbers and expertise, often matched those at the command of the crown itself. Thus, Henry VIII was negotiating for an army of 8,000 men from the Lordship in 1545, which makes less startling the statement that as many as 10,000 accompanied Donald to Harlaw;[24] indeed, Harlaw ranks next to the battles of Bannockburn, Flodden and Culloden in the popular image. Other defeats of apparently substantial royal armies at the hands of the forces of the Lordship occurred at Inverlochy in 1431 and at the battle of Lagebraad in Ross *c.* 1480 where a royal army led by the earl of Atholl was defeated by Angus Óg, son of John, Lord of the Isles, with the loss of 517 men killed, according to Hugh MacDonald.[25] Thereafter, we are told, Huntly and Crawford ignored orders from the king to mount a new expedition against Angus Óg. It is an indication of the military might of the Lordship for much of the fourteenth and fif-

21 A. A. M. Duncan and A. L. Brown, 'Argyll and the Isles in the Earlier Middle Ages', *PSAS* xc (1956–7), pp. 192–218. See also Nicholson, *The Later Middle Ages*, p. 315.

22 *AU*; MacDonald, *Argyll*, p. 196.

23 G. A. Hayes-McCoy, *Scots Mercenary Forces in Ireland* (Dublin, 1937), pp. 15–76.

24 *Henry VIII Letters* xx, part 2, nos. 198 and 294–5; John Major, *A History of Greater Britain* (SHS, 1892), p. 348; G. Buchanan, *The History of Scotland*, translated by J. Aikman (Glasgow and Edinburgh, 1827–9), p. 405.

25 MacDonald, 'History', p. 49.

teenth centuries that almost the only recorded military threat to its borders came from royal armies.

The forces of the Lordship on the other hand made a number of incursions into other areas of Scotland in the fifteenth century besides those primarily aimed at retaining possession of the earldom of Ross; one was made into the earldom of Lennox, for instance, sometime after the death of James I in 1437, and Lachlan MacLean of Duart was said to be among the leaders. An attack on Arran was made *c.* 1443 by an expedition from Knapdale and Kintyre, and in 1453 Donald Balloch harried the islands in the Firth of Clyde and the adjacent mainland districts to the south. An account of this expedition specifically states that Donald Balloch had a fleet of twenty-five galleys at his command.[26] Perhaps nowhere is the importance of the galley in the military organization of the Lordship more clearly indicated than by its ubiquity as a decorative motif on the funerary monuments of the area. The first serious military disturbance recorded within the borders of the Lordship for almost two centuries was the naval battle of Bloody Bay fought off Mull sometime in the period 1481–5 between the Clan Donald led by Angus Óg and the vassal kindreds of the Lordship who supported his father John, Lord of the Isles.[27]

The Lord of the Isles stood in exactly the same relationship to the heads of the important kindreds within his sphere of influence as did the king of Scots to the rulers of provinces in this part of Scotland. The fluctuating fortunes of kindreds within the Lordship were no different from those of the ruling family. In the second half of the fourteenth century the Clan MacLean began to come to the fore in Mull and the fifteenth century saw the expansion of this kindred westwards into the islands of Coll and Tiree and eastwards into the adjacent mainland districts of Ardgour and Morvern; the successive designations of *de Carna*, *de Kilmalew*, and finally, by the beginning of sixteenth century, *de Kingairloch*, of the branch that moved into Morvern are in themselves witness to the process of expansion in this area. We now find that the MacLeans have reformed in five major distinct but related kindreds, namely, the MacLeans of Duart, Lochbuie, Coll, Ardgour, and Kingairloch, all of whom generally but not always followed the lead of MacLean of Duart, and in terms of military power and political influence were beginning to rival the more important Clan Donald kindreds. By 1517 MacLean of Duart could number among his followers the chiefs of neighbouring kindreds, such as MacNeill of Barra and MacQuarrie of Ulva, who were in no way related to his kindred.[28]

26 R. Lindsay of Pitscottie, *The Historie and Cronicles of Scotland* (STS, 1899–1911) I, p. 29; *Asloan Manuscript* I, pp. 216 and 221; *ER* V, pp. 167, 213 and 253.

27 Cameron, *Book of Clanranald*, p. 162; MacDonald, 'History', pp. 49–50.

28 The MacLeans of Lochbuie were in dispute with the MacLeans of Duart in 1506;

Such a process of expansion must be at the expense of the previous inhabitants. The takeover of Ardgour involved the subjugation of 'ane certaine race and clan called Clanmaister alias Mackenis. . . . And this Makmaister being the speciall man of that name' was slain along with his sons 'and the remanent of his friends and kin'.[29] The decimation of the MacMaster or MacInnes kindred implicit in the above account is confirmed for us by the fact that they nowhere appear as a viable political unit in the more detailed records of the following century. Both surnames are, however, still with us, and if there were survivors, we must assume that they either accepted the overlordship of the MacLeans or attached themselves, again in a subordinate capacity, to the chief of a neighbouring kindred.[30]

The fate of the MacMasters was not always experienced by the weaker kindred. Indeed, this was probably an exceptional case in the fifteenth-century Lordship. The MacKinnons suffered at the hands of the MacLeans in Mull but they survived as a kindred, and there is no record of concerted military action against them.[31] The MacKinnons themselves derive from a kindred which had shared in the expansionist policies of Somerled in the second half of the twelfth century, apparently crossing from Knapdale into Mull and Tiree. The curtailment of their power and influence in this area by the MacLeans probably explains their extension into Skye during the fifteenth century, thus illustrating another facet of the rise and decline of kindreds. The replacement of their designation *de Mishnish* in Mull by *de Strathordle* in Skye in the first half of the following century is an indication that they now considered the centre of their power to have been transferred from Mull to Skye.[32] Whom they, in turn, displaced in Skye is not known. Like the king of Scots, the Lord of Isles could only hope to influence trends of this kind for his own benefit. So the crown's fostering of the Campbells as a makeweight to the Mac-Donalds may be compared with the tradition that the Lord of the Isles supported the MacLeans at the expense of the MacMasters in Ardgour.[33]

The level of society beneath that of the heads of important kindreds

ER xii, pp. 709–10. For MacLean of Duart's followers, see *Acts of Council (Public Affairs)*, p. 80.

29 *Geographical Collections relating to Scotland made by Walter Macfarlane* (SHS, 1906–8) ii, 163–4. See also MacDonald, 'History', pp. 26–7.

30 There is a strong tradition today among certain MacInnes families in Skye which maintains that their ancestors came from Morvern. I am indebted to Dr J. MacInnes for this information.

31 Sinclair, *Clan Gillean*, pp. 44–53.

32 *RSS* i, no. 2878; *APS* ii, p. 333; *RMS* iii, no. 2739.

33 *Geographical Collections* ii, p. 164; MacDonald, 'History', p. 27.

is to be seen most clearly in the crown rentals of North and South Kintyre drawn up in 1505 and 1506.[34] Kintyre had been forfeited to the crown since 1475 but it was probably only the execution of John Mór MacDonald of Dunivaig in 1499 that enabled it to enjoy the fruits of that forfeiture. The rentals for South Kintyre are more detailed than those for the North but even so the local landholders of a sizable area, thirteen named holdings amounting to forty merklands in extent, are not recorded because these lands are entered under the name of Alasdair MacAlasdair of Loup as *senescallus* or *ballivus* of Kintyre, an office which Charles MacAlasdair had been granted by the crown for life in 1481 along with these same lands.[35] All the other landholders named seem to be resident in South Kintyre. However, although Kintyre had long been at the centre of Clan Donald power, none except the MacAlasdairs can be certainly identified as a MacDonald. The amount of land held by the MacEacherns of Killellan, six individuals of whom are named including the chief, indicates that they were the most powerful local kindred in the area. Killellan itself and other lands were held in virtue of their chief's position as *maer* of South Kintyre. This office which, we are told, he and his predecessors had held of the Lord of the Isles, had been confirmed to him by the crown in 1499. His opposite number in North Kintyre was MacKay of Ugadale who held lands including Ugadale for his fee as *maer*.[36] Another important kindred in the area were the MacNeills of Carskeich, while five or six individual MacMillans are listed as holding lands including the chief. It has been shown that these were the MacMillans of Knapdale who were probably expelled by the crown from their lands there as a result of their support for John, Lord of the Isles, in a disturbance in 1478 involving the royal castle Sween, of which their chief was then almost certainly the keeper. They seem to have been resettled in South Kintyre in doubtless much reduced circumstances.

A number of professional families can also be identified. The contemporary head of the MacMhuirichs, hereditary poets to the Lords of the Isles, continued to hold five named holdings, eight merklands in extent, *per poetam*, while the MacIlshenaich harpists to the Lords of the Isles are also recorded as holding lands in the area. Another landholder was Moricius MacNeill, parson of Kilblane, who leased the two merklands of the same name as his parish.

The names of all the landholders in the area are not, however, recorded in these rentals. For instance, Lachlan MacEsak was a person of sufficient substance to act as a pledge for the payment of rents from

---

34 *ER* xii, pp. 698–709.
35 *ibid*. xii, pp. 699–700; *RMS* ii, no. 1480.
36 *RSS* i, no 368; *ER* xii, pp. 583–4; see also pp. 702 and 706, and xiii, pp. 222 and 252.

three named holdings in 1505 and yet nowhere is he or any of his surname recorded as landholders. In the corresponding rental of 1541, we actually find these same holdings tenanted by a Donald MacEsak.[37] Colin, chief of the MacEacherns, is credited with fourteen named holdings, twenty merklands in all; many of these will have been let by him to substantial sub-tenants, most of them no doubt members of his own kindred, but not necessarily all. Colin MacEachern, besides acting as surety for named members of his own kindred who held lands of the crown, was pledge for a number of other crown tenants who did not bear his surname. Considered purely in terms of the law tracts of the seventh and eighth centuries, we have probably not yet penetrated to the level of the landholders whom they would have classed as commoners.[38] In other words, apart from the heads of kindreds, the people named in the Kintyre rentals are the nobles, the *daoin-uaisle* or 'gentlemen' of later centuries. This class includes churchmen and members of the professional families who, accorded the status of nobles in these same law tracts, seem to have maintained a similar position in society into our period and beyond.[39]

In 1506 the crown lands of Kintyre were let for terms of three years. On the other hand, the Gaelic charter of 1408 by Donald, Lord of the Isles, records a grant in Islay of twelve named holdings, eleven and half merklands in all, to Vicar Brian MacKay, a person of similar standing to those who appear in the Kintyre rentals, and to his heirs in perpetuity.[40] In terms of continuity of succession, however, the reality probably lay somewhere between these extremes. Thus, it is possible to demonstrate at once that two thirds of the holdings mentioned in 1505 and 1506 were in the hands of kinsmen in 1541. And although MacKays occupied only two of nine or ten holdings mentioned in the Gaelic charter of 1408 which can be identified in the Islay crown rental of 1541, the latter document reveals that they were nevertheless the most numerous kindred in the district at this time.[41]

The basis of the economy of the kin-based society in Scotland and Ireland had long been the *bó* or cow, so much so that the value of any object might be estimated in terms of cattle in the law tracts of the seventh and eighth centuries.[42] It was still possible in Skye in the seventeenth century to value a contemporary manuscript copy of the

37 *ibid.* xii, p.701; xvii, p. 633.

38 *CG*, pp. 77–8 and 98–9.

39 *ALI* v, pp. 52–70 and 91–115. See also K. Hughes, *The Church in Early Irish Society* (London, 1966), pp. 134–6.

40 Watson, *Rosg Gaidhlig*, pp. 182–3.

41 The 1541 holdings are in *ER* xvii, pp. 625–33. For the Islay crown rental, see *ibid.* xvii, pp. 611–13.

42 *CG*, pp. 77 and 105–6.

Gaelic version of Gordon's *Lilium Medicinae*, now in the National Library of Scotland, at sixty milk cows. Another Gaelic translation of the same work cost the earl of Kildare twenty cows in 1500.[43] Brian MacKay paid an annual rent of 'four cows fit to be killed' for the lands in Islay granted to him in 1408, while cattle formed a prominent part of the crown rents of Kintyre in 1505–6. But so did pigs and sheep, and the larger holdings were also expected to produce quantities of white and great oatmeal, as well as oat and barley malt, testifying to the importance of cropping in the agricultural economy of the period. A half century later Donald Monro was able to vouch for the fertility of certain of the Western Isles in terms which are all the more impressive when it is remembered that his place of origin was the rich agricultural area of Easter Ross.[44]

'In case these cows could not be found', the charter of 1408 also gives the value of the rent in terms of money, 'forty-two merks for these same cows'. Money also formed a part of the total rent required of the crown tenants in South Kintyre in 1505. The financial officer of the early law tracts was called a *rechtaire*, synonymous in later times with *maer*, so the continued existence of the office of *maer* in South Kintyre is in keeping with the apportionment of the rents in kind *pro le cane* and *pro le cuddech*. *Cane* or *caín* usually means 'tribute' in the early law tracts, probably in origin that owed by all freemen to the ruler. The term *cuddech* which is *cuid oidhche*, literally, 'share of a night', can also be traced back to the law tracts where the service of *cóe*, 'guesting or a night's entertainment', is recorded.[45] In 1505 the *cuid oidhche* was the more onerous of the two, the cattle being assigned to it, and it seems to have been a burden only on the larger holdings.

In or shortly after 1567 George Buchanan wrote: 'The *Scoti prisci* to the present time elect their chiefs of clans, and having elected them, associate with them a council of elders.' By 1571, for *Scoti prisci* he had substituted 'the men of the Isles,'[46] and perhaps the most conspicuous piece of government machinery within the Lordship of the Isles was the *Concilium Insularum* or Council of the Isles. A number of fifteenth century charters were issued *cum consensu concilii*. Conflating the accounts of Donald Monro and Hugh MacDonald, we find that the heads of kindreds who attended the Council were divided into four

43 J. MacKechnie, Catalogue of Gaelic Manuscripts (Boston, 1973) I, p. 318, col. 1; S. H. O'Grady, *Catalogue of Irish Manuscripts in the British Museum* (London, 1926) I, p. 220.

44 Monro, *Western Isles*, p. 11.

45 *Dictionary of the Irish Language, etc.* (Royal Irish Academy, 1913–57): M: 28; R: 22–3. CG, pp. 79 and 81.

46 Buchanan, *De Iure Regni Apud Scotos* (Edinburgh, 1579), p. 65; H. R. Trevor-Roper, 'George Buchanan and the Ancient Scottish Constitution', *EHR* Supplement 3 (1966), p. 42.

grades with four in each: 'four great men of living of thair royal blude of Clan-donald lineally descendit', namely, MacDonald of Dunivaig, Clanranald, MacDonald of Keppoch, and MacIan of Ardnamurchan; 'four greatest of the Nobles callit Lords', namely, MacLean of Duart, MacLean of Lochbuie, MacLeod of Dunvegan and Harris, and Mac-Leod of Lewis; 'four thanes of les living and estate', namely, MacKinnon, MacQuarrie,[47] MacNeill of Gigha, and MacNeill of Barra; and four 'freeholders or men that had their lands in factory', namely, MacKay of the Rhinns, MacNicol in Portree, MacEachern of Killellan, MacKay of Ugadale, MacGillevray in Mull, and MacMillan of Knapdale.[48] The membership of the Council as enumerated above clearly relates to the fifteenth century rather than earlier, at least in respect of the first and second grades, for the MacDonalds of Dunivaig were not in existence before *c.* 1400, while the MacLean kindreds of Duart and Lochbuie can hardly have been distinguished as such much earlier than this. Furthermore, the grading reflects the relative importance of the kindreds in the contemporary political situation. The prominent place occupied by the MacLeans and the MacLeods no doubt reflects the increasingly significant part they played as the century came to a close.

The division into grades is reminiscent of law tracts on status in society in seventh- and eighth-century Ireland. Nor should we forget that the same classification of nobles held good for Dalriada in Scotland in the seventh century.[49] It was based partly on property qualifications and partly on the number of their rent-paying clients, and although it may never be possible to work out the details, the holding of land, which was synonomous with the possession of clients or vassals by our period, seems to be an important factor in the grading of the heads of kindreds in the fifteenth century. A further reminder of the early law tracts is the numerical schematism so beloved of the native lawman and which often bore no relation to the contemporary situation.[50] Thus, the limit of four to each grade in the fifteenth century would mean the omission of a number of heads of kindreds who ranked in importance with those named. Six names are actually listed in the fourth grade, and even then the wording implies that only a random selection was being made. Moreover, heads of Lordship

47 For this reading see A. Matheson, review of *Monro's Western Isles of Scotland* in *SHR* XLII (1963), p. 50, n. 1.

48 Monro, *Western Isles*, p. 57; MacDonald, 'History', p. 24. The order of the grades in Monro has been altered to take account of the fact that the MacDonald kindreds were likely to be most important. Donald Balloch of Dunivaig, for instance, is described in a deed of 1475 as 'primus et principalis conciliarus': MacDonald, *Clan Donald* I, p. 548.

49 *CG*, pp. 13–17; 'Uraicecht Becc', *ALI* v, pp. 24–50; J. Bannerman, *Studies in the History of Dalriada* (Edinburgh, 1974), pp. 132–40.

50 *CG*, p. xix.

kindreds, who are not mentioned in these accounts, witnessed documents issued with the consent of the Council in the fifteenth century.[51]

Traditionally, the Council is said to have met at Finlaggan in Islay, the island which lay at the centre of Clan Donald power. But, although there is every reason to accept that Finlaggan was its normal setting, it was also peripatetic, Eigg, Aros in Mull, and Oronsay being other places within the Lordship where meetings of the Council were specifically recorded, Eigg *c.* 1387 and the other two in the fifteenth century.[52] No doubt it was held wherever the Lord of the Isles decreed, and this would depend on where he himself was at any given time, which would in turn dictate its membership to some extent at least.

There are also records of Council meetings at Inverness in 1444 and at Dingwall in February, April and November 1463, in January 1464, and in November 1467.[53] But it is nowhere made clear whether this was the Council of the Isles as such or a comital council of the earldom of Ross. Documents issued with the consent of the Council in this area were witnessed by Munro of Foulis and Chisholm of Strathglass, and on two occasions the witnesses occupied official positions apparently specifically associated with the earldom of Ross. The fact that the heads of Lordship kindreds were frequently in the majority, judging by the witness lists, may only reflect the precarious hold that the Lords of the Isles had over the earldom.[54]

It is not easy to decide how far the Lord of the Isles always consulted his Council, whether of the Isles or of Ross. Certainly, it was at a Council meeting that the Commissioners of the Lord of the Isles were appointed to treat with Henry VIII in 1545. And although not mentioned in any of the extant records, we should probably assume that the Council was also involved in appointing the commissioners who negotiated the treaty of Westminster-Ardtornish ratified in London in 1462. They had received their commission in October of the previous year at Ardtornish and it was there in the same month that a charter by the Lord of the Isles was witnessed by people who would normally be members of the Council,[55] including Donald Balloch of Dunivaig who, along with his son John Mór, is actually named in the treaty. But

51 See Monro, *Western Isles*, pp. 140–44.

52 Finlaggan: *ibid.*, pp. 56–7; MacDonald, 'History', p. 24; M. Martin, *A Description of the Western Islands of Scotland Circa 1695*, edited by D. J. Macleod (Stirling, 1934), p. 273. Eigg, Aros and Oronsay: Cameron, *Book of Clanranald*, p. 160; *RMS* II, no. 2286; MacDonald, *Clan Donald* II, pp. 747–8.

53 See Monro, *Western Isles*, pp. 140–43.

54 For positions associated with the earldom of Ross, see below, p. 224. The heads of Lordship kindreds are not always in the majority in witness lists, but such deeds make no mention of a council: MacDonald, *Clan Donald* I, pp. 527–9 and 539–40.

55 *Henry VIII Letters* XX, part 2, no. 1298; *Rot. Scot.* II, p. 407; Transcripts of Argyll Muniments in Inveraray Castle, II: 10 October 1461.

concentrating only on specific or implied references to the Council, it is clear that it was consulted on a wide variety of matters.

It might, for instance, concern itself with the marriage of one of its members. Thus, in 1469 Hugh of Sleat, brother of John, Lord of the Isles, was informed that he should not marry a second time without consulting certain named members of the Council. In the same document Hugh was granted the lands of Sleat by his brother John with the consent of the Council, which is how Celestinus, John's other brother, had been granted Lochalsh in 1463.[56] A grant of lands in Mull to the abbot and monks of Iona was made with the consent of the Council in 1485, and no doubt other matters concerning the church came within its cognizance. The abbot of Iona and the bishop of the Isles were specifically stated by Donald Monro to be members of the Council, and John MacKinnon, abbot of Iona, witnessed a charter issued with the consent of the Council in 1492.[57]

Likewise financial matters must have come within the provenance of the Council. MacKay of Ugadale and MacEachern of Killellan were members of the Council and also hereditary maers of North and South Kintyre respectively; so too, John MacIan of Ardnamurchan, a member of the Council, held lands from the Lord of the Isles in Islay in return for holding the office of *ballivus* of that island, and we find him making the financial returns from there and elsewhere to the crown in 1507. A charter by John as earl of Ross and Lord of the Isles issued at Dingwall in 1463 with the consent of the Council was witnessed by John Monro of Foulis as *ballivus dicti comitis*,[58] and he was no doubt responsible for making the financial returns of the earldom of Ross or of those parts of it currently obedient to the Lord of the Isles. Four years later, also at Dingwall, Thomas Dingwall, subdean of Ross, witnessed a Council charter as *camerarius*. Here we have the administrative financial officer for the earldom of Ross but there is no reason to suppose that his equivalent for the Lordship of the Isles did not exist. Finally, the bailliary of the southern half of Tiree was granted to John MacLean of Lochbuie in 1492 with the consent of the Council.[59]

A matter which concerned the Council was the inauguration ceremony of the Lords of the Isles. The fullest account by Hugh MacDonald tells us that, in the presence of important churchmen, which included the bishop of Argyll as well as the bishop of the Isles, and the

56 *RMS* II, no. 2286; for dating of this document, see E. Beveridge, *North Uist* (Edinburgh, 1911), p. 41n. See also MacDonald, 'History', p. 59. For Celestine's grant, see *RMS* II, no. 806.

57 MacDonald, *Clan Donald* II, pp. 746–8; Monro, *Western Isles*, p. 57.

58 John MacIan's grant and financial returns are in *RMS* II, nos. 2216 and 2895, and *ER* XII, pp. 587–90. For Monro as *ballivus*, see *RMS* II, no. 801.

59 MacDonald, *Clan Donald* I, pp. 545–6: Dingwall; *ibid.* II, pp. 747–8: MacLean.

heads of all the important kindreds, the Lord of the Isles stood on a stone with a footprint carved on it,

> denoting that he should walk in the footsteps and uprightness of his predecessors and that he was installed by right in his possessions. He was clothed in a white habit, to shew his innocence and integrity of heart, that he would be a light to his people, and maintain the true religion. The white apparel did afterwards belong to the poet by right. Then he was to receive a white rod in his hand, intimating that he had power to rule, not with tyranny and partiality, but with discretion and sincerity. Then he received his forefather's sword, or some other sword, signifying that his duty was to protect and defend them from the incursions of their enemies in peace or war.[60]

Martin Martin and the brief description of the inauguration of Donald, presumably c. 1387 in the *Book of Clanranald*, between them confirm MacDonald's account in all its essential details, Martin adding that, during the ceremony of inauguration of the Lord of the Isles, 'the orator rehearsed a catalogue of his ancestors.'[61] These details can be duplicated many times over in accounts of inauguration ceremonies of kings and rulers in Ireland.[62] The white rod, which the MacMhuirichs call 'the staff of lordship', is a particularly ubiquitous feature, as is the sacred stone that reminds us of the Stone of Destiny on which the kings of Scots were inaugurated. Nor should we forget Fordun's account of the inauguration of Alexander III at which a *seanchaidh* recited the pedigree of the kings of Scots back to Fergus Mór, son of Erc, and ultimately to the legendary Scota, daughter of Pharoah.[63] Finally, in the Bannatyne MS. the elevation of John MacLeod of Minginish to the chiefship of the MacLeods of Dunvegan c. 1552 in the presence of the assembled nobles of the kindred included the presentation of the sword of his predecessors.[64] The place of the poet and the *seanchaidh* in this ceremony makes it less surprising to find Lachlan MacMhuirich, *archipoeta*, witnessing a grant of lands in 1485 made with the consent of the Council.[65]

It is also likely that the Council was involved in the election of a successor to the Lordship in the context of the kin-based system of

60 MacDonald, 'History', pp. 23–4.

61 Martin, *Western Islands*, p. 273; Cameron, *Book of Clanranald*, p. 160.

62 K. Nicholls, *Gaelic and Gaelicised Ireland in the Middle Ages* (Dublin, 1972), pp. 25–30. See also F. J. Byrne, *Irish Kings and High-Kings* (London, 1973), pp. 15–27.

63 *Chron. Fordun*, pp. 294–5.

64 I. F. Grant, *The MacLeods* (London, 1959), pp. 120–21. See also Martin, *Western Islands*, p. 166. The Bannatyne MS. is dated c. 1800 but it contains material said to be derived from the classical tradition: R. C. MacLeod, *The MacLeods of Dunvegan* (Edinburgh, 1927), pp. xi–xiv.

65 MacDonald, *Clan Donald* ii, pp. 746–7.

succession which continued into the sixteenth century to be a factor in terms of succession to the headship of a kindred. That it was in some degree an elective process, at least in the circumstances following upon the recapture and imprisonment of Donald Dubh in 1506, is implied in the glimpses of the negotiations vouchsafed to us by Hugh Mac-Donald.[66] Not only were those eligible to succeed, namely, the heads of the important Clan Donald kindreds, members of the Council, but two members who were heads of vassal kindreds, namely, MacLeod of Lewis and MacLean of Duart, are presented as key figures in the process. So too, deposition, for which there is implied provision in the early law tracts, and which George Buchanan indicates was a function of a chief's council in his day, probably also concerned the Council of the Isles.[67] As early as the 1480s dissatisfaction with the leadership of John was stated to be a factor in the political unrest in the Lordship, and the Council's agreement to his deposition *c.* 1494 must surely have been sought.

Other officials with a non-executive function, besides the *camerarius*, witnessed charters issued with the consent of the Council. Thomas Munro, parson of Kilmonivaig, was a witness at Dingwall in 1463 and at Aros, Mull, in 1469 in his capacity as *secretarius noster*, while Colinus, son of Fergus, was designated *domini cancellarius* in a witness list of 1485. Sir James Weik was *clericus et scribus* to John, Lord of the Isles, in 1476, and the offices of *cancellarius et scribus* carried with them the fermes of two merklands in North Kintyre.[68] The *cancellarius* was presumably the person in charge of the seal of the Lord of the Isles, examples of which have survived, and therefore of the chancery or scriptorium. In this case the statement by Hugh MacDonald, to the effect that MacDuffie of Colonsay 'kept the records of the Isles',[69] may refer to the hereditary keepership of official documents of earlier periods. There can be no doubt that the historical records of the Lordship of the Isles, both oral and written, were in the keeping of the MacMhuirich family. We have already noted that the seventeenth-century MacMhuirichs seem to have possessed an annalistic compilation relating to the Lordship. There was also a *senescallus domus nostre* who was Eogan, son and heir of Donald MacLean of Ardgour, in 1463 and Lachlan, son and heir of Lachlan MacLean of Duart, in 1467.[70] This office seems not to have been hereditary or even held for life, if

66 MacDonald, 'History', pp. 56–8.

67 *CG*, p. 19; *ALI* iv, p. 52; Buchanan, *De Iure Regni*, p. 65.

68 *RMS* ii, nos. 801 and 2286; MacDonald, *Clan Donald* ii, pp. 746–7; *RMS* ii, no. 1277; *ER* xii, p. 703.

69 J. H. Stevenson and M. Wood, *Scottish Heraldic Seals* (Glasgow, 1940) iii, pp. 483–4; MacDonald, 'History', p. 25.

70 *RMS* ii, no 801; MacDonald, *Clan Donald* i, p. 545.

we can judge by the fact that Eogan MacLean was not only still alive in 1467 but witnessed the same document as Lachlan in that year. And it may be that the post was filled by the sons of heads of kindreds, possibly of MacLean kindreds in particular by this time.[71]

But in many ways the most interesting official is Willelmus, *archiiudex*, who witnessed the charter issued with the consent of the Council in 1485.[72] The Council had a peculiar competence to deal with legal matters, judging by the weight of extant evidence, and was, we are told, the supreme court of appeal in the Lordship: 'In thair time thair was great peace and welth in the Iles throw the ministration of justice.'[73] We are told further that there was a judge or *iudex* 'in every Isle for the discussion of all controversies who had lands from Mac-Donald for their trouble and likewise the eleventh part of every action decided'. Appeals from these local courts to the council meant that the 'eleventh share of the sum in debate was due to the principal judge' or *archiiudex*.[74] The term *iudex* appears frequently in Latin documents of the twelfth and thirteenth centuries in much of the rest of Scotland and clearly translates Gaelic *brithem*. So too, Donald *Brehiff* (*brithem*) witnessed documents for John, Lord of the Isles, in 1456, probably the same person as Donald *Iudex* who witnessed a charter by Alexander, Lord of the Isles, in 1447.[75] So much of what we have already seen in the Lordship can ultimately be traced back to the early law tracts that it should come as no surprise to us that the *brithem* was at once the custodian and the interpreter of that law in the seventh and eighth centuries. His function was to arbitrate in cases which were submitted to him by agreement of the disputing parties and he received a percentage of the agreed compensation. There was also the *brithem* who acted for the ruler himself and was a constant member of his household.[76] Such no doubt was Willelmus's relationship to the Lord of the Isles.

The Latin charters issued with the consent of the Council and others

71 According to Hugh MacDonald, the Lord of the Isles granted lands to Hector, ancestor of the MacLeans of Lochbuie, and to his younger brother Lachlan, ancestor of the MacLeans of Duart, 'the chamberlainship of his house'; MacDonald, 'History', pp. 22–3. But see Nigellus MacLeod, *senescallus noster*, witness to a charter by Alexander, Lord of the Isles, in 1438; MacDonald, *Clan Donald* i, pp. 530–31.

72 MacDonald, *Clan Donald* ii, pp. 746–7.

73 MacDonald, 'History', p. 25; Martin, *Western Islands*, p. 273; Monro, *Western Isles*, p. 57.

74 For the local *iudex* see MacDonald, 'History', pp. 24–5; see also Nicholls, *Gaelic and Gaelicised Ireland*, p. 47. For the *archiiudex* see Martin, *Western Islands*, p. 273; for the same proportion of the award in medieval Ireland, see Nicholls, p. 52.

75 G. W. S. Barrow, *The Kingdom of the Scots* (London, 1973), pp. 69–82; H. Paton, *The Mackintosh Muniments, 1442–1820* (Edinburgh, 1903), pp. 1–2; MacDonald, *Clan Donald* i, p. 535.

76 CG, p. 79; D. A. Binchy, 'Secular Institutions' in *Early Irish Society*, edited by M. Dillon (Dublin, 1954), pp. 59–64.

like them produced in the chancery of the Lords of the Isles, not to mention those issued by the Campbells of Argyll and other heads of kindreds, are no different in any essential feature from similar documents emanating from central government. Indeed, so accustomed had society become to conducting their official written business in feudal Latin that not only had it become the language of their funerary and commemorative inscriptions on stone but it was a matter of choice whether the Gaelic form of the surname in *mac* was used in these inscriptions or a Scotticized version which had become familiar in the Latin documents of the period. We would have been hard put to it to demonstrate the essential kin-based structure of society, if this had been the only documentary evidence available to us. *Lachlann MacGhill-Eathain* (MacLean), chief of his kindred, is well hidden by *Rollandus Makclane de Dowart* which is how he witnessed a Latin document in 1476.[77]

However, there is one written expression of the kin-based legal system in the fifteenth century and that is the Gaelic charter of 1408.[78] It owes little or nothing to contemporary Latin deeds in terms of language which gives the impression of having evolved in a legal system with a long and secure past. Indeed, in spirit, if not always in terminology, it reminds one of the twelfth-century Gaelic *notitiae* in the *Book of Deer* and the eleventh- and twelfth-century contracts recorded in Gaelic in the *Book of Kells*.[79] The memory of grants of lands in Knapdale made orally by the Lord of the Isles survived into the nineteenth century, and the wording, in so far as it has been preserved, resembles that of the charter.[80] The uniqueness of the latter is itself testimony to the continuing oral tradition of Gaelic law. That this particular transaction was recorded in writing may be because the grantee was a churchman and therefore orientated towards the written word. A similar explanation may be offered to account for the written material in the *Book of Deer* and the *Book of Kells*.[81]

As membership of the council by the abbot of Iona and the bishop of the Isles implies, the association of the church and state in the Lordship of the Isles was a close one. All five medieval monastic communities in the area, namely, the abbeys of Iona and Saddell, the priories of Ardchattan and Oronsay, and the nunnery of Iona were founded by descendants of Somerled and the evidence of the fifteenth century shows the Lords of the Isles continuing to act as principal lay patrons.

77 MacDonald, *Clan Donald* I, p. 545.

78 Watson, *Rosg Gaidhlig*, pp. 182–3.

79 K. Jackson, *The Gaelic Notes in the Book of Deer* (Cambridge, 1972), pp. 30–32; G. MacNiocaill, *Notitiae as Leabhar Chean-annais* (Dublin, 1961), pp. 10–37.

80 *New Statistical Account: Argyle* VII (Edinburgh *c.* 1850), pp. 384 and 635–6.

81 Jackson, *Gaelic Notes*, pp. 85–8.

Of these, the monastery of Iona was by far the most influential. Indeed, the abbot of Iona was more active in the ecclesiastical affairs of the area than was the bishop of the Isles. Iona's pre-eminence derives ultimately from its foundation by Columba and from its central position as head of the widespread Columban *paruchia* of monasteries. Columba continued to be the paramount saint of the Lordship in our period. The Augustinian priory of Oronsay, founded by John, Lord of the Isles, sometime between 1325 and 1353, was dedicated to Columba. Donald, Lord of the Isles, commissioned a shrine 'of gold and silver for the relic of the hand of Columba', while Roderick MacLean, bishop of the Isles, published a book of Latin verse in praise of Columba in 1549.[82]

The abbey of Saddell had almost ceased to function by the opening of the sixteenth century. Significantly its decline may have begun in 1475 when John, Lord of the Isles, suffered the permanent forfeiture of Kintyre.[83] Otherwise these communities continued in good spiritual health up to the eve of the Reformation, as far as one can judge. Indeed, the recovery of Iona from a period of moral and physical decline, so evident in the records of the early decades of the fifteenth century, was complete by *c.* 1450 when the abbey itself was extensively renovated and restored. It was probably the continuing vitality of the monastery and the pre-eminent position of its abbot that persuaded the papal authorities to grant it *in commendam* to the bishop of the Isles in 1499.[84] About this time too, one of the priors of Iona was a bachelor of decreets, and of the seven members of the community of Iona who witnessed a charter in 1532 only one was unable to sign his name.[85] Major schemes of reconstruction were carried out at the nunnery of Iona in the fifteenth century and at Oronsay *c.* 1500.[86] At Ardchattan a building programme begun in the fifteenth century was continued into the sixteenth, in its later stages apparently under the direction of Duncan MacArthur, prior from *c.* 1508 to 1538; Duncan had graduated master of arts at St Andrews in 1497 and was prominent thereafter in that university's affairs.[87] Finally, the number of inscribed grave-slabs and crosses commissioned by members of these communities in the fifteenth and early sixteenth centuries is noteworthy. They include a fine grave-slab and cross commissioned by Anna

82 Cameron, *Book of Clanranald*, p. 160; *Essays on the Scottish Reformation*, edited by D. McRoberts (Glasgow, 1962), p. xvi and opp. p. 224.

83 A. L. Brown, 'The Cistercian Abbey of Saddell', *Innes Review* xx (1969), pp. 135–7.

84 *Highland Papers* iv, p. 185.

85 *The Book of the Thanes of Cawdor* (Spalding Club, 1859), p. 158.

86 RCAHMS, *Inventory of Argyll* iii (forthcoming).

87 *ibid.* ii (1974), pp. 101 and 110. *St Andrews Acta* ii, p. 264; i, p. cxlii.

MacLean, prioress of Iona from before 1509 to 1543. It is perhaps just as much a comment on the continuing vitality of the monastic communities in the area as on the conservatism of society that no friaries were founded and only one collegiate church, that of Kilmun in Cowal by Duncan Campbell of Lochawe in 1442.[88]

Scottish record material in the Vatican archives gives a clearer picture than hitherto of the secular church in the dioceses of Argyll and the Isles. The mobility of personnel between the two dioceses probably reflects the dominance of the Lords of the Isles in the area. But perhaps the most striking feature to emerge is how well supplied they were with clergy in the fifteenth and early sixteenth centuries. For much of the fifteenth century the church of the Lordship remained in close touch with Rome. One indication of this is the amount of litigation decided there, particularly in connection with the possession of parish livings, and another is the frequency with which lay society had recourse to Rome, most commonly for dispensations, especially for marriage within the forbidden degrees of kinship, so irksome a problem in a kin-based society.[89]

As elsewhere plurality was a factor at parish level, but the most extreme case on record was Rodericus Alexandri, dean of Morvern and, by 1545, bishop elect of the Isles, who had simultaneous possession of two parishes certainly, and possibly of four. Appropriation of parishes is also well attested, with Iona taking the lion's share as might be expected.[90] But having said that, there was a greater percentage of independent parishes in these dioceses than elsewhere in the fifteenth century. All three parishes in Islay, for instance, remained independent, while only one of the eight parishes in the deanery of Morvern had been appropriated by 1560. One possible instance of a curate is known to me, but, if such he was, his beneficed employer, Bricius MacPhilip, who held the vicarage of Killean in the early sixteenth century was himself a member of a professional family, and therefore likely to a be a bona fide ecclesiastic.[91] Within the Lordship itself, the only lay patron of an independent parish to appear in the records was the Lord of the Isles.

The secular clergy, like their counterparts in the regular church, seem to have maintained a reasonably high standard of education. It was they, often in the guise of notaries public, who drew up the documents that oiled the wheels of local government. The parish

88 *RMS* II, no. 346.

89 See Nicholls, *Gaelic and Gaelicised Ireland*, pp. 74–5.

90 Rodericus's parishes: *RSS* I, nos. 2670 and 2896. For appropriations, see I. B. Cowan, *The Parishes of Medieval Scotland* (SRS, 1967).

91 I. B. Cowan, 'Vicarages and the Cure of Souls in Medieval Scotland', *Recs Scot. Church Hist. Soc.* XVI (1966–8), p. 111, and see below, p. 232.

priest, Quintinus, who had himself buried in the grounds of Saddell Abbey sometime before 1500 was a master of arts, as were the two parsons who witnessed a charter by Donald, Lord of the Isles, in 1409.[92] The latter were also bachelors of decreets and Michael, bishop of the Isles, witnessed the same document as a doctor of theology. Of the eight incumbents of, or candidates for, the bishopric of the Isles and commendatorship of Iona who were natives of the area and who received their training before 1560, no less than seven were university graduates in arts, while the eighth was Rodericus Alexandri, commissioner to Henry VIII in 1545, and one of the most influential of the group.

The impression is that society was reasonably well served by its church in the century and a half before the Reformation. The monastic communities continued to receive gifts of property and revenue for much of this period, and perhaps even more indicative of the spiritual vitality of the church as a whole is the large number of contemporary funerary monuments and crosses, particularly the crosses; more than sixty of these have been noted to date, erected by individuals, ecclesiastical and lay, to the glory of God and for the salvation of their souls. Indeed, the comparatively healthy state of the church at the Reformation, probably a reflection of the general conservatism of society as much as anything else, may explain, in part at least, why this area, with the possible exception of mainland Argyll, seems to have been so ill served by the reformed church for so long. In such circumstances recruitment of native clergy would necessarily be slow to get under way.

The kindred considerably influenced the staffing of the pre-Reformation church, particularly the monasteries. Thus, whenever a MacKinnon was abbot of Iona in the fifteenth century, the prior was likely also to be a MacKinnon. The MacDuffies, as local lay patrons of the priory of Oronsay, provided many of the officials of that community, while three successive MacDougall priors of Ardchattan are on record between 1489 and 1508, testifying to the continuing close association of the MacDougalls of Dunollie with the priory founded by their ancestor Duncan, son of Dugall, son of Somerled, *c.* 1230.[93]

As a corollary to this there was an almost total lack of regard for clerical celibacy at all levels in the church, whether secular or regular.[94] Andrew MacEachern, parson of Kilkivan, who set up a cross towards the end of the fourteenth century, had no qualms about naming in the inscription his father Ivor MacEachern, onetime parson of Kilcho-

---

92 *RMS* ii, no. 2264.

93 *Extracta e Variis Cronicis Scocie* (Abbotsford Club, 1842), p. 93.

94 See also Nicholls, *Gaelic and Gaelicised Ireland*, pp. 98–102.

man, and no doubt fully expected the spiritual benefits of his action to accrue to both him and his father. Angus, son of Angus, bishop of the Isles from 1472 to 1480, was almost certainly a son of Angus, son of Donald, Lord of the Isles, who was bishop of the same diocese from 1426 to 1438, and indeed in 1465, he petitioned the papacy to succeed to the abbacy of Iona on the grounds that he was the son of a bishop of royal blood. In the period *c.* 1362–1426, father and son were priors of Oronsay,[95] and another inscribed cross set up by Abbot Finguine of Iona *c.* 1400 also names his two sons. Although the influence of the kindred and a disinterest in clerical celibacy are features of the pre-twelfth century church in Scotland and Ireland, they should probably be seen not as survivals of that church into the fifteenth century but rather as the result of the involvement of the existing church in a society which continued to be organized on the basis of kin.

It is possible to identify families who clearly looked upon service in the church as an hereditary profession; such would be the MacPhilips in North Kintyre in the fifteenth and early sixteenth centuries or the MacCauis family of Ardbraknych, of whom no less than five can be identified as parish priests in the records of Mid Argyll and Cowal between 1529 and 1558, while the MacMhuirichs of Colonsay shared the staffing of Oronsay Priory with the MacDuffies from before 1362 through to the Reformation. Here too we can go back in time to find the law tracts of the seventh and eighth centuries deliberately fitting churchmen into the existing professional class, the *aes dána*, literally 'folk of gifts'.[96] These people, who included literary men, poets, genealogists and historians, but also lawmen, physicians, musicians and those whom we today would describe as craftsmen, workers in metal, wood and stone, were accorded the status of nobles in society. By the twelfth century certainly,they were organized in families pursuing their profession or craft on an hereditary basis, and were attached to the courts of the greater nobility. Many of them conducted a *scol* or school, primarily, of course, for the training of members of the family, but lay people might also attend, no doubt for a fee, and it became the custom for already-established practitioners to make circuits of famous schools.[97]

Very little had altered by the fifteenth century and we must give pride of place to the MacMhuirich family of poets.[98] We possess at least twenty poems composed by their progenitor and eponym,

95 Vatican Archives, Registra Avinionensia (Reg. Aven.), 230, f. 183v; 304, ff. 522v–23; *CPL* vii, pp. 457–8.

96 Hughes, *The Church in Early Irish Society*, pp. 134–6.

97 R. Flower, *The Irish Tradition* (Oxford, 1947), pp. 79–99.

98 D. S. Thomson, 'The MacMhuirich Bardic Family', *TGSI* xliii (1960–63), pp. 276–304.

Muredach Albanach, who came over from Ireland to Scotland early in the thirteenth century. He was an Ó Dálaigh, already well established in Ireland as a literary family, and his descendants were to continue the literary tradition in Scotland down to the end of the eighteenth century, a remarkable length of service. During our period they were poets to the Lords of the Isles. It was Lachlan Mór MacMhuirich who composed the *Brosnachadh Catha* or 'Incitement to Battle' before the battle of Harlaw in 1411. We have already seen another Lachlan MacMhuirich witnessing a charter issued with the consent of the Council of the Isles in 1485 as *archipoeta*, while John Mac-Mhuirich composed one of the two laments for Angus Óg (died 1490) in the *Book of the Dean of Lismore*.[99] Finally, we saw that they held lands in South Kintyre of the Lords of the Isles in return for their services.

Hugh MacDonald, describing the order of precedence at a banquet held by a Lord of the Isles in the fifteenth century, places Mac-Mhuirich, the poet, among the most exalted in the land and above him 'Beatton, the principal physician'. The Beatons, or MacBeths as they were generally known before the seventeenth century, rivalled the MacMhuirichs in length of service and surpassed them in numbers recorded.[100] The first Beaton doctor is traditionally supposed to have come over from Ireland in the retinue of Aine Ó Cathán of Keenaght on the occasion of her marriage to Angus Óg (died 1314 x 18). The Beatons settled at Kilchoman in Islay and we are told in 1609 that the ancestors of Fergus MacBeth, who is described as 'chief physician within the bounds of the Isles', had held lands in that parish of the Lords of the Isles beyond the memory of man.[101] Near neighbours of the MacMhuirichs in South Kintyre were the harpists to the Lords of the Isles whose surname was MacIlshenaich, now Scotticized Mac-Shannon. Their proximity to the MacMhuirichs is explained by the duty of the harpist to accompany the recitation of the chief poet's most elaborate poetry.[102] Finally, there is nothing more certain than that Willelmus, *archiiudex*, was also a member of a family practising law on an hereditary basis but, unfortunately, his surname has not yet been securely identified. However, it is worth noting that his forename, an uncommon one in this part of the country, was used by a family of

99 D. S. Thomson, 'The Harlaw Brosnachadh' in *Celtic Studies*, edited by J. Carney and D. Greene (London, 1968), pp. 147–69: and 'The MacMhuirich Bardic Family', p. 23.

100 MacDonald, 'History', p. 45. J. Bannerman, 'The Beatons', *Scottish Gaelic Studies* (forthcoming).

101 *RMS* vii, no. 109.

102 *ER* xii, p. 700. See account by Thomas Smyth dated 1561: H. F. Hore, 'Irish Bardism in 1561', *Ulster Journal of Archaeology* vi (1858), p. 167.

Morrisons in Lewis who were lawmen to the MacLeods of Lewis by the sixteenth century at least.[103]

Nor were hereditary families of smiths, carpenters and stonemasons absent from the scene in the fifteenth century. We see the first two appearing on inscribed monumental sculpture at Kilmory and Keills, Knapdale, which differs little, if at all, from that commissioned by the contemporary nobility. MacMhic-aíd, the kindred surname of the smiths, suggests a connection with a family of smiths working at the Columban monastery of Kells at the beginning of the twelfth century. To Derry, Kells's successor as the head of all the Columban monasteries in Ireland, belong the Ó Brolcháns whose interest in stone-carving is on record there throughout the twelfth century. Becoming domiciled in Scotland at least by the middle of the fourteenth century, they are on record at Iona *c.* 1450. Thus, Donald Ó Brolchán was responsible for the restoration work carried out in the abbey at that time. An inscription on a cross set up at Ardchattan tells us that it was carved by John Ó Brolchán in 1500. Another family of stonemasons were the Ó Cuinns. Mael-Sechlainn carried out the renovations to Oronsay Priory *c.* 1500 and carved the great cross in the graveyard, while an earlier Ó Cuinn of the same forename signed an effigy of a man in armour on Iona.

Besides the professional families whose permanent patrons in the fifteenth century were certainly or probably the Lords of the Isles, there were others supported by lesser people. The MacNab family of smiths at Dalmally were no doubt employed by the MacGregors at this time. A family whose surname was MacBhreatnaich were harpists probably to the MacNeills of Gigha. The Ó Conchobhair, physicians first to the Campbells and then to the MacDougalls of Dunollie, were already established in the area by our period, as were the MacLachlans at Craiginterve, Kilmartin, which they held of the Campbells in return for their services as physicians. The MacEwans, historians, genealogists and poets, first to the MacDougalls and then to the Campbells, were probably a branch of the old established bardic family of Ó hEóghusa (O'Hosey) in Ireland.[104]

Nor were these professions and crafts mutually exclusive. On the contrary, there was much crossing of the demarcation lines, both in terms of personnel and in terms of a culture which, common to all at certain levels, readily allowed participation in more than one profes-

103 D. S. Thomson, 'Gaelic Learned Orders and Literati in Medieval Scotland', *Scottish Studies* XII (1968), p. 60; Nicholls, *Gaelic and Gaelicised Ireland*, pp. 46–7; W. Matheson, *The Blind Harper* (SGTS, 1970), pp. 186–203.

104 The Ó Conchobhair physicians: MacKinnon, *Catalogue*, pp. 5, 63–5, 140 and 273–7; see also Thomson, 'Gaelic Learned Orders', pp. 63–4. The MacLachlans: *Argyll Transcripts*, II: 17 December 1470, 14 May 1493; III: 2 February 1512. The MacEwans: A. Matheson, 'Bishop Carswell', *TGSI* XLII (1953–9), p. 203.

sion. Thus, Gille-Críst MacBhreatnaich was at once a poet and a harpist, while the legal terminology of the Gaelic charter of 1408 was probably the work of Fergus MacBeth, presumably a member of the famous medical family of that surname. The church was an especially popular outlet for members of professional families.[105] No less than five or six Ó Brolcháns can be identified in the church before 1560, and it is perhaps less surprising therefore to find that master stonemasons of the period were literate in Gaelic and almost certainly in the case of John Ó Brolchán in Latin also. John MacMhuirich was dean of Knoydart when he composed his lament for Angus Óg (died 1490).[106] The author of the other lament for Angus Óg in the *Book of the Dean of Lismore* and of a poem deploring the decline of the Clan Donald, presumably since the forfeiture of 1493 and the events that followed, was Gille-Coluim Mac an Ollaimh, clearly a court poet to the Lord of the Isles and probably a Beaton.[107]

The continuity and solidarity of the Gaelic learned orders is matched by the deep-rooted and long-lived culture that they professed. The lawman of the period seems to have interpreted and declared the law of the kin-based society much as his predecessors had done in the seventh and eighth centuries. The medical manuscripts of the Beatons and the Ó Conchobhairs, which form a considerable proportion of the medieval Gaelic manuscripts of Scottish provenance in the National Library and elsewhere, are mainly translations from Latin of standard thirteenth- and fourteenth-century continental works, the product of the medical schools of the southern universities of Salerno, Padua and Montpellier among others.[108] Yet their fame as physicians can hardly rest on other than the eminently realistic and sensible native corpus of medical knowledge of which we catch glimpses in the early law tracts as well as in incidental notes in these same medieval manuscripts.

One of the reasons that John Carswell, bishop of the Isles, gave for publishing his Gaelic translation of the *Book of Common Order* in 1567 was to counteract the many 'vain hurtful lying worldly tales composed about . . . Fionn mac Cumhaill with his warriors'.[109] Fionn was the leader of a band of wandering hunter-warriors who were supposed to have lived in the third century AD and the Ossianic cycle of prose

105 Thomson, 'Gaelic Learned Orders', pp. 66–9.

106 Watson, *Book of Dean of Lismore*, pp. 96–8.

107 *ibid.*, pp. 82–94; J. Bannerman, 'The Beatons'.

108 MacKinnon, *Catalogue*, pp. 5–71, 275–7, 283–5, 295, 298–9 and 324; F. Shaw, 'Irish Medical Men and Philosophers', *Seven Centuries of Irish Learning*, edited by B. Ó Cuív (Dublin, 1961), pp. 93–4; D. A. Binchy, 'Bretha Déin Chécht', *Eriu* xx (1966), pp. 5–8.

109 *Foirm na n-Urrnuidheadh*, edited by R. L. Thomson (SGTS, 1970), p. 11.

sagas, which has been given the name of Fionn's son Ossian, is concerned to tell of their adventures as they moved about Ireland. Some of these tales already formed part of the *seanchaidh*'s repertoire by the eighth century. But Ossianic literature also became the vehicle for a new literary development in Gaelic, namely, the ballad, that had become popular in western Europe by the early twelfth century.[110] It was to give rise to a whole new corpus of poetry confined mainly to the adventures of Fionn and his warriors, now sometimes localized in Scotland. The *Book of the Dean of Lismore* contains some 2,500 lines of Ossianic poetry in ballad form.[111] Also from the continent came the highly stylized courtly love poem that might have been tailor-made for the Gaelic court poet of the period,[112] but as always his real bread and butter was panegyric, eulogy and elegy, in which he celebrated his permanent or temporary patron, their ancestors and kindred. This was what he was paid for and this was considered to be his most elevated poetry.

It has recently been convincingly demonstrated that the classical stansaic metres, based on syllable counting, derived ultimately from pre-Christian metrical forms, influenced by Latin hymn metres of the fifth and sixth centuries[113]. Such was their complexity, not to mention the often esoteric literary language in which they were couched, that a long period of training in a school was necessary to attain the highest rank of poet. Indeed, the ethos of poetry composed in the bardic style is highly literate and could not have been composed, for instance, by a person ignorant of the rules of spelling.[114] It is for this reason that the number of poets represented in the *Book of the Dean of Lismore* who were not members of professional families is surprising. The implication is that laymen, particularly members of the nobility, were not infrequent attenders of such schools in the fifteenth century. The poem in the *Book of the Dean of Lismore*, that urges the compilation of such a collection of poetry, is not by a professional poet but by Finlay MacNab, chief of the MacNabs of Lochdochart (died 1525).[115] In it he suggests that once the collection is completed, it should be brought to

110 G. Murphy, *The Ossianic Lore and Romantic Tales of Medieval Ireland* (Dublin, 1955), pp. 5–16 (*seanchaidh*'s repertoire) and 19–21.

111 N. Ross, *Heroic Poetry from the Book of the Dean of Lismore* (SGTS, 1939), pp. xvii and 70–76.

112 R. Flower in introduction to *Dánta Grádha*, edited by T. F. O'Rahilly (Dublin, 1926), pp. xi–xxxiv.

113 C. Watkins, 'Indo–European Metrics and Archaic Irish Verse', *Celtica* vi (1963), pp. 194–249.

114 W. J. Watson, 'Classic Gaelic Poetry of Panegyric in Scotland', *TGSI* xxix (1914–19), pp. 194–217. See also E. Knott, *An Introduction to Irish Syllabic Poetry* (Dublin, 1957), pp. 1–20. Watson, *Book of Dean of Lismore*, p. xx.

115 *ibid.*, pp. 2–4.

the earl of Argyll for his judgement of its merits: 'Bring unto Mac-Cailein no poem lacking artistry to be read', implying that Argyll, either Archibald, who was killed at Flodden in 1513, or his son and successor Colin, had received bardic training.[116] Nor are women unrepresented; perhaps the best known poem in the *Book of the Dean of Lismore* is Oighreag MacCorquodale's lament for her husband Niall MacNeill of Gigha (died 1455 x 72).[117] Indeed, it is difficult to see how this poetry could be fully appreciated, far less composed, without a period of formal training.

Bishop Roderick MacLean, 'educated in the islands' we are told in a royal letter of 1544, and 'sufficiently learned according to the custom of [his] people', was also a graduate in arts, probably of the German university of Wittenberg at which he matriculated in 1534.[118] But Scotland was unique in the late medieval period in terms of the provision of higher education. It had offered Gaelic-speaking Scots, ever since the foundation of St Andrews University in 1412, the opportunity of attending in their own country either a university on the continental model or a school in the native tradition. Some attended both. Members of professional families were obviously in a good position to take advantage of this. Thus, Duncan Ó Brolchán, parson of Kildalton in Islay, matriculated in Glasgow University in 1453.[119] The most conspicuous example of a layman attending both institutions is John Carswell, whose expertise in the literary dialect of the day implies his attendance at a bardic school and who graduated bachelor of arts at St Andrews in 1542 and master of arts in 1544.[120]

It is perhaps an indication of the relatively peaceful and settled pattern of life within the Lordship for much of the fourteenth and fifteenth centuries that, in marked contrast to the considerable build-ing activity in the ecclesiastical sphere, few castles can be identified as having been built in this period.[121] And although, on occasion, the Lords of the Isles apparently continued to occupy castles of an earlier

116 Probably Colin, for Hector Boece acknowledges his help in the preface to his *Scotorum Historiae* published in 1527: Boece, *Historiae* (Paris, 1527), f. iii. I am indebted to Mr D. Abbott for drawing my attention to this reference.

117 Watson, *Book of Dean of Lismore*, pp. 60–64.

118 *Epistolae Jacobi Quarti, Jacobi Quinti et Mariae Regum Scotorum*, edited by T. Ruddiman (Edinburgh, 1722–4) II, p. 221; J. Durkan, 'The Cultural Background in Sixteenth-century Scotland' in McRoberts, *Essays on the Scottish Reformation*, p. 320.

119 *Munimenta Alme Universitatis Glasguensis* (Maitland Club, 1854) II, p. 61.

120 Matheson, 'Bishop Carswell', pp. 194–205; *Foirm na n-Urrnuidheadh*, pp. 183–6; *St Andrews Acta* II, pp. 396 and 400.

121 The recent establishment of the MacLeans on Coll and the MacNeills on Barra is sufficient explanation for the building of the castles of Breachacha and Kishmul in the first half of the fifteenth century; see D. J. Turner and J. G. Dunbar, 'Breachacha Castle, Coll; Excavations and Field Survey, 1965–8', *PSAS* CII (1969–70), pp. 173–7.

date, such as Aros in Mull and Ardtornish, nevertheless it is a fact that their principal residence at Finlaggan in Islay is described in Fordun's *Chronicle* as a 'mansion', as is 'the town of Kilchomain', also in Islay, in which 'the Lords of the Iles dwelt ofttymes', according to Donald Monro. Indeed, Monro's reference to Finlaggan as 'well biggit in palace-wark according to thair auld fassoun'[122] seems to imply a building or buildings undefended by fortifications, and there is no sign of any such among the ruins on the site today. The native stonemasons of the period are therefore only to be seen working in an ecclesiastical context and, although involved, as we saw, in the programme of restoration and renovation to monastic buildings, their most characteristic product was the sculptured stone monument fashioned either as a religious symbol or as a memorial to the dead. There are more than six hundred of these monuments – richly decorated crosses, grave-slabs, effigies, tomb-chests and one example of a stone font – still in existence. Of the four principal schools of carving which can be identified in the area, that based on Iona was paramount, not only because of the level of excellence attained and the widespread distribution of its carvings but also because a detailed analysis of the decoration shows that the distinctive style of West Highland memorial sculpture in general derives from the Iona school. It is no accident that the Ó Brolcháns and the Ó Cuinns, with one exception the only stonemasons known to have signed their work, are associated directly with Iona or with monuments of the Iona school.

The surname of the Ó Cuinns, not to mention the forename Mael-Sechlainn, betrays their Irish origins, and we can actually see the Ó Brolcháns in their Irish setting.[123] The fact is that Gaelic-speaking Scots shared a common culture with their counterparts in Ireland. There is no more obvious demonstration of this than the number of Irish poets represented in the collection of Gaelic poetry made by the dean of Lismore and his brother. But, although Ireland was and continued to be the metropolitan centre of the common culture (even as late as the second half of the seventeenth century Donald Mac-Mhuirich, like his predecessors, we are told, went to Ireland for part of his bardic training),[124] the traffic was by no means all one way. John Carswell intended his book to be used in Ireland as well as in Scotland. In 1473 Ruairidh MacBeth is recorded as holding lands in Co. Cork in

122 *RMS* ii, nos. 2286 and 2264. *Chron. Fordun* ii, p. 43. Finlaggan and Kilchoman are not mentioned by name there, but the context, and comparison with the account in Monro, *Western Isles*, pp. 56–7, leave us in no doubt as to their identity.

123 *AU*, 1029, 1086, 1097, 1107, 1122, 1158, 1164, 1175 and 1203; *Annals of the Kingdom of Ireland by the Four Masters*, edited by J. O'Donovan (Dublin, 1851), 1095 and 1139.

124 Thomson, 'The MacMhuirich Bardic Family', p. 301.

fee for his medical services. One of the two poems ascribed to Gille-Críst MacBhreatnaich in the *Book of the Dean of Lismore* was addressed to Tomaltach MacDiarmaid of Moylurg in Connaught (died 1458).[125] In it Gille-Críst suggests that the gift of a harp would sufficiently recompense him for the poem. And music, particularly harp music, may be the area of the common culture in which it would be possible to demonstrate that Scotland outstripped her mentor.

The conservatism of society in the Lordship of the Isles has already received comment here and elsewhere but perhaps nowhere is it more strongly stated than in a royal letter of 1532 which reads:

> The people are tenacious of old custom, traditional manners and rites: they cannot tolerate the introduction of anything which menaces ancestral practice, and if any man . . . fails in a matter of accepted custom, they consider it an imperfection or it fills them with aversion and contempt.[126]

Many of the constituent elements in the prevailing kin-based structure of society, in terms of both organization and law, derive from a pre-twelfth century situation and their fullest expression in written-form is often to be found in the seventh- and eighth-century law tracts. A social system with such a long history behind it cannot fail to impose a similar conservatism on the organization and attitudes of its learned orders and therefore on culture in general. This state of affairs was compounded by what seemed to be, even in the glimpses afforded us, a well-organized and highly pervasive administration under a succession of able rulers who, for much of the fourteenth and fifteenth centuries, proved capable not only of preserving internal peace but also of containing any military threat from beyond the borders of their province. The result was certainly a conservative society but there was no sign of decay, and on the contrary it was a vital living organism which the conformist and unitary influences of central government found difficult to penetrate. And yet, paradoxically, the very confidence generated by this combination of circumstances allowed the acceptance of certain developments from outside, but on society's own terms, which left the essential core undisturbed. The use of the written word at a certain level of government and along with it feudal Latin terminology implies no alteration of the existing kin-basis of society, although it would tend to obscure it if we had no other evidence to set beside it. Sometimes too society reacted to foreign influences by reshaping them in its own image to produce something

125 Carswell: *Foirm na n-Urrnuidheadh*, p. 10; MacBeth: BM, Cotton MS. Titus B. xi (part 2) f. 179; I am indebted to Mr K. Nicholls for providing this reference. Watson, *Book of Dean of Lismore*, pp. 32–44.

126 *James V Letters*, p. 209.

quite different and original. There is no more conspicuous example of this process confined to the area dominated by the Lords of the Isles than the monumental stone masonry, which, although firmly rooted in the common past of Scotland and Ireland, nevertheless borrows much from elsewhere; the net result is a style which is new and distinctive, yet in keeping with the spirit of contemporary society.

The concept of the Lordship and what it stood for is a ubiquitous element in later Gaelic literature. It represented a 'Golden Age' to which it was possible to look back with pride. Indeed, the seventeenth century MacDonald historians were unwilling to accept that any material alteration had occurred in the interval and they considered the contemporary Clan Donald ruling kindreds to be direct heirs of the Lords of the Isles in terms of their standing in society. It is perhaps not too fanciful to see the Lordship, a comparatively recent manifestation of a highly successful native political and social unit and only marginally indebted to foreign influences, as a contributory factor in the continuing existence of the Gaelic language and culture in Scotland today. For the historian it holds up a mirror in which is reflected the system of society once common to almost all Scotland.[127]

127 I wish to thank Professor D. S. Thomson, who kindly read this paper in a first draft, for help and advice.

Chronological table

This table covers the period 1424–1488, with brief references to events during the Albany regency and the first half of the reign of James IV. Entries in square brackets refer to the sixteenth-century accounts of some of the well-known events, which may be largely regarded as legend.

1406–24: Regency of the dukes of Albany

Robert, 1406–20; Murdoch, 1420–24. James I (succeeded 1406) a prisoner in England.

1407 Scots staple in the Low Countries transferred from Middleburg to Bruges; throughout the century, moved from Middleburg to Bruges and back; finally established at Campvere.

1411 Battle of Harlaw: Donald, Lord of the Isles, attempting to secure earldom of Ross, defeated by Alexander Stewart, earl of Mar (Donald's son Alexander recognized as earl of Ross from 1438).

1412 Foundation of University of St Andrews by Henry Wardlaw, bishop of St Andrews.

1418 Postcript to ending of Great Schism: withdrawal of support for Benedict XIII and acknowledgement of Martin V, after period when Scotland, almost sole supporter of Benedict, had enjoyed considerable papal interest and favours.

1423 Treaty of London: James I's release agreed, for payment of 60,000 merks, 10,000 of which were remitted as dowry of his bride Joan Beaufort, daughter of John, earl of Somerset. (Only about one sixth of the ransom was ever paid; but used by James I as an excuse for asking for money, and as a political weapon against three Stewart magnates, who were sent as hostages to England and left there until after James' death.)

1424–37: Personal rule of James I

1424 James returned to Scotland: parliament immediately summoned–beginning of a policy by James I–III of using parliament much more extensively; by contrast James IV, like his contemporary monarchs, showed preference for conciliar government, summoning fewer parliaments up until 1509 and none thereafter. In this century a parliamentary peerage was established.

Battle of Verneuil: earls of Douglas (duke of Touraine) and Buchan killed.

Legislation against clerics going abroad (in pursuit of benefices) without royal leave.

1425 Execution of Albany Stewarts–Murdoch, duke of Albany, two sons and his father-in-law Duncan, earl of Lennox; hence removal of powerful Stewart family and significant addition to crown lands.

1426 Creation of new supreme civil court, the 'Session': representatives of the three estates, under the chancellor, to sit three times a year.

Royal foundation of Charterhouse, Perth.

Act attempting to secure personal attendance at parliament of all tenants-in-chief.

Treaty with Eric, king of Denmark-Norway: arrears of the annual (100 merks per annum, due under treaty of 1266) cancelled; regular payments promised–but not paid.

1427 Malise Graham, earl of Strathearn, deprived of earldom; given earldom of Menteith, but sent to England as hostage, remaining there until 1453.

1428 Act attempting to establish shire election of representatives from 'smal baronnis and fre tenandis', and to introduce a speaker; not effective until revived by James VI, 1587. Included first reference to title of 'lord of parliament'.

Act against 'barratry', i.e. creating crime of barratry, unauthorized purchase of benefices in Rome (further acts, 1482 and 1484).

Renewal of Franco-Scottish alliance, with Charles VII; marriage arranged between James' daughter Margaret and the Dauphin Louis (took place 1436).

James I's expedition to Inverness and arrest of about 50 clan chiefs.

1429 First of series of acts (others in 1450, 1469) protecting rights of tenants against landlords.

Submission of Alexander, Lord of the Isles.

Beginning of long and unsuccessful papal attempt to deprive John Cameron, bishop of Glasgow, held responsible for the barratry legislation–and to have that legislation repealed.

1430 Birth of heir, future James II.

From this date, substantial increase in number of notaries public.

1431 Release and restoration of Alexander, Lord of the Isles.

1433 English offer to restore Berwick and Roxburgh, as counter to Franco-Scottish alliance; rejected.

1435 Franco-Burgundian alliance against England, strengthening Scotland's position.

Forfeiture of George Dunbar, earl of March, possibly because of king's suspicion that this southern magnate was favourable to England.

Death of Alexander Stewart, earl of Mar; claim of nearest heir, Robert Erskine, rejected and Mar escheated to crown.
(Both involved further substantial additions to crown lands.)

1436 Well-supported but unsuccessful siege of Roxburgh.
End of restrictions or ban on Scottish trade by the Hanse, imposed because of Scots piracy.

1437 Murder of James I: nominal leader Walter, earl of Atholl, last surviving son of Robert II's second marriage – the one Stewart who had enjoyed James' favour. Principal murderers Robert Graham, uncle of Malise, earl of Menteith, and an opponent of James as early as 1424, and Robert Stewart, Atholl's grandson. No attempt to remove James' heir, which suggests murder for personal rather than dynastic reasons.

1437–49: Minority of James II

1437–9 Government controlled by queen mother, Archibald, earl of Douglas and John Cameron, bishop of Glasgow and chancellor.

1439 Coup d'état after death of Douglas: Cameron replaced as chancellor by Sir William Crichton; custody of king taken over by Sir Alexander Livingston; queen disgraced, retired into obscurity and an impoverished second marriage.

1439–49 Livingston in control, using position to benefit his family; alternatively backed and opposed by Crichton whose opposition was sufficient to save him from the holocaust which overtook the Livingstons at the end of the minority.

1440 'Black Dinner': William, earl of Douglas, his brother David, and ally Malcolm Fleming of Cumbernauld, invited to Edinburgh Castle and there summarily executed; possible instigator Douglas' great-uncle and heir, James 'the Gross', earl of Avandale.
Rapid extension of Douglas power:

by 1442 Archibald, 3rd son of James 'the Gross', married to Elizabeth

Dunbar, co-heiress to earldom of Moray; although she was the younger sister, Archibald recognized as earl, 1445.

1443/4　William, son and heir of James (succeeded 1443), married Margaret, 'Fair Maid of Galloway', sister of the executed earl William and heiress to his Galloway lands; thus the southern Douglas lands were reunited.

1445　Hugh, 4th son of James, created earl of Ormond.

1444/5　Alexander Seton of Gordon created earl of Huntly.

1445　Formation of Scots Guard by Charles VII.

1448　Renewal of Franco-Scottish alliance.

1449　Marriage of James II to Mary of Gueldres.

Fall of Livingstons: most forfeited, two (whose deaths benefited the king financially) executed.

Beginning of the building of Roslin collegiate church, by William lord Sinclair.

1449–60:　Personal rule of James II

1450–60　Burghal development: 11 new burghs of barony (out of total of 68, 1450–1513)

1450　Foundation of St Salvator's College, St Andrews, by James Kennedy, bishop of St Andrews.

Crown's right to present to benefices in episcopal patronage, during vacancies of sees, recognized by bishops.

1451　Foundation of University of Glasgow, by William Turnbull, bishop of Glasgow.

1450/51　William, earl of Douglas went to Rome for jubilee year, visiting Burgundy and England en route.

King seized his Galloway lands, but was forced to restore them, apparently under pressure from the queen (the intended beneficiary) and parliament.

[1450–52　16th-century writers described Douglases in this period as rejecting royal control and acting virtually as kings in the south-west, their final outrage being the execution of one Maclellan, tutor of Bombie, against the command of the king.]

1452

February　Earl William invited to Stirling under safe-conduct; murdered by king.

March　James, brother and heir of earl William, renounced his allegiance to James II.

May　Battle of Brechin: Huntly, who 'displayit the Kingis banere', defeated Douglas's ally Crawford.

Birth of heir, future James III.

June Parliament; exonerated James II; use of patronage – former Douglas allies created lords of parliament.

William Hay, hereditary Constable, created earl of Erroll.

August King and James earl of Douglas reconciled.

1453 Second agreement between king and Douglas, by which – remarkably – king allowed earl to marry his brother's widow, the 'Fair Maid of Galloway', thus again uniting the vast Douglas inheritance.

1453–5 Period of apparent but uneasy peace between king and Douglas.

1455 Final crisis: James' passion for artillery reflected in its use against Douglas castles of Threave and Abercorn; more decisive was the battle of Arkinholm: Douglas and one brother escaped to England; another brother was killed, and the fourth executed.

End of the Douglas earldom.

Act of annexation: king to live of his own, from certain annexed and inalienable lands and lordships as laid down by parliament.

1457–8 Creation of four earldoms: Argyll (Campbell); Marischal (Keith); Morton (Douglas of Dalkeith); Rothes (Leslie).

1458 Parliament: act anent feu-ferme, by which crown was encouraged to 'giff exampill to laif' by feuing lands, thus increasing cash income; advice not followed to any extent until reign of James IV.

Legislation about arrangements for the Session: judges, places and times where court was to sit nominated in Parliament (the subject of legislation also in 1439, 1450, 1456).

Compliment to James II, whose success as king had brought peace to his realm – and whose success would continue if he put into effect the acts of this parliament.

1460 Siege of Roxburgh – successful but king killed by gun exploding.

1460–69: Minority of James III

1460–65 Government controlled by queen mother (died 1463) and Bishop Kennedy (died 1465). Tension caused by Kennedy's support of the defeated Lancastrians finding refuge in Scotland; immediate advantage that Margaret of Anjou ceded Berwick to the Scots (1461) – as against Mary of Gueldres's more far-sighted support of the Yorkists.

1462 'Treaty of Westminster-Ardtornish', between Edward IV, John, Lord of the Isles and James, exiled earl of Douglas: Edward would annex Scotland, which would be ruled as subject kingdom by John and Douglas. A diplomatic counter to Kennedy's policy rather than a genuine military threat.

1466 Coup d'état by Robert Lord Boyd: seized power by getting hold of the king.

Official parliamentary records survive from this date.

1466–8 Boyds in control: like Livingstons, the family benefited, but Lord Boyd made fatal mistake of ignoring former allies who had supported his takeover in 1466.

1468 Marriage of James III to Margaret of Denmark: Orkney (1468) and Shetland (1469) pledged as part of her dowry; failure to redeem pledge gave Scottish crown *de facto* possession of the islands.

1469 Fall of the Boyds.

Burgh legislation, reflecting long process by which merchants had come to dominate burgh affairs: yearly council elections still to be held, but retiring council to choose new council, and both to elect provost, bailies and dean of gild; each craft to have one representative in election.

Followed up, in 1474, by act which stated that four members of retiring council were to serve on new one.

Followed up also by period when crafts fought back, gaining corporate recognition for themselves in the half-century after 1474.

1469–88: Personal rule of James III

1471–3 Proposals by James III for grandiose but risky foreign military expeditions, to annex part of Brittany, the duchy of Gueldres and Saintonge. 1473 parliament opposed these schemes, reminding king of his duty to provide order and justice at home – the first of a series of parliamentary criticisms on this theme throughout the reign. In this parliament came the revolutionary suggestion of peace with England.

1472 Last occasion when the 'Session' nominated in parliament; thereafter, in this reign, lords of session were replaced by lords of council sitting in Edinburgh.

Archbishopric of St Andrews created, ending anomaly by which Scottish sees had been directly subject to pope.

James III acted as intermediary for treaty between kings of Denmark and France.

1473 Birth of heir, future James IV.

1474 Treaty with England: included marriage proposal between Prince James and Cecilia, daughter of Edward IV (with dowry of 20,000 merks, yearly payments of which were duly made until 1479). Represents major rethinking of Scottish foreign policy.

1475–6 Expedition against John, earl of Ross and Lord of the Isles;

forfeiture of earldom; submission of John, 1476, including his resignation of the earldom, in return for crown recognition of his status as baron, lord of parliament with title 'Lord of the Isles'.

c. 1476/8 Blind Hary's epic poem 'The Wallace'; its violent hostility to England is one piece of evidence that James III's new foreign policy was not one which would command widespread support.

1478 First archbishop of St Andrews, Patrick Graham, deprived; replaced by William Schevez, James III's physician and co-adjutor of the see from 1476 – a genuine candidate for the title of favourite of James III (*vide* 1482).

Records of lords of council sitting as supreme civil court survive from this date.

1479 Arrest of king's brothers, Alexander, duke of Albany, and John, earl of Mar. Albany escaped to France and then England; Mar died in mysterious circumstances.
[His death was attributed to his consorting with witches and warlocks; 16th-century writers claimed he had died in 'ane baith fatt' – a brewer's or dyer's vat. This looks like borrowing from the account of the death of George, duke of Clarence, in 1478, drowned in a butt of malmsey after conspiring with sorcerers – with the nice economic touch that an English royal duke could die in malmsey, a Scottish royal earl in at best a brewer's, at worst a dyer's vat.]

Further proposal for marriage alliance with England.

Unusually large parliament: 104, as contrasted to normal average of 50/60; possibly because its business included proposed taxation for the expenses of the English marriage – and new overtures of friendship from France.

1480–82 Period of temporary setback for policy of friendship with England: renewed fighting on the Borders – worsening relations with England; and growing political and economic crisis at home, given expression in violent hostility to heavily debased coinage, the 'blak pennyis'.

1481 Threat of English invasion: commission by Edward IV – Richard, duke of Gloucester and James, former earl of Douglas, to promise lands and lordships to all Scots who would support the English. Arrangements made by Scottish parliament for defence of Berwick and the Borders.

1482

March Further provision for war made by parliament, on very small scale compared to English preparations.

June Alexander, duke of Albany, was promised English help to usurp Scottish throne, in return for homage, surrender of Berwick and border lands, and breaking of the French alliance.

July Scottish army summoned to assemble at Lauder. Group of nobles, led by James III's half-uncles, earls of Atholl and Buchan, and the earl of Angus, seized king, brought him back to Edinburgh and warded him in the castle.

August English army took Berwick, with little resistance; small English force marched to Edinburgh; no support for Albany as king, and no attempt by the English to enforce his claim.

Sept James and Albany reconciled.

Dec Albany demanded office of lieutenant-general, in parliament.
1483

January New conspiracy by Albany against king.

May–July Albany fled to England; forfeited.

1484 Unsuccessful attempt by Albany and Douglas to regain power; Albany fled to France (died 1485); Douglas confined in Lindores Abbey (died 1491).

[The 16th-century writers gradually built up as the major feature of this lengthy political crisis what was originally a minor offshoot: in the skirmish at Lauder, some of James' household servants were, it seems, killed; they became the famous 'low-born favourites', whose hanging at Lauder Bridge was the purpose of the whole episode; they were given names and became the architect, musician etc, of the familiar account. The names were not fictitious; the role of the 'favourites' was, however, at least a massive distortion.]

1485 Petition to Pope Innocent VIII: requested that the king should have six months in which to nominate to benefices, because of 'the gret distaunce of this realme fra the Court of Rome'; this followed a clash between Sixtus V and James III over provisions to the bishoprics of Glasgow and Dunkeld.

1486 Truce with England and new marriage proposal; last years of reign saw peace and stability, now pursued by the English king, Henry VII, as well as the Scottish one.

1487 Indult: pope agreed to delay provision to major benefices until they had been vacant for eight months, while awaiting king's nomination – admission not only of defeat but of *de facto* situation.

1488 Argyll sacked as chancellor; he, Angus and a group of lords with individual grievances, attracted James' heir to their side. James III made two agreements with his opponents (at Aberdeen and Blackness); suspicion that the king had no intention of observing these caused some of his former supporters – the northern magnates – to withdraw to the north and retreat into neutrality. In June the king, still with greater numbers, met the rebel army at Sauchieburn, where he 'happinit to be slane' [probably during the battle rather than, as 16th-century writers claimed, at the mill of Bannockburn by an armed stranger masquerading as a priest, after the king's coward flight].

1488–1503: First part of reign of James IV

1488 Treasurer's accounts survive continuously from this date (an earlier isolated account survives, for 1473/4).

1488–90 New government established itself, with remarkable ease, on the basis of conciliation and effective propaganda, and the fairly easy quelling of two minor rebellions, the only overt sign of hostility.

1492 Treaty with Hans, king of Denmark-Norway, including provision for reciprocal trading.

Renewal of Franco-Scottish alliance.

Archbishopric of Glasgow created, ending period of tension between Glasgow and St Andrews since 1472.

1493 Final forfeiture of John, Lord of the Isles (not accepted in the Isles until after 1545, with death of last claimant, Donald Dubh).

1495 Foundation of University of Aberdeen, by William Elphinstone, bishop of Aberdeen; intended to have strong law school. For the first time, education of laity as well as clerics specifically provided for, in foundation bull.

1496 'Education Act': eldest sons and heirs of all barons and substantial freeholders to go to grammar school; when they had learned 'perfyte Latyne', they were to study arts and law for three years at university.

1497 First recorded Scots mercenaries in Denmark.

1499 Tripartite alliance between kings of France, Scotland and Denmark; made in Edinburgh with James IV acting as procurator for his uncle, Hans of Denmark.

c. 1500–1502 Building of Great Hall at Stirling Castle; the most ambitious and magnificent building of the period, put up, as the building accounts make clear, in the reign of James IV, not by the legendary architect of James III, Cochrane.

1502 Scottish force sent to Denmark to aid King Hans against Norwegian rebellion.

'Treaty of Perpetual Peace' with England (which lasted until the battle of Flodden, 1513).

1503 Marriage of James IV and Margaret Tudor.

Genealogical Tab

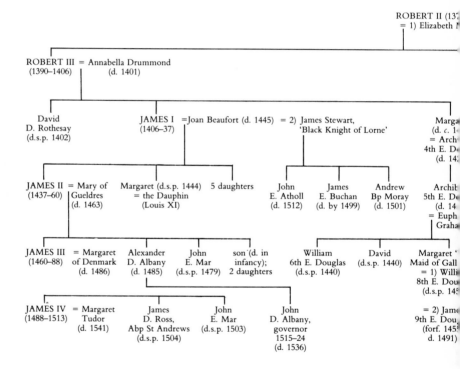

ROBERT II (13?
= 1) Elizabeth N

ROBERT III = Annabella Drummond
(1390–1406)   (d. 1401)

David   JAMES I =Joan Beaufort (d. 1445) = 2) James Stewart,   Marga
D. Rothesay   (1406–37)   'Black Knight of Lorne'   (d. c. 1
(d.s.p. 1402)   = Arch
                                                                                            4th E. D
                                                                                            (d. 14

JAMES II = Mary of   Margaret (d.s.p. 1444)   5 daughters   John   James   Andrew   Archib
(1437–60) Gueldres   = the Dauphin   E. Atholl   E. Buchan   Bp Moray   5th E. D
          (d. 1463)   (Louis XI)   (d. 1512)   (d. by 1499) (d. 1501) (d. 14
                                                                                                  = Euph
                                                                                                  Graha

JAMES III = Margaret   Alexander   John   son (d. in   William   David   Margaret
(1460–88) of Denmark   D. Albany   E. Mar   infancy);   6th E. Douglas (d.s.p. 1440) Maid of Gall
           (d. 1486)   (d. 1485)   (d.s.p. 1479) 2 daughters   (d.s.p. 1440)   = 1) Willi
                                                                                             8th E. Dou
                                                                                             (d.s.p. 14?

JAMES IV = Margaret   James   John   John   = 2) Jame
(1488–1513) Tudor   D. Ross,   E. Mar   D. Albany,   9th E. Dou
            (d. 1541)   Abp St Andrews (d.s.p. 1503) governor   (forf. 145?
                        (d.s.p. 1504)   1515–24   d. 1491)
                                                 (d. 1536)

he House of Stewart, 1371–1513

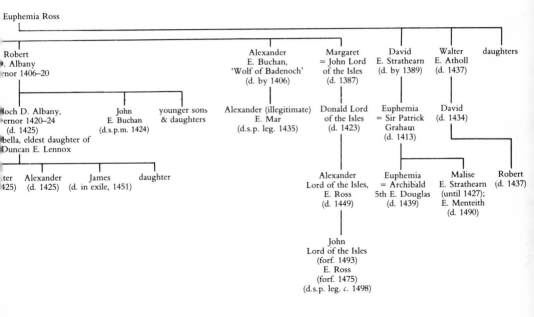

Euphemia Ross

Robert
. Albany
rnor 1406–20

Alexander
E. Buchan,
'Wolf of Badenoch'
(d. by 1406)

Margaret
= John Lord
of the Isles
(d. 1387)

David
E. Strathearn
(d. by 1389)

Walter
E. Atholl
(d. 1437)

daughters

loch D. Albany,
ernor 1420–24
(d. 1425)
bella, eldest daughter of
Duncan E. Lennox

John
E. Buchan
(d.s.p.m. 1424)

younger sons
& daughters

Alexander (illegitimate)
E. Mar
(d.s.p. leg. 1435)

Donald Lord
of the Isles
(d. 1423)

Euphemia
= Sir Patrick
Graham
(d. 1413)

David
(d. 1434)

ter
425)

Alexander
(d. 1425)

James
(d. in exile, 1451)

daughter

Alexander
Lord of the Isles,
E. Ross
(d. 1449)

Euphemia
= Archibald
5th E. Douglas
(d. 1439)

Malise
E. Strathearn
(until 1427);
E. Menteith
(d. 1490)

Robert
(d. 1437)

John
Lord of the Isles
(forf. 1493)
E. Ross
(forf. 1475)
(d.s.p. leg. c. 1498)

duke
earl
archbishop
bishop
died
p.   died without issue
p.m./leg.   died without male/legitimate issue
.   forfeited

Select bibliography

This bibliography is not intended to be comprehensive, but to serve as an introductory guide to work on late-medieval Scotland; it lists the main secondary books. The major journal of Scottish history is the *Scottish Historical Review*, and for ecclesiastical and cultural history, the *Innes Review* is invaluable. The articles on fifteenth-century Scotland which these and other journals contain are not cited individually here; references to them and to primary sources and secondary works on other contemporary societies which are helpful and relevant to a study of Scottish society, are to be found in the footnotes to the essays in this book.

General

G. W. S. Barrow, editor, *The Scottish Tradition: Essays in Honour of Ronald Gordon Cant* (Edinburgh, 1974)

W. C. Dickinson, *Scotland from the Earliest Times to 1603*, revised by A. A. M. Duncan (London, 1977)

G. Menzies, editor, *The Scottish Nation* (BBC publications, 1972)

P. McNeill and R. G. Nicholson, editors, *An Historical Atlas of Scotland, c. 400–c. 1600* (St Andrews, 1975)

Rosalind Mitchison, *A History of Scotland* (London, 1970)

R. G. Nicholson, *Scotland: The Later Middle Ages* (Edinburgh, 1974)

T. C. Smout, *A History of the Scottish People, 1560–1832* (London, 1969 – this contains an introduction on the medieval period)

Political and Legal

E. W. M. Balfour-Melville, *James I, King of Scots, 1406–1437* (London, 1936)

L. A. Barbé, *Margaret of Scotland and the Dauphin Louis* (London, 1917)

Agnes Conway, *Henry VII's Relations with Scotland and Ireland, 1485–1498* (Cambridge, 1932)

W. C. Dickinson, editor, *Barony Court Book of Carnwath, 1523–1542* (SHS, 1937)

　　The Sheriff Court Book of Fife, 1515–1522 (SHS, 1928 – both these books contain long and important introductions)

G. Donaldson, *Scottish Kings* (London, 1967)

Annie I. Dunlop, *The Life and Times of James Kennedy, Bishop of St Andrews* (Edinburgh, 1950)

R. K. Hannay, *The College of Justice* (Edinburgh, 1933)
R. L. Mackie, *King James IV of Scotland* (Edinburgh, 1958)
J. Mackinnon, *Constitutional History of Scotland from Early Times to the Reformation* (London, 1924)
T. I. Rae, *The Administration of the Scottish Frontier, 1513–1603* (Edinburgh, 1966)
R. S. Rait, *The Parliaments of Scotland* (Glasgow, 1924)
An Introduction to Scottish Legal History (Stair Society, 20, Edinburgh, (1958)
J. Maitland Thomson, *The Public Records of Scotland* (Glasgow, 1922)

Social and Economic

M. L. Anderson, *A History of Scottish Forests* (London, 1967)
L. A. Barbé, *Sidelights on the Industrial and Social Life of Scotland* (Glasgow, 1919)
P. Hume Brown, *Early Travellers in Scotland* (Edinburgh, 1891)
    Scotland before 1700 from Contemporary Documents (Edinburgh, 1893)
J. Davidson and A. Gray, *The Scottish Staple at Veere* (London, 1909)
Annie I. Dunlop, *Scots Abroad in the Fifteenth Century* (Historical Association Pamphlet, 1942)
T. A. Fischer, *The Scots in Germany* (Edinburgh, 1902)
    The Scots in Eastern and Western Prussia (Edinburgh, 1903)
    The Scots in Sweden (Edinburgh, 1907)
T. B. Franklin, *A History of Scottish Farming* (Edinburgh, 1952)
I. F. Grant, *Social and Economic Developments of Scotland before 1603* (Edinburgh, 1930)
W. Mackay Mackenzie, *The Scottish Burghs* (Edinburgh, 1949)
H. Marwick, *Merchant Lairds of Long Ago* (Kirkwall, 1939)
W. S. Reid, *Skipper from Leith: the History of Robert Barton of Over Barnton* (Philadelphia, 1962)
R. Renwick, *History of Glasgow* (Glasgow, 1921)
M. P. Rooseboom, *The Scottish Staple in the Netherlands* (The Hague, 1910)
A. M. Samuel, *The Herring: Its Effect on the History of Britain* (London, 1918)
I. H. Stewart, *The Scottish Coinage* (London, 1955)
J. A. Symon, *Scottish Farming, Past and Present* (Edinburgh, 1959)

Ecclesiastical

W. Moir Bryce, *The Scottish Grey Friars* (Edinburgh, 1909)
J. H. S. Burleigh, *A Church History of Scotland* (Oxford, 1960)
I. B. Cowan, *The Parishes of Medieval Scotland* (SRS, 1967)
I. B. Cowan and D. E. Easson, editors, *Medieval Religious Houses in Scotland* (London, 1976)
J. B. Craven, *History of the Church in Orkney* (Kirkwall, 1901)
G. Donaldson, *The Scottish Reformation* (Cambridge, 1960)
J. Dowden, *The Mediaeval Church in Scotland* (Glasgow, 1910)
    The Bishops of Scotland (Glasgow, 1912)

J. Herkless and R. K. Hannay, *The Archbishops of St Andrews* (Edinburgh, 1907–17)
A. R. McEwan, *A History of the Church of Scotland* (London, 1913–18)
D. McRoberts, editor, *Essays on the Scottish Reformation* (Glasgow, 1962)
D. E. R. Watt, *Fasti Ecclesiae Scoticanae Medii Aevi ad annum 1638* (SRS, 1969)

Learning and the Arts

J. W. Baxter, *William Dunbar: a Biographical Study* (Edinburgh, 1952)
R. G. Cant, *The College of St Salvator* (St Andrews, 1950)
    The University of St Andrews (Edinburgh, 1970)
S. H. Cruden, *The Scottish Castle* (Edinburgh, 1960)
J. G. Dunbar, *The Historic Architecture of Scotland* (London, 1966)
J. Durkan and A. Ross, *Early Scottish Libraries* (Glasgow, 1961)
F. C. Eeles, *King's College Chapel, Aberdeen* (Edinburgh, 1956)
H. G. Farmer, *A History of Music in Scotland* (London, 1947)
J. Grant, *History of the Burgh and Parish Schools of Scotland* (Glasgow, 1876)
G. Hay, *The Architecture of Scottish Post-Reformation Churches, 1560–1843* (Oxford, 1957)
A. M. Kinghorn, *The Chorus of History* (London, 1971)
D. Macgibbon and T. Ross, *The Castellated and Domestic Architecture of Scotland* (Edinburgh, 1887–92)
    The Ecclesiastical Architecture of Scotland (Edinburgh, 1896–97)
W. Mackay Mackenzie, *The Mediaeval Castle in Scotland* (London, 1927)
J. Durkan and J. Kirk, *The University of Glasgow, 1451–1577* (Glasgow, 1977)
J. MacQueen, *Allegory* (London, 1970)
    Ballattis of Lufe (Edinburgh, 1970)
    Robert Henryson: A Study of the Major Narrative Poems (Oxford, 1967)
Anna J. Mill, *Mediaeval Plays in Scotland* (Edinburgh, 1927)
J. S. Richardson, *The Medieval Stone Carver in Scotland* (Edinburgh, 1964)
R. S. Rait, *The Universities of Aberdeen* (Aberdeen, 1895)
G. G. Simpson, *Scottish Handwriting, 1150–1650* (Edinburgh, 1973)

The Highlands

Audrey Cunningham, *The Loyal Clans* (Cambridge, 1932)
I. F. Grant, *The Lordship of the Isles* (Edinburgh, 1935)
    The Macleods (London, 1959)
D. Gregory, *History of the Western Highlands and Isles of Scotland from AD 1493 to AD 1625* (Edinburgh, 1881)
K. Jackson, *The Gaelic Notes in the Book of Deer* (Cambridge, 1972)
A. and A. MacDonald, *The Clan Donald* (Inverness, 1896–1904)
C. M. MacDonald, *The History of Argyll* (Glasgow, 1950)
R. C. MacLeod, *The MacLeods of Dunvegan* (Edinburgh, 1927)
R. W. Munro, editor, *Monro's Western Isles of Scotland and Genealogies of the Clans 1549* (Edinburgh, 1961)
A. M. Sinclair, *The Clan Gillean* (Charlottetown, 1899)
K. A. Steer and J. W. M. Bannerman, *Late Medieval Monumental Sculpture in the West Highlands* (Edinburgh, 1977)

Index

J